**W9-CHA-858**

# THE GREENHAVEN ENCYCLOPEDIA OF

# THE VIETNAM WAR

# THE GREENHAVEN ENCYCLOPEDIA OF

# THE
# VIETNAM WAR

# THE GREENHAVEN ENCYCLOPEDIA OF

# THE VIETNAM WAR

Jeff T. Hay

Charles Zappia, *Consulting Editor*

Daniel Leone, *President*

Bonnie Szumski, *Publisher*

Scott Barbour, *Managing Editor*

**GREENHAVEN
PRESS®**

**THOMSON**
™
**GALE**

San Diego • Detroit • New York • San Francisco • Cleveland • New Haven, Conn. • Waterville, Maine • London • Munich

*To the continued evolution of goodwill between
the peoples of the United States and Indochina.*

LIBRARY OF CONGRESS CATALOGING-IN-PUBLICATION DATA

Encyclopedia of the Vietnam War / by Jeff T. Hay.
    p. cm. — (Greenhaven encyclopedia of series)
Summary: An alphabetical presentation of definitions and descriptions of terms
and events of the Vietnam War.
Includes bibliographical references and index.
    ISBN 0-7377-1149-3 (hardback : alk. paper)
    1. Vietnamese Conflict, 1961–1975—Encyclopedias, Juvenile. [1. Vietnamese
Conflict, 1961–1975—Encyclopedias.] I. Hay, Jeff T. II. Greenhaven encyclopedias.
    DS557.7E53 2004
    959.704'3'03—dc21

                                                                    2003005547

Printed in the United States of America

# CONTENTS

The Vietnam War was a turning point in both American history and twentieth-century world history, representing a test of American power and influence. Both were substantial, but neither could prevent the small Southeast Asian nation of South Vietnam (the Republic of Vietnam, or RVN) from falling to the Communist regime in North Vietnam (the Democratic Republic of Vietnam, or DRV). The Vietnam War remains the only war the United States ever lost, a loss that not only resulted in the death of more than fifty-eight thousand Americans but was a crisis of American conscience and credibility. On a broader level the Vietnam War reflected two of the important themes of post–World War II global politics. The first was nationalism, the struggle for independence by peoples who had been colonized by the European powers in the preceding centuries. The second, which inspired direct U.S. involvement in a region of the world of which most Americans knew little, was the ideological struggle known as the cold war, the conflict between Communist totalitarianism as represented by the superpower Soviet Union and liberal democracy as represented by the superpower United States.

American military advisers began training the South Vietnamese army in 1955, and from 1961 they were a significant presence in Vietnam as combat advisers and then regular combat troops. Most American troops were withdrawn from Vietnam in the early 1970s, and by January 1973, when a peace settlement was reached, few Americans remained "in coun-

try." For most Americans, therefore, the Vietnam War lasted from 1961 to 1973.

However, for the Vietnamese people the so-called American War was only one phase of a much larger and longer conflict. North Vietnamese Communists had gone to war against French colonial overlords in the 1920s and 1930s and against the Japanese in the 1940s. From 1946 to 1954, Vietnam was torn by the First Indochina War against French colonial forces who had reoccupied the country after World War II. In the cold war effort to stop the spread of communism, the United States began to provide financial aid to the French in 1948. The 1954 Geneva Accords only temporarily halted the fighting, and by the late 1950s North Vietnamese Communists led by Ho Chi Minh were sponsoring the guerrilla attacks of the Viet Cong in South Vietnam. After American forces left Vietnam in 1973, the fighting between north and south continued until Saigon fell to the armies of the DRV in April 1975. Peace was still not at hand, however. The newly reunified Vietnamese nation fought wars with Cambodia and China in 1978 and 1989, respectively, and Vietnamese armies occupied Cambodia until 1989. To the Vietnamese people, therefore, the Vietnam War lasted nearly forty-five years.

The Vietnam War, as Americans define it, was not limited to Vietnam. The neighboring countries of Laos and Cambodia were drawn in to the fighting as well, first because the North Vietnamese located the Ho Chi Minh Trail, their primary supply line to South Vietnam, through stretches of both countries, and second because Communist guerrilla insurrections were simultaneously occurring there. Massive ongoing U.S. bombing campaigns in both Laos and Cambodia essentially widened the Vietnam War to the entire region, and the extreme political and social upheaval of the period led to the rise of brutal regimes, genocide, and economic stagnation.

In the United States, meanwhile, the Vietnam War was the defining political event of an era of widespread political and social turmoil. It was an overriding concern of three presidents—John F. Kennedy, Lyndon B. Johnson, and Richard M. Nixon—and the center of widespread controversy involving issues of civil rights, morality, military strategy, and financial and human resources. Increasing public opposition to the war inspired some of the largest antiwar demonstrations and civil disturbances in U.S. history. The domestic legacy of the Vietnam War included not only mistrust of governmental institutions and officials (linked to ongoing debate over the limits of presidential and military authority) but uncertainty over the national character and purpose and, some have suggested, lasting unwillingness to risk engaging in another protracted war. Historians, politicians, and ordinary citizens continue to debate the lessons of the war; as presidential adviser

Robert McNamara reflected in his 1995 memoir, *In Retrospect: The Tragedy and Lessons of Vietnam*, "We were wrong, terribly wrong. We owe it to future generations to explain why."

*The Greenhaven Encyclopedia of the Vietnam War* provides students and other readers with an accurate and easy-to-use overview of this fascinating and still controversial subject. The encyclopedic format is designed for easy access, and cross-references included in each entry guide readers to related topics. Entries encompass important figures of the Vietnam War, including military and political leaders, prisoners of war, and antiwar activists; important battles and operations; key military units, equipment, and weaponry; and cultural topics such as the role of women in Vietnam and the influence of television and the antiwar movement on the conflict, as well as the portrayal of the Vietnam War in books, film, and music. Throughout, the text places the Vietnam War within the larger historical and global context. A comprehensive chronology gives readers concise perspective on the arc of the conflict. An extensive bibliography, including many useful Internet websites, points readers to important, specialized sources for further research into this enduringly compelling subject.

## Abrams, Creighton (1914–1974)

Commander of the U.S. Military Assistance Command, Vietnam (MACV), from 1968 to 1972. A graduate of the U.S. Military Academy at West Point and a World War II tank commander, Abrams was first appointed to Vietnam as deputy to MACV commander General William Westmoreland. When Westmoreland was brought home to serve as army chief of staff in 1968, Abrams replaced him.

Between 1968 and 1972 Abrams presided over the withdrawal of American troops from Vietnam and the further strengthening of the South Vietnamese army, as directed by President Richard M. Nixon in his policy of Vietnamization. He accompanied this slow process with basic changes in U.S. military tactics. Abrams believed that both the North Vietnamese and the South Vietnamese, with their American allies, were fighting essentially the same war: for control of the population of South Vietnam. To further that effort, Abrams largely dropped Westmoreland's war of attrition and search-and-destroy missions in favor of a holistic approach aimed at "pacifying" the population of South Vietnam. He realized that, in the south, the North Vietnamese as well as the Viet Cong relied on the infrastructure of the villages, so Abrams took steps to prevent their access to the villages. He also tried to reduce measures such as broad artillery barrages that threatened South Vietnamese civilians directly.

In 1972 Abrams replaced Westmoreland as army chief of staff in Washington, D.C. In this position he focused his efforts on revitalizing the army in the aftermath of the Vietnam experience by developing new strategies and tactics. **See also** Military Assistance Command, Vietnam; Vietnamization; Westmoreland, William.

## Agency for International Development (AID)

The U.S. organization that administered American economic aid to the Republic of Vietnam (RVN) and, as such, one of the most pervasive and important American organizations in the RVN, or South Vietnam. A U.S. government organization, AID's officials were civilians rather than members of the military. AID worked very closely with the South Vietnamese government based in Saigon. Indeed, the Saigon regime ultimately had the power to approve or disapprove specific economic assistance projects, and, until the early 1960s, South Vietnamese officials played a major part in distributing funds and administering specific programs. AID funds provided, depending on the year, approximately 20 percent of the gross national product of the RVN. Between 1955 and 1960 AID funds ranged from $220 to $270 million per year and then slowly increased along with the American military commitment to South Vietnam. After 1965 these funds reached more than $500 million per year. Most of the moneys were used in enterprises that both American and Vietnamese officials hoped would encourage the people of South Vietnam to support the RVN, but many of these backfired as a result of mismanagement, corruption, and conflicting goals. At first, AID was relatively independent of other U.S. agencies in Vietnam, operating through its own U.S. Operation Mission office in Saigon. In 1967, however, its economic assistance programs were placed under the authority of the Civilian Operations and Revolutionary Development Support (CORDS) and a subsidiary branch of the Military Assistance Command, Vietnam (MACV).

Officials used AID funds for a wide variety of projects, including education, public health, public security and police, local government, and economic development. AID sought, among other things, to build schools and factories, construct roads and bridges, establish irrigation and sanitation networks, and provide training for local officials. Among its subsidiary enterprises were the Office of Rural Affairs, formed in the early 1960s, and the International Volunteer Service (IVS), which came under the wing of AID in 1957. The Office of Rural Affairs sent American civilians into rural areas and provincial towns to supervise assistance programs in the hope that raising the standard of living in the villages would ensure the support of their inhabitants for the Saigon regime. Results were often mixed since American officials rarely spoke Vietnamese or had much understanding of local traditions and customs. The IVS, on the other hand, took pains to train volunteers in Vietnamese and send them out to live among villagers, where they taught English or worked on various agricultural or other economic projects. Although it received most of its money from AID, the IVS remained politically independent, viewing its efforts as humanitarian rather than as support for the policies of either Washington or Saigon. In fact, the IVS served as a model for the Peace Corps, which was established in the early 1960s. **See also** pacification.

## Agent Orange

The most well known of the defoliation agents used by U.S. forces during the Vietnam War. Along with Agents Purple and Pink, used until 1964, and White and Blue, used after 1965, Agent Orange provided an effective way for strategists to reduce jungle cover and therefore either uncover enemy emplacements or destroy potential hiding places. The agents were named after the identification stripes painted on their storage containers. Between 1965 and 1972 more than 11 million gallons of Agent Orange were sprayed on Southeast Asian jungles by specially equipped airplanes and helicopters. Agent Orange contained small portions of a poison, a form of dioxin that proved deadly not only to vegetation but to animals and even, perhaps, humans. The Vietnamese alleged that Agent Orange resulted in a number of birth defects in the years during and since the war. Even U.S. veterans of the war complained, beginning in the late 1970s, of various health problems they thought were caused by their exposure to Agent Orange. These included skin problems, cancer, and even birth defects in their children. **See also** defoliation.

## Air America

An air wing of the U.S. Central Intelligence Agency (CIA) during the 1950s, 1960s, and 1970s. Although most of its operations were in Laos, where the CIA took an important role in trying to prevent a Communist takeover, Air America also provided assistance to American forces in South Vietnam.

Originally, Air America was known as Civil Air Transport, a company formed in

*Air force jets spray Agent Orange over the jungle near Saigon. Agent Orange reduced jungle cover, revealing enemy hiding places.*

fight against the Communists. Over the next several years the CIA used Air America for communication with the far-flung Hmong as well as the primary supply line for arms, equipment, and food for displaced refugees. This required expertise in flying in difficult conditions and landing at primitive sites in the Lao highlands. The "air force" included not only numerous small planes but a number of helicopters that were transferred to CIA authority on the orders of President John F. Kennedy in 1961.

After a truce in July 1962, which the Communists failed to observe, fighting in Laos escalated rapidly. Rather than use direct American military aid, however, or station official advisers in Laos as they were doing in South Vietnam, American officials decided to continue to use the CIA to help the locals fend off the Pathet Lao. One reason for doing so was to avoid provoking a confrontation with the North Vietnamese in Laos. Unsurprisingly, the CIA continued to rely on Air America, which rapidly became a paramilitary force providing supplies and transport as well as other assistance to Hmong guerrillas. By the late 1960s, when the official U.S. Air Force was flying missions over Laos, Air America's military role grew even more direct, including flying search-and-rescue missions in support of the air force. Such actions contributed to a growing number of casualties among Air America pilots and crew, most of whom were volunteers with varied backgrounds and not regular military or CIA personnel.

southern China by, among others, General Claire L. Chennault, the top American flier in China during World War II. The CIA purchased the airline in 1950 and used it in covert operations across Asia under the cover of a commercial airline. The organization changed its name to Air America in 1959, retaining a sort of hazy semiofficial status among various branches of U.S. forces.

In 1961, when Communist guerrillas known as the Pathet Lao began to make significant moves against the government of Laos, the CIA took the central role in trying to stop a Communist takeover of the sparsely populated, landlocked country. The agency decided to recruit the Hmong, a large tribal group with a long-time enmity toward the ethnic Lao, to

In 1972, with congressional investigations into the covert activities of the CIA being conducted, director Richard Helms sold the assets of Air America to private investors. Even so, the airline remained a U.S. government contractor and continued to fly missions in Laos until a peace agreement in 1974. Air America's last mission in Southeast Asia was in April 1975, when its aircraft took part in the evacuations of Americans and others from Saigon. It ceased operations in June 1976. **See also** Central Intelligence Agency; Continental Air Services; Laos, secret war in.

## aircraft carriers

Aircraft carriers provided U.S. forces with offshore base capabilities throughout the Vietnam War; in total, nineteen carriers, in rotations of three or four at a time, were stationed off the Vietnamese coast between 1964 and 1975. Among them were the *Constellation*, the *Coral Sea*, the *Enterprise*, the *Intrepid*, and the *Yorktown*. Designated as components of the Seventh Fleet's Task Force Seventy-seven, carriers were posted at Yankee Station and Dixie Station, the two offshore staging areas chosen by U.S. commanders. Navy aircraft flying from carriers played a central role in bombing operations over North Vietnam. They also provided air support for ground operations in South Vietnam and along the Ho Chi Minh Trail. A number of carriers were on hand during the last drama of the American phase of the Vietnam War, the evacuation of Saigon in April 1975. Helicopters from carriers ferried wave after wave of American and South Vietnamese escapees while hordes of South Vietnamese pilots tried to land their planes on carrier decks. Congestion was so bad that a number of aircraft had to be thrown overboard to make way for new arrivals. **See also** Navy, U.S.; Rolling Thunder; Seventh Fleet.

## Air Force, U.S.

The U.S. Air Force played a key role in American operations in Vietnam and the rest of Indochina. Flying from airstrips in South Vietnam, northeastern Thailand, Guam, and the Philippines, air force pilots engaged in two main efforts. One was close air support for ground operations, involving transport, airlift, and bombing and strafing runs using mostly gunships and airplanes. The other was bombing of enemy targets, or perceived enemy targets, ranging from Viet Cong (VC) bases in South Vietnam to military facilities in North Vietnam to the Ho Chi Minh Trail. Air force bomb raids also targeted Laos and Cambodia extensively, especially from 1969 to 1973. The bombing of Cambodia and Laos was in line with the strategic bombing doctrine, a military philosophy adopted by U.S. commanders and officials after World War II, which stated that the key factor in defeating an enemy was the destruction of its industrial, communications, and supply infrastructure.

The first air force unit to be sent to Vietnam was the 4400th Combat Crew Training Squadron, which arrived in South Vietnam in November 1961 to train local aircrews. This small force was followed in 1964 by the Second Air Division, which was followed in turn by the Seventh Air Force, organized in April 1966. The commanders of the Seventh Air Force, of whom there were seven between 1966 and 1973, answered only to the commander in chief of the Pacific Command in Honolulu, Hawaii, not to the commander of the Military Assistance Command, Vietnam (MACV). The major air force effort in Vietnam was Operation Rolling Thunder, the strategic bombing of North Vietnam that began in March 1965 and ended in October 1968. Rolling Thunder involved nearly 500,000 sorties by air force craft. Another important operation was Commando Hunt, an interdiction effort along the Ho Chi Minh Trail begun in November 1968.

U.S. Air Force casualties in Southeast Asia included 1,744 killed in action; 841 nonhostile deaths; and 931 wounded. More than half of American prisoners of war (POWs) in North Vietnam were air force personnel, as were more than half of those designated as missing in action (MIA) after the war. Three air force pilots were named aces for downing five or more enemy aircraft over North Vietnam, and twelve air force men were awarded the Congressional Medal of Honor. **See also** Arc Light; First Aviation Brigade; Rolling Thunder; Seventh Air Force.

## AK-47

The primary battlefield rifle used by North Vietnamese Army (NVA) and Viet Cong (VC) forces during the Vietnam War. It was produced by the Soviet Union and named after its inventor, Mikhail Kalashnikov (AK-47 stands for Avtomat Kalashnikova 1947, or the automatic weapon invented by Kalashnikov in 1947). Lightweight, easy to reload, and usable as either a single-shot or automatic rifle, the AK-47 was known for firing distinctive green tracers, or lighted rounds of ammunition. It provided Communist soldiers with better firepower than U.S. and South Vietnamese infantrymen carried until the latter forces adopted the comparable M-16 in 1966. Many Communist troops carried a Chinese-made copy of the AK-47 known as the T-56. **See also** M-14 and M-16 rifles.

## Ala Moana

A five-month military operation conducted in Hau Nghia Province near Saigon, a major agricultural region that had become a Communist base. The operation, carried out from December 1966 to May 1967, was designed to clear Viet Cong (VC) forces from the region and enable pacification efforts to begin. Most of the forces involved in the operation were American infantry troops of the Twenty-fifth Division, who sometimes worked in concert with counterparts involved in similar actions, notably Operation Junction City around nearby Cu Chi. Infantry troops fought major battles with VC contingents in January and February, although most of their time was spent in searching and clearing actions rather than in battlefield engagements. Operation Ala Moana was thought to have greatly reduced VC activity in Hau Nghia Province and, moreover, denied VC fighters elsewhere of vital resources. **See also** Cu Chi tunnels; Junction City.

## Ali, Muhammad (1942– )

American boxer and prominent opponent of the Vietnam War. Born Cassius Clay, the boxer won his first heavyweight title in 1964 after also receiving an Olympic gold medal. In 1965 he converted to the Nation of Islam and changed his name to Muhammad Ali. He was drafted in 1966 and initially sought conscientious objector status. His claim, like the claims of many American Muslims, was denied. When he was called to report for duty in 1967 he refused to go. His heavyweight title was taken away and in June 1967 he was found guilty of violating the Selective Service Act. The verdict was overturned by the U.S. Supreme Court in June 1970 and Ali returned to the ring, winning the heavyweight title two more times. In the meantime, his charisma and outspoken oratory helped make him a role model for both antiwar protesters and young African Americans. **See also** antiwar movement; conscientious objectors; draft; draft resistance.

## Amerasians

A term applied mostly to the children of American fathers and Vietnamese mothers, one of the unexpected legacies of American involvement in Vietnam. Up to eighty thousand children were born from the unions of, mostly, U.S. servicemen and Vietnamese women forced into prostitution because of the deprivations of the war years. Since servicemen rarely spent more than a year "in country," many were never aware that they had fathered children in Vietnam.

The Vietnamese referred to Amerasians as either "half-breeds" (*con lai*) or, more philosophically, the "dust of life" (*bui doi*). Few Amerasians were accepted into the mainstream of Vietnamese life during or after the war, and often their mothers were targets of unofficial discrimination because of their intimacy with U.S. soldiers. They were also denied the close family support that was characteristic of Vietnamese life.

As soon as the war ended, refugee organizations tried to unite Amerasian children with their fathers, many of whom were willing participants in the effort. To help bring Amerasians to the United States, Congress passed the Amerasian Immigration Act in 1982. The act contained a number of restrictions, however, that made implementation difficult. To prevent immigrants from taking excessive advantage of the U.S. welfare system, for instance, the act required newcomers to have sponsors who were willing and able to support them. Another problem was that the United States and the new Socialist Republic of Vietnam (SRV) did not have formal diplomatic relations, which made it easier for the SRV to deliberately proceed slowly when processing immigration applications. In 1988 Congress passed an extended piece of legislation, the Amerasian Homecoming Act, to facilitate Amerasian immigration to the United States. The new act classified Amerasians and a few family members as a special category of immigrants whose admission was no longer contingent on locating fathers or guaranteed financial support. The act also provided

for federal resettlement assistance. Within three years, more than sixty-seven thousand Amerasians had come to the United States, most accompanied by Vietnamese family members. Refugee organizations estimated that by 1991 there were only some five thousand Amerasians left in Vietnam. **See also** boat people; refugees.

## Americal Division

Officially the Twenty-third Infantry Division of the U.S. Army, the Americal Division was one of the prominent American units in Vietnam from 1967 to 1971. Formed during World War II, the Americal Division was so named because of its staging area in the South Pacific, the island of New Caledonia.

The Americal Division was activated in Vietnam in September 1967, although elements of it had operated earlier as part of a force called Task Force Oregon. Because it was assembled as an ad hoc division from a variety of units already in place in Vietnam, Americal suffered, some claimed, from a lack of effective leadership. The division consisted mostly of light infantry troops but also included artillery, armored, and reconnaissance units. Like many other infantry divisions in Vietnam, Americal also had the support of an aviation group consisting of gunships and assault helicopters. The division's primary area of operations was in I Corps, the northernmost military region of South Vietnam, where its primary task was to contain the advances of North Vietnamese Army (NVA) regulars across either the demilitarized zone or the Laotian border. Other parts of the division were stationed farther to the south. One of these, C (Charlie) Company, First Battalion, Twentieth Infantry, was responsible for the massacre of Vietnamese civilians at My Lai in March 1968.

Most members of the Americal Division were sent home in 1971. The unit was formally deactivated in December 1971. The Congressional Medal of Honor was awarded to eleven members of the Americal Division, which suffered well over seventeen thousand casualties during its service in Vietnam. **See also** My Lai massacre.

## American Friends of Vietnam (AFV)

A nongovernmental organization of Americans that, beginning in 1955, sought to increase support in the United States for the South Vietnamese regime of Ngo Dinh Diem and his successors. The AFV was founded by Leo Cherne and Joseph Buttinger, strong anti-Communists who were members of another organization known as the International Rescue Committee. They worked closely with an American public relations firm that Diem retained. The first two presidents of the AFV were Generals William Donavan and John O'-Daniel, who had contacts among the American military advisers in South Vietnam. The organization attracted support, especially in the 1950s, from a variety of figures, including publisher Henry Luce, Cardinal Francis Spellman, Supreme Court justice William O'Douglas, and then-senators John F. Kennedy and Hubert Humphrey.

The AFV worked to raise funds and disseminate information about the threat of communism in Vietnam through speeches and publications. Its line was generally close to that of the successive presidential administrations of Eisenhower, Kennedy, and Johnson. Like the Kennedy administration, the AFV was divided in the early 1960s over the continued support of the increasingly autocratic and isolated Diem, but after Diem was removed from power, the AFV supported the Johnson administration's military escalation. Although its influence on policy was likely minimal, the high-profile AFV was an easy target of the antiwar move-

ment and others who opposed U.S. policy. During the 1970s, as direct American involvement in Vietnam was greatly reduced, the activities of the AFV dwindled as well. The organization effectively disbanded in 1975. **See also** Michigan State University Vietnam Advisory Group; Saigon Military Mission.

## An Loc, Battle of

One of the last major battles of the Vietnam War in which American forces played an active and important role. The battle was centered around the town of An Loc, some sixty-five miles north of Saigon. It was part of North Vietnam's Easter Offensive of 1972 designed by General Vo Nguyen Giap to split South Vietnam in two.

The North Vietnamese Army (NVA) launched its attack on April 5, 1972, after the Easter Offensive had already succeeded in central Vietnam. The NVA was accompanied by a number of Viet Cong (VC) units. The combined force attacked from across the Cambodian border and quickly captured the town of Loc Ninh, about fifteen miles from An Loc. At that point South Vietnamese president Nguyen Van Thieu ordered the South Vietnamese Fifth Division to An Loc, realizing that the town guarded an essential roadway to Saigon. By April 7 Giap's forces surrounded the Fifth Division in An Loc and began to pound defenders with artillery fire. On April 13 an NVA infantry attack reduced the South Vietnamese position to one square mile. Nevertheless, Thieu's forces were able to hold out thanks to massive American air support from both aircraft and helicopters from navy ships offshore as well as massive B-52 bombing of NVA positions. American forces flew more than nine thousand missions in support of the South Vietnamese at An Loc, and American advisers assisted South Vietnamese officers on the ground. The NVA lifted the siege of An Loc in June 1972 and, for the moment, Saigon and South Vietnam were saved. **See also** Easter Offensive; Linebacker I.

## antiaircraft defenses

Antiaircraft defenses were extensively deployed by the North Vietnamese during the Vietnam War but not by the Americans or South Vietnamese, who had no need to defend the south from air attack because the North Vietnamese used their air force purely for defensive purposes.

The North Vietnamese antiaircraft arsenal consisted of antiaircraft artillery (AAA), surface-to-air missiles (SAMs), and MiG fighter planes, all assisted by electronic communications and radar installations. North Vietnamese leaders determined that such defenses were necessary in 1965 when the Americans began their Rolling Thunder bombing campaign. Most of their equipment was initially supplied by the Chinese; however, the Soviet Union proved to be the source of most of the AAA and SAMs over the course of the war. The former included guns ranging from the 8-millimeter M1944 to the much larger ZU-23, which had a range of up to forty thousand feet. The most frequently used SAMs were the SA-2 and SA-7. Fired from a fixed position, the thirty-five-foot-long SA-2 had a range of over nineteen nautical miles and could hit a target aircraft at a height of up to sixty thousand feet. The SA-7 was a shoulder-fired, infrared-guided SAM first used in 1972. Since its maximum range was only ten thousand feet, its targets were mostly helicopters and low-flying aircraft.

North Vietnamese antiaircraft defenses prevented the United States and South Vietnam from establishing air superiority over North Vietnam until 1972, and they made the skies over the north hazardous for flight crews. Between 1962 and 1973, 990 American and South Vietnamese aircraft were lost over North Vietnam. **See also** artillery; Christmas bombing; Rolling Thunder; smart bombs.

## antiwar movement

Over the years of the Vietnam War a broad-based and vocal antiwar movement arose in the United States representing virtually every segment of American society. It was joined by a broad antiwar movement overseas. The influence of the antiwar movement was so significant that by 1968 it played a central role in the U.S. government's evolving Vietnam policy. Some claim that the movement was the major factor ending American involvement in Vietnam.

A few antiwar protesters emerged in the early 1960s, before American ground troops were sent to Vietnam. They included members of traditionally pacifist groups such as the Quakers as well as members of SANE, an antinuclear peace group. A small student protest organization, the Student Peace Union (SPU), also spoke out against the expanding conflict in Vietnam. All of these groups were small in number, however, and their views remained far from the mainstream of American society. Most Americans knew little about Vietnam and considered it necessary to take strong steps to halt the spread of communism anywhere in the world.

By 1964 antiwar sentiment was being voiced among groups agitating for civil rights, an important domestic concern in an era of social protest. Prominent among these groups was Students for a Democratic Society (SDS), a larger and far more assertive organization than the SPU. The SDS, founded by Tom Hayden and others at the University of Michigan in 1960, issued a manifesto known as the Port Huron Statement in 1962. The Port Huron Statement took direct aim at what Hayden called "the military-industrial-academic complex," which in his view dominated American life and had vested interests in a Vietnam conflict. Another civil rights group that began to take an interest in Vietnam was the Free Speech Movement, founded in 1964 at the University of California, Berkeley, and led by the charismatic Mario Savio.

In February 1965 large-scale U.S. bombing of North Vietnam began and in March the first U.S. ground troops were deployed to Vietnam. These events acted as a catalyst drawing the SDS, the Free Speech Movement, and other organizations together to protest the Vietnam War. The SDS marched on the terminal in Oakland, California, from which U.S. Army troops embarked and in April 1965 staged a March on Washington in which up to twenty-five thousand people took part. At this point the most outspoken antiwar protesters were college students and other young people aware that their lives and futures were being placed on the firing line by men of an older generation. After the March on Washington, student protest groups formed around the country to stage demonstrations, hold teach-ins, and petition government officials. Large numbers of young men also began to seek ways to avoid the military draft. Their methods ranged from trying to acquire medical or student deferments to applying for conscientious objector status to fleeing the country, via underground networks, for countries such as Canada or Sweden.

**The Antiwar Movement Broadens.** Meanwhile, the antiwar movement began to politicize the broader society. Individuals prompted to take an antiwar stand included longtime pacifists such as A.J. Muste, Catholic priests Daniel and Philip Berrigan, other clergymen who provided sanctuary to draft resisters in their churches, and prominent civilians such as pediatrician Benjamin Spock. Influential, widely admired folk musicians such as Joan Baez and Bob Dylan increasingly turned to protest songs with antiwar themes. Civil rights leader Dr. Martin

*Protesters march outside the White House in 1965. Antiwar demonstrators opposed U.S. involvement in Vietnam and urged the government to withdraw U.S. troops.*

Luther King Jr. also spoke out openly against the Vietnam War beginning in early 1967. He criticized the war on moral grounds as well as for the fact that it was draining government resources away from vital domestic programs. Heavyweight boxing champion Muhammad Ali, facing the draft, wondered why he should be expected to travel halfway around the world to fight Vietnamese people with whom he had no quarrel, and thousands of others echoed those sentiments. As the antiwar movement spilled over from student or marginal organizations into the American mainstream in 1966 and 1967, the news media followed. Some reporters had always questioned the accuracy of reports on Vietnam issued by U.S. military or civilian officials, but overall the U.S. media was supportive of the war effort until the antiwar movement had grown too widespread to be ignored.

**The Impact of the Press on Antiwar Sentiment.** By 1965 journalists in Vietnam had begun to speak of their daily briefings by military officials in Saigon as the "five o'clock follies," since these official reports differed widely from what reporters themselves saw in the field. American military policy in Vietnam was to give accredited reporters and photographers complete freedom of movement, and by the mid-1960s journalists were questioning the efficiency and human costs of American efforts in Vietnam. Their reports had a significant impact on the burgeoning antiwar movement at home. Correspondent Neil Sheehan, for example, had written as early as 1963 that South Vietnamese forces at the Battle of Ap Bac had performed poorly (official military reports claimed the battle was a South Vietnamese victory). In 1965 Sheehan, by then a reporter for the *New York Times*, was ready to admit that the war in the Mekong Delta was being lost, and he provided his readers with a graphic account of the Battle of Ia Drang Valley. Sheehan was joined in these efforts by dozens of other journalists, notably David Halberstam, another *Times* reporter who focused, to the chagrin of the U.S. government, on the failings of the Saigon regime, and Harrison Salisbury, who sent back dispatches during a visit to North Vietnam in December 1966 and January 1967 noting that American bombing was having little effect on North Vietnam's morale or ability to conduct the war.

The work of these and other journalists, presented with little whitewashing in newspapers and magazines and on television, helped convince many Americans that not only was the Vietnam War a quagmire, to use Halberstam's phrase, but they were being misled by their government. Some columnists, such as Walter Lippman and James Reston, openly questioned the honesty of Lyndon B. Johnson's administration. By 1968 mainstream publications such as *Time* and *Life* magazines were calling for a withdrawal from Vietnam.

As the unvarnished reports on the Vietnam quagmire and on the misleading messages from government multiplied, the antiwar movement grew larger, and ordinary Americans joined more activist groups. October 1967 marked a vivid turning point in American public support for the Vietnam War; polls showed that 75 percent of the population felt that the war was harmful for their country. Citizens also made it clear that they believed fewer and fewer of the pronouncements of military progress issued by the Johnson administration. That same October one of the largest antiwar demonstrations to date took place in Washington, D.C. Known as the March on the Pentagon, it was organized by the National Coordinating Committee to End the War in Vietnam and by student groups. The event consisted of a rally attended by some

100,000 people followed by the actual march to the Pentagon.

**The Tet Offensive: The Turning Point.** The Tet Offensive of early 1968 seemed to justify the growing antiwar sentiment as Americans heard the news of a lengthy Viet Cong attack on the U.S. embassy in Saigon. After Tet, which was strictly speaking a military victory for the United States and its South Vietnamese allies, Johnson administration officials could no longer convincingly argue that they were winning the war. Important news organizations concurred, and Walter Cronkite, the highly respected anchorman of *CBS News*, voiced the opinion that the Vietnam War might not be winnable.

In 1968 the antiwar movement took a marked turn toward violence as American casualties in Vietnam mounted and military progress appeared illusive. The ground had been laid by the March on the Pentagon, which was characterized by mild rioting and by "guerrilla theater" operations staged by radical peace groups, as well as by a history of violence in the United States over civil rights. The worst of the antiwar rioting took place at the Democratic National Convention held in Chicago in August 1968. There, rock-throwing protesters battled police and National Guard troops wielding clubs and tear gas in the streets. Eight protest leaders (the Chicago Eight, later the Chicago Seven) were later tried for instigating the riots. By 1969 extreme radical groups such as the Weathermen, who appeared to favor a socialist uprising, had sparked a wave of bombings in the name of antiwar protests that caused at least one death and millions of dollars in property damage. Other extreme protesters expressed support for the Hanoi government rather than their own.

In general, the antiwar movement among students and young people had grown far more radical after 1966. The SDS and similar groups dressed and lived respectably and seemed a part of mainstream American life. But beginning in 1967 youth culture took a turn toward a broad rejection of what young people called simply "the establishment." Youthful "hippies" dressed down, grew long hair, took drugs, practiced free love, and listened to antiwar and psychedelic rock and roll songs. They staged "peace-ins" and "love-ins" along with the then-standard teach-ins. Inevitably the hippie movement was connected to the Vietnam War since the war gave young people something vivid and immediate to protest against, and by 1968 hippies and antiwar protesters were closely associated. Meanwhile, the related "Yippie" movement, named after the so-called Youth International Party, emerged. Formed by Muste, radicals Abbie Hoffman and Jerry Rubin, and others, it was the Yippies who staged "guerrilla theater" at both the March on Washington and the Democratic Convention, where they nominated a pig for president.

**Challenging Nixon's Policies.** The growing radicalism and antiestablishment veneer of the antiwar movement did not prevent antiwar sentiment from spreading among ordinary Americans. It should be noted that many young Americans were neither hippies nor protesters, and the baby-boom generation coming of age in the 1960s contained as many conservatives as radicals. Nevertheless, by 1969 broad public rejection of the Vietnam War had resulted in a pledge by new president Richard Nixon to begin to withdraw American ground troops. Antiwar protesters kept the pressure on by staging a nationwide moratorium against the war in October 1969 and a second March on Washington that November. The latter included a rally attended by an estimated half-million people.

News of the bombing and invasion of Cambodia on April 30, 1970, on Nixon's orders inspired still more large-scale protests by people claiming that Nixon had clearly deceived them in his promise to draw down the Vietnam conflict. Clergymen, business leaders, politicians, and others joined student demonstrators on hundreds of college campuses in early May. Another rally in Washington took place, this time at the Lincoln Memorial, where Nixon himself made an odd late-night visit to protesters. The protests turned violent and resulted in the first deaths of antiwar protesters at Kent State University in Ohio and Jackson State College in Mississippi. One political response to these protests, and to Nixon's deceptions, was moves among congressmen to try to limit presidential war-making powers.

Nixon took some of the steam out of the antiwar movement in 1971 and 1972 by withdrawing American troops, engaging in serious peace negotiations with North Vietnam, and promising to end the draft. The last wave of protests took place during the so-called Christmas bombing of 1972, an event that suggested that American bombers were targeting North Vietnamese civilians. After the Paris Peace Accords were signed in January 1973, Americans were more than happy to leave their concerns over Vietnam behind them, and the most active antiwar protesters turned their attention to veterans' affairs and the antinuclear movement. But a legacy of cynicism toward and distrust of government policy and credibility remained. **See also** Democratic National Convention of 1968; March on the Pentagon; media and the Vietnam War; Spring Mobilization to End the War in Vietnam; Students for a Democratic Society; Youth International Party.

## Apache Snow

The military operation conducted to contain North Vietnamese Army (NVA) forces in and around the A Shau Valley in northern South Vietnam during the spring of 1969. The NVA had already established a number of bases in the region and was reinforcing and supplying them from the Ho Chi Minh Trail across the nearby Laotian border. U.S. and South Vietnamese commanders grew concerned that the NVA might use these bases to stage an attack across South Vietnam toward the coast. Operation Apache Snow was designed to prevent such an attack. Using elements of the 101st Army Airborne Division, the Ninth Marine Regiment, and the Third Regiment of the South Vietnamese army, commanders began the operation on May 10. It consisted of a number of skirmishes and one major battle, the so-called Battle of Hamburger Hill. Although the operation failed to regain control of significant territory in the A Shau Valley, it temporarily forced the NVA back across the Laotian border and apparently discouraged eastward Communist attacks. **See also** A Shau Valley; Hamburger Hill, Battle of; Lam Son 719.

## Ap Bac, Battle of

An important engagement on January 2, 1963, centered around Ap Bac, a small village forty miles south of Saigon, where the Army of the Republic of Vietnam (ARVN) hoped to both avenge earlier losses and discourage the spread of Viet Cong sympathies among local villagers. In the end, however, the battle proved to be a public relations loss for the Americans as well as a disturbing example of the type of war that was taking place in Vietnam.

Local Communist forces were forewarned that there was to be an operation against Ap Bac and positioned themselves for a counterstrike. When the ARVN attack came, the Communists proved to be better organized and disciplined than their ARVN counterparts, who at one point refused to advance. In addition, a number of ARVN officers refused to cooperate or commit their forces properly. Even after hundreds of ARVN paratroopers had been dropped in, the greatly outnumbered Communist forces continued to fight effectively, shooting down five American helicopters. When night fell, however, the Communists slipped away rather than take the village.

U.S. commanders proclaimed the battle a victory for the South Vietnamese because the village did not fall to the Communists. American journalists on the scene, however, told a different story: The ARVN, they reported, appeared to be a poor force despite U.S. technology and advice, and the ARVN sustained much higher casualties than the Communists, many of whom were guerrilla fighters rather than army regulars. In the aftermath of the Battle of Ap Bac, the U.S. Army lost some credibility among journalists, who continued to report that the ARVN was a dubious fighting force struggling against a mysterious, determined, and very capable guerrilla movement. **See also** Harkins, Paul D.; Vann, John Paul.

## Arc Light

The code name for B-52 bombing raids over South Vietnam and Laos originating from American bases in Guam, Okinawa, and Thailand. Arc Light missions were designed to both support ground troops and interfere with North Vietnamese operations. Late in the American phase of the Vietnam War they were used for more conventional bombing raids against North Vietnam.

The B-52 was a huge bomber, also known as a Stratofortress, originally designed to deliver nuclear bombs. In 1964 the U.S. Air Force decided to modify the aircraft and train its crews to deliver conventional bombs in support of U.S. efforts in Southeast Asia. B-52s could carry tremendous payloads; the B-52F, for example, could carry fifty-one bombs, twenty-

four of which were 750-pounders. The later B-52D carried 108 five-hundred-pound bombs. The aircraft proved to be devastatingly effective not only because of its huge bomb loads but because it flew at an altitude of thirty thousand feet, which meant that it could not be seen or heard from the ground.

The first Arc Light operation was troop support during the Battle of Ia Drang Valley in November 1965. Over the next years Arc Light bombers continued to support American and South Vietnamese troops at such sites as Khe Sanh and Dak To. Meanwhile, B-52 raids also pounded Viet Cong outposts and the Ho Chi Minh Trail. In 1969 President Richard M. Nixon's Vietnamization policy resulted in a reduction of Arc Light operations in Vietnam proper, but raids continued in Cambodia and Laos, where the war was spreading rapidly. In those two countries, the primary purposes of the missions continued to be support for anti-Communist ground troops as well as the interdiction of enemy positions and supply lines. In 1972 Nixon stepped up Arc Light operations in Vietnam in an effort to keep the North Vietnamese at the negotiating table in Paris. Operation Linebacker I in the spring and summer of that year extended Arc Light's operations to include conventional bombing raids on the North Vietnamese cities of Hanoi and Haiphong. Linebacker II, or the infamous Christmas bombing of 1972, also consisted of numerous B-52 raids. Their precision was such that, even though many military targets had been deliberately located in thickly populated areas, civilian fatalities were estimated at a relatively limited sixteen hundred people. The final Arc Light mission was flown against Cambodia in August 1973.

In total, Arc Light missions numbered over 126,000 between June 1965 and August 1973. Almost all of them resulted in the release of bombs, whose effects can still be seen across Vietnam, Cambodia, and Laos; certain areas contain unexploded bombs to the present day. Remarkably, only thirty-one B-52s were lost during Arc Light operations, eighteen from antiaircraft fire in North Vietnam and thirteen from various operational or mechanical problems. **See also** B-52; bombers; Rolling Thunder.

## Army, U.S.

Almost 67 percent of U.S. military personnel in Vietnam—more than 1.7 million servicemen and servicewomen—served in the U.S. Army, and the commander of the Military Assistance Command, Vietnam (MACV), was an army general. This was a logical reflection of the fact that much of the fighting in Vietnam was on the ground. The first U.S. Army personnel in South Vietnam were members of the Military Assistance Advisory Group (MAAG), formed in 1950. MAAG was replaced by MACV in 1962, and the army component of MACV was designated as the U.S. Army Vietnam (USARV) in July 1965. The USARV, which at its peak strength in 1968 comprised 365,000 men, included seven infantry divisions, four infantry brigades, and an armored cavalry brigade. The army was the dominant U.S. presence in military regions (Corps) II, III, and IV. As organizational counterparts to the four military regions, USARV designated two "field forces" as well as, in 1968, an independent "corps" operational command. Some of the most storied U.S. Army units

*The members of the Ninth Infantry Division take part in a ceremony celebrating their departure from Vietnam. The U.S. Army had up to seven infantry units fighting in Vietnam at one time.*

served in Vietnam, including the 101st Airborne, the Eighty-second Airborne, and the First Cavalry Division (Airmobile).

In Vietnam, the U.S. Army was charged with two primary missions: defeating the North Vietnamese Army (NVA) and Viet Cong (VC) units and building a strong Army of the Republic of Vietnam (ARVN) capable of defending South Vietnam and securing the countryside. The army's record was mixed. Tactical successes were offset by the enemy's ability to retreat behind the Cambodian and Laotian borders, where the USARV could not follow. And ultimately the army advisers were unable to develop the ARVN into an effective force. Combat performance was also mixed; although most conventional engagements the army took part in were, technically, battlefield victories, the guerrilla warfare of the VC made larger victories elusive.

In the field, since most combat actions were relatively small in scale, decisions fell to junior officers rather than colonels or generals, usually captains of infantry battalions or other company commanders. The nature of army organization in the Vietnam years militated against unit cohesion, many have argued, since officers were often rotated in and out of their companies on six-month schedules. This allowed little time for officers and men to gain confidence in one another. Indeed, by 1968, the army was running short of highly qualified officer candidates for combat duty, an issue raised in explanations of the poor leadership that led to the My Lai massacre. In addition, enlisted men, many of whom were draftees, served for only twelve months in Vietnam, further reducing unit cohesiveness.

Of the total of 47,413 Americans killed in action in Vietnam, 30,950 were U.S. Army personnel. The army suffered an additional 7,261 nonhostile deaths and 96,802 wounded. In addition to thousands of other decorations, the Congressional Medal of Honor was given to 155 army men. **See also** Americal Division; First Cavalry Division; 101st Airborne Division.

# Army of the Republic of Vietnam (ARVN)

The South Vietnamese army. Originally formed in July 1949 as the Vietnamese National Army (VNA), the force grew from a mostly volunteer unit of some 100,000 officered by the French to a truly national army of nearly 1 million troops by the early 1970s. Although individual units often fought bravely and effectively, the Army of the Republic of Vietnam was continually hampered by corruption at its highest levels, by poor morale, and by a lack of cohesion.

When the Republic of Vietnam (RVN) took shape in 1954 and 1955, the VNA was in shambles. Training and organization of the new ARVN was taken up by the Americans, who sent a number of officers to military training centers in the United States. Building an effective ARVN also necessitated the presence of military trainers, or advisers, in South Vietnam itself, where advisers set out to shape a Vietnamese force modeled on the American army. Since the ARVN was under the control of the South Vietnamese government, however, the government had the ultimate voice in how the force was managed. Ngo Dinh Diem, president of the RVN from 1955 to 1963, used the ARVN as a place to exercise patronage and foster and reward loyalty. Consequently, top officers gained their positions by demonstrating loyalty rather than skill, and many of them were Roman Catholics in an army whose rank and file were mostly Buddhist. Beyond this, poor oversight often left army officers free to use their positions to enrich themselves through equipment contracts, appropriating material, and the like. Soldiers, for their part, were poorly paid, giving them incentives to pilfer and loot or engage in outside enterprises.

After Diem was ousted in November 1963, and especially after the United States began sending its own ground troops to Vietnam in March 1965, the ARVN became the dominant institution in South Vietnam. Political leaders such as Nguyen Cao Ky and Nguyen Van Thieu were invariably officers who maintained patronage networks within the armed forces. Meanwhile, the ARVN continued to grow, mostly from conscription, and continued to be trained and equipped by the Americans. When the United States began to withdraw its ground forces in 1969, the bulk of the fighting was turned over to the ARVN and its related branches of the South Vietnamese armed forces: the air force (SVNAF), the navy (SVNN), the marines (SVNMC), and the irregulars in the territorial forces and the Civilian Irregular Defense Groups. Only from this point did the ARVN prove to be an effective fighting force, able to halt North Vietnam's Easter Offensive of 1972. Still, the ARVN relied heavily on U.S. training, U.S. equipment, and from 1972 on, massive U.S. bombing runs over North Vietnam.

Organizationally the ARVN was divided into four corps commands, each of which had jurisdiction over a particular area of the country. At full strength the ARVN had nearly a million men, of whom some 450,000 were regular army troops divided into thirteen divisions, seven groups of army rangers, and other elite groups. The others belonged to support units and to the other branches, mostly the territorial forces. By 1972 the ARVN was armed with the latest hand and artillery weapons as well as tanks. The SVNAF, the second largest of the South Vietnamese forces, had at its disposal in 1973 nearly one hundred fighters and fighter-bombers and hundreds of helicopters, mostly Huey UH-1 gunships or transports. Just as the ARVN was one of the largest armies on Earth, the SVNAF was the fourth largest air force.

Neither proved equal to the forces of North Vietnam. In 1974 and 1975 the ARVN paid the price of years of poor leadership, corruption, and overreliance on the United States. Again, although a number of individual ARVN units fought well and bravely, large numbers of troops simply deserted in the face of North Vietnamese onslaughts and roads crammed with refugees, and a number of top officers abandoned their men and fled into exile. RVN president Duong Van Minh, who had taken the post only days earlier, ordered all remaining ARVN troops to stop fighting on April 30, 1975. **See also** Nguyen Cao Ky; Nguyen Van Thieu; North Vietnamese Army; Vietnam, Republic of; Vietnamese National Army.

## artillery

Artillery was widely used by American and South Vietnamese forces during the Vietnam War, and it proved to be effective in the war's characteristic jungle warfare, which lacked conventional front lines. It was generally assumed, in fact, that artillery was responsible for more enemy casualties than all other ground weapons combined. Artillery units accompanied virtually all infantry operations, and all camps and firebases were ringed with artillery weapons, which artillery crews often fired even when no combat was under way in a tactic they called "harassment and interdiction."

The primary artillery piece in Vietnam was the M101 105-millimeter towed howitzer, a mainstay of the U.S. military since World War II that had been improved through various modifications. Weighing several tons, the M101 was capable of rapid fire once secured into the ground. Its primary disadvantage was its inability to pivot 360 degrees, making it cumbersome for artillerymen to move the piece to counter mobile enemy units. The M102, introduced in 1966, was much lighter than the M101 and was able to pivot 360 degrees. It was light enough to be carried by helicopters and was widely used by airborne units. Both guns had an effective range of nearly eight miles and could fire eight 33-pound shells in a single minute. Other artillery weapons used by the Americans and South Vietnamese included the M107, a 155-millimeter gun with a range of nearly twenty-four miles, and the M110, which fired a shell weighing two hundred pounds and was the most accurate, if relatively slow firing, of the artillery pieces. The shells these guns fired ranged from explosive rounds to smoke, phosphorous, and illumination rounds. The M101 and M102 even had the capacity to fire leaflet rounds for the purpose of psychological warfare. **See also** light antitank weapon; mortars; tanks and armored personnel carriers.

## A Shau Valley

A strategically important valley located in northern South Vietnam. The valley, which lay southwest of the city of Hue and ran across the Vietnamese-Laotian border, was the site of frequent and often fierce fighting during the Vietnam War. The region through which it ran was sparsely populated, mountainous, and thick with tropical jungles. On the Vietnamese side its only ground access consisted of a dirt road known as Route 548; on the Laotian side it was not far from the Ho Chi Minh Trail.

American and South Vietnamese strategists recognized that the A Shau Valley was a potential point at which Communist forces could infiltrate South Vietnam as early as April 1963. Therefore, U.S. Special Forces built a camp in the region

staffed primarily by Civilian Irregular Defense Group (CIDG), or Montagnard, troops. Unable to hold the region, Special Forces and CIDG troops abandoned the base in 1966, at which point it became an important outpost of the North Vietnamese Army (NVA). U.S. and South Vietnamese forces tried several times to dislodge the NVA from the area, particularly in 1968 and 1969, but it proved difficult to do because Communist troops could easily withdraw across the border and were also easily resupplied and reinforced thanks to the Ho Chi Minh Trail. The largest single engagement in the valley was the Battle of Ap Bia Mountain, more famously known as the Battle of Hamburger Hill, in May 1969. After bloody fighting, U.S. forces were able to take the mountain but soon relinquished it, allowing the NVA to return. For the remainder of the war, the A Shau Valley remained a sliver of South Vietnamese territory controlled by the Communists. This control made the northern portions of their 1972 and 1974 offensives easier to organize and implement than they otherwise might have been. **See also** Hamburger Hill, Battle of.

## atrocities

A term suggesting a wide variety of abuses against unarmed or otherwise defenseless people, ranging from beatings to intentional deprival of food or other necessities to torture and shootings. Although atrocities are a common feature of all wars, many consider the Vietnam War to be especially "dirty."

Atrocities committed by Americans were often a result of the frustration and uncertainty of the war itself and of the desire for vengeance. Soldiers could rarely be sure whether the Vietnamese people they encountered were friendly or whether they might be carrying grenades or weapons as part of a Viet Cong (VC) ambush. In addition, U.S. troops suffered psychologically from the fear of booby traps, which caused many casualties. Other sources of frustration may have included poor military leadership, especially as the war dragged on, and the soldiers' growing sense that their lives were being endangered in a pointless enterprise. Some have also suggested that atrocities were at least partly encouraged by unit commanders offering rewards, such as increased rest and recreation (R&R) leaves, for units that achieved high body counts.

Examples of U.S. atrocities include the torture of captured VC suspects, "target practice" against villagers or their livestock, and the occasional captured VC fighter thrown alive from a helicopter. In one instance in 1966, members of an off-duty support unit burned a Vietnamese girl to death after staking her to the ground. In 1967 a U.S. Marine contingent entered the village of Thuy Bo after three days of heavy fighting during which they incurred heavy casualties. Reports of their actions in Thuy Bo noted that they had shot anything that moved there. The most infamous example of U.S. atrocities in Vietnam was the massacre at My Lai, where over a period of four hours on the morning of March 16, 1968, an army infantry company killed between two hundred and five hundred Vietnamese women, children, and elderly men in, apparently, a rather casual manner. In addition, a number of women and girls in the village as young as ten years old were raped. Rape, in fact, was not uncommon among American forces in Vietnam. On at least two documented occasions, rape was followed by the murder of the victim. Between 1965 and 1971, 201 army personnel and 77 marines were court-martialed for war crimes, most of them for the My Lai massacre.

South Vietnamese troops were also guilty of atrocities, and their U.S. allies often found it convenient to leave the dirtiest work, such as torture and execution, to the South Vietnamese. One example was the Phoenix Program, the effort to use aggressive intelligence work to root out the VC infrastructure beginning in 1968. Allegedly, interrogation sessions sometimes ended in a suspect's decapitation, and in a pattern seen before and after among both a few Americans and South Vietnamese, troops proudly collected the victim's ears as trophies.

The Viet Cong also committed atrocities, often with political goals in mind. To show that they were in charge in a specific village, for instance, VC troops might publicly decapitate village headmen and then leave their bodies on display. The Viet Cong also targeted South Vietnamese government officials for assassination; tens of thousands were actually killed. The VC was also implicated in one of the largest scale atrocities of the war, the arrest and murder of approximately three thousand civilians during the Battle of Hue in 1968. Their bodies were uncovered when American and South Vietnamese forces retook the city. The North Vietnamese Army was also involved in the actions at Hue as well as atrocities meted out against Montagnards. It was common, moreover, for the North Vietnamese to use torture against prisoners of war and suspected political enemies, even after the war was over. **See also** casualties; Hue, Battle of; My Lai massacre; Phoenix Program.

## attrition strategy

The primary U.S. strategy for winning the Vietnam War, a policy promulgated by General William Westmoreland, commander of the Military Assistance Command, Vietnam (MACV). The strategy was based on a premise used frequently in military history, which was to win by diminishing the enemy's willingness or ability to keep fighting.

For Westmoreland and his political supporters, attrition appeared to be the most effective way to prevent the North Vietnamese Communists from taking over South Vietnam with a minimum cost in U.S. casualties. It depended on drawing both the North Vietnamese Army (NVA) and the Viet Cong (VC) into conventional battles. Then, using vastly superior firepower, American forces could inflict high numbers of Communist casualties. In time, it was presumed, the North Vietnamese government would decide that the high rate of casualties was not worth continuing the fight. Indeed, military studies suggested that enemies usually capitulated when casualties reached a total of 2 percent of the nation's population. Under Westmoreland, the attrition strategy not only relied on this notion but continually employed cold statistical measures such as kill ratios and body counts to demonstrate that the Communists were suffering far more casualties than either the Americans or South Vietnamese and that, therefore, the war was being won.

Although, arguably, variations of the attrition strategy worked for the United States in World War II, it failed in Vietnam. A basic reason for its failure was the willingness of North Vietnam to accept what to American minds were staggeringly high numbers of casualties, measured at up to 3 percent of North Vietnam's prewar population. Indeed, on more than one occasion North Vietnamese leader Ho Chi Minh's comments suggested that he was willing to accept a huge number of casualties, knowing that in time the United States would tire of the effort.

Other factors also contributed to the failure of attrition in Vietnam. The American people hesitated to accept that the war might last a number of years, distaste for long wars being a common thread in American history. The fact that large numbers of American lives were being lost in seemingly pointless engagements only dampened American enthusiasm. For instance, the attrition strategy did not require the taking of territory, a conventional and obvious measure of military success. American soldiers, rather, were sent into battle but told even after successfully taking territory that the territory was strategically insignificant and that they should return to their bases.

The attrition strategy also contradicted another major aspect of U.S. policy in Vietnam: pacification, or the attempt to secure Vietnamese towns and villages by, as was widely quoted, "winning the hearts and minds" of the Vietnamese. Attrition pulled large numbers of U.S. troops away from pacification efforts by sending them on endless search-and-destroy missions or long-range reconnaissance patrols. Moreover, since many killed by U.S. troops were South Vietnamese who had joined the VC, villagers were losing family members and neighbors, leading ordinary Vietnamese to question whether the United States considered them enemies or people to be won over through pacification. Likewise, U.S. field commanders, aware that increased body counts were a measure of their capabilities and prospects for promotion, grew less inclined to distinguish between ordinary villagers and VC insurgents. In some instances, field units became willing to kill civilians to add them to the body counts; in others, commanders simply padded their reports.

The attrition strategy was officially renounced in 1969, by which time Westmoreland had been replaced by General Creighton Abrams. The new overall policy of the United States in Vietnam consisted of stepping up the pacification effort, turning the fighting of the war over to South Vietnam in a process known as Vietnamization, and, for a time, continuing to support South Vietnam with training, supplies, and bombing raids. **See also** body count; kill ratio; search and destroy.

# August 1945 Revolution

The declaration of an independent republic of Vietnam by Ho Chi Minh at the end of World War II. On August 16, 1945, the day after the Japanese surrender, Ho declared himself the president of free Vietnam; at that time he was the leader of the Viet Minh, an informal force that opposed the Japanese occupiers of Vietnam and their French lackeys. The Viet Minh also had the support of the American Office of Strategic Services (OSS), the predecessor to the Central Intelligence Agency, and for a short time Ho was enlisted as an OSS operative. That August, Ho wanted to take advantage of a window of opportunity between the Japanese surrender and the return of stronger French colonial forces. He was able to back up his claim when, on August 19, the Viet Minh took control of Hanoi and when, on August 24, the Viet Minh began its attempted takeover of southern Vietnam from Saigon. On September 2, from the balcony of the French-built Opera House in Hanoi, Ho announced the formation of the Democratic Republic of Vietnam, the regime that provided the focal point of the struggle for Vietnamese independence and unification over the next thirty years.
**See also** Ho Chi Minh; Ho-Sainteny Agreement; Viet Minh.

# B-52

A bomber aircraft closely identified with the Vietnam War. The B-52 Stratofortress, or "buff," was built by the Boeing Corporation beginning in 1952. Its original purpose was to carry nuclear weapons on intercontinental missions, but as the development of long-range missiles and nuclear submarines reduced the need for nuclear bombers, the B-52 was modified to carry more conventional large munitions: A modified B-52 could carry a maximum payload of 108 five-hundred-pound bombs.

The B-52 was a huge aircraft, 156 feet long with eight engines. It required a crew of six, which included a single tail gunner armed with four 4.5-millimeter machine guns. Though not notably maneuverable, the B-52 could cruise at an altitude of thirty thousand feet, a height at which it could not be seen or heard from the ground.

In Vietnam, B-52s were mostly used for the so-called Arc Light missions, the carpet bombing of North Vietnam beginning in 1965 and lasting until 1968. They also played a dominant role in Operation

*A B-52 Stratofortress releases a string of bombs over Vietnam. B-52s played a dominant role in many Vietnam missions, including Operation Linebacker II.*

Linebacker II, the infamous Christmas bombing of 1972, when fifteen B-52s on a single sortie were downed because of misunderstood electronic intelligence data. The craft were also used widely for support of ground troops. Altogether, B-52s from bases in South Vietnam and Thailand flew 125,615 sorties over Vietnam, Cambodia, and Laos. **See also** Arc Light; bombers; Christmas bombing.

## Baby Lift

The April 1975 operation bringing Vietnamese orphans to the United States, where they were adopted by Americans. Over ten days just prior to the fall of South Vietnam, U.S. aircraft transported some twenty-five hundred Vietnamese children to adoptive families. The flights were largely uneventful aside from the very first, on April 4, which crashed soon after taking off from Saigon. Most of the 138 people killed in the crash were children.

Operation Baby Lift was the source of much controversy. Many of the children taken to the United States, some claimed, were not orphans at all. Instead, their Vietnamese parents had simply given them up to get them out of the war-torn country. Other critics, perhaps echoing the fears of Vietnamese parents, wondered whether the operation indicated that both the South Vietnamese and Americans suspected that a bloody reign of terror would follow the fall of South Vietnam. Still others suspected political manipulation, accusing President Gerald Ford, who announced the plan on April 3, of using the children to try to create sympathy for the South Vietnamese regime in hopes of getting Congress to send military aid. **See also** Amerasians; refugees.

## Ball, George (1909–1994)

Adviser to Presidents John F. Kennedy and Lyndon Johnson and the strongest voice within both administrations arguing against the escalation of American involvement in Vietnam. Formerly the head of the U.S. Strategic Bombing Survey, Ball was appointed undersecretary of state by Kennedy in 1961. The number-two man in the State Department, Ball emerged as an early opponent to American involvement in Vietnam; he argued that not only would American forces be drawn into a quagmire, but American interests would be distracted from Europe and from the threat of the Soviet Union, which should take first place among foreign policy priorities. During Kennedy's term, Ball specifically argued against the 1961 introduction of U.S. combat advisers as well as American support for Ngo Dinh Diem, the South Vietnamese president. In fact, Ball urged the United States to stop supporting Diem in hopes that a coup against him would follow. In 1966, under Johnson, Ball expressed opposition to the bombing of North Vietnam on the grounds that it would have opposite effects from what American strategists intended; instead of reducing the North Vietnamese will to fight, the bombing would inspire further resistance.

Ball resigned from the Johnson administration in 1966, dismayed by the course of events in Vietnam and convinced that he had little influence on administration decisions. In 1968, however, Ball served on the senior advisory group convened by Secretary of Defense Clark Clifford. Ball found that many others, including a number of former war hawks, now agreed with him that the United States should seek ways out of the Vietnam conflict. **See also** Johnson, Lyndon B.; McNamara, Robert; Wise Men.

## Ban Me Thuot, Battle of

The battle that marked the beginning of what was to be the final, successful offensive of North Vietnam against South Vietnam. It took place in March 1975 after a number of successful operations in the Central Highlands led the North Vietnamese to believe that U.S. interference would not materialize. On March 10 three divisions of the North Vietnamese Army (NVA) under General Van Tien Dung attacked Ban Me Thuot, a provincial capital north of Saigon. They quickly isolated it from Pleiku, another strategically important city that the South Vietnamese army (the Army of the Republic of Vietnam, or ARVN) under Pham Van Phu had mistakenly believed would be the focus of the attack. ARVN defenses crumbled rapidly, and Dung took control of Ban Me Thuot on March 12.

The ARVN defeat prompted mass desertions among South Vietnamese soldiers who wanted to rejoin and protect their families; even General Phu escaped by plane to Nha Trang. Deserters joined what was turning into a mass exodus southward of ordinary Vietnamese, a situation compounded when South Vietnamese president Nguyen Van Thieu ordered the ARVN to abandon its positions in the Central Highlands and prepare for a defense of Saigon and the coastal regions. The defeat at Ban Me Thuot, therefore, struck a major blow to both the cohesion and morale of the ARVN. On the other hand, it increased the confidence of the political and military leaders of North Vietnam, who responded to the disintegration of the ARVN by speeding up their timetable for the conquests of Saigon and the south. **See also** CBU-55; Frequent Wind; Ho Chi Minh campaign.

## Bao Dai (1913–1997)

The last of the Nguyen emperors of Vietnam, whose reign began in 1802. Bao Dai was also the titular head of various versions of the Vietnamese state that emerged between 1940 and 1954.

Bao Dai was born Nguyen Phuoc Vinh Thuy on October 22, 1913. He was the son of Emperor Khai Kinh, who was largely a ceremonial ruler under French authority. The future emperor spent his childhood in France and was crowned emperor there on January 8, 1926, taking the imperial name Bao Dai, which means "protector of greatness." He traveled to Vietnam for the first time in 1932 after the death of his father; until then the French would not permit him to enter the country for fear that he would be the focus of a nationalist insurgency.

Over the next years Bao Dai tried to reform his court in the hopes of striking a deal with the French that would allow a modernized Vietnam more autonomy. He dismissed many of his court advisers, who were largely sympathetic to the French and had prospered under their rule, and ended such long-standing customs as a vast imperial harem. Arrangements made in 1925, however, had left true authority in the hands of the French, who wanted to limit Bao Dai to a ceremonial role. Finding that his efforts accomplished little, the emperor spent much of the 1930s as a sort of playboy, performing his ritual functions but also indulging his interests in hunting, gambling, and women.

Bao Dai cooperated with the Japanese who occupied Vietnam in 1940 and with the collaborationist French administrators who remained at the end of World War II. In March 1945, still hoping for greater independence for his country, he declared, with Japanese support, that Vietnam was now independent from France. This new government lasted only a few months, during which time Bao Dai tried again to reform and modernize the nation along Western models. The defeat of the Japanese in August, however, meant also the defeat of Bao Dai's new regime. The emperor was thwarted by Ho Chi Minh and the Viet Minh in September 1945, when the Communists proclaimed their own independent Vietnamese republic. Ho had persuaded Bao Dai to abdicate his throne on August 25. Under the name of "First Citizen Vinh Thuy," the former emperor took a position within the new Viet Minh government. He quickly grew disillusioned with communism, however, and finding himself unable to effectively serve his people, he left Vietnam for China in 1946 and Europe the next year.

Over the next few years Bao Dai, still hoping to serve his people and achieve a non-Communist form of independence for Vietnam, found himself a reluctant pawn of the French, who were engaged in a war against Ho and the Viet Minh and who needed an alternative to communism to present to the Vietnamese people. The French convinced Bao Dai to return to Vietnam as head of state in 1949, after the Elysée Agreement established that Vietnam was to be a nominally independent nation within the French Union. Bao Dai set up a government in Saigon that remained in place until after the partitioning of Vietnam by the Geneva Accords of 1954. In effect, since the Viet Minh still controlled the north outside of Hanoi and other cities, Bao Dai led the first version of what was to become the Republic of Vietnam, or South Vietnam. He failed, however, to bring much stability to Saigon or the south, not surprisingly given the war with the Viet Minh and his uncertain position under the French. Bao Dai also established close ties with the Binh Xuyen, a criminal gang engaged in smuggling, the opium trade, prostitution, and other crimes, who maintained what was effectively a powerful private army.

After the Geneva Accords partitioned Vietnam and made South Vietnam an independent nation, Bao Dai remained in place as head of state. To run the government, however, Bao Dai bowed to U.S. pressure and appointed the ambitious Ngo Dinh Diem as prime minister in June 1954. In 1955 Diem ousted Bao Dai through a referendum abolishing the monarchy and making South Vietnam a republic under Diem's authority. Disappointed and frustrated, Bao Dai finally retreated to his estate in the south of France, where he lived until his death in 1997. **See also** Binh Xuyen; Ngo Dinh Diem; Vietnam, historical overview of.

## Barrel Roll

The name for the air support provided by the United States to the Royal Lao government in its attempt to prevent a Communist takeover of Laos. In direct contradiction to U.S. government claims that U.S. forces were not directly involved in the conflict in Laos, and in addition to the more-or-less covert efforts of the Central Intelligence Agency's Air America, Barrel Roll went on from June 1964 to April 1973. It helped turn small, sparsely populated Laos into the most heavily bombed region on Earth; by the time operations ceased, Barrel Roll and similar measures had dropped over 2 million tons of bombs, far more than fell on North Vietnam and more than were dropped by all combatants in World War II.

Operation Barrel Roll was authorized by U.S. president Lyndon B. Johnson soon after the Laotian Communists, the Pathet Lao, violated a 1962 peace agreement. One of Johnson's incentives was the knowledge that the Pathet Lao had the support of the North Vietnamese Communists; another was the fact that long portions of the Ho Chi Minh Trail ran through eastern Laos. In an unusual arrangement, the operation was under the control of the U.S. ambassador in Vientiane, the Laotian capital, rather than a military official. Accordingly, over the years a substantial "air staff" became attached to the U.S. embassy. The ambassadors, in succession Leonard Ungley, William Sullivan, and G. McMurtrie Godley, worked closely with Lao government officials and military leaders as well as with U.S. Air Force officers and their fellow ambassadors in South Vietnam and Thailand. Most of the aircraft used in the operation were flown from either U.S. carriers in the South China Sea or a U.S. Air Force base in Udon Thani, Thailand, some fifty miles from Vientiane.

The most intensive Barrel Roll activity took place in 1969 and 1970, when between two and three hundred sorties per day were launched. By this time, the attacking aircraft included B-52s, which had massive destructive power. In combination with the ground efforts of Royal Lao troops and their allies among the Hmong tribesmen, these B-52 strikes significantly slowed the advances of the Pathet Lao and their North Vietnamese allies, many of whom were regular troops from the North Vietnamese Army. By 1972, however, the Royal Lao government and the Pathet Lao were engaged in peace talks, and Barrel Roll strikes had been markedly reduced. After a peace accord was signed on February 21, Barrel Roll activity ceased aside from tentative reconnaissance flights out to detect violations of the peace in the form of troop or supply movements. **See also** Commando Hunt; Laos, secret war in; Pathet Lao; Steel Tiger.

## beehive shells

Artillery shells consisting of canisters full of small steel arrows known as flechettes. Beehive shells were fired from fixed artillery such as howitzer cannon, from helicopter gunships, from tanks, and from handheld recoilless rifles. Their name came from the fact that, when fired, the arrows produced an ominous buzzing sound. Usually used against large-scale infantry assaults, the beehives, which contained as many as eight thousand flechettes, proved devastatingly effective; a single shot could stop an advancing North Vietnamese unit in its tracks. **See also** artillery; grenades; mortars.

## Berrigan, Daniel (1921– )

Roman Catholic priest, writer, and leading anti–Vietnam War activist. A former U.S. Army chaplain, Berrigan emerged as an antiwar leader in 1964 when he formed the Catholic Peace Fellowship, which used such techniques as fasting and nonviolent protest to draw attention to the war. In 1965 he helped form a larger body known as the Clergy and Laymen Concerned About Vietnam. In 1968 he traveled to the North Vietnamese capital of Hanoi, where he helped gain the release of three American prisoners; he was also shown sites that had been devastated by U.S. bombing raids. Apparently with the encouragement of his brother Philip, also a priest, Daniel Berrigan was moved to more overt action after his return from Hanoi. In May 1968 the two Berrigans, along with seven other Catholic protesters, entered a draft office in Catonsville, Maryland, and burned the draft cards there using napalm. For his actions Berrigan was found guilty of conspiracy and destruction of government property and sentenced to three years in prison. Before his sentence began, however, he went underground. Finally captured and imprisoned in August 1970, Berrigan was released on grounds of ill health in January 1972. He was later named, but never indicted, as a coconspirator in some of the activities of his more radical brother. The actions of both Berrigan brothers gave added credibility to the antiwar movement, since their status as priests carried high moral authority. Other protesters criticized government prosecution of the Berrigans as undemocratic and discriminatory. **See also** antiwar movement; Berrigan, Philip; draft resistance.

## Berrigan, Philip (1923–2002)

Antiwar activist and Roman Catholic priest who proved to be readier to undertake violent protest than his brother and fellow priest, Daniel Berrigan. Philip Berrigan became known as an antiwar activist in 1964, when he helped form both the Emergency Citizens' Group Concerned About Vietnam and, along with his brother, the Catholic Peace Fellowship. His more radical activities began in October 1967 when, along with three other activists, he entered a draft office in Baltimore, Maryland, and poured blood over a number of files. Convicted of destroying government property, Berrigan became the first Catholic priest ever sentenced to prison for political activities in the United States. Before he was sentenced, however, Berrigan staged another draft protest by burning draft cards in a selective service office in Catonsville, Maryland, using napalm, a May 1968 incident in which Daniel Berrigan also took part. At the subsequent trial, Philip was given a second, concurrent sentence. He remained in prison until he was paroled in December 1972. In the meantime, however, Berrigan faced prosecution for other alleged acts, namely plotting the kidnapping of National Security Adviser Henry Kissinger and the destruction of heating systems in federal offices in Washington, D.C. This prosecution, conducted while Philip was in prison, proved unsuccessful. **See also** antiwar movement; Berrigan, Daniel; draft resistance.

## Bien Hoa

A provincial capital city located about twenty miles northeast of Saigon. Established in 1961 as the headquarters of the South Vietnamese army in Tactical Zone III, or III Corps, it served as the major center of military operations in the Saigon region. In addition to the South Vietnamese, American forces based a number of important units in the vicinity of Bien Hoa, including a major combat wing of the air force. Part of the larger Bien Hoa complex was the U.S. Army base at Long Binh, where tens of thou-

sands of American soldiers first set foot in Vietnam. **See also** Long Binh; military regions.

## Binh Xuyen

A criminal gang influential in the politics of southern Vietnam from 1945 to 1955; for a short time, it was also recognized as a legitimate political party. Originating in a group of bandits operating along the Saigon River, the gang emerged to take advantage of the vacuum of authority in Saigon in the aftermath of World War II. It soon established a major presence in the city, headquartering itself in Cholon, Saigon's Chinese district. At first, the Binh Xuyen allied itself with the Viet Minh, but in 1947 it switched loyalties to the French and to the emperor Bao Dai. In return, it received official protection and freedom for its various prostitution, gambling, and opium-trafficking activities. One attraction of the Binh Xuyen to the French and to Bao Dai was its ability to muster a force of up to forty thousand armed men. This force was large enough to exert a major influence on the streets of Saigon. Conversely, many Vietnamese refused to support the Bao Dai regime because of the emperor's close ties with this criminal gang, acknowledging that the relationship represented institutionalized corruption.

The Binh Xuyen, along with the religious sects of the Hoa Hao and the Cao Dai, was one of the major forces discouraging stability in southern Vietnam during the First Indochina War (1946–1954). After the 1954 Geneva Accords divided Vietnam in two, Ngo Dinh Diem took power in the south and forced Bao Dai to resign. To both demonstrate his authority and stabilize South Vietnam, Diem took steps to bring the Hoa Hao, the Cao Dai, and the Binh Xuyen under his heel. After Binh Xuyen leaders refused to take their private armies out of Saigon in April 1955, Diem ordered the national army to attack. The result was a major battle in Saigon that left five hundred dead and rendered thousands homeless. Binh Xuyen fighters retreated to the surrounding countryside, where they continued to fight for another month. By the beginning of June, however, Diem's men had dispersed the Binh Xuyen and its leaders had escaped into exile. At that point it ceased to play a role in South Vietnamese affairs. **See also** Cao Dai; Hoa Hao; Ngo Dinh Diem.

## boat people

Refugees who left Vietnam by sea in the years after the Vietnam War. Although tens of thousands of South Vietnamese left the collapsing nation in April 1975 to seek refuge with the U.S. Seventh Fleet, the mass exodus of so-called boat people began only in the late 1970s after the new Socialist Republic of Vietnam (SRV) stepped up its efforts to transform the south. Those who left fit a range of categories: merchants and businessmen, former South Vietnamese military men or government employees, those who rejected or were oppressed by the new regime, and ethnic Chinese or Cambodians. They left on a wide variety of rickety craft, often after paying substantial sums to boatmen, from ports such as Da Nang and Nha Trang and from the many waterways of the Mekong Delta.

Boat people set out for various destinations, including Thailand, Malaysia, Singapore, Indonesia, the Philippines, and Hong Kong, though the ultimate goal for most was the United States. On the way, the unfortunate suffered at the hands of pirates and opportunistic fishermen in the Gulf of Thailand or the South China Sea, victims of robbery, rape, and murder. Many fishermen they encountered responded with great generosity; still, unknown numbers of boat people were lost at sea. Those who reached foreign shores were sent to refugee camps pending further resettlement.

By 1979 the boat people had become a global refugee problem. At that point, 100,000 boat people had arrived in Hong

*Thousands of refugees known as boat people fled the Socialist Republic of Vietnam in the late 1970s. Many made their way to the United States.*

Kong and more than ten thousand were coming every month, stretching the capacities of refugee camps and local aid agencies. Camps in the Philippines were also full. The United Nations (UN) addressed the problem by raising funding for refugee programs and encouraging potential host countries to raise the number of refugees they would accept. The United States, for instance, doubled its admissions from seven thousand to fourteen thousand per month. The UN also asked the SRV to step in to help contain the problem, and the number of boat people fell drastically in the early 1980s.

Nonetheless, into the 1990s, groups of boat people continued to leave the SRV, and the refugee camps remained full. By 1995 an estimated 480,000 Vietnamese had been resettled in the United States, and an additional 210,000 had found homes in other countries. More than 200,000 were in refugee camps when, that year, the UN and the various Southeast Asian governments made the decision to close the camps. Some of the remaining refugees would be resettled, but others would be forced to return to Vietnam. Many refugees, however, refused to consider going back. In 1996 the last boat people camps, in Hong Kong, were closed when the British Hong Kong government agreed to accept the remaining refugees. **See also** reeducation camps; refugees.

## body count

One of the statistical measures used by U.S. commanders and officials to judge their success in the Vietnam War, used primarily from 1965 to 1969. Since commanders had settled on a policy of attrition, or winning the war by killing so many enemy soldiers that their leaders would surrender or negotiate for peace, military units in the field were encouraged to maintain high body counts, or large numbers of enemy dead. This encouragement inspired field commanders

to inflate their body counts or otherwise file misleading reports. In any case, large body counts had little effect on Communist morale or decision making, and U.S. commanders acknowledged by 1969 that the strategy of attrition had failed. **See also** attrition strategy; kill ratio; search and destroy.

## bombers

Aircraft designed mostly for the purpose of dropping bombs; that purpose, however, varied from support of ground troops to electronic intelligence to carpet-bombing missions. Bombers were generally equipped with guns for defense. The bomber most used during the Vietnam War was the B-52 Stratofortress, a craft originally designed in the early 1950s to carry nuclear weapons that was modified for use in Vietnam and surrounding regions. The huge craft, powered by eight engines, carried a crew of six; it had a range of over seven thousand miles. Another advantage of the B-52 was that it could cruise at an altitude of thirty thousand feet, making it impossible to see or hear from the ground. B-52s, often flying in groups of three, dropped hundreds of thousands of tons of bombs on North Vietnam, Laos, and Cambodia. They were also used in an air support role for combat operations. Other bombers widely used in Vietnam include the A-4 Skyhawk, the "workhorse" of navy and marine pilots, and the A-1 Skyraider, a dive-bomber. The Grumman A-6, later modified to the EA-6A Intruder and the EA-6B Prowler, was the most versatile bomber in wide use in Vietnam. It was an attack bomber as well as an effective airplane for electronic intelligence and reconnaissance. **See also** B-52; fighter-bombers.

## booby traps

Relatively simple devices used to devastating effect by North Vietnamese Army (NVA) and Viet Cong (VC) forces on jungle paths, roads, bridges, and waterways.

U.S. statistics suggest that booby traps caused 11 percent of the deaths and 17 percent of the wounds among army troops between 1965 and 1970. In addition to the casualties they inflicted, booby traps caused psychological harm and forced the diversion of resources to counter them.

Many booby traps were simple, even primitive, contraptions. Examples include bear traps, whose "mouths" full of sharp steel teeth snapped quickly shut; crossbows set in trees or brush and triggered by trip wires; and mud balls that hid sharp spikes. Communist forces even deployed boxes full of scorpions. Among the most damaging of the booby traps were pungi stakes, sharpened sticks of bamboo placed upright in a disguised pit. One particularly dangerous booby trap was the so-called Malay whip, a log fifteen meters long that was tied to trees by extremely tight ropes. The log was so heavy that elephants had to be brought in to hoist it into place. If someone stepped on a trip wire, the ropes broke apart and the log was released. In one instance a Malay whip killed all thirteen members of a South Vietnamese patrol.

Some booby traps were explosive. These included coconuts filled with gunpowder, grenades hidden in tin cans, and even, apparently, discarded bicycles that triggered an explosive device when picked up. The NVA and VC also frequently deployed so-called mud-ball mines, grenades with safety pins removed that were buried in mud to prevent detonation. When a footstep cleared away the mud, the grenades exploded. Larger booby traps, such as five-gallon oil drums filled with explosives, were used against personnel carriers and other transport vehicles. **See also** casualties; pungi stakes.

## Bouncing Betty

A type of antipersonnel land mine used mostly by U.S. and South Vietnamese forces, although Communist troops also used stocks of mines that were left behind or captured. Its name came from the fact that, when triggered by the pressure of a footstep, the three-pronged conical device bounced up in the air to about waist level. Then, too quickly to dodge, it released a sixty-millimeter mortar round. **See also** mines; unexploded ordnance.

## Buddhists and Buddhist protest

Buddhism, a major world religion, has been the predominant religion of Vietnam for nearly two thousand years. It was introduced in the second and third centuries by Chinese monks and missionaries. Probably as a result of Chinese influence, Vietnam adopted the Mahayana ("greater path") form of Buddhism, which focused on communal rituals as well as the individual search for nirvana, the Buddhist state of nonexistence and bliss. Mahayana Buddhism, in Vietnam and elsewhere, also provided for the appearance of bodhisattvas, enlightened souls who remained in their earthly form to help others achieve enlightenment. Many traditional Vietnamese heroes were considered to be bodhisattvas. As it was practiced, Vietnamese Buddhism also included many long-standing animist beliefs and rituals such as the belief in the presence of various spirits. In the nineteenth century, due largely to the arrival of the French, many Vietnamese adopted Roman Catholicism. Nevertheless, Buddhism remained the professed faith of as much as 80 percent of the population and a fundamental force in Vietnamese culture.

Beginning in the years of the First Indochina War (1946–1954) and for much of the remainder of the larger Vietnam conflict, many Buddhists felt they were under increasing fire from two sides. The North Vietnamese Communists were largely opposed to organized religion as a matter of doctrine, while the South

*In an act of protest that shocked the world, Buddhist monk Thich Quang Duc burns himself to death at a busy Saigon intersection.*

Vietnamese regime of Ngo Dinh Diem, in place from 1955 to 1963, actively supported Catholics, to the detriment of Buddhists. Diem himself was a devout Roman Catholic who encouraged hundreds of thousands of fellow Catholics to move from North Vietnam to South Vietnam during a brief period after the First Indochina War when such migration was permitted. Once they arrived, he awarded them grants of land and other privileges. As early as 1951 Vietnamese Buddhists had organized themselves into the General Association of Buddhists to defend their forms of worship. As a matter of custom and belief, Buddhist leaders, who were generally high-level monks in charge of monasteries and temples, avoided politics, but the upheavals of the war years forced the Buddhists to become politicized.

Buddhist protest reached its peak in 1963, sparked by an incident that took place in May of that year, when monks and worshipers gathered in the city of Hue to celebrate the birthday of Siddhartha Gautama, the original Buddha and founder of the faith. Diem's police opened fire on the assemblage, killing nine people. Diem blamed the deaths on Communist terrorists, but the lie fooled no one. Buddhist leaders demanded an end to religious oppression and, when Diem chose not to respond, called for him to leave office. As tensions mounted, Buddhist protests spilled over into the streets. Then on June 11, an elderly monk, Thich Quang Duc, staged an elaborate ceremony in the middle of a busy intersection in Saigon in which, doused with gasoline, he set himself on fire. A journalist's photograph of the burning monk made its way to the front pages of newspapers the world over. The shocked global reaction to the story, however, did not inspire Diem to end his persecution or even meet with leading Buddhists, and in August Diem used regular troops to arrest and imprison more than one thousand Buddhists in Hue and Saigon. Quang Duc's self-immolation was followed by similar suicides, and Buddhist protests spread. People around the world began to question a regime that would oppress peaceful Buddhists and provoke such shocking sacrifice. The U.S. government, for its part, considered the protests a major challenge to its support of the Diem regime. Through the U.S. ambassador, Henry Cabot Lodge, the administration of President John F. Kennedy demanded that Diem and his brother, Ngo Dinh Nhu, find a way to end the protests. The brothers refused, claiming that Communist infiltration lay behind the Buddhist protests. Although no religious leaders played a direct role in the coup that overthrew Diem and his brother on November 1, 1963, Buddhist protests had prepared the way by fatally undermining what little support for the regime remained in place. Moreover, Diem's treatment of Buddhists offended a number of politicians and military officers who were themselves Buddhist.

The South Vietnamese regimes that followed Diem tried to accommodate the Buddhists. More Buddhists, for instance, were raised to high positions in the government and armed forces, and successive Vietnamese leaders pledged to respect the independence of the temples and monasteries. In 1966, however, Buddhist protests began anew, led by Thich Tri Quang and taking place mostly in Hue and Da Nang. Thich Tri Quang denounced the United States as an accomplice to the oppressive South Vietnamese government and targeted an American library in Hue for protests. In addition, the Buddhists objected to the recent ouster by leader Nguyen Cao Ky of an important official, General Nguyen Chanh Thi, who was closely allied with the Buddhist movement. By May 1966, ten monks and nuns had burned themselves to death and the Buddhist protests threatened to undermine the combined South Vietnamese–U.S. military efforts in central Vietnam. Ky tried at first to crush the protests by force but ultimately entered into negotiations with Buddhist leaders, and the protests subsided. Thich Tri Quang, for his part, was arrested while staging a hunger strike. No large Buddhist protests took place after these incidents, although individual monks continued to speak out against the Saigon regime until 1975. **See also** Ngo Dinh Diem; Thich Quang Duc.

# Bundy, McGeorge (1919–1996)

Presidential special assistant for national security affairs from 1961 to 1966. John F. Kennedy appointed him to the post out of academia, and Bundy went on to be part of the inner circles of advisers to both Kennedy and Lyndon B. Johnson. Intelligent and articulate, he generally supported the U.S. effort to help the South Vietnamese build an independent, democratic regime but was hesitant to fully commit American forces.

In the fall of 1963, when Vietnam began to take a prominent place among presidential concerns, Bundy advised Kennedy to take a wait-and-see stance during the coup against Ngo Dinh Diem. In late 1964 and early 1965, under Johnson, Bundy supported the general policy of the new administration, which was to expand American troop involvement while beginning bombing strikes against North Vietnam both in retaliation and in hopes of forcing the Communists to negotiate. In 1965 Bundy was in Vietnam when a Viet Cong (VC) raid against an American installation at Pleiku killed nine Americans. The event helped convince him that the presence in the field of a large American force was necessary, if for no other reason than to discourage North Vietnamese or VC attacks and to provide South Vietnam with a strong negotiating tool. He understood that a political victory in Vietnam might be more attainable than a military victory, and he also encouraged Johnson to strengthen the various pacification efforts directed at the South Vietnamese populace. Nevertheless, Bundy took an active role in selecting and reviewing bombing targets and in ensuring that the role of politicians and managers in Vietnam was not subordinated to the military effort.

Bundy resigned from his position in 1966, largely over Vietnam policy. He had grown skeptical of the escalation of American military involvement, suggesting that escalation was rash at best and would only undermine pacification programs. **See also** Ball, George; Bundy, William; Johnson, Lyndon B.; McNamara, Robert.

## Bundy, William (1917–2000)

Presidential adviser on Vietnam policy from 1961 to 1969. The brother of McGeorge Bundy, William Bundy held lower-level offices but arguably had a stronger influence on Vietnam policy than his brother. A Central Intelligence Agency (CIA) official since 1950, Bundy was appointed deputy assistant secretary of defense for international security affairs with the Kennedy administration in 1961. Familiar with Southeast Asia, Bundy was asked to analyze the South Vietnamese government and advise the administration. He became a strong supporter of both Ngo Dinh Diem's regime and the U.S. hope to stall the spread of communism in the region by supporting South Vietnam. At various points he proved to be in favor of counterinsurgency and other covert operations, bombings of North Vietnam, and the escalation of an American military presence.

Bundy was one of the important figures behind the Gulf of Tonkin Resolution of 1964, which gave the president the authority to approve military action in Vietnam without a congressional declaration of war. Early in 1964, when he was promoted to assistant secretary of state for Far Eastern affairs, he came to believe that America needed to make offensive moves against North Vietnam rather than simply react to Viet Cong actions in the south. To that end he wanted to prevent access to the North Vietnamese port of Haiphong and attack North Vietnamese military installations. Such actions would require congressional authorization, and in May 1964 Bundy helped write a rough draft of the Gulf of Tonkin Resolution, which Congress quickly ratified.

Bundy also helped draw up plans and explanations for a graduated bombing campaign against North Vietnam, as well as considering other options, as part of a special National Security Council working group established by President Lyndon B. Johnson. Bundy submitted a report to his superior, Secretary of State Dean Rusk, in May 1966. In this report he made recommendations that effectively became U.S. policy until after Johnson left office. These included expanding the bombing of North Vietnam in hopes of forcing the Communists to negotiate. Bombing operations would cease only when the North Vietnamese stopped sending troops and equipment to South Vietnam and, according to an assumption that remains controversial, used their authority to halt the activities of the Viet Cong. Like many others, Bundy presumed that Hanoi had complete control over the guerrillas in the south.

U.S. management of the war effort and President Johnson's management style left Bundy disillusioned by 1967, when he began to advocate deescalation of the American effort on the grounds that the effort was having little effect on North Vietnam. After the Tet Offensive of early 1968 he grew even more cautious about continued U.S. involvement in Southeast Asia. Bundy left the State Department with the rest of Johnson's administration in January 1969. **See also** Bundy, McGeorge; Gulf of Tonkin Resolution; Johnson, Lyndon B.; Rusk, Dean.

# Bunker, Ellsworth (1894–1984)

U.S. ambassador to South Vietnam from 1967 to 1973. After serving in a number of foreign service posts beginning with ambassador to Argentina in 1950, Bunker replaced Henry Cabot Lodge in the Saigon embassy in April 1967. Along with military commander Creighton Abrams, Bunker tried to persuade American policy makers to coordinate their efforts rather than working at cross-purposes on such efforts as military action and assistance, pacification, and public relations.

Bunker developed great respect for the South Vietnamese people and their leaders, particularly Nguyen Van Thieu, and he strongly supported the policy of Vietnamization, according to which the Americans sought to shift more of the burden of fighting North Vietnam onto the South Vietnamese. Bunker backed the invasion of Cambodia in 1970, believing that it would help Vietnamization by relieving the immediate burdens on South Vietnamese forces from North Vietnamese bases in Cambodia. Meanwhile, he also supported increased American air strikes, both against military positions in South Vietnam and along the Ho Chi Minh Trail and against targets in North Vietnam, convinced that such measures would ensure that Communist representatives would remain at the negotiating table. Bunker's respect for the South Vietnamese was reciprocated, and he was able to work closely with Thieu and other South Vietnamese political leaders. After serving for six years in Saigon, longer than any other top American military or diplomatic official, Bunker resigned in March 1973. **See also** Abrams, Creighton; Lodge, Henry Cabot; Vietnamization.

## Calley, William (1943– )

A U.S. Army lieutenant who was the only soldier convicted of criminal charges for participation in the My Lai massacre of March 1968. Calley joined the army in 1967. After an undistinguished graduation from officer candidate school, he was commissioned as a second lieutenant and sent to Vietnam, where he took a position as a platoon leader in the C (Charlie) Company, First Battalion, Twentieth Infantry, Americal Division. His commanding officer was Captain Ernest Medina.

On March 16, 1968, Calley took his platoon into a hamlet known as My Lai in Song My village in Quang Nai province in central Vietnam, where the unit engaged in a massacre of villagers. The news of the events at My Lai was leaked to the U.S. Congress in April, and soon reached the media. After an investigation, Calley was arrested and indicted by the army on the charge of murdering 109 Vietnamese civilians. Calley pled innocent but was found guilty by a court-martial and sentenced to life imprisonment at hard labor in an army stockade. On the orders of President Richard Nixon, however, he was freed from the stockade after only three months and confined to his quarters, pending further investigation. Findings reduced Calley's sentence to twenty years and then to ten. After serving thirty-seven months in his quarters, a U.S. district court judge overturned the court-martial's earlier conviction, indi-

cating that Calley had been the victim of unjust publicity stemming from public outrage over the massacre. The army objected mildly to the interference of a civilian court in military legal proceedings, but Calley was not subjected to any further legal action. Calley was released in November 1974 and dishonorably discharged from the army. **See also** My Lai massacre.

## Cambodia, invasion of

An expansion of the Vietnam War into neighboring Cambodia in April 1970. The immediate cause of the invasion, carried out by a combined force of South Vietnamese and American troops, was a set of actions taken by the new Cambodian prime minister Lon Nol, who replaced Norodom Sihanouk on March 18. In contrast to Sihanouk, Lon Nol proved unwilling to cooperate with the North Vietnamese Communists, who received supplies through Cambodia and manned a stretch of the Ho Chi Minh Trail in the mountainous eastern regions of the country. Lon Nol closed the port of Sihanoukville, through which supplies were taken to the Ho Chi Minh Trail, and attacked North Vietnamese encampments. The Communists counterattacked and quickly threatened to overwhelm Lon Nol's small, underequipped army.

Small South Vietnamese forces, and American advisers, had by this point already entered Cambodia from border areas in central Vietnam, an expansion of covert operations that were long under way. Military commanders, however, including General Creighton Abrams, the chief of the Military Assistance Command, Vietnam (MACV), wanted to send in a larger force to support Lon Nol's anti-Communist government. Although American political leaders hesitated to jeopardize official Cambodian neutrality, President Richard M. Nixon authorized an invasion, which began on April 30.

This Cambodian incursion, as some called it, comprised a sizable force of fifty thousand South Vietnamese and thirty thousand American troops. The attack was divided along three sectors. The first was an operation against Communist sanctuaries in a region known as the Fishhook. The second was a riverborne expedition sent up the Mekong River to establish control of the vital waterway as well as repatriate the thousands of ethnic Vietnamese who lived in Cambodia. The third sector was designed to cut the Ho Chi Minh Trail. All three, using Cambodian Army forces where appropriate and necessary, achieved some measure of success, but as in most military operations in the Vietnam War, this success was temporary. American troops left Cambodia, in fact, by June 30, satisfied with the recovery of tons of Communist supplies and interference with the regular operations of the North Vietnamese. South Vietnamese troops remained for much longer, supported by a controversial American bombing campaign and intelligence operations until August 1973.

The Cambodian invasion was a public relations disaster for Nixon and his administration. The president announced it in a televised address on May 1, and the revelation of this "secret" operation inspired some of the largest and most violent antiwar protests yet staged, including clashes at Kent State University and Jackson State College in which National Guardsmen and police shot and killed protesters. In 1969 Nixon had promised to gradually end American involvement in Indochina and withdraw American troops. To many Americans, the Cambodian invasion seemed to belie those promises by expanding the war to a new country. The president tried to justify the invasion by arguing that it allowed U.S. troop withdrawals to continue safely and encouraged the policy of Vietnamization, but few were convinced. Public outcry led the U.S. Congress to seriously consider ways of limiting Nixon's warmaking powers, as well as his tendency to engage in secret diplomacy and military operations.

Although Nixon's national security adviser, Henry Kissinger, proclaimed the invasion a great success, North Vietnamese Army (NVA) forces soon regained lost territory. NVA retreats in the face of the invasion had actually worked to their advantage, allowing Communist forces to disperse throughout the country. To counter this penetration, American strategists widened their areas of bombing raids, eventually turning Cambodia into one of the most heavily bombed countries in the history of warfare. The upheaval caused by the raids turned many Cambodians into supporters of the Khmer Rouge, the country's largest indigenous Communist insurrectionist group. After the withdrawal of the Americans and South Vietnamese, Lon Nol's army proved unable to stop the North Vietnamese, who successfully enlarged the Ho Chi Minh Trail. It could also not contain the expanding Khmer Rouge, which took the capital, Phnom Penh, in April 1975 after seizing control of much of the rest of the nation. **See also** antiwar movement; Khmer Rouge; Lon Nol; Sihanouk, Norodom.

## Cam Ranh Bay

The largest deepwater port on the coast of South Vietnam, located south of the

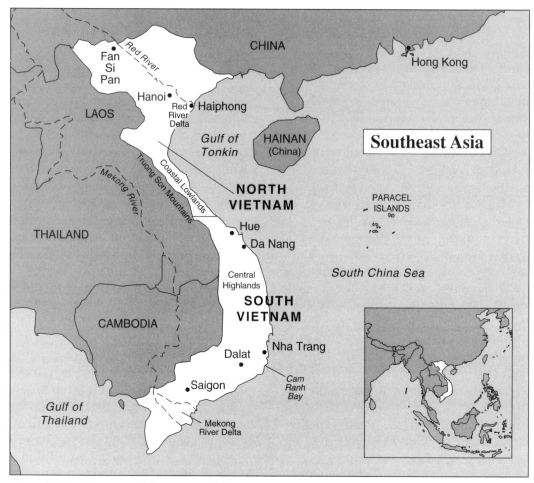

Southeast Asia

city of Nha Trang, and for cargo ships an easier and safer target than the upriver port of Saigon. An important stopping point for sailors for centuries, Cam Ranh Bay became the major port for the importation of American supplies during the Vietnam War. American forces took charge there in 1965 when the decision was made to commit American combat troops to the long-standing conflict. In addition to stationing combat troops there, and in time constructing a military airfield, the U.S. Army Corps of Engineers worked to expand the port's facilities, ultimately turning it into one of the largest and most modern ports in Southeast Asia. A contingent of South Korean troops provided security for the port facilities. Because of the heavy military presence, many considered Cam Ranh Bay the safest place in South Vietnam, and President Lyndon Johnson made two visits there.

Cam Ranh Bay was turned over to the South Vietnamese in 1972, as were the surrounding military installations. In April 1975 it fell, like the rest of South Vietnam, to Communist forces, who now found themselves in possession of a highly valuable port. According to the terms of a 1978 treaty between Communist Vietnam and the USSR, Cam Ranh Bay was turned over to the Soviet Union for use as a naval base in exchange for much-needed financial aid. **See also** Bien Hoa; Saigon.

## Cao Dai

A major religious sect that emerged in southern Vietnam in the late 1920s.

Along with another sect, the Hoa Hao, and the criminal Binh Xuyen, the Cao Dai was a major challenge to the stability of the South Vietnamese regime in 1954 and 1955.

Cao Dai, short for Dai Day Tam Ky Pho Do (the Third Revelation of the Great Path), was founded on the belief that all religions are fundamentally the same. Its teachings combined aspects of Christianity, Buddhism, Taoism, animism, and Confucianism, the main schools of thought and religion in Vietnam. Cao Dai followers believed that those five schools had been founded by prophets during the so-called First Revelation. During the Second Revelation, it was believed, they were altered by human shortcomings and therefore inspired conflict instead of unity. Ultimately, in the present period of the Third Revelation, the god who was the source of all belief systems and prophets would once again bring all schools of thought into a final unity. The term *Cao Dai*, meaning "high palace," is how followers referred to this god. Teaching also that all living organisms possess a part of the spirit of god and are therefore one, Cao Dai had a great appeal: The sect reinforced traditional Vietnamese beliefs about the everyday presence of the spirit of god and about reincarnation, or the movement of this spirit from body to body through a number of lives and deaths, which was also an aspect of Vietnamese Buddhism.

Cao Dai leaders' involvement in politics began in the late 1920s, when they took part in the general movement to oust French colonial rule. They continued to resist the French during World War II by building a private army with Japanese support. Then, during the First Indochina War (1946–1954) the Cao Dai, now in possession of its own military bases and territory, fought on the side of the French against the Communist Viet Minh. When the war ended, Cao Dai officials were well placed to take high positions within the new South Vietnamese government of Ngo Dinh Diem in return for turning over Cao Dai military forces and territories.

Members of the Cao Dai continued to play important roles in the South Vietnamese government and armed forces throughout the long Vietnam conflict, and millions of Vietnamese continued to follow Cao Dai teachings. After the North Vietnamese victory in 1975, many Cao Dai chose to join the hordes of refugees fleeing the country, but others remained in Vietnam. **See also** Binh Xuyen; Buddhists and Buddhist protest; Hoa Hao; Ngo Dinh Diem.

## Case-Church Amendment

A notable June 1973 addition to a U.S. State Department appropriations bill introduced in the Senate. Sponsored by Senators Clifford P. Case and Frank Church, the amendment was designed to cut off funding for U.S. military actions in Vietnam, Laos, and Cambodia unless such funding was specifically approved by Congress. Case and Church, along with many other senators and representatives, disagreed not only with the seemingly unending U.S. military involvement in Southeast Asia but with what they saw as potential misuses of presidential authority. According to the U.S. Constitution, only the U.S. Congress has the right to declare war. But John F. Kennedy, Lyndon B. Johnson, and Richard M. Nixon had continually sidestepped that issue by approving military actions in Southeast Asia on presidential authority alone. In particular, Case and Church were responding to Nixon's decision to continue the bombing of Cambodia in early 1973 as well as the president's June veto of legislation that would immediately have ended the bombing.

The appropriations bill, with the Case-Church Amendment attached, was passed by the Senate and then approved by the

*South Vietnamese refugees hurry past the bodies of three North Vietnamese soldiers in the street. Estimates of total casualties in the Vietnam War reached several million.*

House of Representatives. Nixon signed it into law according to a compromise he reached with congressional leaders: Further funding for operations in Vietnam, Laos, and Cambodia would be ended pending further authorization from Congress, but the bombing of Cambodia would continue until August 15, 1973. **See also** Cooper-Church Amendment; War Powers Resolution.

## casualties

Though exact figures vary, Department of Defense statistics report that the United States suffered a total of 211,501 casualties in the Vietnam War, including 47,413 killed in action, 10,785 nonhostile deaths, and 153,303 wounded in action. Over 65 percent of American servicemen killed in Vietnam served in the army, more than 25 percent in the marines, 4.4 percent in the

navy, 4.4 percent in the air force, and 0.01 percent in the Coast Guard. Free world forces casualties included 4,407 Koreans, 351 Thais, 83 New Zealanders, and 423 Australians.

By far the largest number of casualties were Vietnamese. Estimates of totals vary widely, but at least 110,000 South Vietnamese troops were killed and at least 500,000 wounded. For North Vietnamese and Viet Cong forces, the generally accepted estimate is some 660,000 killed, which may or may not include 300,000 missing in action. Large numbers of civilians also died during the Vietnam War, although exact totals can never be known. In the 1990s the Vietnamese government suggested that at least 2 million civilians died between 1954 and 1975. The lowest reliable estimate is 415,000. Civilians died not only from combat-related problems but from hunger and disease. Of the total of North Vietnamese civilian casualties, the U.S. government estimates that 30,000 deaths resulted from bombings.

These numbers do not include the tens of thousands who died in Laos, the up to 2 million Cambodians whose genocide was a by-product of the Vietnam War, or the thousands of casualties whose numbers continued to climb into the twenty-first century because of land mines and other unexploded ordnance left over from the war. **See also** *specific service branches.*

## CBU-55

The most powerful weapon used in the Vietnam War. The CBU was a cluster bomb consisting of three one-hundred-pound BLU-73 fuel-air bombs packed in a large metal cylinder. Airplanes had to be fitted with special bomb racks in order to carry it. After the cylinder was released, the three smaller devices parachuted to the earth. Upon impact they projected a huge cloud of ethylene dioxide fuel eight feet thick and fifty feet in diameter. The layer of fuel was then ignited. The resulting flaming mass produced an intense down-pressure heavy enough to kill anyone or anything beneath it. In a few seconds the flames consumed all the oxygen in a wide area, producing a vacuum that was itself lethal. The CBU-55 was used only once during the war, even though it was available by 1970. In April 1975, during the last days of the war and hours after South Vietnamese president Nguyen Van Thieu resigned, Americans gave one of the devices to the South Vietnamese in lieu of a B-52 raid. The South Vietnamese subsequently dropped it on a North Vietnamese contingent that had taken possession of a government encampment near Saigon. **See also** dumb bombs; smart bombs.

## cease-fire war

One name for the renewed fighting between North and South Vietnam after the signing of the Paris Peace Accords in January 1973. Although the Americans and other foreigners were gone, the fighting continued almost without a break despite the cease-fire called for in the accords. Since the accords failed to specify where the armed forces of the Republic of Vietnam (RVN, or South Vietnam) and Democratic Republic of Vietnam (DRV, or North Vietnam) were to stand at the moment the cease-fire took effect, both sides took advantage of a brief window of opportunity to quickly grab more territory before the cease-fire hour struck. The North Vietnamese Army moved more quickly, marching south from the demilitarized zone (DMZ) to seize hundreds of towns and villages. South Vietnamese president Nguyen Van Thieu refused to accept this, and even after the cease-fire was supposed to take effect ordered his forces to retake the territory. They succeeded, but the time it took, nearly two weeks, allowed the DRV to claim that the RVN had violated the cease-fire, and the DRV chose to retaliate in kind. U.S. president Richard Nixon tried to remain true to his pledge to support Thieu but found very quickly that both the American public and Congress were tired of Southeast Asian troubles.

The North Vietnamese launched a major offensive against South Vietnam in late 1974 and, surprised by the ease of their success, sped up their timetable for the conquest of the south. The final attack of the cease-fire war was the Ho Chi Minh campaign, directed against Saigon in March and April 1975. Overall, the period produced some of the bloodiest fighting of the entire thirty-year Indochina conflict and filled Vietnam's roads with refugees. **See also** Ho Chi Minh campaign; Paris Peace Accords; Xuan Loc, Battle of.

## Cedar Falls

A major military operation conducted in January 1967. It was directed against the so-called Iron Triangle, an area near Saigon that was largely controlled by the Viet Cong (VC) and was the center of its local command and intelligence operations. Cedar Falls was an attempt to remove the VC threat from the Saigon region. To accomplish the task, U.S. forces were joined by South Vietnamese army units as well as thousands of civilians drafted into service units.

Operations commenced on January 8, when American forces began an attack on the village of Ben Suc, thought to be the location of VC headquarters. After an intense but brief firefight, U.S. forces secured the village and discovered a wide network of VC tunnels. In their effort to clear the area around Ben Suc of all VC outposts, the U.S. forces destroyed several villages and cleared away acres of trees and vegetation. Some six thousand villagers were forcibly resettled.

The second phase of Operation Cedar Falls, beginning on January 9, consisted of search-and-destroy missions beginning at the edges of the Iron Triangle. As in Ben Suc, there were several firefights in this phase, but U.S. and South Vietnamese forces quickly found that many VC units simply slipped away rather than confront them head-on. To secure the area, more jungles and villages were cleared to make way for landing zones and other outposts. Finally winding down by January 26, Operation Cedar Falls was largely a success from the standpoint of the United States and South Vietnamese. Not only did they loosen the VC stranglehold on the area, they learned valuable lessons about VC tactics, including tunnel warfare. In addition, the VC had left behind large amounts of documentation for use by intelligence services. In contrast to the claims of some commanders, however, the operation did not end the threat of the VC in the region around Saigon, as the next year's Tet Offensive would make all too clear. **See also** Iron Triangle; Viet Cong.

## Central Highlands

A large area in the interior of Vietnam stretching, east and west, from the coastal plain to the mountainous regions along the Cambodian and Laotian borders and, north and south, between the towns of Kontum and Ban Me Thuot in South Vietnam. The Central Highlands consisted of some fifty-four hundred square miles of territory thick with mountains as high as eight thousand feet. It was sparsely inhabited by various Montagnard tribes who shared a mutual, traditional dislike of lowland Vietnamese. During the Vietnam War the area was the scene of extremely heavy fighting. Not only did portions of the Ho Chi Minh Trail pass through the highlands, but North Vietnamese offensives tended to begin there and strike in the direction of the coast in the hope of splitting South Vietnam in two. Among the important battles taking place in the region was the Battle of Ia Drang Valley in 1965, the first engagement involving American combat troops. Other decisive battles in the Central Highlands included the Battle of Dak To in 1967, the Battle of Kontum in 1972, and the Battle of Ban Me Thuot in 1975. **See also** Ban Me Thuot, Battle of; Ia Drang Valley, Battle of; military regions.

## Central Intelligence Agency (CIA)

The U.S. government branch responsible for all overseas intelligence operations. From 1945 to 1975 it played a wide and varied role in the long Indochina conflict, operating as one of the major arms representing American interests.

The CIA, strictly speaking, was formed in 1947. Its predecessor was the Office of Strategic Services (OSS), which in the summer of 1945 sent agents into northern Vietnam from its base in Kunming, China, to help in the effort to oust the Japanese. Among those whom OSS agents befriended was Viet Minh leader Ho Chi Minh, who worked alongside the OSS for a number of months and used the help of an American agent to draw up a Vietnamese declaration of independence that borrowed wholesale from the American model. Some OSS men, in fact, felt that the United States lost an opportunity in 1945 to turn Ho Chi Minh into an ally. Instead, the OSS, and later the CIA, supported the French in the 1946–1954 war. After the Geneva Accords of 1954 divided Vietnam, the CIA acted covertly to strengthen the South Vietnamese regime of Ngo Dinh Diem. For a number of years the head of the CIA's Saigon station was Lieutenant Colonel Edward Lansdale, who came to Vietnam with experience in counterinsurgency operations against Communists in the Philippines. Among other activities, Lansdale mounted a major propaganda campaign against North Vietnam that helped inspire hundreds of thousands of North Vietnamese to migrate south. In addition, he tried to reduce the threat of social instability represented by the Cao Dai and Hoa Hao sects by tying them to the Diem government. In time, however, the CIA withdrew its support from Diem, believing that his autocratic rule was enlarging rather than reducing the ranks of the Viet Cong. From 1960 to 1963 the CIA either stood aside during the various coup plots or rebellions against Diem or assured the generals who wanted to replace Diem that the United States would support them.

From 1959 to 1962 the head of the CIA's Saigon station was William Colby, who assembled continuing covert operations directed against the Viet Cong and its North Vietnamese supporters. With marginal success, he tried to instigate a guerrilla war in the north using CIA-trained South Vietnamese agents. Meanwhile, CIA agents also backed up U.S. Special Forces in their effort to establish effective alliances with the Montagnards, the non-Vietnamese hill tribes, in the nation's Central Highlands.

In addition to these field efforts, the CIA continued its intelligence-gathering activities using as many as four hundred American and Vietnamese agents. Colby frequently forwarded intelligence reports to decision makers in Washington; therefore, the efforts of the CIA contributed broadly to the American debate over Vietnam policy. By 1965, in fact, thanks to inside knowledge of the corrupt and inefficient workings of the South Vietnamese government and military command, the CIA took the position that the United States was not likely to win the war. Nevertheless, CIA agents did not make policy and for the remainder of the war continued to support the American and South Vietnamese effort. Among their major aims was forcing a collapse of the Viet Cong from within by arresting as much of its leadership as possible. To that end, in connection with South Vietnamese soldiers and police, the CIA set up the infamous Phoenix Program in 1968. The Phoenix Program established interrogation centers across South Vietnam where, allegedly, torture and other forms of abuse were rampant. Tens of thousands of ordinary Vietnamese as well as Viet Cong cadres were arrested, imprisoned, "reeducated," or killed. The effect on the structure of the Viet Cong was mixed; although certainly a number of Viet Cong leaders were rounded up, the corruption and brutality of the program may have increased peasant sympathy for the Communists.

The CIA actually had a freer hand in a secondary theater of the Indochina conflict, Laos, than it had in Vietnam. As early as 1960, when Communist insurgents known as the Pathet Lao threatened to overrun the country, President John F. Kennedy authorized the CIA to take steps to stop them. Over the next years the CIA fought a so-called secret war in Laos. It involved mostly the arming, training, and supplying of hill tribes in Laos, notably the Hmong, to oppose the Pathet Lao, although CIA efforts were also directed against the stretch of the Ho Chi Minh Trail that ran through Laos. One of the agency's major tools was Air America, a quasiprivate airline that ran supplies to Lao resistance fighters while conducting a variety of other missions.

In the early 1970s CIA operations came under the microscope of congressional investigators, and its freedom of operation was soon restricted. News about the Phoenix Program inspired concern, as did the revelation that the CIA was involved in surveillance of Americans who opposed the Vietnam War, domestic activity in violation of CIA authority. In addition, leaks and rumors indicated that the CIA may have been involved in illicit drug production and trade in Laos in order to help finance its secret war, activities that some believed increased the drug problem in the United States, especially the increase in heroin addiction. The result was increased congressional oversight of CIA activities as well as strict confirmation that the agency was to operate only outside U.S. borders.

Meanwhile, in Vietnam the CIA station was forced to evacuate Saigon along with all other U.S. agencies in April 1975 with the approach of the North Vietnamese Army. The rapid fall of Saigon meant that the CIA was forced to leave behind a considerable paper trail, as well as a number of Vietnamese colleagues and informers. CIA agents played an important role in helping former president Nguyen Van Thieu and other South Vietnamese notables escape, often with loads of luggage and treasure. **See also** Air America;

Colby, William; Helms, Richard; Phoenix Program.

## Central Office for South Vietnam (COSVN)

The name given by the North Vietnamese to the office controlling all Viet Cong military operations in South Vietnam. It acted as an effective liaison office between Democratic Republic of Vietnam (DRV, or North Vietnam) government officials and military leaders and the leadership of the Viet Cong, although often, sometimes because of other circumstances, the Viet Cong operated independently of DRV command. In addition, the COSVN represented the Central Committee of the Vietnamese Communist Party (the Lao Dong) in the south.

The COSVN headquarters generally lay somewhere in Tay Ninh Province near the Cambodian border; its exact location shifted to elude South Vietnamese and American forces. It was almost necessarily a shoestring operation, rather than a complete military or political headquarters, given the nature of Viet Cong operations and the danger of attack and the resulting need for invisibility and mobility. Generally, COSVN personnel consisted of a small group of military officers along with their staff and intelligence people.

The COSVN became an important target of U.S. military operations in their hope to sever the ties between the Viet Cong and the Hanoi government. Operation Junction City in 1967 as well as the invasion of Cambodia in 1970 were both directed specifically at the COSVN. Throughout the war, however, the COSVN remained independent and intact. **See also** National Liberation Front; Viet Cong.

## Chicago Seven

The group of protest leaders placed on trial for their roles in the violence surrounding the 1968 Democratic National Convention in Chicago. The trial of the Chicago Seven was a central event in both the anti–Vietnam War movement and the counterculture and protest movements of the 1960s in general. It provided many Americans with the illusion that the antiwar and social protest movements amounted to a coordinated conspiracy.

The Chicago Seven were originally the Chicago Eight. They were Abbie Hoffman and Jerry Rubin, leaders of the Youth International Party, or Yippies; Tom Hayden and Rennie Davis, both formerly of the Students for a Democratic Society (SDS); Lee Weiner and John Froines, two academics; Dave Dellinger, a top antiwar organizer as cochairman of the Mobilization Against the War; and Bobby Seale of the Black Panthers, a radical African American group. All were indicted on March 16, 1969, on charges of conspiracy and crossing state lines with intent to riot. The presiding judge was Julius Hoffman

of the U.S. Federal Court in Chicago. The defendants, except for Bobby Seale, were represented by William Kunstler and Leonard Weinglass.

The trial lasted from September 1969 until February 1970. During its first weeks Seale's critical outbursts proved so disruptive that the judge had him gagged and bound to a chair; soon after, Seale's trial was declared a mistrial and he was removed to be tried separately, already carrying a four-year sentence for contempt of court during the original proceedings. The remaining Chicago Seven also engaged in frequent ridicule of the court and its efforts, as did their attorneys. Moreover, all seven defendants were released daily, allowing them further access to and exposure in the media. Hoffman and Rubin, in particular, saw the trial as an opportunity for what they called "guerrilla theater," staged antics ridiculing the American establishment and its institutions.

*The Chicago Seven. Standing, from left, are Abbie Hoffman, John Froines, Lee Weiner, Dave Dellinger, Rennie Davis, and Tom Hayden. Jerry Rubin is seated (with his girlfriend, who was not involved in the trial).*

The defendants were found not guilty of conspiracy; all except Froines and Weiner, however, were declared guilty of intent to riot and sentenced to five years in prison and fines of $5,000. In addition to these verdicts, the seven defendants and their attorneys were handed a total of 175 contempt-of-court charges, resulting in prison sentences ranging from two to four years. In 1972 an appeals court overturned the riot convictions, and most of the contempt-of-court charges were also dismissed in time. Of the original defendants, only Bobby Seale served time in prison. **See also** antiwar movement; Democratic National Convention of 1968; Youth International Party.

## Chieu Hoi Program

A campaign by the South Vietnamese government to encourage Viet Cong (VC) or North Vietnamese Army (NVA) soldiers to desert their cause by ensuring them amnesty. The title meant "open arms," and the program was also known as the Great National Solidarity campaign. It was begun by President Ngo Dinh Diem in April 1963 and lasted until 1973. For much of that period the program was run by its own governmental agency, the Chieu Hoi Ministry.

Chieu Hoi officials used various means to encourage desertion by Communists. Some had an ideological and cultural focus. Using radio broadcasts, loudspeakers, pamphlets, and other means of communication, officials informed potential deserters that they were fighting their brothers and that such fighting should cease in favor of building the nation through cooperation. The program also sometimes used family or village contacts to get across the same message. In addition, the Chieu Hoi Program promised potential defectors job training, education, reunification with their families, and even such rewards as free land or cash. Although such measures increased the number of defectors, a certain percentage, officials discovered, were simply ordinary peasants who were forced into the program by corrupt officials seeking rewards.

The Chieu Hoi Program was believed to have resulted in nearly 160,000 defectors from the Communist cause between 1963 and 1973, many of whom were placed into either the South Vietnamese armed forces or the civil service. Indeed, American forces did not hesitate to use defectors as guides or intelligence agents such as the so-called Kit Carson scouts. In addition, the Chieu Hoi Program uncovered hundreds of VC weapons caches and likely did a great deal to undermine the VC infrastructure, particularly by the late 1960s. Despite the corrupt aspects of the program, and despite the occasional tendency of officials to use coercion along with encouragement, the South Vietnamese government considered the Chieu Hoi Program a success. **See also** desertion; pacification; psychological operations.

## China Beach

A stretch of beach along the South China Sea coast south of Da Nang. China Beach was a well-known rest and recreation (R&R) center approved for U.S. troops stationed in Vietnam. Another "in country" R&R center was located at Vung Tau, a beach resort outside of Saigon; others lay elsewhere in Southeast Asia, East Asia, or Hawaii. Because China Beach lay close to the fighting at Marble Mountain and other areas around Da Nang, it provided only a limited sense of escape from the rigors of duty in Vietnam. **See also** Da Nang; Marble Mountain; rest and recreation.

## Chinook

The workhorse helicopter of both U.S. Army and South Vietnamese forces. Built by Boeing, the CH-47 Chinook had two twenty-two-hundred-horsepower engines and horizontal rotor blades at both ends. Its range was between 150 and 200 miles and it could carry up to thirty-three passengers. Frequently used for troop transport and evacuation, the ungainly craft was also employed in medical evacuation, supply and equipment retrieval, and artillery emplacement missions. One unique feature of the Chinook was its two external slings, or panniers, which allowed it to carry heavy loads such as large artillery pieces. **See also** Cobra; Huey.

## Chou En-lai (1898–1976)

Top diplomatic and foreign affairs official of the Communist People's Republic of China (PRC), a nation that had very uneasy relations with North Vietnam despite the fact that both professed communism. Chou urged the PRC to recognize Ho Chi Minh's Democratic Republic of Vietnam (DRV, or North Vietnam) in 1950, one of the few nations to do so, and he attended the negotiations in Geneva, Switzerland, in 1954 that divided French Indochina into four nations: the DRV, the Republic of Vietnam (South Vietnam), Cambodia, and Laos. Chou approved of the Geneva settlement, hoping to keep Indochina separated into smaller, more manageable states rather than a single entity under the control of either Hanoi or Saigon. DRV officials were upset at the Chinese stance, but over the next years found the need to create a viable North Vietnamese state more pressing than the desire to once again exercise their thousand-year-old hostility against China. In fact, following a visit to Hanoi in 1956, Chou promised DRV officials that the PRC would support them with financial and technological aid.

The old enmity arose once again, however, in the 1960s when the DRV began to look to the Soviet Union rather than China as its main patron. For much of the world, in fact, Moscow was the home of global communism rather than Beijing, and Chou found himself presiding over a drastic split between the Soviet Union and China. Seeking to strengthen the PRC's position with regard to the Soviet Union, Chou began around 1970 to sound out possible improved relations with the United States, a nation with which it had had no formal diplomatic relations since 1949. Happy to promote a Sino-Soviet split, although hesitant about Chinese intentions, the Americans slowly became more open to Chou's overtures. In April 1971 U.S. national security adviser Henry Kissinger accepted Chou's invitation to visit China, and in February 1972 President Richard M. Nixon shocked the world by visiting China himself and opening formal diplomatic relations. Among the many advantages of this new openness for the United States was an assurance that the PRC would likely no longer support the DRV, eliminating from the American perspective the risk that all of Southeast Asia would fall to communism under the umbrella of the PRC. Nixon was therefore free to pursue policy that would allow the United States to disengage, honorably and finally, from Vietnam. **See also** Mao Tse-tung; Nixon, Richard M.; Paris negotiations.

## Christmas bombing

Officially known as Operation Linebacker II, the Christmas bombing was a massive aerial bombardment of North Vietnam by American B-52 bombers and F-111 and A-6 fighter-bombers taking place from December 18 until December 29, 1972. U.S. president Richard Nixon ordered the bombing not for strategic or tactical military reasons but to convince North Vietnamese politicians to return to peace negotiations in Paris, which had broken down on December 13.

Having received an ultimatum from Nixon to return to the negotiating table "or else," North Vietnamese leaders began to evacuate Hanoi and Haiphong on December 14. Nixon ordered the harbor at Haiphong remined the same day. After further preparations, the first B-52 strikes took place just after dark on December 18. Temporarily halted on Christmas Day, the strikes continued until Hanoi agreed to resume negotiations on January 2. U.S. strategists launched a total of 739 B-52 sorties and over a thousand more fighter-bomber sorties, dropping more than twenty thousand tons of bombs on North Vietnamese targets, mostly industrial, storage, or military facilities. To counter the attacks, the North Vietnamese used up almost their entire stock of surface-to-air missiles, downing in the process fifteen B-52s, nine fighter-bombers, a navy reconnaissance plane, and a rescue helicopter. North Vietnamese MiG fighters helped in the defense.

The Christmas bombing was heavily criticized by many who viewed it as a return to World War II–style carpet bombing. Thanks, however, to advanced electronic and laser guidance systems, bombs were delivered with great accuracy. Even Hanoi officials noted that there were only some sixteen hundred civilian casualties in Hanoi and Haiphong, a relatively low number. In any case, unwilling to risk further destruction to their nation's infrastructure, North Vietnamese negotiators returned to the Paris talks. Bombing runs continued at a reduced level to ensure that the talks proceeded quickly and in good faith; the attacks stopped only when the Paris Peace Accords were signed on January 27, 1973. **See also** B-52; Linebacker I; Paris Peace Accords; smart bombs.

## Civic Action

Broad term for pacification actions carded out by U.S. military personnel as opposed to civilian or South Vietnamese organizations. Military strategists often referred to Civic Action as a second war waged alongside the conventional military effort against the Communists. Civic Action teams performed a wide variety of tasks, including building schools, roads, bridges, and clinics; distributing medical supplies and food to villagers; and teaching English. The largest Civic Action projects were the medical Civic Action programs (MEDCAPS) in which military doctors, medics, and nurses supplied modern health care services, including improvements in sanitation and disease prevention, to villagers. Civic Action projects had the added benefit of supplementing the military effort when, for instance, Civic Action teams collected intelligence on Viet Cong (VC) activities. **See also** Civilian Operations and Revolutionary Development Support; pacification.

## Civilian Irregular Defense Groups (CIDGs)

Irregular forces made up of Montagnards, members of Vietnam's seminomadic, mountain-dwelling tribal groups. In 1961 U.S. Special Forces organized units of Montagnards known as Civilian Irregular Defense Groups to be used for patrol and border defense. Special Forces expanded the program over the next three years by establishing twenty-seven CIDG camps spread across the mountainous Central Highlands. These camps were inhabited by as many as forty thousand highlanders, accompanied by regular South Vietnamese troops. Since they were constructed near villages, the CIDG camps also served to discourage Viet Cong infiltration.

Many Montagnards took advantage of participation in the CIDG program: The arms and military training they received were considered useful preparation against future encroachments by any Vietnamese government, whether based in Saigon or Hanoi. The South Vietnamese government, for its part, grew concerned about the growing military ability and assertiveness of the Montagnards. These concerns resulted in the abandonment of the stationing of CIDG forces near villages; the CIDG fighters were subsequently placed under the control of U.S. military commanders. CIDGs were then used for patrol and reconnaissance missions in the border regions of Cambodia and Laos. Often, teams of Montagnard trainees would accompany U.S. and South Vietnamese Special Forces on their long-range reconnaissance patrols; their knowledge of the mountains and jungles and techniques for survival in harsh conditions were vital to the success of the patrols. In the later years of the war, CIDG units were generally integrated into regular South Vietnamese army units, although a number of the CIDG camps were simply abandoned. **See also** long-range reconnaissance patrols; Montagnards; Special Forces, U.S. Army.

# Civilian Operations and Revolutionary Development Support (CORDS)

A large American organization that oversaw an elaborate network of aid and information programs directed at South Vietnamese civilians, an effort broadly known as pacification. Its responsibility was to win over the "hearts and minds" of the South Vietnamese people in order to ensure their support for the American and Republic of Vietnam (RVN) war effort and to discourage Communist infiltration and recruitment.

Replacing the earlier Office of Civilian Operations, a branch of the U.S. embassy, CORDS was formed in May 1967 to coordinate a number of existing pacification efforts with military efforts. CORDS was placed under the Military Assistance Command, Vietnam (MACV). Its first director was a civilian official, Robert

Komer, who also held ranks equivalent in level to the U.S. ambassador and to a three-star general. After Komer (an appointee of Lyndon Johnson) left in November 1968 he was replaced by William Colby. The staff of CORDS was both civilian and military.

The main centers of CORDS operation were South Vietnam's innumerable villages, where most of the population lived and where the threat of Viet Cong (VC) infiltration was greatest. CORDS officials adopted the view that the best way to win over the South Vietnamese villager was to foster social and economic development. To that end, they created six named subdivisions. The Open Arms program encouraged VC cadres and North Vietnamese soldiers to defect on the promise of aid and resettlement. Revolutionary Development focused on training teams of villagers to both provide security and foster economic development. Psychological Operations involved propaganda through education, speeches, publications, and broadcasts, while Public Safety sought to improve water-supply and sanitation facilities. The refugee program worked with the U.S. Agency for International Development to help settle villagers who had been displaced. Finally, New Life Development hoped to foster social and economic change through education, local government, and various small-scale economic enterprises. Throughout, the coordination of the pacification efforts with military operations ensured that CORDS enjoyed substantial military protection, including, by 1969, some six thousand U.S. military advisers, three U.S. Army companies, and nearly 500,000 local troops.

The efforts of CORDS, along with various other measures such as the Phoenix Program undertaken by the CIA and the Army of the Republic of Vietnam (ARVN), appear to have had some effect in reducing the appeal of the VC to South

Vietnamese villagers. Indeed, after the Tet Offensive of 1968, the VC ceased to be a major military threat. It remains arguable, however, whether CORDS helped win over the South Vietnamese or simply helped keep them reasonably compliant. The organization was dismantled after the withdrawal of U.S. forces began in early 1973, and some of its operations were turned back over to the U.S. embassy. **See also** Civic Action; Colby, William; Komer, Robert; pacification.

## claymore mines

The most common antipersonnel mine carried by American and South Vietnamese forces. Along with the M-16 rifle, claymores were part of an infantryman's standard equipment after 1966. The 3.5-pound mine could be detonated either by a trip wire or by a remote electrical circuit in a procedure known as commander detonation. Once detonated, the claymore would release up to seven hundred steel ball bearings in a circular spray over a range of up to two yards high and fifty-four yards in diameter. The claymores proved to be among the most effective infantry weapons in the jungle warfare of Vietnam. **See also** booby traps; grenades; mines.

## clear and hold

A term used to describe a basic tactic adopted by American and South Vietnamese forces during the Vietnam War. The clear-and-hold strategy was fundamental to pacification efforts, by which the Americans and South Vietnamese meant securing areas against Viet Cong (VC) guerrillas while ensuring the support of local populations. The strategy required forces to station garrisons of troops in regions that had been "cleared" of VC fighters, and resembled the conventional warfare strategy of taking and holding territory.

Clear and hold proved unsuccessful. Though American forces often succeeded in clearing areas, holding them was a much more difficult task. VC guerrillas could fairly easily disguise themselves among village populations, and VC units were often small enough that they could simply escape into the jungles during attacks and return later once American or South Vietnamese forces departed. In addition, villagers feared the possible revenge of the Viet Cong if they cooperated with the Americans or South Vietnamese.

The only way to make the strategy work, as top commanders understood, would be to station permanent, if unwelcome, garrisons of American or South Vietnamese troops in "cleared" villages. The total number of American troops needed to do this would be overwhelming, and neither the administration of President Lyndon B. Johnson nor the American public would have accepted the calling up of reserves or vast conscription in order to secure hundreds of small Vietnamese villages. Moreover, General William Westmoreland, the top American military commander in Vietnam, adopted the tactic of search and destroy rather than clear and hold, asserting that the only realistic way to victory was by destroying VC or North Vietnamese Army units. Thus, "holding" operations were generally left to the South Vietnamese, either regular army units or local civil forces. From a military standpoint, they often proved unreliable. Meanwhile, both American soldiers and the American public increasingly questioned the purpose of a war in which battles were won and ground taken but only temporarily and to no clear end. **See also** enclave strategy; pacification; search and destroy.

## Clifford, Clark (1906–1998)

Adviser to U.S. presidents John F. Kennedy and Lyndon B. Johnson and secretary of defense in 1968 and 1969.

Clifford played a central role in U.S. government debates over the direction of American policy in Vietnam. He was the most vocal moderate of all top advisers.

Clifford, a "grand old man" among Democratic officials due to his close relationship with Harry S. Truman in the 1940s, first served as an informal adviser to both the Kennedy and Johnson administrations. Like most others in these two presidents' circles of advisers, he supported the gradual buildup of U.S. advisers and special forces in Vietnam in the early 1960s. But in 1965, when pressures arose to send large numbers of American combat troops to Vietnam, Clifford, along with George Ball, recommended instead a negotiated settlement with North Vietnam. He was concerned that U.S. forces might be drawn into a conflict they could not win. Once American leaders decided on a policy of escalation in Vietnam, however, Clifford abandoned his misgivings and argued for a strong, focused military effort, including large-scale bombing raids, and he grew confident that the United States could win the war after visits with American and South Vietnamese officials in Saigon as the chairman of the Foreign Intelligence Advisory Board.

Clifford's concerns resurfaced in 1967 after visits to Australia, New Zealand, and the Philippines, three countries that now refused to send any more troops to Vietnam and appeared unalarmed by the prospect of a Communist takeover. Clifford began to wonder whether the United States might be expending its energy and finances supporting a lost cause in South Vietnam. Nevertheless, he continued to argue publicly that as long as American forces were in Vietnam, they should try their utmost to win. Because of this pronouncement, he came into increasing opposition with Secretary of Defense Robert McNamara, who now encouraged bombing halts and negotiations. President Johnson, more comfortable with Clifford's advice as well as his style, replaced McNamara with Clifford as defense secretary early in 1968.

Clifford's immediate problem in his new position was to formulate a response to the Tet Offensive, which began soon after he was confirmed. General William Westmoreland, the commander of U.S. forces in Vietnam, responded by requesting more than 200,000 more U.S. troops. Rather than simply provide them, Clifford set up a new Vietnam Task Force, which learned quickly that military leaders in Vietnam had no effective plan for victory. Consequently, he recommended to Johnson that the United States send no new forces. Soon after, in March 1968, Clifford convened another meeting of the so-called Wise Men, a group of Vietnam policy advisers who included William Bundy, McGeorge Bundy, and McNamara, among others. Most members of the group reported to Johnson that the Vietnam War was unwinnable and that the United States and South Vietnam should enter into peace negotiations with North Vietnam. As a gesture in that direction, Clifford suggested to Johnson that the president state publicly that he was going to stop all bombings of North Vietnam above the demilitarized zone. Johnson took the occasion of the speech, which was made on March 31, 1968, to announce that he would not seek a second term as president. Clifford left office, along with the rest of Johnson's administration, in January 1969. He had spent much of the previous year working with other administration officials organizing peace talks with the North Vietnamese to be held in Paris. **See also** Johnson, Lyndon B.; McNamara, Robert; Rostow, Walt; Wise Men.

## cluster bombs

A group of bombs released in a cluster from an airplane. Along with standard, or general practice, bombs, cluster bombs were the main munitions dropped by American aircraft over North Vietnam, Laos, and Cambodia. Generally delivered by B-52 bombers, most cluster bombs released smaller explosives known as bomblets, which exponentially increased the damage a single B-52 sortie could inflict. One cluster might contain more than twenty-five thousand bomblets; one bomblet, such as the BLU-26B, or "guava," released three hundred steel pellets. Therefore, over 7 million steel pellets could be projected over an area as small as one square mile. Noteworthy cluster bombs included the MK20 Rockeye, an antitank cluster that released 247 arrow-shaped bomblets, and the BLU-73, a fuel-air explosive capable of releasing an intensely flammable cloud over a wide area. **See also** CBU-55; dumb bombs; smart bombs.

## Coast Guard, U.S.

The U.S. Coast Guard, whose ostensible duty is to guard the U.S. coastlines, has historically been under the control of the Departments of the Treasury, Transportation, and Homeland Security, but in wartime control of the Coast Guard can be transferred to the U.S. Navy by executive order. Lyndon Johnson issued such a presidential order in 1965, and Coast Guard commanders were asked to send seventeen cutters, or patrol boats, to Vietnam. The Coast Guard went on to play an important role in the American war effort. Its initial task was to assist the navy in surveillance activities and interdiction of enemy supplies along the South Vietnamese coast. The cutters, armed with machine guns and mortars, were divided into two divisions. One was given the responsibility of patrolling the coast along the Gulf of Thailand. The second was positioned to the north of Da Nang up to the demilitarized zone (DMZ). In 1967 they were joined by a third division of nine more cutters sent to

patrol the Mekong Delta south of Saigon. All played a major part in Operation Market Time, the effort to maintain control of the South Vietnamese coastlines. Their responsibilities included boarding ships and junks in search of smuggled weapons or other supplies intended for the Viet Cong (VC). Coast Guard vessels also supported land actions with mortar fire, assisted in medical service and evacuation, and provided aid to pacification efforts. In 1968 the Coast Guard's fleet in Asian waters was expanded to include three large high-endurance cutters. That same year Coast Guard helicopter pilots were asked to join in the rescue and recovery missions mounted to recover pilots downed over North Vietnam. A total of eight thousand Coast Guardsmen served in Vietnam and seven were killed in action. **See also** Market Time; Navy, U.S.; Sea Dragon.

## Cobra

One of the primary attack helicopters used by the U.S. Army in Vietnam. The AH-1G Cobra, first used in 1967, was built by the Bell Helicopter Company to replace slower helicopters in the combat tasks of offensive and close air support for troops delivered by helicopter to designated landing areas, escort missions, and armed reconnaissance. The helicopter carried a crew of two and was equipped with various weapons: automatic miniguns, a grenade launcher, antitank missiles, and rockets. After proving its efficacy in support missions, both the army and the marines began to use the Cobra in a more aggressive attack role. **See also** Chinook; gunships; Huey.

## Colby, William (1920–1996)

Important Central Intelligence Agency (CIA) official in Vietnam. A member of both the World War II–era Office of Strategic Services and its successor, the CIA, Colby was first sent to Vietnam in 1959 as chief of the CIA station in

Saigon. Over the next three years he was instrumental in devising and implementing counterinsurgency strategies ranging from participation in the strategic hamlet program to the use of Montagnard troops. In 1962 he was named head of the Far East Division of the CIA, a post based in Washington, D.C. The new position required him to take a perspective broader than that concerned with the spread of communism in Vietnam alone, and he came to believe that counterinsurgency and pacification were the most effective ways to halt communism's growth throughout the region.

Colby returned to Saigon in November 1968 as deputy to the commander of the U.S. Military Assistance Command, Vietnam, as well as a high-ranking diplomat. In this post he presided over a stepped-up pacification program intended to secure South Vietnamese villages against Communist infiltration. Colby had long believed in the importance of pacification measures, but it was not until late 1968 that a large-scale pacification program truly began. Among its important aspects was the Phoenix Program, which was directed at undermining the support for Viet Cong (VC) insurgents in the villages. Mostly using the enforcement power of the South Vietnamese, the Phoenix Program apprehended, and allegedly tortured and assassinated, large numbers of villagers suspected of having ties with the VC. Colby testified before the U.S. Congress in 1971 that many of the deaths were in battle.

Colby returned from his posts in Vietnam in 1971 because of both an illness in his family and the turning over of the pacification effort to the South Vietnamese as part of the larger policy of Vietnamization. As director of the CIA from 1973 to 1976, however, he was called to testify before Congress about the CIA's global actions, some of which violated the CIA's charter. These included involvement in foreign intelligence schemes and plots to assassinate foreign leaders. In effect, Colby admitted the CIA's involvement in such actions in hopes of steering the agency through a difficult period brought on by its alleged participation in the domestic Watergate scandal that brought down the Nixon administration as well as what some saw as its questionable actions in Vietnam.

In later years Colby argued that South Vietnam could have survived if the United States had followed through on the pacification measures begun in 1968 and continued to support the South Vietnamese army with supplies, training, and bombing raids. He claimed that the Vietnam War was lost, in other words, only because the United States withdrew support from Saigon in an effort to end the unpopular war. **See also** Central Intelligence Agency; Helms, Richard; Phoenix Program.

## cold war

The name given to the state of global politics between the world's two superpowers from the end of World War II in 1945 to the breakup of the Soviet Union in 1991. The cold war was an ideological struggle between communism, as represented by the Soviets, and democracy and free-market capitalism, as represented by the United States. Many of the battlefields of the limited conflicts of the cold war lay in nations that, like Vietnam, tried to establish themselves as independent nations after decades of colonial administration. Cold war antagonists appeared to believe that victory in Vietnam could represent an expansion of their respective ideologies.

At various periods and to varying degrees, the USSR and China both provided support to the Communist North Vietnamese, during the First Indochina War (1946–1954) and thereafter. Meanwhile, the United States pledged its support to independent South Vietnam as early as 1950, seeing in Vietnam an opportunity to redeem the cause from what many referred to as the "loss of China." This led to direct U.S. military involvement beginning in 1965. Larger cold war concerns remained at the forefront of the U.S. approach to the Vietnam War. Although decision makers were criticized during the Vietnam War and ever since for not devoting the full power of the U.S. military to defeating North Vietnam, they had to keep in mind the larger context. A broader conflict might risk drawing either the USSR or China directly into the war, and focusing full resources on Vietnam risked a weakening of the U.S. presence elsewhere in the world, most importantly in Europe, where communism also had to be contained. U.S. policy makers therefore committed the country to a "limited war" in Vietnam.

Ironically, the Vietnam War played itself out while tensions were lessening between the United States and both the USSR and China. By the early 1970s, in fact, the United States and USSR had entered a period of détente, or a relaxation of tensions. This involved greater trade and cultural exchange, as well as the beginning of discussions designed to pare down the size of nuclear arsenals. The United States also opened up formal diplomatic relations with China. The lessening of tensions had an important impact on the Vietnam War since, by 1972, American leaders were no longer afraid that the conflict would expand and therefore could bomb North Vietnam with impunity. The North Vietnamese, now realizing that they were on their own, proved more willing to take peace negotiations seriously. **See also** containment policy; domino theory.

## combined action platoons (CAPs)

Special units of the U.S. Marine Corps and local forces formed in 1967 to engage in combat and security operations in I Corps, the northernmost of the four military regions in South Vietnam. The combined action platoons were an offshoot of the Civic Action program, which attempted to link pacification with military efforts. The CAPs were mixed units of marines and members of the South Vietnamese regional forces. They were believed to not only provide a vital link between U.S. and South Vietnamese personnel but also assure ordinary people that U.S. motives were sincere and generous. The CAPs were credited with dismantling a substantial part of the Viet Cong infrastructure in I Corps. **See also** Civic Action.

## Commando Hunt

Lasting from November 1968 to February 1973, Operation Commando Hunt was the descendant of Operations Steel Tiger and Tiger Hound, all of which were designed to halt the flow of supplies on the stretch of the Ho Chi Minh Trail that ran through eastern Laos. In combination with earlier operations, Commando Hunt and its predecessors dropped hundreds of thousands of tons of bombs on Laos.

Commando Hunt was designed to be a consolidation of the earlier operations using stronger, more efficient firepower. Most of its missions were carried out by U.S. Air Force planes based in South Vietnam or northeastern Thailand, although occasionally navy, marine, or Laotian aircraft took part. The operation also marked the first time that B-52s were widely used in Laos; at its height, thirty B-52 sorties per day were flown against concentrated points along the Ho Chi Minh Trail. The use of the B-52s was a sign that U.S. officials were less concerned than they had been earlier about the political dangers of bombing a technically neutral country.

Like its predecessors, however, and like its counterpart in North Vietnam, Operation Rolling Thunder, Commando Hunt had little effect on the flow of supplies and personnel down the Ho Chi Minh Trail. Parts of the trail that were damaged could be easily repaired, and the Communists maintained no large supply depots or trans-shipment points that could be identified and targeted. Military and government statisticians attempted to measure the success of the operation by counting the number of trucks supposedly destroyed or damaged, but their estimates varied widely. In any case, Commando Hunt had so little lasting effect that the North Vietnamese had little trouble moving tens of thousands of soldiers to South Vietnam in preparation for the Easter Offensive of 1972. Soon after, the operation was canceled, leaving little legacy other than hundreds of acres of destroyed jungle and thousands of tons of unexploded ordnance and military wreckage scattered across eastern Laos. **See also** Barrel Roll; Ho Chi Minh Trail; Laos, secret war in.

## Conein, Lucien (1919–1998)

Central Intelligence Agency (CIA) agent in Vietnam. In 1943, after joining the army and reaching the rank of second lieutenant, the French-born Lucien Conein was recruited by the Office of Strategic Services (OSS), the predecessor of the CIA. He participated in a number of operations in World War II Europe and postwar Asia. From 1954 to 1956 he was an important member of Edward Lansdale's CIA team that was sent to Vietnam to advise the South Vietnamese regime of Ngo Dinh Diem and perform covert sabotage activities against North Vietnamese Communists. In 1956 Conein returned to the United States and joined U.S. Army Special Forces.

After retiring from the army in 1961 Conein returned to the CIA. The agency sent him back to Saigon under the cover, unsurprisingly, of an army officer and ad-

viser. His job was to maintain contact with important officers in the South Vietnamese army, many of whom he had known during his earlier days in the country. This long acquaintance apparently made Conein one of the few Americans many South Vietnamese generals felt they could truly rely on. During the summer and fall of 1963 Conein acted as an intermediary between the generals who were plotting to overthrow Diem and U.S. officials, notably Ambassador Henry Cabot Lodge. Conein made it known to the generals, apparently, that the United States would not interfere with a coup. After Diem was dislodged and assassinated in early November 1963, Conein left Vietnam and the CIA. **See also** Lansdale, Edward G.; Ngo Dinh Diem; Saigon Military Mission.

## conscientious objectors (COs)

Persons who achieved exemption from the Vietnam War–era draft, or from combat duty, because of moral or religious opposition to war or service in war. As American participation in the Vietnam War escalated beginning in 1965, ever larger numbers of young men sought to establish conscientious objector status in order to avoid being sent to fight in Vietnam.

Traditionally, COs were members of pacifist religious groups such as Quakers and Jehovah's Witnesses. Qualifications for CO status were strict: Candidates had to document their religious beliefs with the support of a legitimate clergyman and declare an opposition to all war, not just the American war in Vietnam. Various legal challenges complicated the definition of CO status, however, as more and more young men sought it. Courts established that specific religious affiliation need not be necessary, for instance, nor did a potential draftee even have to declare a belief in a god. Complicating matters even further was the fact that the decision regarding CO status was left to local draft boards, who applied the criteria inconsistently. Recognizing the philosophical variation among applicants, the Selective Service Agency devised three categories of conscientious objector in 1965. Some COs were drafted but restricted to noncombat roles such as clerks or orderlies. Ironically, COs in this first category were among the draftees most likely to be sent to Vietnam. Despite their noncombat assignments, some found themselves in combat situations in Vietnam, and a number were killed or wounded. A second category of COs declared themselves willing to be drafted into civilian public service work at some unspecified time. Finally, a third category of COs immediately entered public service work voluntarily under the supervision of their local draft board. About 170,000 young men took the second option; 100,000 accepted the third because it meant an immediate, concrete assignment that fulfilled their service commitment (with no possible conscription in the future).

One noteworthy group who sought CO status were American Muslims, who declared themselves opposed to all war except that waged in the name of their faith. Most of them were denied CO status and a number were sent to prison for refusing the draft. In addition to potential draftees, approximately twenty thousand active-duty military personnel tried to establish CO status during the Vietnam War. Some two thousand of them were granted it and either discharged or transferred to noncombat posts. **See also** draft; draft resistance.

## containment policy

The primary U.S. strategy toward the global spread of communism during the cold war (ca. 1945–1991) and the fundamental basis of U.S. decision making in Vietnam. The containment policy was first articulated by George F. Kennan, a foreign service officer whose experiences in Moscow convinced him that the Soviet Union was bent on expansion. Upon returning to the United States he wrote an article titled "The Sources of Soviet Conduct." That article, published in the journal *Foreign Affairs* in July 1947, is generally seen as the first major description of the containment policy.

Kennan argued that, given the Soviet Union's expansionist tendencies, the democratic West, led by the United States, had to take strong action to contain the Soviet Union. In so doing, the West would also discourage the spread of communism. Kennan believed that in time the Soviet Union would collapse, break up into a number of independent states, or simply cease being an expansionist threat. In the meantime, the rest of the world needed to strengthen itself to the point where Soviet expansionism would be discouraged. Kennan's theories were taken up by officials in the administration of President Harry S. Truman, who, given political realities and the devastation of the just-completed World War II, hesitated to express a willingness to take on the Soviet Union with military action. In the late 1940s and early 1950s, and despite the transition from Truman to Dwight D. Eisenhower, the containment policy remained the lynchpin of American cold war policy.

The containment policy also explained the beginning of U.S. involvement in Vietnam. The United States made the decision to support the French in the First Indochina War (1946–1954) for two main reasons. The first was the desire to maintain France as a powerful ally in containing the spread of communism in Europe. The second was the fact that the United States considered Ho Chi Minh, the leader of the Vietnamese Communists, to be a lackey in the expansionist desires of the Soviet Union and China who could, conceivably, be stopped without drawing either the Soviet Union or China into a larger conflict.

When the 1954 Geneva Accords split French Indochina into four countries— Laos, Cambodia, an independent South Vietnam, and a Communist North Vietnam under Ho Chi Minh—American officials modified their strategy toward the region. Nonetheless, the new approach was still informed by the containment policy. Among the new measures was the formation of the Southeast Asia Treaty Organization (SEATO), a regional counterpart to the North Atlantic Treaty Organization (NATO). Another was the advancement of the domino theory, a complement to the containment policy that suggested that Asian nations could be seen as dominoes; if one was allowed to fall to communism, the others would soon follow. To the Americans, South Vietnam became the essential first domino, the nation that could not be allowed to be overcome by communism. Accordingly, the United States took steps to strengthen the government of South Vietnam through supplies, weapons, and military advisers so that it could resist a takeover by North Vietnam.

These steps were escalated in the 1960s by Presidents John F. Kennedy and Lyndon B. Johnson, who remained committed to the containment policy. Both presidents were criticized for what was, in fact, the limited nature of the war in Vietnam despite the fact that by 1968 there were a half-million U.S. troops there. One source of criticism was that neither considered an actual invasion of North Vietnam. Many critics came out of military circles, people trained to win whatever conflict they were engaged in. Such critics argued that American forces never lost a major conventional battle in Vietnam. However, the containment policy required that the Vietnam War itself be contained, meaning that it had to be fought in such a way that neither the Soviet Union nor China would step in in Viet-nam or cause trouble elsewhere, namely in Europe. Kennan, commenting on Vietnam in the late 1960s, argued that Southeast Asia was a minor concern and that the focus of containment should indeed have remained in Europe. **See also** cold war; domino theory.

# Continental Air Services (CAS)

A subsidiary of the commercial carrier Continental Air Lines that was contracted out to the U.S. government in Southeast Asia during the Vietnam War. It began operations in September 1965, when the president of Continental, Robert Six, took possession of the assets of a small airline known as Bird and Sons. Since 1960 Bird and Sons had been flying various covert operations for American agencies in Laos, and Six maintained the practice using the newly named Continental Air Services. CAS was also used for regular commercial business and by the Agency for International Development, a civilian organization affiliated with the U.S. military effort in Southeast Asia.

Along with Air America, an airline that was wholly owned by the Central Intelligence Agency (CIA), CAS supported the counterinsurgency war in Laos as well as Vietnam. Indeed, the president of CAS was Robert Rousellot, former chief pilot for Air America. At the height of its activities, CAS airplanes carried twenty thousand passengers and six thousand tons of cargo per month. These passengers and cargoes included military advisers and trainers as well as weapons and ammunition. As did Air America, CAS pilots and crews suffered losses due to combat conditions and the rather primitive nature of air travel in inland Southeast Asia. CAS activity declined as American involvement in the region diminished in the early 1970s. It was closed down in December 1975. **See also** Air America; Laos, secret war in.

# Cooper-Church Amendment

An amendment to a Department of Defense appropriations bill in 1970 that proposed limiting the president's authority to maintain U.S. military activities in Cambodia. Introduced by Senators John Cooper and Frank Church in response to the U.S.-sponsored South Vietnamese invasion of Cambodia in the spring of 1970, the amendment was a sign that many members of Congress had had enough of war in Vietnam and elsewhere in Indochina.

Specifically, the Cooper-Church Amendment proposed to bar the use of funds, without specific congressional authorization, for the purposes of military instruction or advice in Cambodia after June 30, 1970. It also prohibited American air support to Cambodian troops unless, again, such measures were specifically authorized by Congress. The proposed amendment inspired a major debate in the Senate over the way the presidential administration of Richard M. Nixon was conducting the war in Indochina. The bill including the amendment was finally approved by the Senate but was voted down in the House of Representatives. A later version of the amendment attached to a foreign aid appropriations bill, however, passed both the House and Senate in December 1970. It was no longer relevant to Cambodia, since U.S. troops had since been withdrawn, but it prohibited the use of U.S. combat troops in either Laos or Thailand.

The Cooper-Church Amendment, which Nixon loudly denounced on the grounds that it would weaken his bargaining position with North Vietnam, was the first of a number of congressional attempts to block further American involvement in Indochina by denying funding. Congressional debate over the amendment, moreover, gave new confidence to the nationwide antiwar movement. **See also** Case-Church Amendment; War Powers Resolution.

# counterinsurgency

The central approach taken by American political and military officials in the 1960s to stop the global spread of communism. Since many Communist movements were insurgencies mounted by loosely organized nationalist forces in places that had only recently been freed from European colonialism, counterinsurgency was viewed as a way to encourage local nationalists to change their minds about communism. It thus added to conventional warfare a political component: winning the hearts and minds of the people. Counterinsurgency also altered U.S. military doctrine. From the massive nuclear deterrent built up in the 1950s by the administration of Dwight D. Eisenhower, John F. Kennedy switched to a military built around "flexible response," or the ability to adjust to circumstances in various regions around the globe, in effect to fight smaller wars. Another advantage of counterinsurgency warfare was that it could be carried out in various unconventional ways: providing aid and military advisers, using ostensibly nonmilitary bodies such as the Central Intelligence Agency, and mustering support for local anti-Communist forces. Significantly, such means allowed the president to respond quickly and commit U.S. military force without a formal declaration of war from Congress.

Counterinsurgency doctrine was devised by British expert Robert G.K. Thompson, who had helped guide a counterinsurgency effort that defeated Communist guerrillas in Malaysia in the 1950s. Thompson, who also advised the South Vietnamese government for a time in the 1960s, established five central rules for a successful counterinsurgency effort: Establish a stable, democratic government; operate within the law; have a consistent plan of action; defeat opposing political leaders rather than their fighters; and secure base areas. Thompson also emphasized that any successful counterinsurgency effort depended on the support of ordinary people.

American and South Vietnamese forces tried to uphold most of Thompson's rules, but they failed to build a stable government in the south, to be consistent in their operational plans, and to effectively challenge opposing politicians. Various pacification efforts also had little effect in winning over the South Vietnamese population to more than grudging support. **See also** guerrilla warfare; Thompson, Robert G.K.; Viet Cong.

## Cu Chi tunnels

A vast Viet Cong (VC) tunnel complex located in and around the village of Cu Chi, twenty-five miles north of Saigon in an area known as the Iron Triangle. VC officials chose the location because of its proximity to both important supply lines from Cambodia and the South Vietnamese capital. Construction of the underground VC base, largely carried out by local forced labor, was made possible by the hard, compact soil of the region. Begun in the early 1960s, the Cu Chi tunnels were a remarkable engineering feat. Nearly 120 miles of tunnels 3 feet high and 2.5 feet wide were constructed in three or four connecting levels. They contained supply depots, weapons depots, and even craft shops for building new weapons. Sections were equipped as living areas, classrooms, kitchens, and hospitals, well supplied to enable hundreds of people to live underground for months. Ventilation was provided by numerous special shafts leading to the surface, and the tunnel openings were well camouflaged. For a number of years, Cu Chi provided the VC with a secure base from which to mount guerrilla warfare operations against Saigon and surrounding areas as well as funnel supplies and personnel to other regions.

American forces discovered the Cu Chi tunnels early in 1966. U.S. commanders quickly established a surface camp there for the purpose of clearing the tunnels. Given the labyrinth of zigzagging tunnels, secret passageways, and hidden doors, this difficult task took well over one year. VC guerrillas, for instance, adopted the effective tactic of concealing themselves inside the tunnels, emerging at U.S. soldiers' backs, and then, following an assault, retreating into the underground passageways. To defeat them, American strategists used tear gas, explosives, and, in time, small-framed, minimally armed soldiers known as "tunnel rats." By the middle of 1967, VC units were thought to have been removed from the tunnels altogether and the operation was closed.

The Cu Chi tunnels were only one of a number of tunnel networks maintained by Communist forces and by ordinary North Vietnamese civilians during the war. There were smaller tunnel structures throughout VC-held areas in South Vietnam, while in North Vietnam tunnels were built so that villagers could survive American bombing raids. In the 1990s parts of the Cu Chi tunnels were restored and reopened by the government of the Socialist Republic of Vietnam, both as a memorial to their long struggle for reunification and as a tourist attraction. **See also** Iron Triangle; Viet Cong.

## daisy cutter

A bomb known technically as the BLU-82B. Dropped from aircraft, the fifteen-thousand-pound bomb released a parachute to slow its descent. The bomb's charge consisted of a compound of ammonium nitrate and other chemicals that had twice the power of TNT. Its explosion could flatten an area with a radius of up to four hundred meters. Known as the daisy cutter because it was often used to clear jungle in order to create helicopter landing sites, the bomb was also used against concentrations of enemy troops. **See also** cluster bombs; defoliation; Rome plows.

## Da Nang

The second largest city in South Vietnam after Saigon. It was known as Tourane during the French colonial era. Because it stood along the coast of the South China Sea and was close to the demilitarized zone (DMZ), Da Nang was a logical center of military operations during the Vietnam War. It was the headquarters of one of the major South Vietnamese army groups and, at various times, the home of a number of U.S. military installations, including the First and Third U.S. Marine Divisions and the U.S. Army's XXIV Corps. Da Nang also contained major port facilities as well as several airfields. The first U.S. combat troops in Vietnam, in fact, were sent to Da Nang in March 1965 to defend a local airfield.

Da Nang was the center of more than military activity, however. In 1966 a major uprising of Buddhists against the government of General Nguyen Cao Ky was based in the city. They were joined by contingents of South Vietnamese army troops, and only the intervention of U.S. Marines helped bring peace back to the streets. Meanwhile, refugees flooded into Da Nang from the surrounding regions, which were subject to firefights, defoliation, and bombing raids.

Da Nang's proximity to the DMZ made it a target of attacks by both Viet Cong and North Vietnamese Army (NVA) forces. It was bombarded heavily in 1967 and attacked in several areas during the Tet Offensive of 1968. Da Nang was taken fairly easily by the NVA during its final assault on South Vietnam in the spring of 1975, when even more refugees streamed into the already choked city. In later years, many of these refugees fled Vietnam from the coast around Da Nang, forming a substantial portion of the so-called boat people. **See also** Hue, Battle of; military regions.

## d'Argenlieu, Georges Thierry (1889–1964)

French high commissioner for Indochina from 1945 to 1947. Sent to Saigon by General Charles de Gaulle, d'Argenlieu torpedoed the attempt by Ho Chi Minh and French liberals to establish a semi-autonomous Vietnamese state. Maintaining order in the cities with the help of British troops and, ironically, Japanese soldiers awaiting repatriation, d'Argenlieu slowly reestablished a facade of French authority in late 1945. In much of the countryside, however, especially in the north, the Viet Minh exercised great influence, and Ho refused to acknowledge the return of French overlordship. D'Argenlieu, for his part, refused to negotiate with the Viet Minh and, in hopes of forestalling Ho, d'Argenlieu declared a Republic of Cochin China in southern Vietnam in June 1946, thus negating the agreement that Ho had already worked out with French officials. Not long after, perhaps believing that he could treat the Vietnamese with the alacrity and disdain of his colonial predecessors, the high commissioner made it clear to his military commanders that they were free to use force against the Viet Minh. The subsequent shelling of the North Vietnamese port of Haiphong by a French naval vessel in November 1946 led to the beginning of the war between the Viet Minh and the French on December 19. As a result of a change of government at home, d'Argenlieu lost his post

and returned to France in February 1947. **See also** August 1945 Revolution; Ho-Sainteny Agreement.

## Dean, John Gunther (1926– )

American diplomat who served in Laos and Cambodia as well as South Vietnam. John Gunther Dean first served in South Vietnam, from 1970 to 1972, as a regional director for Civilian Operations and Revolutionary Development Support (CORDS), a U.S. organization charged with conducting pacification operations. In 1972 he was transferred to Vientiane, the capital of Laos, where he served as deputy chief of mission, or second in command under the U.S. ambassador. Remaining in Vientiane until 1974, Dean played a major role in removing the last elements of American support from the region and in seeking the freedom of American prisoners of war allegedly held by the Pathet Lao, the nation's Communists. In late 1974 Dean was appointed

*U.S. Marines from the First Battalion, Ninth Regiment land at Da Nang. Because the city was close to the demilitarized zone and contained ports and airfields, Da Nang became a center of U.S. military operations.*

ambassador to Cambodia. From the U.S. embassy in Phnom Penh, he unsuccessfully negotiated to halt the advance of the Khmer Rouge and prop up the government of Lon Nol. On April 12, 1975, as Khmer Rouge forces surrounded the city, he ordered the evacuation of the embassy. Allegedly, Dean clutched an American flag and wept as his helicopter rose above the defeated and devastated city. **See also** Eagle Pull.

## Defense Attaché Office (DAO)

An organization that provided for a continued but small U.S. military presence in South Vietnam even after almost all troops were withdrawn in accordance with the January 1973 Paris Peace Accords. The accords limited the United States to only fifty official military personnel, but the presence of the Defense Attaché Office allowed that number to be supplemented by civilian personnel. The DAO was designed to both work with the U.S. embassy in Saigon and provide a means by which any military support to South Vietnam might be arranged. Its headquarters were at Tan Son Nhut air base outside Saigon. The major operation the DAO was involved in, as it happened, was helping to arrange for the evacuation of Saigon during the final North Vietnamese offensive in April 1975. **See also** Frequent Wind; Paris Peace Accords.

## defoliation

The effort to prevent the growth of plants and trees by using strong chemical herbicides. Defoliation was employed widely by American forces in Vietnam, who used some 19 million gallons of herbicides in the process of clearing hundreds of thousands of acres of farmland and jungle. The purposes of defoliation were military. By clearing jungles, U.S. strategists hoped to eliminate hiding places where their enemies in the Viet Cong (VC) and North Vietnamese Army (NVA) main-

tained supply depots and trails, garrisons, and weapons emplacements. In addition, defoliants were used to kill crops that enemy forces might rely on to feed themselves.

The preferred defoliant compounds were known as Agents Orange, White, and Blue. Agents Orange and White were used to reduce jungles, while Agent Blue was used to discourage crops from growing. All three had the effect of reducing the products of plants, namely leaves, fruits, or grains; plant roots were killed less effectively.

From a military standpoint, the defoliation program was a success. The clearing of forests made military movements safer, and the observation of enemy movements from both the ground and the air was far easier. However, defoliation, a frequent practice in the history of warfare (although generally done by simply using fire), has been highly criticized on environmental and humanitarian grounds. Acres of old-growth forest were destroyed in the inland mountain ranges, and mangrove fields along the coast, which helped prevent erosion, were also eliminated. Destruction of these sophisticated habitats killed a wide variety of animals, insects, and, in the case of the mangrove forests, sea life. Defoliant residues also polluted soil and water.

Reforestation efforts since the end of the war were only partially successful, and sometimes misguided or badly handled; the effects of defoliation across South Vietnam were still obvious more than twenty-five years after the end of the war. Meanwhile, the effects on human beings of toxic chemicals used in the defoliant compounds, notably dioxin, were the subject of some pointed questions at an informal international war crimes tribunal staged by the philosopher and mathematician Bertrand Russell in 1971. Large numbers of South Vietnamese people are thought to have suffered health problems, including various permanent physical and mental disabilities, from their contact with defoliants. The postwar government of the Socialist Republic of Vietnam, for its part, long continued to cite defoliation as one of the "crimes" of the Americans and their South Vietnamese allies. It claimed that the United States used 75 million liters of defoliating agents during the war years. **See also** Agent Orange; napalm.

## demilitarized zone (DMZ)

A five-mile-wide buffer zone between North Vietnam and South Vietnam. It stretched for thirty-five miles east to west from the coast of the South China Sea to the Laotian border. At its center was the Ben Hai River, which stretched inland to the village of Ho Su.

The demilitarized zone was created by the 1954 Geneva Accords, which recognized the two independent Vietnamese nations. Originally the border between North and South Vietnam was placed along the seventeenth parallel of latitude, a temporary border pending future elections that, it was hoped, would reunite the country. Neither nation, nor any of their allies, would be permitted to place any military garrisons in the DMZ or move military supplies through the area. The hoped-for elections, however, never took place, and by 1956 the DMZ was considered the northern border of South Vietnam. The North Vietnamese, for their

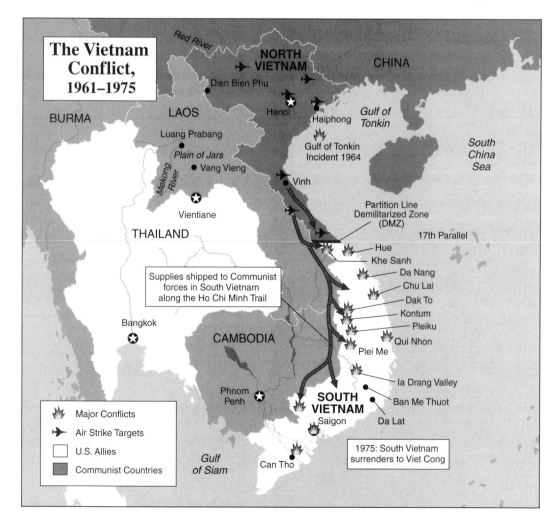

The Vietnam Conflict, 1961–1975

part, considered it merely a temporary hindrance rather than a proper borderline. The nearest large city on the South Vietnamese side was Hue, and Da Nang lay not much farther to the south. To the north, the nearest major town was Vinh.

Both sides completely disregarded the neutrality of the DMZ during the Vietnam War. It became one of the most heavily bombed areas of the conflict and the site of frequent violent battles. Strings of small outposts were constructed on both sides of the Ben Hai River; more substantial outposts were located to the rear of the DMZ. To the north, along the coast, Communist forces built up an extensive tunnel network to house villagers and supplies and to aid intelligence gathering. Meanwhile, in anticipation of a major North Vietnamese offensive, American and South Vietnamese forces established a major line of defense only a few miles south of the DMZ. It stretched from the coast through several U.S. Army and Marine bases to Khe Sanh and the Laotian border. The bases were close enough to the DMZ to regularly pound it with artillery fire directed at Communist positions. **See also** McNamara Line; military regions; Quang Tri, Battle of.

# Democratic National Convention of 1968

A symbolic event in American policy making that had a great impact on American attitudes toward the Vietnam War. As they did every four years, in 1968 delegates of the Democratic Party held their national convention to select the party's candidate for president of the United States in that year's election. The 1968 convention was to take place August 26–29 in Chicago, a city tightly controlled by Democratic mayor Richard Daley, who supported the Vietnam War and opposed the various civil actions that had been staged by antiwar protesters over the preceding several years.

Democratic Party delegates faced a fairly straightforward choice for the presidential nomination, although many antiwar protesters disagreed. The incumbent president, Lyndon B. Johnson, had announced at the end of March that he would not run again, leaving the field open for a newcomer. Johnson, whom many people held responsible for the quagmire in Vietnam, chose to withdraw partly because of the strong showing of the vocally antiwar senator Eugene McCarthy during the March New Hampshire primary. McCarthy remained the prime antiwar candidate, although he was too left-wing for the tastes of the Democratic establishment. For a time, in April and May, the expected Democratic nominee was Robert F. Kennedy, younger brother of John F. Kennedy and a popular candidate among both the antiwar movement and the Democratic mainstream. Kennedy, however, was assassinated on June 5 following an important victory in the California primary. At the convention, Democrats were likely to settle on Hubert H. Humphrey, senator from Minnesota, who had entered the race in late April and who stood to inherit Johnson's mantle as the representative of the Democratic establishment. The antiwar faction of the party divided its loyalty, meanwhile, between McCarthy and another antiwar candidate, George S. McGovern.

Outside the convention hall, thousands of antiwar protesters gathered to publicize their views on both the nomination and the party's platform on Vietnam. As more and more protesters were drawn to Chicago, rumors began to spread about possible radical plans to put the hallucinogen LSD in the city's water supply or stage race riots to disrupt the convention. Daley's political machine tried to contain the protest rallies in Chicago's Lincoln Park and refused to issue demonstration permits to protest leaders. Tensions mounted when thousands of Chicago police were joined by thousands of National Guard troops in riot gear and combat vehicles. Most of the protesters, certainly, planned only peaceful rallies, but others were bent on more radical action, and events spun out of control on the evening of August 27. The protest turned into a riot, protesters ignored police orders to remain in Lincoln Park, and the streets of Chicago were filled with fistfights and other confrontations as the police and National Guard used tear gas and truncheons to restore order.

Around the United States, television viewers were presented with alternating scenes of the political debate inside the convention hall and the violent upheaval on the Chicago streets. Inside, Humphrey was duly selected as the Democratic nominee, but the main event was the vote on the Democratic Party's official position on the Vietnam War. Late at night on August 27–28, a delay designed to limit TV coverage, the delegates voted to support the policy of the Johnson administration, which at the time was to continue intensive bombing of North Vietnam while keeping American forces in place. The decision further enraged the protesters and the riot escalated outside. At one point Democratic senator Abraham Rubicoff took the floor to denounce the "Gestapo tactics" of Mayor Daley. In the end, innumerable protesters and a few innocent bystanders were injured, and Chicago police and the National Guard arrested well over six hundred people. It was the largest series of riots of the anti–Vietnam War movement, and some suggest that the entire unsettling experience may well have lost the presidency for the Democratic Party in November, when voters elected Republican Richard M. Nixon by one of the narrowest popular-vote margins in U.S. history. **See also** antiwar movement; Chicago Seven; Humphrey, Hubert H.; McCarthy, Eugene.

## desertion

Leaving an active-duty military unit for a specified period of time without express permission. In the American armed forces, desertion was officially defined as an absence longer than thirty days or as gone with the clear desire to stay away permanently. A desertion of shorter periods was considered absent without leave, or AWOL. During the years of the Vietnam War some 500,000 incidents of desertion occurred among the approximately 8.7 million American military personnel on active duty worldwide. Fewer than 94,000 deserters stayed away longer than thirty days, however.

Rates of desertion in the Vietnam War compared favorably with those in World War II and the Korean War, although they rose markedly from 1965 to 1971, from 1.5 percent to 7.4 percent. This was attributed mostly to the rising tide of antiwar sentiment in the United States. Approximately thirty-two thousand recorded cases of desertion were connected specifically to Vietnam service, including twenty thousand desertions of military service after one's tour of duty in Vietnam ended. There were only twenty-four recorded cases of desertion from the field of battle or Vietnam itself. Motivations for desertion included financial and family problems, inability to adjust to military life, and antiwar views. Estimates varied, but up to ten thousand deserters were never located and were listed as fugitives after the war. Many others who returned or were found took advantage of amnesty programs offered by Presidents Gerald R. Ford and Jimmy Carter in the late 1970s. This generally involved a change in discharge status from undesirable to honorable.

South Vietnamese armed forces suffered much higher desertion rates, attributable to low pay, corruption, and the various hardships that went along with being a South Vietnamese soldier. It was also reasonably easy for a South Vietnamese deserter to blend in to a village locality; few deserted to join the Communists. Most South Vietnamese deserters were regular army troops rather than the regional or popular forces, which were generally stationed closer to home. As the North Vietnamese overran South Vietnam in 1974 and 1975, desertion became the norm rather than the exception, even among officers, in the south's forces.

Relatively few North Vietnamese regulars deserted, largely because strict government controls over food and other basic resources offered little enticement to go home. Viet Cong forces deserted in greater numbers, especially after Saigon's Chieu Hoi (Open Arms) Program began to encourage desertion. Those who joined the Chieu Hoi Program were granted immunity from charges, given access to training and education, and granted other privileges provided that they declared their loyalty to South Vietnam. Some Chieu Hoi "graduates" even served on the U.S. and South Vietnamese side. **See also** Chieu Hoi Program; draft resistance.

## Dewey Canyon I

A major operation carried out from January 22 to March 18, 1969, in the A Shau Valley in northern South Vietnam. It was designed to discourage the buildup of Communist supply depots and base areas in this critical region. American and South Vietnamese strategists knew the Communists could easily infiltrate the area from across the Laotian border and threaten the populated areas along the coastal plain, such as the cities of Hue and Da Nang.

Dewey Canyon I was an airmobile operation involving the insertion and recovery of U.S. Army and Marine units by helicopter. Since it took place during the winter monsoon, helicopter operations were hampered by rain and poor visibility. Nonetheless, U.S. troops, working their way outward from specially designated fire support bases, managed to uncover a number of North Vietnamese Army (NVA) outposts and capture large amounts of supplies and armaments. Frequent small firefights with NVA troops resulted in an estimated 1,617 Communist casualties. U.S. forces suffered losses of 121 dead and 803 wounded. Though the operation was a success at forestalling Communist activity in the A Shau Valley, it had little long-term effect because U.S. or South Vietnamese troops did not remain in the area, thus enabling the NVA, over time, to return. **See also** A Shau Valley; Khe Sanh, Battle of; Lam Son 719.

## Dewey Canyon II

The attempt by U.S. forces to support the Army of the Republic of Vietnam (ARVN) during its invasion of Laos in February 1971, the so-called Operation Lam Son 719. It involved such measures as helicopter and air support; securing Highway 9, which ran east-west from the South China Sea to the Laotian border past such sites as Khe Sanh; and a diversionary attack to the north in the A Shau Valley. Since the U.S. Congress had forbidden the use of ground troops in Laos and Cambodia a year earlier, only American aircraft were able to support ARVN forces as they proceeded into Laos. Such support included bombing strikes by B-52s. The goal of ARVN troops during Operation Lam Son 719 was to reach the Laotian town of Xepon, some twenty miles inside the border. Along the way they hoped to destroy the stretches of the Ho Chi Minh Trail that ran through the region. **See also** Barrel Roll; Commando Hunt; Lam Son 719.

## Dewey Canyon III

An anti–Vietnam War protest that, satirically, adopted the name of two military operations in Vietnam. Operation Dewey Canyon III took place in Washington, D.C., from April 19 to April 23, 1971. It was organized by Vietnam Veterans Against the War, a protest group made up mostly of those who had fought in Vietnam. Many participants brought their discharge papers with them to prevent any accusation that they were not truly veterans. Other demonstrators were the parents and other relatives of young men who had died in Vietnam. The protest involved a march from the Lincoln Memorial to Arlington National Cemetery as well as a sit-in outside the Supreme Court building intended to underscore what some considered the unconstitutionality of the war. Some protesters also threw their medals and other military insignia on the ground in front of government buildings. **See also** antiwar movement; March on the Pentagon; Vietnam Veterans Against the War.

## Dien Bien Phu, Battle of

The battle that ended the First Indochina War (1946–1954) and knocked the French out of Southeast Asia. After years of inconclusive fighting, the French commander General Henri Navarre decided to try to draw the army of the Viet Minh, led by General Vo Nguyen Giap, into a decisive engagement. The site he chose was a valley near the village of Dien Bien Phu in the mountains of northwestern Vietnam. The village lay along the traditional invasion route from Vietnam into Laos, where the Viet Minh had already begun to support local Communists. Navarre built a substantial series of fortifications in the valley supported by numerous outlying posts. He staffed them with some sixteen thousand French troops, some of them the elite of the French force in Indochina and others colonial troops from Vietnam and Africa. Navarre considered the post impregnable, since he believed that Giap lacked the firepower to dis-

*Paratroopers land near a bunker during the Battle of Dien Bien Phu.*

lodge such a huge garrison. The French commander erred, however, in siting his garrison nearly two hundred miles from the nearest French outpost and constructing only a rudimentary airstrip, isolating Dien Bien Phu and making reinforcement and resupply difficult. Moreover, Giap outsmarted his French counterpart. Using peasant labor, Giap had huge artillery pieces dragged up the mountains surrounding the French base, much to the surprise of Navarre. He also surrounded the area with nearly 100,000 troops and support personnel along supply lines stretching all the way to the Chinese border.

Preceded by skirmishes in the outlying areas, the siege of Dien Bien Phu began on March 13, 1954, and lasted until May 7.

Giap's artillery continually pounded the French base and greatly interfered with aerial resupply efforts, and slowly the circle around remaining French troops was closed. Reinforcements had to generally parachute in and, by the beginning of May, most supplies were falling into the hands of the Viet Minh. Last-ditch efforts to mount a rescue mission from Laos, or stage a massive retreat of the garrison, were too late. The French and the Americans, who by this point were supplying the French with most of their military equipment, considered massive bombing runs, and some American officials reportedly considered using nuclear bombs to save the day at Dien Bien Phu. But U.S. president Dwight D. Eisenhower decided against American military involvement.

The final French forces surrendered on May 7. The French had suffered sixteen hundred killed, a like number missing, and forty-eight hundred wounded. Viet Minh casualties were even higher, with an estimated eight thousand killed and fifteen thousand wounded. Eight thousand French troops were captured and marched off to prison camps. Only half of them survived the experience. The defeat convinced the French to acquiesce to the proposed settlements for Indochina already being discussed at the Geneva Conference. The Battle of Dien Bien Phu, meanwhile, provided an object lesson for Americans in later years and partly explains the bitter American defense of Khe Sanh, a similar isolated mountain outpost, in 1968. **See also** First Indochina War; Geneva Conference on Indochina; Khe Sanh, Battle of.

## Dixie Station

A staging area and coordination point for U.S. naval forces in the South China Sea. It was located at 11 degrees north latitude and 110 degrees east longitude some miles off the South Vietnamese port of

Cam Ranh Bay. Its primary military purpose was to support air operations of carriers in the U.S. Seventh Fleet, along with its counterpart, Yankee Station, located to the north in the Gulf of Tonkin. Aircraft flying from Dixie Station were sent in the directions of South Vietnam and, when called for, Cambodia and Laos; those operating from Yankee Station generally targeted North Vietnam. **See also** aircraft carriers; Seventh Fleet; Yankee Station.

## domino theory

A cold war theory first developed in the late 1940s, although the phrase itself was not used until a speech by U.S. president Dwight D. Eisenhower in April 1954. According to the domino theory, the fall of one country to communism meant a far greater likelihood that its neighbors would likewise fall to communism. The spread of communism must therefore be contained by preventing the first domino from falling and then toppling the others. The idea was supported by Communist rhetoric, which maintained that communism was a monolithic movement that expanded regardless of traditional borders, historical or cultural differences, ethnic conflicts, or national hatreds. It was also supported by the general tendency, in the late 1940s and early 1950s, of Communist nations across the world supporting one another. As became apparent after 1960, however, Communist movements varied greatly depending on the nations in which they were based, and cultural and historical differences, such as longstanding distrust between Russia and China, or between China and Vietnam, made any talk of "monolithic communism" misguided.

Eisenhower's first use of the term, in an April 7, 1954, speech, directed the domino theory at Vietnam, where the imminent victory of Ho Chi Minh's Viet Minh over the French suggested that the first Southeast Asian domino was about to fall. After the Geneva Accords split Vietnam into two, American officials determined that South Vietnam was the domino that had to be kept standing, and Eisenhower approved the decision to send financial and military aid to the South Vietnamese government. During the 1960s, Presidents John F. Kennedy and Lyndon B. Johnson continued to subscribe to the domino theory. They based their expanding support for South Vietnam, and the eventual arrival of American combat troops, on the fear that, if South Vietnam fell, it would soon be followed by Laos, Cambodia, Thailand, Malaysia, Indonesia, and the Philippines. The threat was not, however, a foreign Communist invasion of countries beyond Vietnam but the encouragement of local insurgency movements such as the Viet Cong. **See also** cold war; containment policy.

## Dong Ha, Battle of

An important battle between the regular North Vietnamese Army (NVA) and a combined force of the Army of the Republic of Vietnam (ARVN) and U.S. Marines. The battle took place from April 29 to May 15, 1968, shortly after the Tet Offensive. It was therefore the first guide to Communist intentions after the failure of Tet.

The battle was fought in the regions around the town of Dong Ha, which stood on the juncture of Highway 1, Vietnam's main north-south artery, and Highway 9, which ran east-west from the South China Sea to the Laotian border. The town lay just south of the demilitarized zone (DMZ) and thus was in easy reach of a number of U.S. and ARVN bases and defense facilities. These included an important marine headquarters known as the Dong Ha Combat Base. The entire region acted as the first defense in the event of a major NVA thrust across the DMZ and into South Vietnam.

The fighting around Dong Ha began on April 29 as part of a larger Communist strategy to ensure a strong bargaining position at the Paris peace talks, which were scheduled to begin in May. Communist strategists thought that they would do so with a show of force, and since the beginning of April, NVA units had made a number of small attacks on positions across the DMZ. On April 29, a group of marines spotted units of the NVA only four miles away from the Dong Ha Combat Base. The American and ARVN forces knew that defense of the base was vital, and the fighting that ensued to protect it was intense, most of it taking place in the vicinity of villages to the north and east of Dong Ha itself. Since the NVA attack was largely a show of force rather than an offensive thrust, and perhaps also since NVA casualties were substantial, the Communist retreat began on May 16.

The Battle of Dong Ha was a relatively bloody engagement from the American standpoint. American casualties included 233 marines killed and 821 wounded. In addition, 42 ARVN troops were killed and 124 wounded. North Vietnamese casualties numbered nearly 2,500 dead, and many more were taken prisoner. The Dong Ha Combat Base was successfully defended, and it remained the main forward marine base until it was turned over to the ARVN as part of the Vietnamization plan in November 1969. **See also** Hamburger Hill, Battle of; Tet Offensive.

## draft

The term used to signify required conscription into the American armed forces. During the Vietnam War, the United States relied heavily on the draft to fill the ranks of the armed forces, and the manipulation of various exceptions to draft eligibility left a long legacy of bitterness and contributed to the war's unpopularity.

According to the U.S. Constitution, only the U.S. Congress has the right to raise an army. It first used the draft during the Civil War (1861–1865) and again during the years of American participation in World War I (1917–1918) and World War II (1941–1945). After those wars, however, Congress ended the forced conscription of young American men. In 1948, with the cold war looming, Congress revived the peacetime draft, a step begun tentatively in the months before the United States entered World War II according to the so-called Selective Training and Service Act. It remained in place until 1973, and millions of young Americans came to expect military service to be a part of their process of coming of age. At no point were young women drafted, although women could voluntarily join some fields of military service.

The Vietnam War was a war fought mainly by draftees, or by those who joined the armed forces just to avoid being drafted, since volunteering was likely to ensure a less dangerous posting and a choice of service branch. The average age of those who fought in Vietnam was nineteen years (one became eligible for the draft at eighteen), in comparison to twenty-six years in World War II. Of an estimated 26.8 million young men who turned eighteen during the Vietnam War, 2.2 million were drafted and another 8.7 million joined the armed services voluntarily. Most of the rest enjoyed draft deferments of one sort or another. The most common form of draft deferment was enrollment at a college or university; not surprisingly, college enrollments boomed as young men sought to avoid the draft. Other deferments included having children, teaching in public schools, or serving in the U.S. National Guard or reserves. It was also possible to avoid being drafted by claiming conscientious objector status or through certain physical ailments or limitations.

The various draft deferments helped produce armed forces that were somewhat unbalanced demographically, especially at the level of the U.S. infantry, which conducted most of the ground fighting in Vietnam. Those most apt to get deferments were white and relatively well-off financially. This meant that a disproportionate number of those drafted, and thus of casualties, were African Americans, Latinos, and poor, less well educated whites. The sons of the wealthy and powerful, meanwhile, often found it easy to get slots in the National Guard or reserves. The unfairness of the draft system, along with the draft itself, added greatly to opposition to the Vietnam War among ordinary Americans.

To rectify this unfairness and in the hopes of increasing the manpower pool, U.S. officials modified draft requirements beginning in 1967. By December 1971, when American forces were being withdrawn from Vietnam anyway, all college and teaching deferments had been lifted. In addition, a draft lottery was instituted in 1970, requiring anyone whose number came up to serve provided that they were physically able. In January 1973, after the signing of the Paris Peace Accords, President Richard M. Nixon ended the draft. In its place arose an all-volunteer armed forces, the product of both the political unpopularity of the draft and, in the opinion of many top military men, the relative lack of quality and cohesiveness that the draft provided. In the late 1970s President Jimmy Carter reinstituted the requirement that all young men complete a selective service registration, but no formal draft was reinstituted. **See also** conscientious objectors; draft resistance.

## draft resistance

Although resistance to the draft has existed in all times, far larger numbers of young men became draft resisters during the Vietnam War than in any other American war. Most cited the injustice and alleged illegality of the conflict as well as the unfairness of the draft system itself. Forms of draft resistance included simply refusing to report when called, departing for other countries such as Canada, and burning draft cards. Notably creative means included faking medical problems, using drugs to give misleading health reports, and concocting records as homosexuals or others considered social undesirables. An underground network within the antiwar movement sprang up to provide young men with advice on how to resist the draft. An estimated 570,000 young men found some way to avoid the Vietnam-era draft. Tens of thousands of others were charged with draft evasion; most of these cases were settled, pardoned, or amnestied in the 1970s, but nearly nine thousand resisters were convicted and spent time in prison. A few draft dodgers remained on the run, technical fugitives for decades after the war. **See also** Ali, Muhammad; conscientious objectors; desertion; draft.

## drug use in the armed forces

The issue of drug abuse by American servicemen in Vietnam arose when the traditional, noncontroversial off-duty use of alcohol in the ranks was increasingly supplemented by the use of illicit drugs. The most popular drug in Vietnam, as in the United States, was marijuana. After 1968, in fact, it was normal for U.S. servicemen, at least at the enlisted level, to smoke marijuana regularly. Marijuana was cheap: $5 could buy a sealed pack of marijuana cigarettes, which, apparently, the Vietnamese sometimes even gave away for free. Also popular was methamphetamine, or speed. Often used in liquid form, methamphetamines were used by soldiers to stay awake and alert on patrol. Most alarming was the epidemic-level use of opium

and heroin, especially in forward areas. Those addictive substances were also cheap and widely available, and many servicemen turned to heroin when military officials aggressively clamped down on the more easily detectable marijuana in 1969. Controversy remained alive for years over whether the Central Intelligence Agency processed and transported opium and heroin, using poppies grown by hill tribes in Laos and upper Burma, to help support their "secret war" in Laos.

Estimates indicate that, after 1968, nearly 70 percent of U.S. servicemen in Vietnam used illegal drugs at some point. Explanations include not only the cheapness of the substances but the extreme stress and boredom of serving in Vietnam and the growing rebelliousness and indiscipline in the armed forces after 1970. Few of those who used drugs carried their habits back home after being discharged. **See also** desertion; draft resistance; fragging.

## Dulles, Allen (1893–1969)

Head of the Central Intelligence Agency (CIA) from 1952 to 1960 and brother of John Foster Dulles, secretary of state during the same period. Allen Dulles played a central role in devising America's Vietnam policy after the 1954 Geneva Accords. He helped convince President Dwight D. Eisenhower to throw his support behind South Vietnamese president Ngo Dinh Diem, particularly in 1955 when Diem removed or co-opted his enemies in the Hoa Hao, Cao Dai, and Binh Xuyen. One of Dulles's operatives, Edward G. Lansdale, became the most influential American in Vietnam between 1954 and 1956 and represented a sure sign that the CIA would have an increasing, if covert, role in the region. **See also** Central Intelligence Agency; Dulles, John Foster; Lansdale, Edward G.; Saigon Military Mission.

# Dulles, John Foster (1888–1959)

U.S. secretary of state during most of the presidency of Dwight D. Eisenhower (1952–1960) and a major figure behind the U.S. decision to commit itself to supporting the regime of South Vietnamese president Ngo Dinh Diem.

As secretary of state, Dulles was a major U.S. proponent of a strong nuclear deterrent in what he considered the global effort to stop the spread of communism. He considered the policy of the prior Truman administration, which was based on the containment of communism, somewhat too weak, believing that the United States should take a more aggressive stance toward the Communist threat. When the French came to U.S. officials in 1954 to help them maintain their fight against the Communist Viet Minh in Vietnam, Dulles urged a full American military intervention and even considered the possibility of a tactical nuclear attack. President Eisenhower was hesitant to commit American forces without the cooperation of allies such as Britain, Australia, and New Zealand or without the support of the U.S. Congress. Dulles was unable to secure either, and direct military intervention in Vietnam was delayed for more than ten years.

After the French lost to the Viet Minh at the Battle of Dien Bien Phu in 1954, the concerned nations met in Geneva, Switzerland, to draw up peace arrangements. Dulles, however, opposed the negotiations, and while American observers were present, the United States did not take a direct part in the construction of the Geneva Accords, nor did it sign the agreement. Nevertheless, Dulles followed the Geneva Accords with an announcement that the United States would consider any violation of them, most importantly a military incursion by the Communist North Vietnamese against South Vietnam, to be grounds for U.S. intervention,

since such a violation would constitute a threat to "international peace and security." Meanwhile, following partly the advice of his brother, Central Intelligence Agency director Allen Dulles, the secretary of state made plans to send both economic aid and military advisers to Diem. **See also** containment policy; Eisenhower, Dwight D.

## dumb bombs

Conventional bombs not equipped with electronic guidance systems. A wide variety of these weapons were used in Vietnam, ranging from standard general-purpose bombs weighing up to three thousand pounds to cluster bombs weighing up to fifteen thousand pounds. Their munitions included standard blasts, antipersonnel steel fragments, fuel explosives, and, notoriously, napalm and phosphorus charges. In some cases, single dumb bombs such as the BLU-82B daisy cutter or the CBU-55 were responsible for hundreds of casualties. Dumb bombs were also used to destroy supply depots and other facilities and to clear away jungle. **See also** cluster bombs; Rolling Thunder; smart bombs; unexploded ordnance.

# Duong Van Minh (1916–2001)

South Vietnamese military officer and politician who served as the final president of the nation. After helping President Ngo Dinh Diem solidify his government in 1955, Minh proved very popular among the rank and file of the South Vietnamese army. By the early 1960s, in fact, Diem had grown concerned that Minh, now a general, might be a threat to his authority. To reduce that threat, Diem removed Minh from his military command and gave him the largely useless post of "special adviser." Disgruntled, Minh went on to play a key role in the coup that overthrew Diem in November 1963. Familiar among American

*Duong Van Minh addresses guests after accepting the presidency of South Vietnam in 1975.*

advisers and other officials, who referred to him as "Big Minh," Minh met with CIA man Lucien Conein, who acted as a sort of intermediary between the plotters and the American government between July and October 1963. Minh assured Conein that the plotters did not require American support for the coup, just the assurance that the United States would not interfere with it and that afterward, hopefully, the flow of financial and military aid would continue. Minh's assur-

ances were thought to have encouraged U.S. officials, notably ambassador Henry Cabot Lodge, to give tacit approval to the coup.

Minh emerged as the head of the so-called Military Revolutionary Council, which governed South Vietnam after the coup, but his leadership did not last long. In any case, most observers concurred that, despite his best efforts, the affable Minh was more interested in his personal pastimes than in day-to-day leadership. Further plotting among the Military Revolutionary Council had Minh placed in a figurehead position as head of state on January 30, 1964, and then removed from office altogether.

Minh reappeared on the scene in 1971 when he ran for president against Nguyen Van Thieu. He withdrew from the race after coming to the realization that his cause was hopeless. He, in effect, volunteered for the presidency on April 27, 1975, six days after Thieu resigned in the face of a massive North Vietnamese onslaught. Minh's supporters and other politicians thought that Minh might be their best choice to negotiate some sort of settlement with the North Vietnamese; he was appointed president on April 28. On April 30, however, Minh found he had no choice but to surrender his government and army unconditionally, and he waited peacefully for the arrival of North Vietnamese Army representatives in Saigon's presidential palace. **See also** Ho Chi Minh campaign; Military Revolutionary Council; Ngo Dinh Diem.

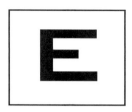

## Eagle Pull

The code name for the plan to evacuate American diplomatic and military personnel from Phnom Penh, the capital of Cambodia. Operation Eagle Pull was originally devised in June 1973 by U.S. Air Force personnel based in Thailand. At the time, the Communist Khmer Rouge threatened to take over all of Cambodia, and U.S. officials wanted to ensure that American citizens, as well as some Cambodians who had aided the United States, could be safely brought out of the country. The Khmer Rouge offensive bogged down by August, however, and the plans for Operation Eagle Pull were suspended and revised.

By April 1975 the Khmer Rouge was again encircling and shelling Phnom Penh, and the forces of the Cambodian government were retreating and dispersing. Following the announcement by President Gerald R. Ford on April 11 that the embassy was to be closed, U.S. ambassador to Cambodia John Gunther Dean called for Operation Eagle Pull to be carried out on April 12. According to the revised plan, a small unit of U.S. Marines flew to Phnom Penh to prepare while a fleet of helicopters, stationed on U.S. Navy ships from the Seventh Fleet in the Gulf of Thailand, readied itself to carry out a relatively small number of evacuees. The evacuation began early on April 12, when a small air force team arrived to manage the operation. The helicopters landed on a soccer field near the embassy that had been turned into a landing zone by the advance team of marines; the first helicopter to arrive carried a larger contingent of marines to provide security and defense, if necessary. By 10:00 P.M. 276 people had been evacuated, including 82 Americans (mostly embassy employees and their families), 159 Cambodians, and 35 other foreign nationals. The last to leave were the U.S. Marines. A few Americans, mostly journalists, remained in Cambodia of their own accord. **See also** Khmer Rouge; Lon Nol.

## Easter Offensive

A major offensive launched by North Vietnam against South Vietnam in the spring of 1972. North Vietnamese leaders' reasons for the Easter Offensive, known to them as the Nguyen Hue campaign, were political as well as military. They wanted to disrupt the programs of Vietnamization and pacification that had taken the place of direct American military involvement in the south, and in so doing further discredit the Americans in the eyes of ordinary Vietnamese. They also calculated that the political climate in the United States in 1972 was such that President Richard M. Nixon would be unable to commit further U.S. ground troops. Ideally, according to some reports, top military commander Vo Nguyen Giap and other strategists thought that if the campaign worked it would turn Americans away from Nixon, who would indeed lose the presidency in the 1972 election. At the very least, Hanoi leaders understood that a strong military showing on the part of the North Vietnamese Army (NVA) would strengthen the North Vietnamese position in peace negotiations.

The overall military plan for the offensive was to use conventional ground attacks to eliminate as much of the Army of the Republic of Vietnam (ARVN) as possible. That would allow the NVA to seize control of the major cities of South Vietnam and, perhaps, incite an overthrow of South Vietnamese president Nguyen Van Thieu. If these goals proved impossible to reach, Giap hoped that NVA forces might be able to take control of enough territory to, again, strengthen Hanoi's negotiating position. In preparation for the offensive, the NVA received a substantial amount of military aid from both the Soviet Union and China, including the latest tanks and antiaircraft guns. The NVA's forces were massive. Altogether, over half a million troops took part in the offensive.

The attack was to take place in three stages in three different areas. The first, and most successful in the end, was a strike against Quang Tri Province, the northernmost part of South Vietnam. It involved an attack across the demilitarized zone (DMZ) as well as an approach from the A Shau Valley in the west. Both were directed, ultimately, at the strategically vital cities of Hue and Da Nang. Giap planned for this northern prong of the offensive to be massive enough that it would divert ARVN forces from their defenses farther south. Once Thieu sent reserves to reinforce the north, Giap would launch the second prong of the attack, which was directed at An Loc, a provincial capital not far from Saigon. Forces for this part of the offensive would attack from across the Cambodian border. The third prong of the attack would take place in between the other two geographically.

It was an attack on the Central Highlands from across the border in Laos. The initial target was the provincial capital of Kontum, but Giap planned for this third prong to ultimately strike across South Vietnam for the coast, thereby cutting the nation in two.

The initial attack on Quang Tri Province from across the DMZ was successful, partly because of the inexperience of newly formed ARVN units stationed in the region. The NVA thrust was halted, however, before it reached Hue. Meanwhile, the attack on Kontum was also contained by a stout ARVN defense and, although An Loc in the south was besieged for several months, it too held. Throughout, ARVN forces were supported from the air by massive American bombing raids. In addition, on May 8, 1972, Nixon ordered a renewed bombing campaign against North Vietnam itself in order to draw attention away from the offensive. He also, for the first time, instructed U.S. and South Vietnamese forces to mine the North Vietnamese harbor at Haiphong as well as other ports.

From a military standpoint, and like a number of other NVA efforts, the Easter Offensive failed. By September 1972, NVA troops even lost the territory they had taken in Quang Tri Province. NVA casualties were heavy, including an estimated 100,000 killed. Moreover, the stand taken by the ARVN was an indication that, thanks to the various Vietnamization programs, South Vietnam was able to defend itself, provided it also had air support from the United States. **See also** Linebacker I; Paris negotiations; Quang Tri, Battle of.

# Eisenhower, Dwight D. (1890–1969)

President of the United States from 1953 to 1961. During World War II Eisenhower rose to the post of supreme commander of the Allied Expeditionary Force in Europe. His wartime fame, and his avuncular personality, encouraged the Republican Party to nominate him for president in 1952, and he went on to defeat Democrat Adlai Stevenson. Eisenhower was reelected in 1956. His vice president for both terms of office was Richard M. Nixon.

As president, Eisenhower continued the policy of containing communism that was adopted by his predecessor, Harry S. Truman, emphasizing the development of a nuclear deterrent rather than the buildup of conventional armed forces. When he took office, the First Indochina War between the French and Ho Chi Minh's Viet Minh was still raging. Eisenhower elected to continue American support for the French. When the war ended in 1954, the United States was providing most of the funding for the French effort. Eisenhower also privately urged the French to grant independence to Vietnam. On the urging of his secretary of state, John Foster Dulles, Eisenhower briefly considered sending direct American military support to help lift the siege of the French at Dien Bien Phu, including the possible use of nuclear weapons. But in the end he held back military support because of the advice of General Matthew Ridgway, chairman of the Joint Chiefs of Staff, and because the British refused to provide similar aid.

Eisenhower refused to send an official American delegation to the Geneva Conference of 1954, which created the Geneva Accords separating Vietnam into two nations. He hesitated to give American approval to an agreement that allowed North Vietnam to establish a Communist regime. On the other hand, and again on the urging of Dulles, Eisenhower was quick to send both economic and military aid to the South Vietnamese government. To prevent the further spread of communism in the region, Eisenhower also supported the establishment of the Southeast Asia Treaty Organization (SEATO), a body designed to provide collective security to the area. From 1955 to the end of his presidency, Eisenhower was occupied with matters other than Vietnam, and, in any case, American aid seemed to be helping to stabilize the South Vietnamese government of Ngo Dinh Diem.

Eisenhower continued to comment on the Vietnam conflict after leaving the presidency in 1960, about the same time that North Vietnam stepped up its campaign against South Vietnam. He reminded his successor, John F. Kennedy, of the need to present a strong front against communism and expressed dismay over the fact that the next president, Lyndon B. Johnson, hesitated to use overwhelming force to win. He also questioned the patriotism of some members of the antiwar movement. **See also** containment policy; Dien Bien Phu, Battle of; Southeast Asia Treaty Organization.

## electronic intelligence (ELINT)

A term referring to the gathering of intelligence about the enemy's electronic equipment rather than the use of advanced electronics in intelligence gathering. During the Vietnam War, ELINT became a highly specialized activity designed to counter the air defenses mounted by North Vietnam. American commanders and technicians used ships and aircraft equipped with special avionics equipment to gather and collect information on North Vietnamese radar capabilities and habits beginning in 1964 and lasting till the end of U.S. involvement. The equipment included highly sensitive antennae, pulse analyzers, and recorders that could track North Vietnam's radar and allow U.S. equipment to match its frequencies and pulse patterns exactly. Then, the North Vietnamese radar networks could be jammed using equipment carried on special aircraft.

Using this technique, American technicians could trick North Vietnamese radar operators into mistaking their locations. ELINT was also employed to determine the frequencies used by guided surface-to-air missiles. ELINT proved to be of marginal effectiveness because the North Vietnamese could easily change their frequencies or pulse patterns, and therefore ELINT computers had to constantly play catch-up. **See also** antiaircraft defenses; Operation Plan 34A; smart bombs.

## Ellsberg, Daniel (1931– )

Intelligence analyst who worked for both the RAND Corporation, a private consultancy, and the U.S. Defense Department. Ellsberg's fame came from his release of the so-called Pentagon Papers, a private Defense Department record of Vietnam policy during the presidency of Lyndon B. Johnson, to the *New York Times* in 1971.

Trained in economics, Ellsberg joined the Defense Department in 1964, where he took a special interest in Vietnamese affairs. In July 1965 he traveled to South Vietnam to study the pacification programs then under way and to try to ensure the support of civilian villagers for the Saigon regime. He also worked for a time as part of the staff of Deputy U.S. Ambassador William Porter. Ellsberg's experiences in Vietnam changed his mind about U.S. policy in the region, convincing him of not only the ineffectiveness of pacification but the corruption of the Saigon regime.

After returning to Washington, D.C., Ellsberg informed Secretary of Defense Robert McNamara of his views, but he was simply one of many trying to influence McNamara. In late 1967, the secretary of defense commissioned a group of researchers and analysts to assemble a history of U.S. policy toward Vietnam since 1945, the so-called Pentagon Papers. Only sixteen copies were made of the final study, which comprised copies of original records and commentary by analysts. Copies were divided among the Defense Department and Pentagon. Ellsberg, meanwhile, began working for the RAND Corporation in 1968 and continued to be one of the few people with a high enough security clearance to have access to the Pentagon Papers. By this time he was strongly opposed to U.S. efforts in Vietnam, believing that U.S. involvement was prolonging and worsening the conflict rather than resolving it. In late 1969, with the help of a colleague named Anthony Russo, Ellsberg began making secret photocopies of parts of the Pentagon Papers. He believed that they demonstrated that U.S. policy toward Vietnam had been made in consistent disregard of both local history and the wishes of the Vietnamese people and that, moreover, American officials had misled the public about Vietnam.

Ellsberg first took his photocopies to members of Congress known to be opposed to the war, including Senator William Fulbright. They refused to act on the information. In 1970, frustrated by the continuation of the war, Ellsberg resigned from RAND and began to take part in antiwar activities. In the summer of 1970 he leaked parts of the Pentagon Papers to reporter Neil Sheehan of the *New York Times*. Sheehan and other *Times* staffers agreed to publish portions of the history, along with supporting documentation, on June 13, 1971. President Richard M. Nixon was infuriated by the leak and tried to stop continued publication. Court decisions, however, favored continued publication.

Ellsberg did not conceal the fact that he was the source of the information. A federal grand jury brought charges against him, including conspiracy, theft, and illegal possession of government documents. He was tried twice. The first, in late 1972, ended in a mistrial. The second, held from June to May 1973, resulted in the dismissal of all charges against Ellsberg. Among the judge's reasons for dismissal was the news that the Nixon administration, angered over Ellsberg's leak of classified government information relevant to national security, had taken steps to destroy his reputation. Most important among these were the illegal tapping of his telephones and a break-in of Ellsberg's psychiatrist's Los Angeles office in search of damning information. **See also** Pentagon Papers; Watergate scandal.

## Elysée Agreement

A 1949 attempt to create a semi-independent Vietnamese nation. The agreement was signed at the Elysée Palace in Paris by French president Vincent Auriol and, representing Vietnam, the former emperor Bao Dai. No Viet Minh representatives were involved, although the French remained at war with the Vietnamese Communists in the so-called First Indochina War. The agreement was ratified by the French government in January 1950. It was followed by similar agreements with Cambodia and Laos.

According to the Elysée Agreement, Vietnam was to be considered an associated nation within a larger entity known as the French Union. It confirmed the borders of the Vietnamese nation by including within the new Vietnam the "Republic" of Cochin China, the southern state that had been declared independent by French high commissioner Georges Thierry d'Argenlieu in 1946. In reality, however, Bao Dai's Vietnam was to be extremely limited in its freedom. The French maintained the right to control Vietnam's armed forces and foreign policy, and the new nation was to be allowed to maintain diplomatic relations only in Thailand, the Vatican, and India (although India refused to recognize the state). In addition, the agreement provided for continued French economic domination of Vietnam. Bao Dai himself

recognized that the arrangement benefited the French far more than it did the Vietnamese.

One of the great advantages of the Elysée Agreement to the French, in fact, was diplomatic. The establishment of a semi-independent Vietnam allowed them to claim that the First Indochina War was not a struggle to maintain possession of colonies. France's American allies, in particular, opposed the continuation of colonialism. Instead, the French could now claim that the war was a civil war between a free Vietnam and a Communist Vietnam, which placed the struggle there firmly within the global cold war. The United States, for its part, had already committed itself to containing the spread of communism. **See also** Bao Dai; First Indochina War; Ho-Sainteny Agreement.

## enclave strategy

The first strategy adopted by American politicians and military commanders following their decision to commit American combat troops to Vietnam in 1965. The enclave strategy, favored by former chairman of the Joint Chiefs of Staff and current U.S. ambassador to Vietnam General Maxwell Taylor, was designed to limit American involvement while also strengthening the ability of the Army of the Republic of Vietnam (ARVN), or South Vietnam, to fight effectively. Taylor was hesitant to call for too broad an American commitment and was convinced that the war could only truly be won by the ARVN. The enclave strategy called for U.S. troops to control important areas along the South Vietnamese coast, generally areas that were densely populated. This would then free the ARVN to fight both the Viet Cong (VC) and the North Vietnamese Army (NVA) in inland areas. A further advantage of the enclave strategy, Taylor argued, was that it would help strengthen and stabilize the South Vietnamese government by giving people confidence that their major cities and ports were secure.

The first regular U.S. ground troops in Vietnam were deployed along the lines of the enclave strategy. More than three thousand U.S. Marines were sent to secure the airfield, and a few other locations, in the coastal city of Da Nang in March 1965. They were ordered not to actively engage any VC troops.

General William Westmoreland, commander of the Military Assistance Command, Vietnam (MACV), rejected the enclave strategy before it was even fully implemented. Westmoreland argued that it would turn U.S. troops into an occupying force and eliminate the great advantages in firepower and airpower held by American forces. Meanwhile, by June 1965, ARVN forces proved only marginally capable of dealing with the threat of increased VC attacks, turning more strategists and politicians over to Westmoreland's view. The MACV commander asked for, and received, a much larger contingent of U.S. troops, and by the middle of June 1965 American forces were shifting toward the more aggressive strategy of search and destroy. **See also** clear and hold; search and destroy; Taylor, Maxwell.

## Enhance and Enhance Plus

Two plans to strengthen the South Vietnamese army in the wake of two threatening developments: the departure of most U.S. combat troops and the massive Easter Offensive mounted by North Vietnam in March 1972. Operation Enhance was announced by U.S. president Richard M. Nixon that March in the effort to replace military equipment that the South Vietnamese had expended or lost during the Easter Offensive. Its sequel, Operation Enhance Plus, was derived from Nixon's desire to strengthen the negotiating positions of both the United States and South Vietnam in the peace talks then taking place in Paris. By supplying the South Vietnamese with millions of dollars worth of military equipment, including tanks and planes, Nixon hoped that he could enable South Vietnam to successfully defend itself against any North Vietnamese incursion, and therefore be in a better position to bargain even after the projected Paris Peace Accords were signed. Nixon also hoped, apparently, that this infusion of aid would help convince South Vietnamese president Nguyen Van Thieu to accept a peace settlement. As it happened, the two operations constituted the last major American effort to support South Vietnam, even though sporadic air and intelligence support continued until August 1973. **See also** Easter Offensive; Linebacker I; Vietnamization.

# F-4 Phantom

The top fighter aircraft used by U.S. forces during the Vietnam War. The F-4 was a twin-engine, supersonic aircraft made by the McConnell Douglas Corporation. It was equipped with four guided missiles whose type and range varied depending on the craft's mission. It also carried extra fuel tanks that could be jettisoned for greater maneuverability. Flown by pilots from the air force, navy, and Marine Corps, the F-4 was most often used on bomber support missions, also known as MiG combat air patrol (MIGCAP). MiGs were the common fighters flown by North Vietnamese pilots. The majority of downed MiGs, an estimated total of 137, were downed by F-4s, and all American aces, or pilots who downed at least five MiGs, flew F-4s. In addition to MIGCAP missions, F-4s were used for reconnaissance patrols. The craft were flown by the air force from bases in both Vietnam and Thailand, by the navy from aircraft carriers offshore, and by the marines from their air bases at Chu Lai and Da Nang. **See also** bombers; fighter-bombers.

# Fairfax

A year-long campaign begun in December 1966 by General William Westmoreland, commander of the Military Assistance Command, Vietnam (MACV), to improve security in the Saigon area and provide a model of cooperation between U.S. and South Vietnamese military forces. West-moreland's immediate concern was the continued and intensive Viet Cong (VC) operations around Saigon, which neither American nor South Vietnamese intelligence or military activity seemed to affect. Indeed, Saigon was beset by frequent bombings or other attacks, and many ordinary people in the region faced constant pressure to join or support the VC. The American response was to connect specific U.S. Army units to a designated district, each unit being connected to three of its South Vietnamese counterparts. Westmoreland's hope was that the South Vietnamese might soon be able to take over the security effort entirely.

VC forces mostly worked around Operation Fairfax instead of being limited by it. They altered their tactics, shifted locations, or went underground. Meanwhile, it proved difficult for American and South Vietnamese units to coordinate their activities, especially with regard to intelligence collecting. The lessons of Operation Fairfax led, in later years, to the Phoenix Program. **See also** Cu Chi tunnels; Phoenix Program; Viet Cong.

# Farm Gate

The name for the broad American effort to support and develop the air combat capabilities of the South Vietnamese. It lasted from 1961 until 1967, when the U.S. Air Force (USAF) assumed direct control of most air operations in Vietnam. Until 1965, when the first American combat troops arrived, Farm Gate provided a vehicle by which the United States slowly and steadily increased both its presence and its role in the growing Vietnam conflict.

Operation Farm Gate began in October 1961 as part of U.S. president John F. Kennedy's attempt to use counterinsurgency movements to stem the spread of communism in Vietnam. That month he sent a small USAF combat team to South Vietnam. Stationed at the Bien Hoa combat base near Saigon, its assignment was initially to train South Vietnamese pilots and ground crews, but the USAF team, known as the 4400th Combat Crew Training Squadron, soon found itself carrying out other missions as well. These included combat support for U.S. Special Forces contingents on the ground and, by December, actual combat missions, provided that at least one Vietnamese national was on board each plane. During 1962, Farm Gate missions expanded to include air strikes against suspected Viet Cong outposts, although U.S. aircraft were restricted to sorties that the South Vietnamese were unable, for whatever reason, to carry out. Despite the presence of American crews, the planes sported the insignia and colors of the Republic of Vietnam.

Operation Farm Gate expanded markedly in 1963. The 4400th Combat Crew Training Squadron was officially attached to the U.S. Pacific Air Force, and the facilities at Bien Hoa were supplemented by smaller bases at other sites, notably the Central Highlands town of Pleiku. Crews had access to more than forty aircraft, most of which were transport planes or older, propeller-driven fighters. The crews also found themselves in greater demand as a result of the expansion of the ground war and the need for both transport and air support. By 1964 problems with spare parts, as well as structural flaws in some of the aircraft, inspired U.S. commanders to assign more modern aircraft, notably the A-1E, to the operation. By the end of 1964 there were two squadrons of A-1Es based at Bien Hoa, and they were flying far more missions than the crews of the South Vietnamese air force.

In 1965 American officials took steps to "Americanize" Operation Farm Gate. They ended the "training" requirement, stating that all aircraft on assignment had to carry at least one South Vietnamese national and replaced the South Vietnamese markings on the planes with those of the USAF. In 1966 and 1967 the arrival of more USAF planes, crews, and support operations made Operation Farm Gate irrelevant. **See also** Flaming Dart; Harkins, Paul D.; Kennedy, John F.; Pierce Arrow.

## Field Force I

One of the two larger designations into which U.S. Army forces in Vietnam were divided for tactical and organizational reasons. Commanders used the term *field force* rather than *corps* to differentiate American from South Vietnamese commands; the South Vietnamese had designated four "corps tactical zones," or military regions, prior to the arrival of U.S. troops. Field Force I, or "Eye" Field Force, was officially organized in March 1966. Originally known as Task Force Alpha, its first units had arrived in South Vietnam in August 1965. Field Force I was based in Nha Trang in South Vietnam's II Corps and its area of operations included the Central Highlands. Beyond its basic artillery and support units, Field Force I deployed, at various points depending on needs and strategy, such U.S. Army units as the First Cavalry Division (Airmobile); the First and 173rd Brigades, the 101st Airborne; and the Fourth Infantry Division. Field Force I was closed down on April 30, 1971. **See also** Field Force II; military regions.

## Field Force II

The second designation into which U.S. Army forces in South Vietnam were divided. After its original components arrived in South Vietnam in March 1966, it grew to be far larger than Field Force I and was based at Bien Hoa, the massive military installation near the outskirts of Saigon. Field Force II was designated to support operations in South Vietnamese military regions I, III, and IV, which included the area just south of the demilitarized zone (DMZ) as well as the Mekong Delta and the regions around Saigon. Field Force II commanders, depending on strategic needs, deployed such U.S. Army units as the First Infantry Division, the 101st Airborne, and the First Cavalry Division (Airmobile). It was deactivated on May 2, 1971. **See also** Field Force I; military regions.

## fighter-bombers

Aircraft that in addition to fighter capabilities were able to engage in bombing missions. Fighter-bombers were heavily used in Vietnam. The U.S. Air Force most commonly employed the F-105 Thunderchief, a supersonic airplane designed in the 1950s to deliver nuclear weapons that was modified for Rolling Thunder missions in Vietnam. The navy and marines generally flew the A-4 Skyhawk. Other commonly used fighter-bombers were the F-100 Super Sabre, which was the first supersonic fighter, having passed the sound barrier in the mid-1950s, and the F-101 Voodoo, a so-called penetration fighter capable of tactical bombing missions. More unique fighter-bombers included the closely related F-111 Aardvark and EF-111A Raven. These were capable of flying long-distance bombing missions at low levels and, in the case of the Raven, carried extensive electronic intelligence equipment for reconnaissance purposes. **See also** Air Force, U.S.; B-52; fighters.

## fighters

Agile, maneuverable aircraft designed primarily to engage in combat with enemy aircraft, although they were effective in reconnaissance roles as well. The most successful fighter used by American forces in Vietnam was the F-4 Phantom. Others included the F-102 Delta Dagger, used in the early years of the war as support for bomber missions, and the Vought F-8 Crusader, another supersonic fighter, which was capable of carrying four 20-millimeter guns in addition to

*The F-105 Thunderchief was one of several types of fighter jets used in the Vietnam War.*

missiles. F-8 pilots downed an alleged nineteen North Vietnamese MiGs, the second largest total after the F-4s. The South Vietnamese air force used a number of F-5 Tiger fighters supplied by the United States. **See also** Air Force, U.S.; F-4 Phantom; fighter-bombers.

## film and the Vietnam War

The Vietnam War inspired hundreds of films, documentaries, and television series. Even before American involvement began, popular films were made of the novels *The Quiet American* (1958) and *The Ugly American* (1963), both based on the dangers and opportunities of American interference in Indochina. During the war itself, few films appeared, perhaps a Hollywood acknowledgment of the American public's polarization over Vietnam. The most well known of the time was probably *The Green Berets* (1968), a World War II–style glorification of U.S. military men starring John Wayne.

Only in the years after the fall of Saigon did large numbers of films about the Vietnam experience appear. The first wave of dramas reflected mostly the negative effects of the war on individual soldiers. Among the most highly praised were *Taxi Driver* (1976), starring Robert De Niro as a disturbed Vietnam veteran; *Coming Home* (1978), the story of the challenges faced by a paralyzed veteran; and *The Deer Hunter* (1978), director Michael Cimino's examination of the dehumanizing aspects of Vietnam service among a group of friends from small-town Pennsylvania, which won several Academy Awards, including best picture. *Apocalypse Now* (1979), Francis Ford Coppola's complex portrayal of the insanity and futility of the war, has been called one of the key films of the twentieth century for its striking imagery and insights into war's horrors.

During the early 1980s the Vietnam War provided some filmmakers with the context for action films of comic book–style adventure and heroism. Among the most popular of these was *First Blood* (1982), which introduced Sylvester Stallone as Rambo, a character so popular he appeared in a sequel called simply *Rambo: First Blood Part II*. *Uncommon Valor* (1983) and *Missing in Action* (1984) featured heroes returning to Vietnam to rescue Americans left behind there, unlikely exploits, and daredevil escapes. By the mid-1980s the trend had swung toward the production of presumably realistic battlefield films. One of the most famous and vivid of these was Oliver Stone's *Platoon* (1986), which won the Academy Award for best picture. Notable others included Stanley Kubrick's *Full Metal Jacket* (1987) and Brian De Palma's *Casualties of War*, which like *Platoon* pitted good American soldiers against bad American soldiers in Vietnam. Movies about veterans' experiences continued as well with, notably, *In Country* (1989), starring Bruce Willis, and Stone's second Vietnam film *Born on the Fourth of July* (1989), starring Tom Cruise. The Vietnam experience even inspired a few comedies, perhaps most memorably *Good Morning Vietnam* (1987), starring Robin Williams as a nonconformist military disk jockey, and *Air America* (1990), a satiric account of the secret war in Laos starring Mel Gibson.

Far fewer films explored the Vietnam War from the Vietnamese perspective. Stone completed his so-called Vietnam trilogy, however, with *Heaven and Earth* (1992), based on the story of a Vietnamese village girl, torn between the Viet Cong and loyalty to her family, who marries a U.S. military man. Not strictly Vietnamese but a noteworthy document of the long years of warfare in Indochina was *The Killing Fields* (1983), the story of the conquest of Cambodia by the Khmer

Rouge and the subsequent genocide of the Cambodian people. A popular French film released in 1992, *Indochine*, attempted to depict the rise of communism in Vietnam from both the French colonial and Vietnamese perspectives. **See also** literature and the Vietnam War; music and the Vietnam War; television and the Vietnam War.

## fire support bases

Temporary base areas that U.S. and South Vietnamese forces established at the beginning of military operations. Fire support bases formed a mobile front line that suited the random nature of a war that lacked traditional fronts where artillery pieces could be placed. Locations of fire support bases were often determined by helicopter-borne "pathfinders" who were dropped to designate effective landing sites. After the ground was suitably cleared of foliage, artillery was brought in by Chinook helicopters to provide a defensive perimeter. Often infantry units were stationed at the perimeters as well to provide security. Once the fire support bases had been established, infantry units were helicoptered in to commence attacks. Networks of such bases often took shape to provide support for larger operations, and communications often enabled strings of fire support bases to provide effective, yet temporary, front lines. Some of them, such as Firebase Bastogne near the A Shau Valley, remained in place for months and provided artillery support for a variety of operations. **See also** pathfinders.

## First Aviation Brigade

The largest U.S. aviation group in South Vietnam. At its height in 1967 and 1968 the First Aviation Brigade had at its disposal more than six hundred airplanes and over thirty-five hundred helicopters in addition to tens of thousands of troops. Its duties varied from reconnaissance to combat missions, from troop support to medical evacuation, and even included logistical responsibilities such as hauling equipment. The brigade was formed at Tan Son Nhut air base near Saigon in May 1966; moved to Long Binh, the huge airfield near the Bien Hoa base outside Saigon, in December 1967; and returned to Tan Son Nhut upon the imminent withdrawal of U.S. troops in December 1972. The last components of the First Aviation Brigade left Vietnam on March 28, 1973. **See also** Air Force, U.S.

## First Cavalry Division (Airmobile)

A U.S. Army division with a storied history and the first division to be deployed to Vietnam. It arrived in Vietnam from its base in Fort Benning, Georgia, on September 11, 1965, and was involved in the Battle of Ia Drang Valley that November, the first encounter between American troops and North Vietnamese regulars. The First Cavalry Division, which was designated as Airmobile in July 1965, consisted of nine infantry battalions, six artillery battalions, an air combat wing flying helicopters and gunships, and various support units. At various points the First Cavalry Division was deployed to all four military regions in South Vietnam and in addition to Ia Drang took part in the Battle of Hue in 1968 and the relief of Khe Sanh that same year. It also participated in the 1970 Cambodian "incursion." Aside from its Third Brigade, which remained until June 1972, the First Cavalry was withdrawn from Vietnam in April 1970. In later years it was based at Fort Hood, Texas. The unit suffered more than thirty thousand casualties, both killed and wounded, in Vietnam, and individual members as well as the division itself won numerous decorations, including twenty-five Congressional Medals of Honor. **See also** Army, U.S.; Ia Drang Valley, Battle of.

# First Indochina War

The eight-year conflict that provided the prelude to the Vietnam War. It was fought between the Viet Minh, seeking national independence for Vietnam, and France, trying to regain control of one of its richest colonies.

After Viet Minh leader Ho Chi Minh proclaimed an independent Democratic Republic of Vietnam (DRV) in early September 1945, weeks after the end of the Japanese occupation of the region, the French acted quickly. A French expeditionary force under the leadership of General Jacques-Philippe Leclerc was dispatched to Vietnam early in 1946. It quickly reestablished French control throughout the south, in Cambodia, and in the large cities, including Saigon and Hanoi. The Viet Minh was forced into the countryside. Hoping to take advantage of global sympathy and, especially, the U.S. dislike of colonial empires, Ho tried at first to establish independence through diplomatic channels despite the return of French forces. Over the spring and summer of 1946, however, the French government shifted toward the right, which meant that top officials had little interest in establishing an independent Vietnam, especially one under a professed Communist like Ho Chi Minh. On June 2 the French high commissioner to Vietnam, Admiral Georges Thierry d'Argenlieu, outflanked both Ho Chi Minh and his own government by proclaiming a semi-independent Republic

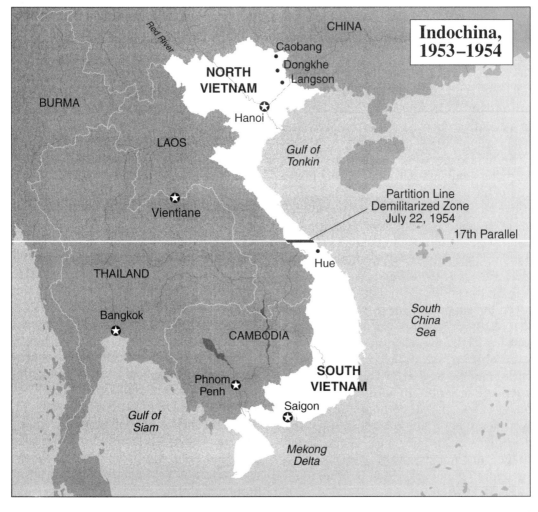

of Cochin China in southern Vietnam. Soon after he took steps to establish a similar semi-autonomous state, Annam, in central Vietnam. An ardent nationalist posted to the area by France's World War II savior, Charles de Gaulle, d'Argenlieu refused to even consider negotiating with the Viet Minh. Ho Chi Minh spent part of the summer of 1946 in France, hoping to extend the privileges granted to the DRV by the earlier Ho-Sainteny Agreement. But the talks proved fruitless, and he returned to Vietnam in September prepared to take more drastic action. General Leclerc, meanwhile, frustrated by the drift of events, resigned his post over the summer and was replaced as head of the French expeditionary force by a succession of generals. On November 23, a French naval vessel, the *Suffren*, launched an artillery barrage against the port of Haiphong. The French followed the attack by placing what DRV leaders considered unreasonable limitations on their autonomy. By the end of December the First Indochina War was under way.

French leaders imagined at first that Vietnam, and indeed all of Indochina, could be resecured fairly easily. They began to implement their long-tested "oil slick" method, which involved ensuring control of major cities first and then expanding their authority into the countryside. The strategy, however, was effective only in the south, where the French enjoyed the support of local religious sects that exercised great power, the Hoa Hao and Cao Dai. In the north the French were able to maintain control of only Hanoi and the Red River Delta as well as a few other towns. In addition, and in a manner somewhat comparable to the American approach to their own Indochina conflict twenty years later, France did not devote its full military strength to winning the war or employ its most effective strategies.

Perhaps the largest error committed by the French, however, was that they underestimated the Viet Minh. Its military leader, Vo Nguyen Giap, proved again and again that he was a capable strategist, while the propaganda efforts of Ho Chi Minh and others demonstrated to many ordinary Vietnamese that the Viet Minh were true nationalists. As the years of the war passed, in fact, the Viet Minh found itself able to secure more and more territory in the countryside. Much of the fighting that took place resembled the guerrilla warfare that the Viet Minh proved far more capable at than the French, who possessed no concrete plan for gaining territory. Instead, the French seemed to settle on a sort of war of attrition, hoping that one day the Viet Minh would abandon its cause and make a settlement. Instead, the Viet Minh simply grew stronger.

The French war effort also suffered from indifferent political leadership in Paris and a revolving door of military commanders in Vietnam, resulting in constantly shifting strategies and poor coordination among units. General Jean de Lattre de Tassigny, commander in 1951 and 1952, had taken major steps to solidify control of the Red River Delta, but his successor, Raoul Salan, had little success against Viet Minh guerrillas. In July 1953 General Henri Navarre arrived to assume command of French operations. He appeared hopeful that his so-called Navarre Plan, along with, by now, huge amounts of American aid, could turn the tide by mounting offensives against the Viet Minh. Behind this outward confidence, however, Navarre suspected that the war could not be won, and reported as much to his government.

In January 1954, in response to a second, and far deeper, invasion of Laos by the Viet Minh, Navarre began the operation that was to end up characterizing French failures in the First Indochina

War. The plan was to establish a major outpost near a village called Dien Bien Phu, located in the mountainous northwestern corner of Vietnam along the traditional invasion corridor between northern Vietnam and Laos. Navarre hoped, apparently, to draw the Viet Minh forces that had engaged in the invasion of Laos into a conventional battle, which he was confident they would lose thanks to massive French firepower.

Giap, however, outsmarted Navarre. He proved ready to engage his forces in a set battle with the French, but mustered four divisions, far more than Navarre had envisioned. In addition, Viet Minh leaders collected hundreds of laborers to drag artillery pieces up the mountains surrounding Dien Bien Phu. Navarre found himself in a long siege, lasting from March 13 to May 7, 1954. Viet Minh artillery continually pounded the base, both causing damage and making airlifts difficult. Briefly, the United States considered sending military aid to save the garrison at Dien Bien Phu, including, apparently, the possibility of nuclear weapons. U.S. president Dwight D. Eisenhower, however, rejected both the use of nuclear bombs and, after the British refused to help out, the deployment of American military forces. The French surrendered the base on May 7 and the war was over. The Geneva Conference, already under way, turned its attention to a peace settlement that divided the former colony of French Indochina into North Vietnam, South Vietnam, Laos, and Cambodia.

In addition to some of their richest colonial territory, the First Indochina War cost the French over seventy-five thousand dead and more than sixty-five thousand wounded. Many of the casualties were so-called French Union troops from the various French African or Asian colonies or members of the French Foreign Legion; unlike the Americans later, the French did not use draftees in Indochina. The Vietnamese nationalists fighting on the side of the French lost nearly twenty thousand dead and over thirteen thousand wounded. The Viet Minh was thought to have lost many more, and tens of thousands of Vietnamese civilians died in the fighting as well. **See also** Dien Bien Phu, Battle of; Elysée Agreement; Geneva Conference on Indochina; Ho-Sainteny Agreement.

## Fishhook

A region of Cambodia that bordered South Vietnam, only sixty miles from Saigon, the South Vietnamese capital. American and South Vietnamese strategists believed that the Fishhook was a major sanctuary for Viet Cong (VC) and North Vietnamese Army (NVA) forces as well as the headquarters for the Central Office for South Vietnam (COSVN), the Communist organization that coordinated VC efforts with those of Hanoi. The first of these assumptions was borne out, but U.S. president Lyndon Johnson refused to consider incursions across the border to close down the sanctuaries. Richard Nixon, however, was of a different mind; in 1969 he ordered B-52 bombing raids over the Fishhook. When American and South Vietnamese forces crossed into the Fishhook during the so-called Cambodian incursion of 1970, they found a number of large supply depots and military base areas. COSVN headquarters, however, was never located. After the Cambodian incursion ended, Communist forces reoccupied the area. **See also** Cambodia, invasion of; Central Office for South Vietnam; sanctuaries.

## five o'clock follies

The sarcastic name reporters gave to the daily briefings of the press corps given by U.S. military information personnel in Vietnam every day at 5:00 P.M. The epithet reflected the sense of many journalists that they were not being told the entire truth behind U.S. or South Vietnamese military efforts. The custom for military information officers since the Kennedy administration, in fact, had been to present such efforts in as positive a light as possible. As early as 1963, correspondent Neil Sheehan published an account of the Battle of Ap Bac that quoted military adviser John Paul Vann criticizing the South Vietnamese effort as "a miserable damn performance" (Sheehan, *A Bright Shining Lie*). Sheehan's report differed greatly from that of U.S. Commander in Vietnam general Paul D. Harkins, which proclaimed the battle a decisive victory for the South Vietnamese. By 1965, when Lyndon Johnson was president, the United States was escalating its commitment to Vietnam, and the regular five o'clock briefings had begun, many reporters assailed what they later called a "credibility gap" between military briefings, which till 1968 were almost invariably optimistic, and the realities of the Vietnam War.

The briefings themselves were held by the staff of the Office of Information of the Military Assistance Command, Vietnam (MACV). The information they dispensed was compiled by Office of Information staff from daily communications sent from officers in the field. The reporters then gathered in central Saigon at the Joint U.S. Public Affairs Office (JUSPAO) to hear that day's news. The widening credibility gap may have been the result of differing assumptions on the part of independent reporters and military information officers. The latter, as well as many of their sources of information, were encouraged to "sell" the war to the public, whereas reporters sought to tell the public the whole, unvarnished story. **See also** Joint U.S. Public Affairs Office; media and the Vietnam War.

## Flaming Dart

The true beginning of American bombing operations in Vietnam and the precursor to Operation Rolling Thunder, the name given to years of bombing raids against North Vietnam. The operation was an outgrowth of the rising use of American aircraft in Vietnam as part of Operation Farm Gate. Allegedly, U.S. president Lyndon B. Johnson signaled for it to begin in December 1964, considering that a massive display of U.S. airpower could be both a reprisal against North Vietnamese actions and a possible deterrent to further aggression.

The occasion to implement Operation Flaming Dart, which had been developed as a contingency plan some weeks earlier, came early in February 1965 when a Viet Cong (VC) attack on an American helicopter base near Pleiku killed eight Americans and wounded more than one hundred others. The attack also crippled twenty aircraft. In agreement with South Vietnamese officials, Johnson ordered bombing raids against four sites in North Vietnam as both reprisal and warning. The air strikes were carried out by U.S. Navy jets from aircraft carriers in the Seventh Fleet stationed in the South China Sea. Johnson ordered a second series of strikes after a VC attack killed twenty-three Americans at Qhi Nhon.

The use of Operation Flaming Dart was a turning point in American involvement in Vietnam, committing U.S. military assets to an attack on North Vietnam for the first time. It also signaled a willingness to attack North Vietnam in response to VC attacks. **See also** Gulf of Tonkin Resolution; Rolling Thunder.

## Fonda, Jane (1937– )

Actor and anti–Vietnam War activist. In her early career as an actress and sex symbol, Fonda appeared in army recruiting programs, but by the late 1960s she had become an outspoken opponent of the Vietnam War, so much so that the Federal Bureau of Investigation (FBI) allegedly tried to trump up criminal

*Jane Fonda sings an antiwar song to North Vietnamese soldiers and reporters in Hanoi. An extreme antiwar activist, Fonda was condemned by many Americans, particularly U.S. soldiers.*

charges against her. In 1972 Fonda made a controversial trip to Hanoi, where she met with North Vietnamese politicians, was posed with American prisoners of war, and broadcast a number of propaganda messages; the trip earned her the lasting enmity of U.S. soldiers. Fonda was only the most famous of those who were so radicalized by the Vietnam War that they grew sympathetic to the Communist cause, but many Americans, civilian as well as military, considered her a traitor and referred to her as Hanoi Jane. In 1973 she married Tom Hayden, another prominent activist and one of the Chicago Seven. She made a second trip to Hanoi in 1974 to shoot a documentary called *Introduction to the Enemy*. For these trips Fonda faced no charges, and her film career suffered only a temporary setback. In 1978 she was nominated for an Academy Award for her performance in *Coming Home*, the story of a disabled Vietnam veteran. **See also** antiwar movement; Hayden, Tom.

## Forces Armées Nationale Khmer (FANK)

The new armed forces of Cambodia in the regime of Lon Nol, which toppled the government of Norodom Sihanouk in March 1970. The Forces Armées Nationale Khmer, or the Khmer National Armed Forces, were largely trained and equipped by the United States, South Vietnam, and their allies and represent a major escalation of the Vietnam War into Cambodia.

Sihanouk had struggled to maintain Cambodian neutrality as the conflicts in Vietnam and Laos raged; Lon Nol, in contrast, pledged to support both U.S. and South Vietnamese efforts to halt the spread of communism in the region.

FANK was evidence that U.S. officials were ready to return the favor, a direct result of the decision by President Richard M. Nixon to begin providing military and financial aid to Lon Nol in April 1970. Three training bases established for the purposes of preparing FANK were staffed by personnel from U.S. Special Forces, who taught Cambodians loyal to Lon Nol modern methods of strategy, organization, and how to use weapons. As U.S. troops, including Special Forces, were withdrawn from Southeast Asia according to Nixon's policy of Vietnamization in 1971, the training bases were turned over to the control of the U.S. Army and staffed, by and large, by Australians and New Zealanders. The training sites were closed at the end of January 1973 in line with the decision to remove American forces and other foreign troops from Southeast Asia after the Paris Peace Accords took effect. Lon Nol thus found himself in control of a substantial new national army equipped, for the time being, with modern equipment. FANK proved of little use, however, in ultimately preventing the takeover of Cambodia in April 1975 by Communist Khmer Rouge guerrillas. In various engagements up to that point, like the South Vietnamese army, it had fought well. According to some, and again like the South Vietnamese army in the same months, FANK proved much less effective once the United States discontinued its resupply and air support. **See also** Khmer Rouge; Lon Nol; Sihanouk, Norodom.

## Ford, Gerald R. (1913– )

President of the United States from August 9, 1974, the day the resignation of Richard M. Nixon took effect, to January 20, 1976. Ford was therefore president at the time of the final North Vietnamese conquest of South Vietnam and the end of the Vietnam War.

The Republican Party leader in the House of Representatives from 1965 to 1973, Ford took a special interest in national defense policy. He openly supported America's growing involvement in the Vietnam War and even urged President Lyndon B. Johnson to commit more money and equipment to the conflict. When Nixon's original vice president, Spiro Agnew, resigned in the face of numerous personal scandals in October 1973, Nixon asked Ford to step in. Less than a year later, when Nixon himself faced impeachment because of various misdoings, the president resigned and was replaced by Ford. Thus, Ford was a rare U.S. president who took office without having been on any national election ticket.

As president, Ford proved hesitant to restart American support to South Vietnamese president Nguyen Van Thieu, despite promises that Nixon had reportedly made to Thieu. Ford also rejected the advice of his inherited secretary of state, Henry Kissinger. When the final North Vietnamese offensive threatened to take Saigon in the spring of 1975, Ford made it clear, against Kissinger's wishes and against another promise made by Nixon, that American forces would not return and that American involvement in Vietnam was over. The president did seek further funding from Congress to send to Thieu but the funding was denied.

One of Ford's last important decisions with regard to the long Indochina conflict was to pull American diplomats out of Phnom Penh, the capital of Cambodia, in the face of a Khmer Rouge onslaught. Ford's April 11, 1975, decision was fairly easy since the United States had no firm or long-term commitments to a free Cambodia. Ford also called for the abandonment of the U.S. embassy in the South Vietnamese capital of Saigon on April 29. Finally, in May, Ford chose a show of force to retrieve the crew of an American merchant ship, the *Mayaguez*, that had been captured off the shore of Cambodia by Khmer Rouge forces.

Ford lost the presidential election of 1976 to Georgia governor Jimmy Carter, a newcomer to national politics not implicated in either the various misdoings of the Nixon administration or the quagmire of the Vietnam War. **See also** Eagle Pull; Frequent Wind; *Mayaguez* Incident; Nixon, Richard M.

## Fort Hood Three

The name given to three U.S. Army privates—James Johnson, Dennis Mora, and David Samas—who were the first members of the U.S. military to publicly refuse to be sent to Vietnam. The three men, stationed at Fort Hood, Texas, refused to follow when their unit was called up to go to Vietnam in June 1967. Instead, they contacted a peace organization based in New York City that helped them arrange a press conference. At the press conference, the newly dubbed Fort Hood Three denounced the Vietnam War as both illegal and immoral. They also filed a lawsuit against the U.S. government claiming that the orders sending them to Vietnam were invalid since no war had been declared by Congress. The soldiers were absent without leave (AWOL) throughout these events and therefore subject to military discipline.

Over the summer of 1967, the Fort Hood Three faced arrest and trial in military courts, their lawsuit having been rejected by a U.S. district court judge on the grounds that civil courts had no jurisdiction over this particular military matter. Military authorities finally caught up with them on July 7, and they were detained at Fort Dix, New Jersey. On August 14, the three men again refused to be transported to Vietnam, and the next day they were all charged, separately, with insubordination. Following courts-martial in September, military judges convicted all three and sentenced them to terms in the army prison at Fort Leavenworth, Kansas.

For the antiwar movement, the Fort Hood Three became a cause célèbre. The actions of the three soldiers, military insiders who conventionally simply followed orders, gave credence to the movement's views about the Vietnamese conflict, and protesters realized they had thousands of potential allies in uniform. Soon, incidents of other soldiers refusing Vietnam service, even soldiers already in Vietnam, came to light, and the Fort Hood Three proved to be on the leading edge of what became a broad protest movement inside the U.S. military. Johnson, Mora, and Samas were released into civilian life after serving their sentences, and all became involved in the antiwar movement. **See also** antiwar movement; desertion; draft resistance.

## Four-Party Joint Military Commission (FPJMC)

The temporary arrangement designed to restore stability in Vietnam after the Paris Peace Accords, signed on January 27, 1973, took effect. The four parties were the United States, the government of North Vietnam, the government of South Vietnam, and the Provisional Revolutionary Government, which represented South Vietnam's Communists. The commission's specific tasks, to be accomplished within sixty days, were to preserve the cease-fire, provide for the return of prisoners of war (POWs), develop a strategy to deal with those missing in action (MIA), and oversee the departure of remaining Americans and other Free World troops. The FPJMC only succeeded in exchanging POWs and withdrawing troops. The MIA issue was never resolved, and contradictory ambitions quickly had the North and South Vietnamese firing at each other again. The FPJMC was disbanded on March 29, 1973, according to the sixty-day calendar. It was replaced by a much smaller Four-Power Joint Military Team (FPJMT), which kept lines of communication open between Hanoi and Saigon. The FPJMT managed to locate twenty-three U.S. MIAs before it was disbanded with the Communist takeover of Saigon in April 1975. **See also** Paris Peace Accords.

# fragging

An extreme form of antiwar protest associated exclusively with American forces in the last years of the Vietnam War. Generally fragging involved the intentional use of fragmentation grenades by enlisted men against noncommissioned officers or officers. Those insubordinate soldiers who resorted to such actions preferred fragmentation grenades because they could be tossed anonymously and left no fingerprints or other damning evidence. Other weapons were used as well, however; smoke grenades, for example, might be left burning under a sergeant's or an officer's bunk as a warning. Fragging resulted in dozens of deaths and injuries inflicted by American troops against their own leaders.

Many incidents of fragging were thought to have been incited by the sense among soldiers that their leaders were incompetent and therefore put troops in unnecessary danger on the battlefield. Most fragging occurred, however, in units that were not involved in fighting: Sometimes, for example, unit leaders were "fragged" for being too strict. Other fragging incidents were associated with illicit drug use by troops in rear areas.

Fragging was encouraged, many argued, by the fact that both officers and enlisted men in Vietnam shifted posts regularly, preventing the development of unit cohesion and loyalty. Other factors that may have encouraged fragging include the soldiers' sense, widespread by 1969, that they might be risking their lives in a pointless conflict that many of

their countrymen did not support and the fact that, with the policy of Vietnamization beginning in 1969, most troops knew that U.S. forces were on their way out of the country.

No reliable total of fragging incidents has been calculated. Nonetheless, most historians seem to think that there was more of this type of activity in Vietnam than was considered normal for an army in combat. In 1971, the year most incidents were reported, there were 333 episodes of fragging resulting in twelve deaths. **See also** draft resistance; drug use in the armed forces.

## free-fire zones

A term used early in the Vietnam War to designate areas in which U.S. and South Vietnamese forces were free to use heavy firepower to eliminate supposed Viet Cong (VC) strongholds. The areas were declared by military officials more or less free of civilian populations, but this estimation was often incorrect, and reports that tens of thousands of Vietnamese civilians were being killed led many Americans to conclude that the so-called free-fire zones were evidence of a careless and indiscriminate approach to the war. Concerned by the negative publicity, in 1965 the U.S. Department of Defense changed the name of such designated areas to "specified strike zones," but the earlier name was still more commonly used.

The free-fire zones were chosen by South Vietnamese officials, a number of whom were from Saigon and did not really know the areas that they cleared for massive bombing and artillery strikes. In a continuation of practices begun during the regime of Ngo Dinh Diem, many South Vietnamese villagers were forcibly evacuated from areas designated as free-fire zones. Others were urged to leave by loudspeakers on trucks traveling through the zones or by leaflets dropped by aircraft, which many could not read. Those who chose to remain in their home villages, or who returned after having been evacuated, were sometimes automatically viewed as VC sympathizers rather than ordinary villagers caught in dangerous circumstances, and were therefore treated badly. **See also** friendly fire.

## Free World Assistance Program

A plan designed in 1965 by U.S. president Lyndon B. Johnson in an effort to give international sanction to his decision to send regular American combat troops to Vietnam to support the South Vietnamese government. From 1965 to 1973 the Free World Assistance Program included forty nations that sent some form of aid to South Vietnam.

Five countries provided troops, who joined their American counterparts in South Vietnam in an alliance that came to be known as the Free World Military Forces. The largest numbers were from South Korea, which had nearly fifty thousand troops in Vietnam in 1969, and Thailand, which had over eleven thousand. Australian and New Zealand together sent nearly eight thousand troops, many of them experts in jungle fighting or other specialized fields. There were also about fifteen hundred troops from the Philippines, although their number was reduced drastically after 1968. Small groups of advisers and volunteers from other countries such as Taiwan and Spain and a few mercenaries from around the world also joined in the fight.

The Free World Military Forces were under the operational command of the U.S. Military Assistance Command, Vietnam (MACV), and all long-term strategic decisions were made jointly by the MACV commander, the top officer in the South Vietnamese army, and the commander of

*Members of the Royal Australian Air Force arrive in South Vietnam as part of the Free World Military Forces. Australia and New Zealand sent a combined eight thousand troops, many of them specializing in jungle warfare.*

forces from South Korea. As a group, the three were known as the Free World Military Assistance Council. The council produced an annual combined campaign plan that outlined larger goals but did not provide specific assignments to troop contingents; these remained largely in the hands of local commanders from the respective Free World nations.

More than thirty other nations participated in the Free World Assistance Program in nonmilitary ways. Some of the richer and more powerful nations of the world, including Great Britain, Canada, the Netherlands, Belgium, and Japan, provided humanitarian, medical, or advisory help. France, notably, did not take part in the Free World Assistance Program. Others that did included Iran, Turkey, Israel, Ireland, Brazil, and Venezuela. The large assembly of nations allowed the United States and South Vietnam to assert that the effort to stop the spread of communism in Southeast Asia reflected global concerns. **See also** Military Assistance Command, Vietnam; Southeast Asia Treaty Organization.

## French Indochina

A colony consisting of territory that would become the nations of Vietnam, Cambodia, and Laos. Established beginning in the 1860s by France, which in the nineteenth century sought to counter the expanding British colonial empire with an empire of its own. The nature of French rule and the reluctance of France to withdraw from the area were important factors in the thirty-plus years of warfare in Indochina from 1946 to 1980.

The French arrived in Indochina in the 1860s as the latest in a long series of European merchants, explorers, and missionaries. The first were the Portuguese and the Dutch, who arrived in Vietnam in the 1500s to set up trading posts. Beginning in the early 1600s the Portuguese merchants were joined by

Roman Catholic missionaries, who, over the years, had some success in converting the Vietnamese to the foreign religion. The term *Indochina*, meanwhile, was first used by mapmakers and sailors in the 1600s to denote the vast areas in between India and China that included—in addition to Vietnam, Cambodia, and Laos—Thailand (Siam) and Burma.

European colonialists grew far more aggressive in the mid-1800s, and by this time they enjoyed a vast technological superiority over any of their Asian foes. The French government sent warships to Vietnam in 1845 in response to anti-Catholic measures taken by the Nguyen emperors based in Hue. They sank four Vietnamese vessels in 1846 in an attempt to free a church official who had been imprisoned. In 1858 the French made their second incursion into Vietnamese waters. They landed at the port of Tourane (later Da Nang) and then moved south to Saigon, which possessed a relatively protected deepwater port, where they established a permanent outpost. By 1862 the Vietnamese emperor, Tu Duc, signed a treaty recognizing French suzerainty over Cochin China, the southernmost region of Vietnam. Over the next years, and in the face of constant, if small-scale, guerrilla resistance, the French established control over Annam, the regions of central Vietnam, and Tonkin, the far north. Despite their plans to negotiate a means to colonize Thailand as well, the French failed; they were outsmarted by the Thais, who remained among the few Asian peoples to fend off European colonization. As part of the negotiations, however, the Thais ceded vast regions in Cambodia in 1863. The final piece was added in 1893 when the French took possession of Laos.

The colony of French Indochina was formally established in 1887. It consisted of only one official colony, Cochin China, which was directly ruled by the

French. The remaining four territories—Annam, Tonkin, Cambodia, and Laos—were ruled as protectorates under members of the local ruling families. These protectorates, however, were for all intents and purposes dominated by the French despite their nominal autonomy. The top official in the region was the French governor-general, who maintained offices in Hanoi. The governor-general answered only to the Ministry of Colonies in Paris and had the right to station troops in Cochin China or any of the four protectorates.

Indochina became the richest of the French colonies. It was a center for the production of rubber and other vital industrial commodities and remained a major rice-growing region. French colons, as they were known, dominated the important plantations, mines, and towns, often exploiting cheap local labor. In addition, the French took steps to ensure the loyalty of traditional Vietnamese, Cambodian, or Laotian landlords and nobles by granting them political or economic privileges, including the right to collect rents from tenants and to staff certain civil service posts. In this sense, much of the traditional ruling class of Indochina underwent a fundamental transformation; in the past its education and system of values were largely Chinese in orientation. Under French rule, by contrast, many ruling elites found themselves beholden to the French, learned French in place of Chinese, and sent their offspring to be educated in France.

The French claimed to be conducting a "civilizing mission" in Indochina as part of their justification for seizing the region. But their efforts to "Europeanize" the local peoples were limited to the traditional ruling elites, although thousands of Indochinese of all classes converted to Roman Catholicism. For instance, the French built few schools in Vietnam. By 1940, in fact, there were only fourteen French-speaking high schools and one university in Vietnam. In all, only 10 percent of Vietnamese who had access to education, a small number in any case, were educated in the French manner. Those Vietnamese who did make it into and through the French educational system often found themselves, upon graduation, barred from any significant position within the colonial administration. Their frustration sometimes took them into anti-French resistance groups.

The Vietnamese, moreover, never lost their strong sense of nationalism, forged over centuries of conflict with China. Major rebellions took place, for instance, in 1888 and 1913. The Vietnamese hoped that their cause might be heard at the Paris Peace Conference, held after the end of World War I in 1919, when U.S. president Woodrow Wilson proclaimed that all peoples should enjoy the right to self-determination. Ho Chi Minh was among several Vietnamese nationalists present at the conference, but he found that the French were not interested in letting go of their colony. During the 1920s the Vietnamese nationalist movement emerged in force. It generally followed two strains. One took China as its model, particularly the nationalist Chinese government of Chiang Kai-shek. These nationalists, who formed a body known as the Vietnam National Party (VNP), wanted both strength and autonomy for Vietnam under a centralized and somewhat traditional government. The other strain took the Communist Soviet Union as its example, and many young, educated Vietnamese, like Ho Chi Minh, looked to communism as the way to not only free Indochina from French rule but free ordinary people from their domination by landlords and officials. After the French violently crushed a VNP uprising in 1931, more and more Vietnamese opted for the nascent Indochinese Communist Party (ICP). Others, such as Ngo

Dinh Diem, came to rely, for now, on the more traditional nationalists rallying under Emperor Bao Dai. During the 1930s the French faced constant trouble from both factions, and many Vietnamese nationalists and Communists found themselves placed in prison for anti-French activities ranging from distributing pamphlets to staging strikes and riots.

In June 1940 the French government fell to an invasion by Nazi Germany. A new regime, known as Vichy France, was formed to replace the deposed government. Vichy was nominally semi-autonomous but truly a puppet of Germany and, in Asia, of Japan. The Japanese began to move into Indochina in the summer of 1941, seeking control of both its natural resources and bases for attacks on other regions in Asia. Vichy France was left nominally in control of Indochina, but the true authorities there until the end of World War II were the Japanese occupiers. They coexisted reasonably peacefully, and with cooperation in such matters as military bases and jurisdictions, until March 1945. During that month the French authorities, who possessed new confidence now that the Vichy regime at home had been overthrown, staged an uprising against the Japanese. It was easily averted, and the Japanese installed a puppet regime in Vietnam under Bao Dai. Meanwhile, a substantial anti-Japanese guerrilla movement had emerged in the years since 1940. It was dominated by the Viet Minh, headed politically by Ho Chi Minh and militarily by Vo Nguyen Giap, and it had harassed the Japanese occupiers in various small actions beginning in 1944. The Viet Minh stood strongly for Vietnamese independence, and Ho Chi Minh wanted to find a way to establish that independence when the Japanese left. During the summer of 1945 he began to work with American intelligence personnel from the Office of Strategic Services (OSS), the

predecessor to the Central Intelligence Agency (CIA). Many of the Americans, who generally opposed colonialism as a matter of course, were sympathetic to Ho's desire to rid Vietnam of not only the Japanese but the French as well.

After the Japanese surrendered on August 15, 1945, ending World War II, British forces arrived in southern Vietnam to secure it under an agreement that had been made in July. Chinese forces accepted the Japanese surrender in the north. Both released French prisoners, and the new French government under Charles de Gaulle began sending over new troops to resecure their colony. Ho Chi Minh, however, saw the period immediately following the Japanese surrender as a window of opportunity. Viet Minh contingents, accompanied by bemused OSS officers, hurried to Hanoi, where on September 2 Ho proclaimed the independence of Vietnam under a new regime to be known as the Democratic Republic of Vietnam (DRV). He could only rely, however, on solid support north of the sixteenth parallel. In southern Vietnam other nationalists held sway.

The French, ironically, had planned to grant the peoples of Indochina more autonomy, but they failed to work closely with nationalist leaders and were unwilling to grant complete independence. Events of 1946 further alienated the French from Ho Chi Minh and other nationalist leaders. After an agreement in March, the Ho-Sainteny Agreement, the French agreed to recognize the DRV as a member state within the French Union. A planned vote on independence with the south, however, was never allowed to take place because of the actions of a new French high commissioner, Admiral Georges Thierry d'Argenlieu. D'Argenlieu hesitated to negotiate at all with Vietnamese nationalists. Ho responded to the high commissioner's intransigence by making an appeal to the French government in Paris, since d'Argenlieu's actions clearly violated the March agreement. A new, more strongly nationalist government in Paris, however, failed to respond to his complaints and d'Argenlieu took another fateful step. He proclaimed the independence of Cochin China, thus negating the possibility that Vietnam would be unified. Ho now felt that only war could free French Indochina. The fighting began on December 19, 1946, after negotiations failed to settle accounts following d'Argenlieu's bombing of Haiphong in late November. By the time this First Indochina War was over in 1954, the French had been soundly defeated and removed as colonial overlords, leaving behind them the independent nations of North Vietnam (the DRV), South Vietnam, Cambodia, and Laos. **See also** Vietnam, Democratic Republic of; Vietnam, historical overview of; Vietnam, Republic of; Vietnam, Socialist Republic of.

## Frequent Wind

The elaborate plan to evacuate American diplomatic and military personnel, as well as select South Vietnamese nationals, from Saigon before the South Vietnamese capital fell to the forces of North Vietnam. Contingency plans for Operation Frequent Wind were drawn up long before the final North Vietnamese assault on Saigon in April 1975, but, as it happened, those on the scene were forced by circumstances to improvise. The plans called for the use of assets of the U.S. Seventh Fleet, stationed off South Vietnam in the South China Sea, to both carry out the evacuation and provide air cover if necessary. Planners also hoped to use the facilities of Tan Son Nhut airport, some five miles from the center of Saigon, for the evacuations, and the Defense Attaché Office at Tan Son Nhut was designated the command post of the operation.

U.S. ambassador to South Vietnam Graham Martin had the authority to call for the operation to begin. He did so on April 29, 1975, upon learning of a massive North Vietnamese artillery attack at Tan Son Nhut, which was thought to signal a broad assault on Saigon itself. The artillery attack, however, had provoked a number of South Vietnamese pilots to jettison bombs and extra fuel tanks on the runways before fleeing in their planes, which rendered the runways unusable. Martin learned that, instead, people would have to be evacuated from Tan Son Nhut by helicopter, one of the options provided for in the contingency plans but hardly the optimal one. After a force of U.S. Marines was gathered together from ships in the Seventh Fleet and flown in to provide security, the operation began. The first helicopters landed at Tan Son Nhut at approximately 3:00 P.M., and the evacuations continued until 9:00 P.M. During those hours CH-53 helicopters took some 4,500 Vietnamese and 395 Americans from the Tan Son Nhut site. The last to leave, in the hours before midnight, were the marines, who had struggled all day to secure the site against hordes of Vietnamese clamoring to get in to Tan Son Nhut and onto the helicopters, and a special demolition team that blew up the Defense Attaché Office headquarters and other U.S. facilities. Some of the shells of these buildings remained standing over twenty-five years later.

The operations at Tan Son Nhut were only one of the methods by which people left Saigon. A second evacuation site was the U.S. embassy itself in central Saigon, which had not been figured into any contingency plans. The rising chaos on the streets of Saigon and outside Tan Son Nhut, however, had made it impossible for many people to get to the airport, and they fell back upon the embassy. The marine commander in charge of Operation Frequent Wind, Brigadier General

Richard Carey, was forced to devise a new plan to evacuate hundreds of people from the embassy compound. After again sending in a marine contingent to provide security, Carey ordered in the helicopters. Some, CH-53s, could land in the courtyard, but only one at a time. Smaller helicopters, CH-46s, could use the helipad on the embassy roof. Nightfall, bad weather, and the possibility of North Vietnamese artillery fire made this part of the operation hazardous, but it continued as long as U.S. officials dared. President Gerald R. Ford, paying close attention from the White House, ordered Martin to leave at 5:00 A.M. on April 30, after Carey had ordered that only Americans be evacuated after 4:30. The last to leave the embassy was Marine Master Sergeant Juan Valdez, part of the security force. He boarded the last CH-46 at 7:53 A.M. Several hundred Vietnamese remained in the compound. Over 2,000 people had been evacuated from the embassy, including 978 Americans and some 1,100 Vietnamese.

Those evacuated from Tan Son Nhut and the U.S. embassy were joined on the ships of the Seventh Fleet by tens of thousands of South Vietnamese soldiers, sailors, and refugees. Nearly one hundred South Vietnamese aircraft, for instance, had been cleared to land on U.S. aircraft carriers along with their crews and the crews' families. More than fifty of the airplanes were thrown over the sides of the carriers into the ocean to make room for the waves of helicopters coming in from Saigon. The news footage of valuable aircraft being flung into the sea brought home the reality of the fall of Saigon to a watching world. Meanwhile, much of the South Vietnamese navy, carrying up to thirty thousand sailors and their families, joined the evacuation fleet. So also did a huge number of small craft: barges, junks, tugboats, fishing boats, and even pleasure craft. Altogether, an estimated eighty

thousand people, fewer than fifteen hundred of whom were Americans, made their way to evacuation centers in Guam and the Philippines. **See also** Duong Van Minh; Ho Chi Minh campaign; refugees.

## friendly fire

The term used in wartime to describe accidental injuries and deaths caused by one's own forces. It was difficult for American or South Vietnamese forces to avoid friendly fire in Vietnam given the lack of conventional front lines and the mountainous, jungle terrain. In dense jungle fighting conditions, a patrol might easily misjudge the identities of other units it encountered, and miscommunication among artillerymen, ground troops, and air support units led to errors in calculating strike positions. Exact figures for friendly fire casualties in Vietnam are uncertain; some evidence suggests that field commanders sometimes failed to report friendly fire as a cause for fear victims or their families would lose recognition or benefits. Estimates range from 1,326, a figure referring to those killed in what the Department of Defense classified as "misadventures," to over 8,000, which includes those classified as killed in accidents and other nonhostile deaths. One well-known incident involving friendly fire deaths was the 1967 Battle of Dak To, in which 42 of the total of 76 U.S. deaths were caused by U.S. bombs. **See also** casualties; free-fire zones.

## Fulbright, J. William (1905–1995)

An influential opponent of the Vietnam War in the U.S. Senate. Long interested in fostering international understanding, Fulbright, a Democratic senator from Wisconsin, was the guiding force behind the Fulbright program for student and scholarly exchange.

Fulbright questioned American policy in Vietnam as early as 1961. A supporter of Lyndon B. Johnson, however, Fulbright voiced his concerns privately. Johnson, in fact, convinced Fulbright to introduce into the Senate the Gulf of Tonkin Resolution in August 1964, figuring Fulbright's powerful voice on foreign affairs would ease the passage of the resolution. The senator continued to support Johnson's Vietnam policy until early 1965, but he publicly disagreed with the notion that the North Vietnamese attack on South Vietnam constituted the front end of a larger, Chinese-backed, Communist assault on the region.

By 1966, with American involvement in Vietnam escalating rapidly, Fulbright became a vocal opponent of Johnson's Vietnam policy. He claimed that Vietnam did not represent a vital U.S. interest and that, instead of being a cold war conflict, the war was a localized insurgency directed against the corrupt and inept South Vietnamese government. As head of the Senate Foreign Relations Committee, Fulbright called for hearings on Vietnam policy in February 1966. The Fulbright hearings, which were televised nationally, allowed Americans for one of the first times to actually hear a high-level debate over the conflict.

Fulbright, for his part, began to argue that the Vietnam War was the product of American overconfidence and aggression. He warned against such dangers in his 1967 book, *The Arrogance of Power*, raising a number of the same concerns that prompted the Fulbright hearings. The senator claimed in his book that the American involvement in the Vietnam War reflected no vital national interest and, in fact, was weakening democracy at home as well as abroad. He also noted that the Vietnam effort was drawing resources and attention away from domestic reforms such as civil rights legislation. In 1968 Fulbright staged another round of hearings, this time behind closed doors, to determine whether the United States had actually been attacked during the Gulf of Tonkin Incident, as administration spokesmen had always asserted, or whether the United States had instead provoked the incident to justify its military response. In the end, Fulbright claimed that the Johnson administration had intentionally misled both him and the Congress when the Gulf of Tonkin Resolution was introduced.

Fulbright continued to speak out against the Vietnam War after Richard M. Nixon took office as president. Although he approved of Nixon's plan to withdraw American troops, he criticized the president's policy of Vietnamization on the grounds that it merely continued the war in new ways. By 1971, the involvement of U.S. forces in incursions into Cambodia and Laos inspired Fulbright to initiate legislation that would reduce the president's ability to conduct a war without the approval of Congress. Meanwhile, Fulbright remained very concerned about what the Vietnam War had done to democracy, the rule of law, and honorable behavior in the United States, even at the highest levels of government. He addressed these concerns in a 1972 book titled *The Crippled Giant*. **See also** Case-Church Amendment; Cooper-Church Amendment; Gulf of Tonkin Resolution.

## Geneva Conference on Indochina (1954)

An international conference addressing the crisis in Indochina left by the long First Indochina War (1946–1954). When it began on April 26, 1954, its original goal was to change the armistice that had ended the Korean War into a permanent peace settlement. Unable to settle the Korean issues, representatives turned their attention to Indochina on May 8. A day earlier the remnants of the French garrison at Dien Bien Phu had surrendered to the Communist Viet Minh.

The Geneva Conference was originally chaired by the United States and the Soviet Union. Representatives were also present from France, China, Great Britain, and the concerned Indochinese regimes: the Democratic Republic of Vietnam (DRV), the State of Vietnam (later the Republic of Vietnam, or RVN), Cambodia, and Laos. U.S. secretary of state John Foster Dulles, however, left Geneva even before formal negotiations began; subsequent U.S. officials remained present only as observers.

The representatives concluded their agreements on July 20, 1954, including an armistice between France and the Viet Minh formally ending the First Indochina War. Separate peace agreements were concluded between France and, respectively, Laos, Cambodia, and Vietnam. Laos and Cambodia were granted independence under their present governments (which had been devised in the late 1940s as associates of the French Union). Moreover, both countries were forbidden from entering military alliances, a decision implying neutrality in any further conflicts.

The peace treaty with Vietnam was less decisive, reflecting the fact that Vietnam was represented by two different regimes. The Geneva Conference in effect created North and South Vietnam, or the DRV and RVN, although the split, along the seventeenth parallel, was to be only temporary. The accords provided for a demilitarized zone (DMZ) five miles above and below the line. In 1956 supervised elections would be held in which the Vietnamese people would determine the course of their own reunification. In the meantime, the north would be governed by the DRV and the south by Bao Dai's puppet regime within the French Union. Vietnam was also forbidden from participating in military alliances, and an International Control Commission, involving representatives from the theoretically disinterested nations of Poland, Canada, and India, would supervise the implementation of the accords. For three hundred days after July 20, also, civilians would be free to move from north to south or vice versa.

Neither U.S. nor South Vietnamese representatives signed the accords, and in any case few believed even in 1954 that the 1956 election would ever take place. It never did, and by 1956 the DRV had consolidated its rule over the north while Ngo Dinh Diem, with American support, had become the unchallenged president of the RVN. In later years the United States proclaimed that the Geneva Accords had created an independent South Vietnamese nation. **See also** First Indochina War; Vietnam, Democratic Republic of; Vietnam, Republic of.

## Geneva Conference on Laos (1962)

A meeting that sought to ensure the stability and borders of Laos in the face of a large-scale insurgency conducted by the Pathet Lao, the local Communists. The Geneva Accords were the product of a conference called together in May 1961 attended by representatives from fourteen concerned nations, including the United States. U.S. president John F. Kennedy had already made the decision to not intervene militarily in Laos, despite the danger of a Pathet Lao takeover.

The results of the Geneva Accords were limited and mixed. They arranged for an International Control Commission (ICC) to work with the three competing factions in Laos: the Royal Lao government, its enemies the Pathet Lao, and the so-called neutralists under Souvanna Phouma. The three Laotian factions, however, rarely worked together and the ICC was able to accomplish little. The accords also required that all foreign military personnel leave Laos within seventy days after they were signed on July 23, 1962. This provision was aimed at the North Vietnamese, who already had hundreds of troops in Laos.

While these provisions were being negotiated, the Pathet Lao took advantage of the slowness of the talks by extending its range of control over much of southeastern Laos. In response, Kennedy sent a contingent of U.S. troops to northern Thailand, across the border, and ordered the Seventh Fleet to the Gulf of Thailand. This show of force worked to halt the Pathet Lao advance temporarily and en-

abled a neutralist government, headed by Souvanna Phouma, to take office in the capital, Vientiane. The expansion of the war in Vietnam, however, proceeded to absorb more and more of the attention of American leaders. Though Souvanna Phouma's regime remained in place in Vientiane, much of the rest of Laos was in a state of civil war until 1972. American involvement in this "secret war" mostly consisted, until 1970, of covert CIA support of anti-Communist factions. **See also** Laos, secret war in; Pathet Lao; Souvanna Phouma.

## Goldwater, Barry (1909–1998)

U.S. senator from Arizona from 1953 to 1964 and from 1969 to 1987; also the Republican candidate for U.S. president in the 1964 election. The most prominent spokesman for the conservative wing of the Republican Party, Goldwater consistently supported more decisive military action during the Vietnam War.

As a candidate for president, Goldwater found that the escalating conflict in Vietnam was a major issue. He strongly supported a powerful U.S. military presence but urged that the United States should leave Vietnam if American leaders were not willing to make that commitment. He also strongly supported any measure to stop the spread of communism. Goldwater argued that the United States should be prepared to invade North Vietnam if necessary, and even considered that low-level nuclear weapons might be used for the purposes of defoliation. Goldwater lost the presidency to Lyndon B. Johnson in a landslide, 39 to 61 percent.

Goldwater continued to speak out against the American strategy in Vietnam while out of office, and was reelected to the Senate, in a landslide of his own, in 1968. In a message that was to resonate among Americans long after, Goldwater criticized the Johnson administration and military leaders for failing to support the soldiers in the field, a criticism he also leveled at war protesters. At various points he called for stepped-up bombing campaigns against North Vietnam and for the expansion of the war into Cambodia. Goldwater opposed the various congressional attempts, beginning in 1970, to limit the president's war-making capacity, such as the Cooper-Church Amendment, and even after the signing of the Paris Peace Accords in January 1973 he urged the United States to continue sending military aid to South Vietnam. **See also** Johnson, Lyndon B.

## Great Migration of 1954

The departure of some 800,000 Vietnamese people from the northern part of the country to the south. Such a departure was provided for by the Geneva Accords of 1954, which opened a three-hundred-day window for migrations. Many of the migrants were Roman Catholics spurred by fears of oppression under the new Democratic Republic of Vietnam. The Catholics were welcomed in the south by Ngo Dinh Diem, at that time a prominent politician but within months the unchallenged leader of South Vietnam. Diem, himself a Catholic, recognized the importance of the support these migrants might provide and he was generous in offering them land, government jobs, and other privileges. **See also** Geneva Conference on Indochina; Ngo Dinh Diem; Vietnam, Republic of.

## Green Berets

The nickname for U.S. Army Special Forces troops. Among the first Americans to take an active part in the Vietnam War, Special Forces engaged in various covert and unconventional operations. President John F. Kennedy granted them the right to wear green berets as a distinguishing feature of their uniform in 1961. **See also** Army, U.S.; Special Forces, U.S. Army.

## grenades

One of the common weapons used by all sides during the Vietnam War. Standard hand grenades can be divided into two categories. Defensive grenades, built only to blast, posed less risk to the infantrymen using them than offensive grenades, meant to be planted or thrown a good distance, which released hundreds of antipersonnel fragments. The workhorse hand grenades used by U.S., South Vietnamese, and other Free World forces included the MK2 defensive grenade; the M33 baseball grenade, which was also defensive; and the MK3, an offensive grenade used mostly in clearing operations. North Vietnamese forces used similar weapons, usually made by the Soviets or copied from Soviet models. All variants could be thrown distances ranging from fifteen to twenty meters.

Other hand grenades used in Vietnam included smoke grenades, incendiary grenades, and antitank grenades. Some specialized devices included "irritant" grenades filled with tear gas, poisonous chemical agents, and the M34 phosphorous grenade. When detonated, the M34 released a phosphorous cloud to a radius of twenty-five meters. It burned, briefly, at nearly five thousand degrees Fahrenheit.

Launched grenades included those fired from the M79, a shoulder-mounted weapon mainly used by the Americans, and the RPG2, the Soviet-made counterpart to the M79 used by the North Vietnamese. The M79 could fire a single forty-millimeter grenade to a range of four hundred meters. Most rounds fired were explosive grenades, but the M79 was also used to fire antitank, smoke, and tear gas grenades. The M79 proved useful not only in combat operations but to mark targets and even as a form of communication among separated units. **See also** light antitank weapon; mines; mortars.

# Guam Conference

A meeting among top American and South Vietnamese officals taking place in the U.S. protectorate of Guam in the western Pacific on March 20 and 21, 1967. Those in attendance included U.S. president Lyndon B. Johnson, Secretary of State Dean Rusk, Secretary of Defense Robert McNamara, and Ambassador to South Vietnam Henry Cabot Lodge. The top South Vietnamese officials at the time, Premier Nguyen Cao Ky and Chief of State Nguyen Van Thieu, also attended.

The purpose of the meeting was to assess the progress of the Vietnam War, address the strength of the Saigon regime, and, from the American standpoint, inform South Vietnam of some important changes in top personnel. Though the U.S. officials reaffirmed their commitment to supporting South Vietnam, Johnson committed only fifty-five thousand new troops to Vietnam, far fewer than U.S. commander William Westmoreland requested. Johnson also refused to increase American bombing raids along the Ho Chi Minh Trail in Cambodia and Laos, as Ky had hoped. Meanwhile, Ky and Thieu took advantage of the opportunity to show Johnson the new constitution they had drafted, seeking to convince the U.S. president that South Vietnam was making steady progress toward democracy. Among the new appointments that the United States made known at Guam, Ellsworth Bunker was to replace Lodge as ambassador in Saigon; General Creighton Abrams would arrive soon as Westmoreland's assistant and, in time, his replacement; and Robert Komer would take over the pacification program. It was the pacification effort, which had been proceeding haphazardly, that was the main change being noted at the Guam Conference. Under Komer, pacification would proceed under the aegis of the military rather than as a civilian operation, and it would proceed without the necessary guarantees of land reform and other measures on the part of South Vietnam. **See also** Honolulu Conferences; Midway Island Conference.

# guerrilla warfare

The form of warfare conducted by the Viet Cong (VC) in South Vietnamese territory, a form of fighting that challenged the notion that wars could be won simply with overwhelming firepower and high technology. Guerrilla warfare involved the use of irregular forces rather than regular army units, often organized as small, mobile groups and at times operating as individuals. Guerrilla fighters attacked the means by which the enemy waged war rather than the enemy itself, seeking

*Holding an infant, a young girl stands in the ruins of her home after a Viet Cong guerrilla attack.*

to destroy roads, bridges, and supply depots; cutting communication lines; and engaging in small-scale bombings or other attacks. Since they were irregulars, many guerrilla fighters in Vietnam found they could, in effect, fight a part-time war and disguise themselves and their efforts with relative ease. In terms of large-scale military goals, guerrilla warfare was most useful in harassing the enemy in preparation for an assault by regular army troops and equipment. The North Vietnamese used this strategy very effectively.

U.S. troops found the continual guerrilla attacks mounted by the VC, who would often disperse and disappear before they could be located or defeated, extremely frustrating. They were also understandably stressed by the uncertainty over whether South Vietnamese civilians were friend or foe, which probably played a role in the atrocities committed by some U.S. troops. In combat terms, U.S. and South Vietnamese forces tried to counter the guerrilla war with a wide range of tactics, including the use of massive firepower to root out guerrilla base areas and small-unit actions rather than large set-piece battles. In some ways U.S. forces and their allies adopted their own versions of guerrilla warfare, such as long-range reconnaissance patrols. **See also** counterinsurgency; long-range reconnaissance patrols; search and destroy; Viet Cong.

# Gulf of Tonkin Incident

A mysterious series of events that prompted the Gulf of Tonkin Resolution, the measure that gave U.S. president Lyndon B. Johnson the authority to send regular ground troops to Vietnam. The events gave the impression that U.S. naval vessels had been attacked by North Vietnamese boats, but it was later determined that most of the attacks had not, in fact, occurred. Questions also arose as to whether it was the Americans or North Vietnamese who provoked the incident.

The beginnings of the Gulf of Tonkin Incident, named for the body of water bordered by Vietnam and China in which it took place, came in late July and early August 1964. Over those days U.S. officials planned a series of investigations to determine the extent of North Vietnamese coastal defenses as part of a program named Operation Plan 34A. Using vessels manned by South Vietnamese crews, but following American orders, Operation Plan 34A mounted a series of small attacks on North Vietnamese targets. These included the shelling of islands off the North Vietnamese coast on July 30 and 31 and shelling of sites on the Vietnamese mainland on August 3 and 4. The South Vietnamese crews also planned to capture and interrogate the crew of a fishing boat. These moves were apparently not intended to provoke the North Vietnamese into an actual fight but to simply motivate them to mobilize their coastal defenses, thus making them easier to find and identify.

Meanwhile, the U.S. Navy destroyer *Maddox* was sent into the Gulf of Tonkin, equipped with high-tech radio gear, to monitor North Vietnamese coastal preparations. On August 1, it approached one of the islands that was shelled the day before. The next day the North Vietnamese outpost on the island attacked the *Maddox* using three small torpedo boats. This attack, which was easily repelled, was the only confirmed North Vietnamese attack in the entire convoluted series of events. President Johnson learned of the attack but decided that it did not merit large-scale retaliation.

On August 3, the *Maddox* was joined in the gulf by a second destroyer, the *C. Turner Joy*. They were given orders that, apparently, kept them far away from the North Vietnamese coastline, thus reducing the risk of an armed encounter. The night of August 4, however, both destroyers took actions that suggested that a

North Vietnamese attack was under way, although later investigations uncovered some fundamental inconsistencies in their reports. The *Maddox*, for instance, claimed to pick up the sound of North Vietnamese torpedo boats on its sonar equipment, although sonar operators on the *C. Turner Joy* could not hear the same sounds. In addition, radar operators on the *Maddox* failed to locate the objects that gunners on the *C. Turner Joy* fired at on the basis of its radar findings.

Despite these inconsistencies, U.S. officials back in Washington determined that an attack on American naval vessels had taken place. They were confirmed in this view, apparently, by intercepts of North Vietnamese radio transmissions acknowledging the attack, although it was possible that the transmissions referred to the earlier encounter on August 2. Now ready for a larger and more forceful retaliation, Johnson authorized American air strikes on North Vietnam, and on August 5 U.S. planes began bombarding North Vietnamese coastal defenses as well as an oil storage facility near the town of Vinh according to a plan named Operation Pierce Arrow. Soon after, the U.S. Congress passed the Gulf of Tonkin Resolution, giving Johnson the authority to use American force to repel attacks against U.S. forces in Southeast Asia, noting that the United States considered "security" in the region "vital to its national interest and to world peace."

The American public, echoing the sentiments of Congress, at first overwhelmingly supported Johnson's desire to take a strong stand against communism in Vietnam. In time, however, the truths and misunderstandings about events in the Gulf of Tonkin between July 30 and August 4 became widely known, and many people began to accuse Johnson of misleading both Congress and the American people. **See also** Gulf of Tonkin Resolution; Operation Plan 34A; Pierce Arrow.

# Gulf of Tonkin Resolution

The congressional resolution authorizing U.S. president Lyndon B. Johnson to use all necessary measures to stop attacks on the U.S. forces in Vietnam and preserve the security of Southeast Asia in accordance with the United Nations charter and with regional defense treaties. It was passed by Congress almost unanimously on August 7, 1964, under the official title of the Southeast Asia Resolution.

The Gulf of Tonkin Resolution was presented to Congress in the aftermath of alleged attacks on U.S. Navy destroyers in the gulf on August 2 and August 4, followed on August 5 by a retaliatory bombing strike by U.S. aircraft against North Vietnam. The Johnson administration presented the alleged attacks as acts of war against the United States, justifying an appropriate response. No one voted against the resolution in the House of Representatives, where the vote was 416 to 0; it passed in the Senate 98 to 2. Congressmen were apparently reassured that the resolution did not signify any intention by the administration to escalate the Vietnam conflict despite language in the resolution suggesting that the president had the authority to take measures to support the South Vietnamese regime.

Administration officials may not have intended an escalation of the conflict, but the escalation took place anyway. Perhaps not taking into account the North Vietnamese response to both the resolution and the bombing raid on August 5, U.S. officials were surprised to learn of open attacks on U.S. bases and other sites in November and December 1964 and February 1965 by North Vietnamese troops and their Viet Cong allies. The American response was to send regular U.S. ground troops to Vietnam. Johnson cited the Gulf of Tonkin Resolution as giving him the necessary legal authority to send U.S. soldiers, who began to arrive in Vietnam in March 1965.

The resolution quickly became controversial despite the overwhelming approval it had attracted in August 1964. Some claimed that it did not grant the U.S. president the right to conduct a war since only Congress has the right to declare war according to the Constitution. Others noted that Johnson's administration had prepared such a resolution earlier than the alleged attacks in the Gulf of Tonkin, suggesting that the president had been looking for a pretext to expand U.S. presence in Vietnam. Johnson was accused by several congressmen of having misled them about the incidents and thus expanding the Vietnam conflict under false pretenses. In 1966 Wayne Morse, one of the two senators who opposed the initial resolution, tried to have Congress repeal the resolution. Although few supported him at first, Congress finally repudiated the Gulf of Tonkin Resolution in 1970. **See also** Gulf of Tonkin Incident; Johnson, Lyndon B.; War Powers Resolution.

## gunships

Airplanes or helicopters fitted with large caliber artillery or machine guns. Gunships were a new weapon developed during the Vietnam War. According to U.S. strategists, they were well suited to such tasks as close air support of ground troops and the harassment of enemy positions and supply lines. Fixed-wing gunships included the AC-47, or "puff," and the AC-119, or "shadow." The latter carried three 7.62-millimeter machine guns able to fire six thousand rounds per minute. As the utility of gunships became apparent, the U.S. Air Force added the AC-130 "spectre" to its arsenal in 1968. The spectre was equipped with six machine guns and two cannons. It also carried electronic equipment such as infrared sensors and laser designators to locate and mark targets as well as radar equipment that could jam enemy radar. The AC-130 was used heavily in Operation Commando Hunt, an interdiction operation along the Ho Chi Minh Trail, where gunships destroyed hundreds of supply trucks and, reportedly, inspired much fear among Communist troops.

Helicopter gunships were mostly used by the U.S. Army and Marine Corps for close air support. The earliest were modified versions of helicopters already in use, such as the UH-1 Huey and the CH-47 Cobra, both of which were equipped with machine guns, cannons, and occasionally rocket launchers. In 1967 the AH-1 Cobra, a specially designed helicopter gunship, came into widespread use. It featured a multibarreled machine gun mounted at the bow as well as grenade and rocket launchers. **See also** Cobra; fighters; Huey.

# Haiphong Harbor, mining of

The controversial 1972 operation to bomb Haiphong, the major port of North Vietnam, and mine its harbor to cripple the NVA fuel supply and advance stalled peace negotiations in Paris. Haiphong is located on a tributary of the Red River about sixty miles from Hanoi and about ten miles inland from the Gulf of Tonkin. Built by the French in the late 1800s, Haiphong was directly connected to Hanoi by a dedicated rail line. As the source of most supplies that entered the North Vietnamese capital, Haiphong was naturally a military target and a flash point for conflict. Indeed, an attack by French vessels and troops on Haiphong in late November 1946 was considered to be the event that led to the First Indochina War (1946–1954).

During the Vietnam War (1959–1975), the North Vietnamese received nearly 80 percent of their supplies, including war matériel, via the port at Haiphong, at least partly because air strikes damaged rail connections with China. The South Vietnamese and Americans refused to attack the port, however, for fear of escalating the conflict. Some thought that attacks might result in the sinking or damaging of ships from the Soviet Union or China, thus encouraging deeper involvement from them. Other officials noted that Haiphong still received merchant ships from such nations as France, which was a U.S. ally in Europe.

In the aftermath of North Vietnam's Easter Offensive of 1972, however, the United States decided to mine the harbor to close it to shipping and, it was hoped, force the North Vietnamese to negotiate at the Paris peace talks. On May 10, U.S. aircraft dropped hundreds of mines into the water which were timed to arm after three days. Within those three days, U.S. officials made clear, all foreign shipping had to leave the harbor or risk explosion. The mining largely worked to close the harbor to large ships, although smaller ships often learned to avoid the mines. Like Hanoi itself, Haiphong city, which had a population of some 180,000 people, was targeted by the Christmas bombing of 1972, suffering major damage and hundreds of civilian casualties.

Haiphong was reopened to cargo ships in July 1973. The Paris Peace Accords, signed that January, provided for U.S. assistance in helping the North Vietnamese clear the area of mines. The operation took approximately six months. **See also** Easter Offensive; Linebacker I.

# Hai Van Pass

An important passageway in the northern part of South Vietnam. The Hai Van Pass ran roughly north-south along the borders of Thua Tiem and Quang Nam Provinces; it connected the ports of Da Nang and Chu Lai with the cities of Hue, Dong Ha, and Quang Tri as well as the extensive American and South Vietnamese military installations along the demilitarized zone (DMZ). Highway 1, Vietnam's only significant north-south roadway, ran through the pass. Since it provided the only ground supply line to the extreme north of South Vietnam, the Hai Van Pass became a major target of attacks by North Vietnamese and Viet Cong forces. For their part, American and South Vietnamese forces made keeping the pass open a major priority. **See also** demilitarized zone; Highway 1; military regions.

## Hamburger Hill, Battle of

Also known as the Battle of Ap Bia Mountain, the Battle of Hamburger Hill from May 11 to May 20, 1969, was one of the most violent engagements of the Vietnam War as well as one of its few examples of a conventional, set-piece battle. The relatively high number of casualties, among both American forces and their North Vietnamese enemies, and the repeated, intense firefights that characterized the battle inspired observers to dub the site Hamburger Hill because of the "meat-grinder" nature of the fighting. It was also one of the last important battles in which regular American ground troops took part.

The Battle of Hamburger Hill was part of Operation Apache Snow, a large effort by combined American and South Vietnamese forces to prevent North Vietnamese Army (NVA) troops from expanding from their strongholds in the A Shau Valley. The A Shau Valley, in the northernmost part of South Vietnam along the Laotian border, had grown to be a major area of conflict, not only because of its proximity to the demilitarized zone (DMZ) but because it was well connected to the Laotian portion of the Ho Chi Minh Trail. By bottling up NVA forces in the valley, Operation Apache Snow could prevent them from driving eastward to the coast and cutting South Vietnam in two.

On May 11, a task force of combined U.S. and South Vietnamese troops encountered a large NVA contingent entrenched in various points on Ap Bia Mountain. Over the next several days they tried to take the mountain in the face of staunch resistance. Finally, in the tenth major assault, a force consisting of, among others, two battalions of the 101st Army Airborne, was able to reach the summit of the hill. As was their common practice, the NVA troops simply retreated into their sanctuaries across the border, and Ap Bia Mountain was secured.

It proved to be a temporary victory with unexpected results, however. U.S. and South Vietnamese forces did not stay on the mountain, since the purpose of Operation Apache Snow was not to seize territory but to reduce the NVA's ability to mount a sustained offensive. After the ground was abandoned, the NVA soon returned. The battle, moreover, was the subject of a report in *Life* magazine, which described vividly, with photographs, the course of events that had resulted in 241 American deaths for, to many minds, no gain whatsoever. The bad publicity resulted in a new understanding among American military commanders that ground battles were to be avoided and that they were to focus on "Vietnamization," turning the fighting over to the South Vietnamese. **See also** Apache Snow; A Shau Valley.

## Hanoi

The capital of the Democratic Republic of Vietnam, or North Vietnam, from 1945 to 1976, and the capital of the Socialist Republic of Vietnam thereafter. Hanoi lay in the Red River Delta, the traditional agricultural heartland of the Vietnamese people and the home of numerous earlier Vietnamese kingdoms. During the era of French colonialism, Hanoi was the center for the French administration of the "protectorate" of Tonkin China, or northern Vietnam. During the Vietnam War, Hanoi was not seriously targeted by U.S. bombers until 1972 for fear that large numbers of civilians would be killed and that such actions might bring China or the Soviet Union into the conflict. Hanoi thus remained relatively unscathed and a much "older" city than its brash southern counterpart, Saigon. **See also** Saigon.

## Hanoi Hannah (1929– )

The name American forces used to refer to Ngo Thi Trinh, a North Vietnamese radio host who broadcast a program in English over the Voice of Vietnam, a propaganda and communications tool of the Hanoi government. The purpose of her program was to demoralize American soldiers and sow dissension in the ranks. Her program typically listed American casualties, praised the efforts of the global and American antiwar movements, and called on Americans to reconsider what they were fighting for. It also emphasized the racial problems in the United States in order to stir discontent among African American or Latino soldiers. Trinh also broadcast American statements she thought might be useful, such as antiwar speeches or the forced statements of prisoners of war. To attract listeners, she filled her program with American pop music. Most American soldiers tuned in to the program for amusement and because they liked the rock and roll songs, and few took her statements seriously. American prisoners of war in North Vietnam could also listen to the program, which was canceled after the departure of most American troops following the Paris Peace Accords of 1973. Ngo Thi Trinh went on to work for Vietnamese state television.

## Hanoi Hilton

The name used by Americans to refer to Hoa Lo Prison in Hanoi, one of the most notorious sites in North Vietnam, which held prisoners of war (POWs). Standing in central Hanoi, Hoa Lo was originally built by the French in the late 1800s as an

*American prisoners look out from their cells in the North Vietnamese prison known as the Hanoi Hilton.*

incarceration center. It was thought to have housed some 360 American POWs between 1964 and 1970 and several hundred more thereafter. Robert Schumaker, the second American imprisoned there, was the first to call it the Hanoi Hilton. American POWs went on to give all of the cell blocks American-style names, including Heartbreak Hotel and, for recent arrivals, New Guy Village.

Although the POWs in the Hanoi Hilton suffered regular torture and interrogation as well as poor food, vermin infestation, and a lack of medical care, they maintained a semblance of regular life as much as possible in order to prop up morale and pass the time. Sometimes they held church services or gave one another lessons. They even tried to entertain each other by remembering movie dialogue and comedy routines. This cohesion and mutual support was strengthened by the fact that from 1967 to 1973 many of the POWs were pilots and therefore shared similar backgrounds, educational levels, and rank. The prison population at the Hanoi Hilton increased after an American raid at another facility, Son Tay prison camp, failed to free the POWs there. Prison officials responded by concentrating American POWs in sites in central Hanoi, including the Hanoi Hilton, both for security purposes and to discourage American bombing raids. Despite the overcrowding, however, conditions in the Hanoi Hilton improved markedly beginning in 1970 thanks to an American letter-writing campaign.

The Hanoi Hilton stopped functioning as a POW center when, allegedly, all U.S. POWs were freed after the signing of the Paris Peace Accords in January 1973. Among those who were finally freed was U.S. Navy captain Jeremiah A. Denton, who had spent seven years in the Hanoi Hilton. **See also** McCain, John, III; missing in action; prisoners of war; Stockdale, James.

## harassment and interdiction (H&I)

A form of fire meant to distract enemy forces, prevent them from achieving their goals, and lower their morale. H&I fire was part of standard tactical procedure in Vietnam, used to protect fire support bases, patrols, and other jungle operations. The tactic accounted for as much as 70 percent of all artillery ammunition fired in the war. It was thought to have been effective in minimizing U.S. casualties while increasing those of the North Vietnamese Army or Viet Cong and in achieving favorable kill ratios. **See also** artillery; kill ratio; mortars.

## Harkins, Paul D. (1904–1984)

U.S. Army general and the first commander of the Military Assistance Command, Vietnam (MACV), when President John F. Kennedy reorganized the earlier Military Assistance Advisory Group (MAAG) into the MACV. Harkins arrived in Saigon on February 8, 1962, ready to take over an expanding American role in the affairs of South Vietnam. In office Harkins proved to be a strong supporter of South Vietnamese president Ngo Dinh Diem and of an intensified military campaign. The latter of these included the use of napalm against villages suspected of Viet Cong (VC) infiltration. In addition, Harkins believed that military and pacification efforts could not work hand in hand; in other words, he thought that, with U.S. help, Diem's armies had to first establish firm control of the countryside before beginning economic or political reforms. This was Diem's instinct as well.

Harkins continued believing in Diem even when the South Vietnamese leader's regime fell apart over the summer and fall of 1963. Indeed, the generals who plotted to overthrow Diem hestitated to do so for fear that Harkins might withdraw American support in response. Harkins also came into conflict with U.S. ambassador to South Vietnam Henry Cabot Lodge, who favored dislodging Diem. Harkins proposed that, instead of Diem, the president's brother Ngo Dinh Nhu and his wife, Madame Nhu, be forced into exile. The proposal proved unworkable, and both Diem and Nhu were assassinated on November 2, 1963.

The downfall of the brothers constituted the eclipse of Harkins's authority in Vietnam. He did not get along well with most members of the junta that replaced Diem, opposing its efforts to restrict MACV influence. Harkins was replaced by William Westmoreland on the approval of President Lyndon B. Johnson in June 1964, at which point Harkins retired from the army. **See also** Ap Bac, Battle of; Military Assistance Command, Vietnam; Ngo Dinh Diem.

# Hatfield-McGovern Amendment

A major attempt in the U.S. Senate to bring a quick end to American involvement in the Vietnam War by restricting the president's war-making abilities. It was sponsored by Senators George McGovern and Mark Hatfield and introduced into the Senate in the summer of 1970. The two men were among many lawmakers who were upset at the secrecy of President Richard M. Nixon and outraged by U.S. participation in the Cambodian invasion. As part of the reaction to this, the Senate repealed the 1964 Gulf of Tonkin Resolution.

Known by journalists as the "amendment to end the war," the proposed amendment was tied to a military appropriations bill. It required Nixon to end all U.S. military operations in Vietnam by the end of 1970 and remove all U.S. forces by the middle of 1971. This timetable was too radical for many senators, and the amendment was also the target of vocal criticism by the Nixon administration. It went down to defeat, even after the troop withdrawal deadline was extended. Nixon was able to convince enough senators that the Hatfield-McGovern Amendment would limit his ability to conduct peace negotiations with the North Vietnamese. **See also** Case-Church Amendment; Cooper-Church Amendment; War Powers Resolution.

# hawks and doves

Labels in common usage in American debate over the Vietnam War, denoting the level of one's support for the conflict. Hawks were those who favored escalation of military involvement as the best way to resolve the Vietnam conflict, while doves preferred to seek peace, primarily through diplomatic negotiation. The terms were most frequently applied to government officials.

# Hayden, Tom (1940– )

Leading anti–Vietnam War activist. While a student at the University of Michigan in the early 1960s, Hayden became involved in the Student Nonviolent Coordinating Committee (SNCC), an organization dedicated to civil rights. He was also one of the founders of a second group, the Students for a Democratic Society (SDS). In 1962 the SDS issued the Port Huron Statement, one of the major documents inspiring various social and protest movements in the 1960s. The Port Huron Statement called for Americans to take a greater individual involvement in policy making. It also criticized what it saw as the intolerance, secrecy, and hypocrisy of the U.S. government.

Hayden's activities led logically to an interest in the escalating Vietnam War, a conflict he vocally opposed. Twice he traveled to North Vietnam during the American phase of the Vietnam War. The first time, in December 1965, he was part of an informal delegation of American antiwar spokesmen. The second time, in 1967, he helped gain the release of three American prisoners of war from Cambodia. In 1968 Hayden was one of the planners of protests to be staged at the Chicago Democratic National Convention, now in the capacity of one of the directors of the National Coordinating Committee to End the War in Vietnam. His involvement in the Chicago protests, which turned violent, as well as his visibility, led to his arrest as one of the so-called Chicago Eight (later the Chicago Seven). In March 1969 he and seven others were put on trial on the charge of crossing state lines with intent to riot and conspiracy to begin riots. He was convicted, along with six other protest leaders, in February 1970, although his conviction was overturned on appeal.

In January 1973 Hayden married Jane Fonda, an actress heavily involved in antiwar activities who had herself visited

Hanoi. Even though the Paris Peace Accords ostensibly ended American involvement in Vietnam that month, Hayden and Fonda continued to speak out against potential hidden support for the South Vietnamese regime as well as any overt aid. **See also** antiwar movement; Chicago Seven; Fonda, Jane.

## helicopters

The aircraft most closely identified with the American effort in Vietnam, where helicopters were fully realized as combat machines for the first time. U.S. forces extensively used a wide variety of helicopters to perform missions ranging from troop and equipment transport to close air support to medical evacuation to search and rescue. Records show that all four U.S. service branches used thousands of helicopters in more than 36 million sorties in Vietnam. More than forty-five hundred helicopters were lost either to enemy fire or to crashes or accidents, and more than one thousand helicopter pilots died in Vietnam. **See also** Chinook; Cobra; Huey; search and rescue.

## Helms, Richard (1913–2002)

Director of the Central Intelligence Agency (CIA) from 1966 to 1973. The CIA had been at the center of America's presence in South Vietnam for twelve years before Helms was appointed head of the CIA; thus, Helms was a central figure in the evolution of U.S. policy in Vietnam. He often differed with his counterparts in the State and Defense Departments as well as with military officers since he suspected that the United States might not win the war and because his intelligence estimates clashed with those of the military. In 1967 he found himself forced to reduce his estimates of the total strength of North Vietnamese and Viet Cong (VC) troops from 600,000 to 334,000 to come closer to the military's more positive estimates, a fateful capitulation on his part.

During his years in office, Helms presided over a huge range of operations, including covert activity in Vietnam, participation in the Phoenix Program directed at the VC infrastructure, and the conduct of the "secret war" in Laos. In contradiction to the CIA's charter, which

*Helicopters, like this U.S. Army Sky Crane, were used to their full military capacity for the first time during the Vietnam War.*

mandated only offshore intelligence activities, Helms's CIA also launched operations against members of the antiwar movement in the United States. In 1971 the CIA was forced to account for a number of these operations before the U.S. Congress. Testifying on behalf of the CIA was William Colby, former CIA station chief in Saigon. Although President Lyndon B. Johnson valued Helms, Richard M. Nixon took steps to distance himself from the CIA in the early 1970s, and in 1973 Helms was replaced as director by Colby. **See also** Central Intelligence Agency; Colby, William.

## Highway 1

The only continuous north-south roadway in Vietnam, Highway 1 stretched from the Chinese border to the Mekong Delta. Initially built by the French during the colonial era, the highway was improved and widened by the Americans south of the demilitarized zone (DMZ) in the early 1960s. Control of Highway 1 near the DMZ was key to both defending and attacking the south, and it was the site of heavy fighting, often in the area of the Hai Van Pass. Refugees made up much of the traffic along Highway 1, especially in 1974 and 1975 when the North Vietnamese began their final offensive against South Vietnam. **See also** Hai Van Pass; Highway 9.

## Highway 9

A roadway stretching east-west from the city of Dong Ha, in the coastal plain of the northernmost part of South Vietnam, to the Laotian border. Thanks to American aid, it was paved until it reached the foothills of the Annamite chain of mountains. After that it was a dirt road often rendered impassable because of mud, landslides, or destruction caused by combat activity. Since Highway 9 was the logical route by which North Vietnamese or Communist troops might strike across

the Laotian border, and since it lay only twenty kilometers south of the demilitarized zone (DMZ), the roadway was heavily defended by American and South Vietnamese forces, who constructed a network of base camps roughly parallel to or along the highway. The largest of these was the U.S. Marine base at Khe Sanh. For much of the Vietnam War, stretches of the highway lay under the control of Communist troops. In Dong Ha, Highway 9 intersected Highway 1, thereby making the town one of the key strategic sites of the war. **See also** demilitarized zone; Dong Ha, Battle of; Highway 1.

## Hilsman-Forrestal Report

An important document in forming official American understanding of the conflict in Vietnam. It was written by Roger Hilsman, director of the Bureau of Intelligence and Research in the U.S. State Department, and Michael Forrestal, an aide to President John F. Kennedy, after the two made a fact-finding mission to South Vietnam in December 1962. Kennedy dispatched them to Saigon hoping to get a clearer view of the situation, since he was hesitant to fully trust information from American reporters, who tended to be pessimistic, or American military officials, who appeared overly optimistic.

The Hilsman-Forrestal Report concluded that the South Vietnamese regime of Ngo Dinh Diem was unlikely to survive, much less contain the Communist insurgency then being mounted by both the Viet Cong (VC) and the North Vietnamese Army (NVA). The report blamed the corruption of the Diem regime itself, which contributed to a lack of support among both ordinary people and the South Vietnamese army. Consistent with Hilsman's earlier view that the Vietnam conflict was political as well as military, the report also criticized the mismanaged strategic hamlet program, noting that it was failing to achieve any of Saigon's goals of rural pacification. In a prescient way, the Hilsman-Forrestal Report also indicated that U.S. involvement in Vietnam might be longer and more expensive than originally thought, although it expressed confidence that the war could be won. **See also** Kennedy, John F.; Ngo Dinh Diem; Taylor-Rostow Report.

## Hmong

The Hmong were one of the major tribal groups of Laos, numbering several hundred thousand during the 1960s. Like most of the other tribal groups in Indochina, the Hmong had little conception of the meaning of national borders. Most of those living in Laos had migrated from China in the nineteenth century, where other groups of Hmong, also known as Meo, remained. Branches of the larger tribe could also be found in Thailand and Vietnam. In Laos the Hmong lived mainly around the so-called Plain of Jars in the north-central region of the country, where they practiced a seminomadic lifestyle based on hunting and slash-and-burn agriculture. Their large numbers and lifestyle, as well as fundamental ethnic differences, brought the Hmong into conflict with the lowland Lao who controlled the country politically.

Outsiders in Laos learned to take advantage of this enmity. The Hmong generally supported French colonial rule, even during the First Indochina War (1946–1954), when Viet Minh soldiers from Vietnam frequently crossed the border. Beginning in 1961, Hmong fighters were deeply involved in a fight to prevent a Communist takeover of Laos during the so-called secret war in that country. They struggled against the Pathet Lao, the local Communist insurgency group, as well as the North Vietnamese. The Hmong were actively recruited by the U.S. Central Intelligence Agency (CIA), which largely handled the American end of the secret war since American military involvement was prohibited. Much of the fighting took place around the Plain of Jars, which remained for years a site of massive bomb craters and unexploded ordnance.

In becoming more effective fighters, the Hmong were wrenched out of a preurban, traditional lifestyle. They were given modern weapons and training and often supplied with food and medicine by the CIA and its auxiliaries, such as Air America. When Laos fell to the Pathet Lao after a series of halting cease-fires beginning in 1972 that removed the CIA and its support networks from the country, the Hmong were left to their own devices. While some, using weapons they had acquired during the secret war, continued to try to protect their mountain villages from the lowland Lao, others escaped into Thailand. Some were able to immigrate to the United States, France, or Australia. The new Communist regime in Laos, unsurprisingly, considered the Hmong for years to be "enemies of the people." **See also** Central Intelligence Agency; Laos, secret war in.

## Hoa Hao

A major religious and social movement in Vietnam that played an important part in both the resistance to French colonialism and the attempt to prevent a Communist takeover of the south in the years before 1954. Hoa Hao was founded in 1939 by Huynh Phu So, who named the movement after his home village in the Mekong Delta. On its surface the movement was based on a sort of reformation of Buddhism, Vietnam's major religion. So wanted Buddhist thought to be translated into the kind of action that would improve life on Earth rather than focus on achieving individual nirvana, the goal of most forms of orthodox Buddhism. He wanted his followers to renounce their preoccupations with wealth and tradition and give up such vices as opium, alcohol, and gambling. He thought that Western influence, in fact, was partly responsible for the demoralization of the people. Along more practical lines, the Hoa Hao also argued for the end of the traditional privileges of the elite, especially landowners. The formula proved a popular one: By the end of 1941 Hoa Hao had some 2 million followers.

So, for his part, was a thorn in the side of both the French and the would-be emperor Bao Dai because of his anticolonial and anti-imperial ideas. In 1940 the French arrested him, but rather than put him in prison they placed him under house arrest in the town of Bac Lieu northwest of Saigon. The town became the Hoa Hao base, as So received unlimited visitors and took advantage of the opportunity to lobby against French control. The countryside around Bac Lieu largely fell under the control of the Hoa Hao, and in that region the movement effectively replaced French imperial control by restaffing bureaucratic offices, infiltrating army units, and even giving supplies, during World War II, to Japanese occupiers. After the war was over So founded a political party, the Social Democrats, which was to play a role in South Vietnamese political debate until 1954. Although he despised Marxism and Hoa Hao forces fought widely against Viet Minh infiltrators in the south, So favored a complete redistribution of land along the lines of common ownership. His party also tried to provide social welfare to villagers. In time the Hoa Hao built a vast network of support across southern Vietnam, including both bureaucrats and military units. The movement's leadership splintered after So's death, but it remained one of the largest political and social organizations in the nation.

After the formation of the Republic of Vietnam in the south in 1954, both Bao Dai and the new president Ngo Dinh

Diem tried to break the power of the Hoa Hao. Indeed, Diem saw the movement (along with the Cao Dai, another sect, and the criminal Binh Xuyen) as the greatest challenge to his authority. By the end of 1954, thanks to both military action against the Hoa Hao base and political dealings with various Hoa Hao officials, Diem managed to break the organization. Later, Hoa Hao leaders and fighters emerged as members of the Civilian Irregular Defense Groups and as anti–Viet Cong soldiers in the Mekong Delta. **See also** Binh Xuyen; Cao Dai; Ngo Dinh Diem.

## Ho Chi Minh (1890–1969)

The guiding force behind the North Vietnamese Communist regime known as the Democratic Republic of Vietnam (DRV) and the man considered by his countrymen to be the founding father of modern, unified Vietnam.

Ho Chi Minh was born under the name Nguyen That Thanh in 1890 in the central Vietnamese province of Nghe An. His forebears were minor noblemen during the Nguyen regime, now impoverished by the decline in power of the royal family. In 1911 the young man, taking Van Ba as the first of a number of aliases, took a job in the French merchant fleet as a cook's assistant. Among his ports of call were cities in the United States, where Ho grew acquainted with the ideals of the U.S. Declaration of Independence and Constitution and became interested in political reform.

During World War I (1914–1918) Ho lived in Paris under the name Nguyen Ai Quoc (Nguyen the Patriot). There he met Vietnamese nationalists working toward independence from France. He also grew interested in communism, particularly the Marxist-Leninist version that emphasized anticolonialism. Ho grew to believe that national independence and the liberation of the masses from class oppression were goals that could be achieved in concert. With others, he attended the Paris Peace Conference in 1919 and 1920, which reconstructed the world after World War I, hoping to advance the cause of Vietnamese independence.

Finding that the Western powers at the conference were opposed to colonial independence, Ho then turned to the Communist Soviet Union for education and support, attending the Congresses of the Communist International (Comintern) in 1924 and 1925, where he was exposed to revolutionary theory and technique. The Soviet-dominated Comintern sent him to Guangzhou, China, in 1924, a base from which he could work to organize the Vietnamese Communist movement. He stayed in China until 1926 writing his first manifesto, a document called "Revolutionary Path." During the same years he also founded the first version of the Vietnamese Communist Party: the Vietnam Revolutionary Youth League. Forced to leave by the nationalist Chinese government, Ho then settled briefly in Hong Kong, at that time a British colony. There he helped found the Indochina Communist Party, which he was to lead in its various forms until his death in 1969. Among his tasks at this early stage were propaganda and education, recruiting new members skilled in organization, and bringing together the disparate elements of the Vietnamese Communist movement.

In 1941 the former Nguyen That Thanh took the name Ho Chi Minh, which means "Ho the Enlightened One." In May of that year, he returned to Vietnam to reassert his place within the Indochina Communist Party and began the League for Vietnamese Independence, or Viet Minh, an organization devoted to direct political action as well as theoretical debate. After the Japanese occupied Indochina, Ho left again for China, where in the new circumstances of World War II

he hoped to acquire the support of the nationalist Chinese in his anti-Japanese efforts. The Chinese, fearful of their own Communists under Mao Tse-tung, imprisoned him instead. He was released, however, in 1943. By then the tide of war was turning and the Chinese, as well as their British and American allies, understood Ho's potential as an anti-Japanese resistance leader. Fully aware of the opportunity to work for Vietnamese independence, Ho reconstituted the Viet Minh as a nationalist force fighting for Vietnam against both the Japanese and their French collaborators.

In the later months of World War II, the spring and summer of 1945, Ho was believed to have worked closely with the American Office of Strategic Services (OSS), the predecessor of the Central Intelligence Agency (CIA), in maintaining contacts between Allied authorities and Viet Minh underground operatives. Ho was apparently involved in jobs ranging from coordinating logistics to helping rescue American pilots downed in northern Vietnam. Although records are unclear, Ho may have been recruited by the OSS as an official counterintelligence agent. When Allied forces entered Hanoi on August 19, four days after the Japanese surrender, Ho went with them, the OSS apparently realizing that the Viet Minh was their best hope for an immediate, post-Japanese leadership. Again, Ho seized his opportunity, staging the so-called August Revolution. On September 2, 1945, Ho proclaimed the independence of Vietnam from both Japan and France and announced the formation of the DRV. His statements included phrases taken verbatim from the American Declaration of Independence, and OSS agents were in attendance during the proclamation. Always mindful of practical necessities, Ho took steps over the next months to ensure that the Viet Minh was seen as a legitimate government, including sending comrades to assert Viet Minh authority in the southern city of Saigon.

The French, however, wanted their colony back. They returned early in 1946 to reassert control over Vietnam and the rest of Indochina. After Ho was unable to reach a compromise with the French in the so-called Ho-Sainteny Agreement, which would have made Vietnam an autonomous state within the French Union, talks broke down. By the end of 1946 the First Indochina War, an eight-year struggle between the Viet Minh and the French, was under way. It marked the beginning of nearly thirty years of warfare before Ho's vision of an independent, unified Vietnam was realized.

During the war Ho once again found himself forced into the arms of his Communist compatriots elsewhere. The only nations that recognized the DRV as a legitimate state, and Ho himself as a national leader, were most of the Soviet-bloc nations of Eastern Europe and, after 1949, Mao Tse-tung's People's Republic of China. This fact made it easy for the French to claim that they were fighting the spread of communism, a goal shared by the United States, Great Britain, and the other Western powers. Ho Chi Minh was therefore placed alongside Mao, Joseph Stalin, Tito, and other Communist leaders as a potential threat to democracy and freedom, and the Indochina conflict became a cold war battle. Meanwhile, Ho continued to be an effective organizer and propagandist as well as a leader of men. To the surprise of much of the world, the Viet Minh was able to hold off the French for years, despite the influx of American money and war matériel to aid the French. Finally, Ho's military leader, Vo Nguyen Giap, ended the war by engineering a decisive victory over the French at Dien Bien Phu. The two sides entered into a truce, the Geneva Accords, on July 20, 1954. Four years earlier, in 1950, Ho had reasserted the position that the De

mocratic Republic of Vietnam, with he himself as president, was the legitimate government of the nation. The Geneva Accords confirmed that. The Geneva Accords represented a major step for Ho Chi Minh by removing the French from Indochina and establishing not only independent nations in northern and southern Vietnam but also independent regimes in Cambodia and Laos.

After 1954 Ho consolidated his authority in North Vietnam as the leader of the Lao Dong, as the Indochina Communist Party was renamed in 1951. He also set about to reform society along lines laid out by himself and other Communist theoreticians. He instituted land reform by dissolving the estates of large landlords and attempted to nationalize both agriculture and manufacturing. Oppressive measures followed against those who resisted, and thousands of North Vietnamese were imprisoned or sent to reeducation camps.

By 1959, Ho was ready to take action to reunite North and South Vietnam. He had already helped form groups of Communist cadres in the south, and that year he authorized them to join in a "political struggle" to depose the South Vietnamese regime of Ngo Dinh Diem. With the help of former Viet Minh fighters living in the south as well as unorganized individuals opposed to Diem, these cadres constituted the first versions of the Viet Cong (VC). By 1960 Viet Cong fighters had their political struggle well under way by recruiting villagers and assassinating local authorities loyal to Diem. In December 1960 the National Front for the Liberation of South Vietnam (National Liberation Front, or NLF) was formed to provide political leadership to the VC as well as coordination between the southern cadres and the Hanoi government, although the precise relationships and responsibilities of the various parties remained unclear. Meanwhile, Ho extended his efforts in 1959 and 1960 to include the expansion of the Ho Chi Minh Trail to provide communications and supplies to the south as well as support for the Pathet Lao, the Communists in Laos. The Second Indochina War, the one in which the United States was to become deeply involved, was under way.

From Ho's perspective, the Second Indochina War proceeded slowly, which was very much to his taste. Its first major victim was the Diem regime in Saigon, toppled by Diem's own corruption and incompetence as well as by expanding support in the south for the NLF. Soon after, however, the United States made its commitment to prop up the Republic of Vietnam (RVN, or South Vietnam) by bringing in American combat troops and engaging in "nation building." This provided Ho with the most difficult challenge he had yet faced, although he remained confident that his ultimate goal of reunification was in reach. He had learned from his experiences with the French that Westerners had little stomach for a long, protracted fight in difficult terrain and among peoples who were culturally very foreign. He was also prepared to accept huge numbers of casualties on his own side. Although American president Lyndon Johnson made it known as early as 1965 that he was prepared to enter into peace negotiations with Ho, the Communist leader laid down very stringent conditions, including the recognition of the NLF as the political and military leadership of South Vietnam. This condition made no sense to the Americans, who assumed, rightly or not, that the NLF was under the command of Ho's regime and that acquiescing to NLF leadership in the south would mean allowing Vietnam to be reunified under Communist control.

As the American military effort bogged down after 1965 along with its diplomatic feelers, Ho's prestige grew both

*As president of the Democratic Republic of Vietnam, Ho Chi Minh was a hero to his people.*

within Vietnam and across the globe. Indeed, he reached his greatest fame in the three or four years before his death in 1969, when he was considered by many to be a major world leader despite the fact that he came from a nation few could locate on a map before 1965. Among many people, in fact, "Uncle Ho" became a sort of counterculture hero along with such revolutionaries as Che Guevara in Bolivia, Fidel Castro in Cuba, and Mao Tse-tung in China. At home, moreover, Ho had become a true national hero. Although he was weakening with age, Ho tried to use his prestige to maintain the war effort and, during the preparations for the 1968 Tet Offensive, made his first public appearances in months. He also remained influential enough to quell, at least temporarily, the squabbles among other DRV leaders. In foreign policy he proved deft as well, steering a middle course between the two Communist superpowers, the Soviet Union and China, who by the late 1960s were enemies of each other rather than allies. When peace talks among the DRV, the RVN, and the United States finally began in May 1968, Ho worked with the negotiators to fine-tune DRV demands while pledging to continue the struggle on the battlefield.

Ho Chi Minh died on September 2, 1969, and therefore did not survive to see Vietnam reunified. He remained important as a symbol, however, and the Lao Dong leadership as well as his old comrade, Vo Nguyen Giap, added to the reasons for their ongoing struggle the need to honor the memory and accomplishments of Uncle Ho. After North Vietnamese tanks rolled into Saigon in April 1975, Ho's vision of a reunified Vietnam was achieved, and to help consolidate the new, larger Democratic Republic of Vietnam, Lao Dong leaders continued to use the name and prestige of Ho Chi Minh. Saigon, for instance, was now known as Ho Chi Minh City. In Hanoi the leader was deified in memorials, including a house where he briefly lived, a huge museum commemorating both his life and his role in the history of international communism, and, most popular, a vast mausoleum where his embalmed body remained open to view during most of the year. Tens of thousands of people visited the mausoleum every year. **See also** Viet Minh; Vietnam, Democratic Republic of.

## Ho Chi Minh campaign

The North Vietnamese name for their final offensive. Hanoi strategists decided to launch the Ho Chi Minh campaign, which had long been in the planning, in early April 1975. Surprised by the collapse of South Vietnamese forces in an earlier attack, planners were able to speed up their timetable, which had originally placed the attack on Saigon in early 1976.

They now intended to capture Saigon before the onset of the rainy season, which usually began in May or June, and before the May 19 birthday of Ho Chi Minh himself. Their main concern, and the main hope of the South Vietnamese government, was that the United States might launch a last-ditch military effort to save Saigon.

The campaign began in early April with the shelling of important sites in the Saigon region such as the Bien Hoa air base and with battles in towns such as Xuan Loc. By April 21 North Vietnamese forces had cut off most of the roadways into Saigon, including Highway 1 from the north, Highway 4 from the Mekong Delta, and Route 15 from the seacoast, and still they continued to shell the city itself. Meanwhile, explosives experts and political cadres infiltrated the city to take control of the streets. The encirclement of Saigon inspired the resignation of South Vietnamese president Nguyen Van Thieu, who turned over his office to Vice President Tran Van Huong on April 21. Thieu had hoped for American aid, but the U.S. Congress refused to consider it. The North Vietnamese, meanwhile, were fairly certain that the United States would not intervene after April 12, when the U.S. embassy in Phnom Penh, Cambodia, was abandoned in the face of a Khmer Rouge assault. Now, refugees were streaming into Saigon from the countryside, and a mass exodus of foreign nationals out of the country was also taking place. Many top South Vietnamese politicians and military officers also made plans to get their families and, in some cases, their treasure out of the country before Saigon fell. Still, and despite the abandonment of many top leaders, units of the South Vietnamese army fought on heroically, defending Xuan Loc until April 21 and even, for a time, reopening some of the roadways.

On April 28 Tran Van Huong resigned as president in favor of Duong Van Minh, an old political hand thought by many South Vietnamese to be their best hope for a negotiated settlement with Hanoi. That same day, Communist forces attacked Tan Son Nhut air base with captured aircraft and began placing their forces for a final assault. U.S. ambassador Graham Martin finally ordered the evacuation of all remaining U.S. personnel, and the U.S. embassy was abandoned, along with thousands of South Vietnamese employees of various American organizations, early in the morning of April 29.

General Van Tien Dung, the top North Vietnamese field commander, launched his final assault on Saigon on April 29. While some of his army held down remaining South Vietnamese units in sporadic combat, other troops sped toward the presidential palace in the center of the city. On April 30, after Minh ordered his army to stop fighting, Communist tanks, in a largely symbolic gesture, crashed down the gates of the palace. Saigon had fallen, and Vietnam was soon to be unified under the Hanoi regime. **See also** Duong Van Minh; Frequent Wind.

## Ho Chi Minh Trail

The extensive network of roads, trails, caves, supply depots, and tunnels that connected North Vietnam to South Vietnam after passing through the eastern portions of Laos and Cambodia. The continued expansion of the Ho Chi Minh Trail, which allowed the North Vietnamese Communists to move ever-larger numbers of troops and ever-greater amounts of supplies to the south, was one of the major reasons why the Communists were able to prevail in the Vietnam War. Although U.S. and South Vietnamese officials understood the importance of the route and mounted massive attacks, they could never stem the flow of troops and supplies.

Footpaths through the mountainous inland regions of Indochina had long connected regions in Vietnam, Laos, and Cambodia, and those footpaths existed long before the borders of those modern nations. On May 19, 1959, North Vietnamese Army (NVA) major Vo Ban was given an order to establish a supply route to the south using some of those ancient footpaths. North Vietnam had decided to foment an aggressive war of insurgency in South Vietnam, and Hanoi officials realized that supplies were essential, as were troops and intelligence information. Using a workforce of some thirty thousand civilians and five hundred regular NVA troops, Vo Ban set to work enlarging and connecting footpaths along the Annamite chain, a range of mountains in the border regions. His team, known as Unit 559, also built supply depots and command posts. By the end of 1959 their work had enabled the first supplies to be delivered to Viet Cong (VC) fighters in the south. In addition, nearly two thousand NVA regulars made their way down the Ho Chi Minh Trail to infiltrate South Vietnam, a flow of troops that was to remain steady for the next fifteen years.

Between 1960 and 1963, the original Ho Chi Minh Trail was much expanded. A second major route was established to the west of the original, through the Truong Son Mountains in Laos. Branches of the trail were also built to stretch into strategically important areas, such as the Ia Drang Valley and the A Shau Valley, to ensure the flow of supplies and men to the insurgents in those regions. By the end of 1963 the entire network consisted of more than six hundred miles of roads, almost all of them impossible to see from the air because of jungle cover. This expansion made possible much more efficient uses of the trail. At first a footpath, the trail was soon given over to bicycle traffic. Specially trained couriers using reinforced bicycles could carry hundreds of pounds of supplies, although it took them months to travel all the way south. By 1962, trucks and troop transports were able to use the trail, replacing the bicycles where possible, and NVA commanders had stationed a permanent contingent of five thousand troops and engineers to maintain this vital roadway.

The NVA continued to expand the Ho Chi Minh Trail for the rest of the war, in parallel to the continuing escalation of the conflict. Engineers and workers paved certain parts of the route, forded rivers, built extensive supply depots and tunnel networks, and maintained a system of communications as the Ho Chi Minh Trail became a major part of the North Vietnamese war effort. By 1970, for instance, seventy thousand NVA troops defended the trail while an estimated ten thousand tons of supplies, and eight thousand men, moved along it every month. In one week, trucks could travel the distance that used to take six months for marchers or bicycle couriers. For a time the trail was supplemented by the so-called Sihanouk Trail, which connected the Cambodian port of Sihanoukville (later Kompong Som) with the Ho Chi Minh Trail in eastern Cambodia, and by attempts to land supplies from the sea using South Vietnam's elaborate labyrinth of waterways. But the Sihanouk Trail closed when Cambodian president Norodom Sihanouk fell from power in 1970, and the seaborne supply lines were limited by U.S. and South Vietnamese naval interdiction efforts. This made the Ho Chi Minh Trail all the more important to North Vietnam.

U.S. officials, notably Secretary of Defense Robert McNamara, understood the importance of the Ho Chi Minh Trail as early as 1964, and closing the trail down became one of the major goals of U.S. military activity. The first U.S.-supported attacks, using small units of combined American and South Vietnamese person-

nel, including Montagnards, were made in 1964. These were ground attacks, which proved unsuccessful. Also in 1964 U.S. Air Force bombers tried to destroy parts of the trail from the air, despite the dense jungle cover. These attacks, likewise, enjoyed limited success. American forces were to continue to use both strategies, although ground interdiction of the trail was necessarily limited by the fact that it generally required troops to cross the borders of Cambodia or Laos. The major air attacks on the trail came in 1968, when U.S. officials switched from bombing North Vietnam to bombing the

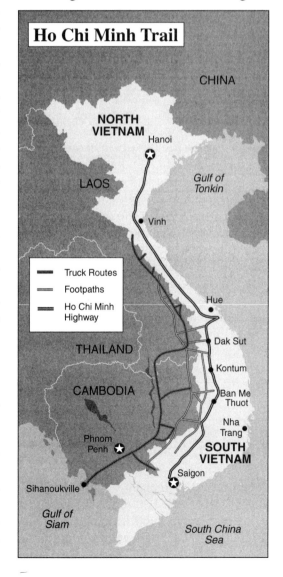

**Ho Chi Minh Trail**

CHINA

NORTH VIETNAM
Hanoi

LAOS

Gulf of Tonkin

Vinh

Truck Routes
Footpaths
Ho Chi Minh Highway

Hue

THAILAND

Dak Sut

Kontum

CAMBODIA

Ban Me Thuot

Nha Trang

Phnom Penh

SOUTH VIETNAM

Saigon

Sihanoukville

Gulf of Siam

South China Sea

trail itself; the largest single operation in this effort was known as Commando Hunt. The bombings were supplemented by attempts to cause landslides in order to create blockages, defoliation of jungle areas, and even attempts to seed clouds to lengthen the rainy season, which for parts of the year made the route impassable. One of the more unusual attempts to slow the flow of supplies along the trail was the dropping of electronic sensors at various points as part of a 1967 effort to construct a network of electronic defenses. The sensors, when stepped on or driven over, would send the location information back to computers at U.S. Air Force bases, thus alerting pilots to bombing sites.

These efforts had little overall effect, however, and the Ho Chi Minh Trail remained North Vietnam's greatest military asset. By 1973, the year the last American ground troops left Vietnam, the trail was in effect a highway connecting North Vietnam with various points in the south, and supply traffic had become routine. The extensive, well-maintained trail also allowed the NVA to move much faster than the South Vietnamese army; when Hanoi launched its final offensive against Saigon in 1975, hundreds of thousands of NVA soldiers found it fairly easy to move to their strategic destinations in the south. After the war was over, most of the Ho Chi Minh Trail fell into disuse, since it was far from important population centers. Plans emerged, however, to use portions of it to build an extensive highway system in the interior of Vietnam. **See also** Commando Hunt; Sihanouk Trail.

# Hoffman, Abbie (1936–1989)

Prominent anti–Vietnam War activist. After earning a master's degree in psychology from the University of California, Berkeley, in 1960, Hoffman became not only a vocal antiwar spokesman but also a representative of the emerging "counterculture" of mostly antiestablishment younger people who rejected American norms and who were known in general as hippies. Part of what made Hoffman visible was his choice of tactics. He staged events designed to be both outrageous and dramatic, often under the umbrella of the Youth International Party, or Yippies, which he cofounded in 1967 with Jerry Rubin. The Yippies marched to the Pentagon in Washington, D.C., where they staged an odd ceremony to exorcise the facility of its war-making demons. As preparation for the Democratic National Convention in 1968, the Yippies nominated a pig for president. Meanwhile, Hoffman himself published a book titled *Revolution for the Hell of It.* The Democratic Convention itself, held in Chicago, provided Hoffman with his greatest notoriety. Along with his fellow Yippies, Hoffman made plans to upstage the convention, which they labeled a "festival of death," with their own "festival of life," featuring rock concerts and other events as well as antiwar demonstrations. After the demonstrations outside the convention turned violent, Hoffman was arrested as one of the Chicago Seven, a group of protest leaders who were later indicted on charges of crossing state lines to incite a riot as well as conspiracy to begin riots. During his trial, Hoffman continued his absurdist protest tactics, refusing to take the proceedings seriously and staging what was known as "guerrilla theater" as a kind of insidious protest against an "establishment" he did not believe in. His antics resulted in a number of contempt-of-court charges. Along with some of the others Hoffman was found guilty, although the charges were later overturned on appeal.

After the trial, and as American involvement in Vietnam dwindled, Hoffman's fame faded. He was dismissed from the Yippies partly on the grounds that, as a man pushing forty, he was too old. He continued, however, to speak out as a radical, sometimes in staged debates with a reformed, conservative, and prosperous Jerry Rubin, until his suicide in 1989. **See also** antiwar movement; Chicago Seven; Rubin, Jerry; Youth International Party.

## Homecoming

The name given to the return to the United States of hundreds of prisoners of war (POWs) by the North Vietnamese regime and its allies. Operation Homecoming took place from February 12 to March 29, 1973, after the Paris Peace Accords, taking effect on January 27, provided for the release of all POWs within sixty days. Altogether, 591 POWs were released. Most had been prisoners of the North Vietnamese, although substantial numbers had been held by the Viet Cong. Three, who were initially sent to Hong Kong following their release, had been prisoners in China. After brief receptions in Hanoi or Saigon, all freed POWs were flown to Clark Air Force Base in the Philippines, where they were debriefed and given medical examinations. Soon after, most returned home. Most of the prisoners had been officers, and many had been pilots. There were also twenty-five enlisted men among the POWs.

Operation Homecoming was the only official "welcome home" tribute offered by the American government, commemorating the end of years of conflict in Vietnam. Unlike most other returning Vietnam veterans, who received at most subdued welcomes and too often scorn, the released POWs, some of whom had been imprisoned for as long as eight years, were hailed as heroes. Questions remained, however, whether the Vietnamese Communists had actually released all of their American prisoners, an issue that remains unresolved. **See also** Hanoi Hilton; missing in action; prisoners of war; Stockdale, James.

*Former prisoners of war celebrate their homecoming as they fly from Hanoi back to the United States.*

# Honolulu Conferences

Meetings held at the headquarters of the Pacific Command of the U.S. Navy in Honolulu, Hawaii, from 1962 to 1966. It was at these meetings that the overall American strategy for fighting the Vietnam War was determined. The conferences were attended by those in high-level government and military positions, including the secretary of defense, the chairman of the Joint Chiefs of Staff, the U.S. ambassador to South Vietnam, the chief of the U.S. Military Assistance Command, Vietnam (MACV), and the commander of the Pacific Command.

Up until 1964 the Honolulu Conferences were mainly occupied with implementing the counterinsurgency strategy preferred by President John F. Kennedy, the attendees agreeing to the steady increase in the numbers of military advisers and amounts of equipment that were sent to Vietnam. Beginning in 1964 the conferences were characterized by a new debate over how to best understand the conflict, a decision that would determine the American military approach. Some attendees argued that the Vietnam War was turning into a widespread war thanks to the infiltration into South Vietnam of regular North Vietnamese troops. In such a scenario, they claimed, attacks on North Vietnam were justified. Others, however, still believed in the notion that they were involved in a limited guerrilla war and that continued counterinsurgency measures would be most effective.

The most important, and last, of the Honolulu Conferences was held in February 1966. U.S. president Lyndon B. Johnson took advantage of the opportunity to propose a meeting with South Vietnamese leaders, a move he had been urged to make by his advisers. He also hoped, apparently, to forestall the growing criticism of his Vietnam policy in Congress. Therefore he arranged to join the regular attendees at Honolulu accompanied by his secretary of state, Dean Rusk. He also invited South Vietnamese premier Nguyen Cao Ky and Chief of State Nguyen Van Thieu.

The results of the conference, published in a joint communique on February 9, consisted of a decision that the preservation of an independent South Vietnam depended on social and political development as much as military action. U.S. officials stepped up their commitment to the pacification of South Vietnam by establishing an organization that became, in time, Civilian Operations and Revolutionary Development Support (CORDS). Ky and Thieu, for their part, made it plain that they wanted to create a democratic political system in which social injustice and economic inequality were minimized. They promised, in fact, to prepare a constitution and plan for elections.

The Honolulu Conference of 1966 did not neglect military matters. Ky and Thieu promised to eradicate the Viet Cong and provide incentives for soldiers who defected from the Communist side. Johnson, in fact, exhorted them to step up their military efforts. U.S. officials, meanwhile, provided MACV commander William Westmoreland with more troops to carry out his larger search-and-destroy methods of securing South Vietnamese territory. This final Honolulu meeting, therefore, laid out what was to be the combined U.S. and South Vietnamese strategy: a "limited" war, at least from the American standpoint, combined with an extensive pacification effort. **See also** Guam Conference; Midway Island Conference; Pacific Command.

# Ho-Sainteny Agreement

A pact signed on March 6, 1946, after a conference held at the Fontainbleau chateau outside Paris. The agreement might have prevented the First Indochina War if it had been allowed to stand. Signed by Ho Chi Minh as a representative of the Democratic Republic of Vietnam (DRV), Jean Sainteny of the French Fourth Republic, and Vo Hong Khanh for the Vietnam National Party (VNP), the agreement recognized, with important conditions, the existence of an independent nation in northern Vietnam under Ho Chi Minh. The DRV would have its own parliament, its own army, and its own financial system, although it would remain connected to France as a member of an organization to be called the Indochinese Federation of the French Union. Moreover, the agreement also provided for a plebiscite to be held in southern Vietnam to see if southerners wanted to be unified with the north. However, it set no date for the vote.

Ho Chi Minh was unhappy with the agreement, despite the fact that it would at least partially recognize the state that he had declared late in 1945. Ho may have felt pressured into signing it, since he could rely on little help from the outside world, even the Americans who generally opposed colonialism. In exchange for recognition Ho would have to accept, in addition to a still-divided Vietnam, a heavy French military presence in the north until 1951. Nonetheless, the Ho-Sainteny Agreement may have made it possible for Ho and the French to develop an effective working relationship.

The agreement was made irrelevant, however, by the actions of French admiral Georges Thierry d'Argenlieu, the French high commissioner for Indochina. Unwilling to consider working with "natives," in June 1946 d'Argenlieu outflanked both the Viet Minh and his home government by declaring an independent Republic of Cochin China, based in Saigon, which would govern the south. Under these circumstances, a future plebiscite would have no power since the DRV and Cochin China would be separate nations. D'Argenlieu's actions suggested to Ho that negotiations with the French offered little hope, and he returned to Vietnam prepared to take drastic action. **See also** August 1945 Revolution; Elysée Agreement; First Indochina War.

## hot pursuit policy

An early acknowledgment by American military commanders that events in Cambodia had a great significance in Vietnam. The hot pursuit policy was the name given by the Military Assistance Command, Vietnam (MACV), to its 1965 request to allow South Vietnamese and American forces to follow Communist troops who escaped from South Vietnam into Cambodia, where they were thought to have sanctuaries. MACV also called for a naval blockade of the Cambodian port of Sihanoukville (later Kompong Som) because supplies for the Communists were imported there before being transported overland.

The hot pursuit policy was not approved by either President Lyndon Johnson or the U.S. State Department. Neither wanted to violate Cambodia's neutrality or widen the war. The lack of official approval, however, did not prevent units from occasionally crossing the border, a line on maps that in truth meant little and was not well guarded. Meanwhile, debate over hot pursuit continued, and when President Richard Nixon approved the invasion of Cambodia in 1970, his goal was indeed to close down Communist sanctuaries and cut off supply lines. **See also** Cambodia, invasion of; sanctuaries; search and destroy.

## Hue, Battle of

The largest fixed battle of the 1968 Tet Offensive and one of the major conventional engagements of the Vietnam War, as opposed to guerrilla fights, jungle missions, or bombing raids.

The city of Hue, in central Vietnam, was one of the nation's major cultural centers. It contained the vast Citadel, modeled after China's Forbidden City, which housed the Nguyen kings in the nineteenth century, and was surrounded by other structures and relics ranging from temples to royal mausoleums. The city was also economically important, located near the mouth of the Perfume River, which stretched deep into lush countryside. Hue was also a potential battlefield because it was the nearest big city to the demilitarized zone (DMZ). In 1968, thanks in part to a vast influx of refugees, Hue was the third largest city in South Vietnam after Saigon and Da Nang. Most inhabitants lived in the old city, north of the Perfume River, where the Citadel stood. South of the river, there was a new, more modernized city. Until 1968 Hue was fairly peaceful; the Viet Cong (VC) left it alone and there

was a heavy South Vietnamese military presence there, including the headquarters of the First Division of the Army of the Republic of Vietnam (ARVN). The American military presence was somewhat less, although the city did contain an important Military Assistance Command, Vietnam (MACV), compound. Most Americans in Hue worked for civilian organizations.

On January 30, 1968, the local ARVN commander heard news of sporadic attacks by combined VC and North Vietnamese Army (NVA) forces on cities south of Hue. In response he put his troops, many of whom were stationed along Highway 1 north of the city, on alert. Meanwhile, Communist infiltrators made their way into the city for the attack on Hue, which was to commence on Jan-

*Refugees cross the Perfume River to flee the city of Hue, site of the largest battle of the Tet Offensive.*

uary 31. These infiltrators included elements of the VC as well as NVA sappers, following plans that had been laid out several months earlier.

The formal attack began early on the morning of January 31 when, partly hidden by a thick fog, two NVA regiments marched into the city. By noon the Communists had taken the new city and the southern part of the Citadel in the old city. They had also surrounded the MACV compound. They were unable to consolidate a victory, however, because ARVN troops still controlled the northern part of the Citadel and a group of some two hundred Americans, along with a few Australians, held out inside the MACV compound. Their actions were enough to delay the Communist conquests until ARVN and American reinforcements could arrive.

For several weeks the fighting continued indecisively, and the battle became a house-to-house and street-to-street struggle. U.S. Marine reinforcements entered the city at a haphazard pace and enjoyed numerous, if often temporary, victories. Although the marines were able to rescue the MACV compound and, at one point, cross the river to join up with ARVN forces still defending the northern half of the Citadel, they could not dislodge the Communists. U.S. commanders were slow to recognize the scale of the threat to Hue, also, and were reluctant to send in U.S. firepower for fear of damage to Hue's architectural treasures and because of the danger of killing U.S. or ARVN troops engaged in close combat. MACV commander William Westmoreland believed that the main Communist thrust would come at Khe Sanh, a comparatively meaningless mountain base some fifty miles to the northeast of Hue, and he kept his reserves located in that region rather than commit them to the city. Meanwhile, the Communists were able to keep their main supply line, running westward into the A Shau Valley, open. In addition, they took control of a huge ARVN weapons depot; emptied the prison of its inmates, many of whom chose to join the fight; and were reinforced by large numbers of fresh troops.

American and ARVN commanders finally decided, early in February, to commit the necessary resources to saving Hue by, first, cutting off Communist supply lines and, second, reinforcing the combat units already there. It took until February 21 before the American 101st Cavalry Division was able to close off the last supply route. Meanwhile, U.S. Marine reinforcements joined the fight for the Citadel, helping the ARVN clear it of Communist troops between February 11 and 25. Again, much of the fighting was extremely bitter and face-to-face, for one of the rare times in the Vietnam War both sides used tear gas, and casualties mounted on all sides. On February 24, an ARVN battalion overran the last NVA stronghold in the Citadel and found, the next day, that the remaining Communist troops had left during the night.

The Battle of Hue was very costly. There were a total of 212 American dead and 1,364 wounded. Within the ARVN, losses were 384 dead and 1,830 wounded. Over 5,000 NVA and VC fighters were killed, and thousands more wounded. Only 89 were captured. Numerous civilians were caught in the crossfire. Furthermore, much of the city was destroyed, including a number of the monuments in the Citadel. Estimates claim that over 100,000 people were left homeless, at least temporarily. American and South Vietnamese officials also uncovered mass graves in which they found the remains of nearly 3,000 people who had been executed by the Communists during their brief occupation of Hue. These included intellectuals, religious leaders, and foreigners from various countries. **See also** atrocities; Tet Offensive.

# Huey

The main helicopter used by U.S. forces in Vietnam. Produced by the Bell Helicopter Company, the Huey's distinctive long tail and loud "thwop-thwop" rotor noise were among the most well-known symbols of the war. Known also as the Iroquois, the Huey performed a variety of functions, ranging from troop transport to medical evacuation to resupply and reconnaissance missions. Depending on the mission, Hueys carried a crew of two to four, with room for about a dozen troops or six stretchers. The UH-1D Huey, an advanced model, was one of the most effective helicopter gunships deployed in the war, equipped with two 2.75-inch rocket launchers, a 40-millimeter grenade launcher, and machine guns mounted at the doors. Some UH-1Ds were also equipped with television systems that enabled them to mark targets and fire at night. **See also** Cobra; gunships.

# Humphrey, Hubert H. (1911–1978)

Vice president under Lyndon B. Johnson and Democratic presidential candidate in the election of 1968. After becoming vice president in 1964, Humphrey opposed Johnson's efforts to escalate the Vietnam War. He was vocal enough in his criticism that, after a time, the president declined to ask for his opinions. Humphrey made a trip to South Vietnam in February 1966 as part of an extensive tour of Asia. The visit changed his mind about the war, and Humphrey returned to Washington, D.C., full of praise for the American military and civilian efforts. This turnabout was a major disappointment to Humphrey's supporters and liberal Democrats.

In 1968, after Johnson chose not to run again, Humphrey emerged as the leading possible Democratic candidate. His main rivals were Eugene McCarthy, who ran on an antiwar platform, and the popular favorite Robert F. Kennedy. After Kennedy was assassinated in early June, Humphrey was the clear frontrunner. Still, he faced major problems. The largest was to distance himself from Johnson, whose Vietnam policies had become extremely unpopular and which Humphrey had supported since his return from Saigon in 1966. A second problem was the disunity within the Democratic Party, a problem that was exacerbated by the violence at the Democratic National Convention in August. On the campaign trail, Humphrey frequently found himself the target of antiwar spokesmen, and the many Americans who opposed the war found themselves with no satisfactory presidential options. Humphrey found it difficult to separate himself from Johnson, while his major opponent, Republican Richard M. Nixon, said little that was specific regarding his plans for Vietnam.

During the last weeks of his campaign, Humphrey tried to run as the peace candidate, promising to end the bombings of North Vietnam and continue the peace negotiations then under way. Johnson, as it happened, tried to give him a hand by ordering a bombing halt on October 31. It was to little avail. While the popular vote was close, 43.3 to 42.7 percent, Nixon defeated Humphrey by a wide margin in the electoral college. Humphrey was reelected to the Senate in 1970 and remained there until his death in 1978. **See also** Democratic National Convention of 1968; Johnson, Lyndon B.; McCarthy, Eugene.

# Huston Plan

An effort by the presidential administration of Richard M. Nixon to gather intelligence on members of the antiwar movement in the United States. The plan was devised by a special advisory body and named after one if its sponsors, Tom Huston, although it was officially known as the "Domestic Intelligence Gathering Plan: Analysis and Strategy." In the aftermath of the massive antiwar demonstrations in the spring of

1970, which were mounted in opposition to what appeared to be the extension of the war into Cambodia rather than the deescalation of conflict Nixon had often promised, Nixon staffers decided it was time to track American "subversives." The Huston Plan called for the collection of intelligence information using wiretaps and other electronic surveillance, operatives to infiltrate antiwar groups, and even property break-ins and the opening of private correspondence. In addition, the plan wanted to create a separate office to act as a liaison on domestic surveillance among the Central Intelligence Agency (CIA), Federal Bureau of Investigation (FBI), the Defense Intelligence Agency, and the White House.

The surveillance techniques proposed in the plan were all illegal. Nevertheless, Nixon signaled his approval on July 14. Only the intercession of Attorney General John Mitchell and FBI head J. Edgar Hoover got Nixon to change his mind, and the Huston Plan, as it stood, was shelved. As it happened, Nixon's White House simply made plans to gather intelligence on its domestic enemies in other ways, including a special Intelligence Evaluation Committee and the infamous "plumbers," whose efforts to gather information as well as plug leaks were to play a major part in Nixon's downfall. **See also** antiwar movement; Nixon, Richard M.; Watergate scandal.

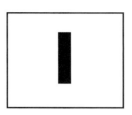

## Ia Drang Valley, Battle of

A major battle in November 1965 that marked an important change in the nature of the Vietnam War. For the first time, regular American combat troops, as opposed to Special Forces or military advisers, were deployed in a pitched battle. Moreover, the American troops faced regular units of the North Vietnamese Army (NVA) rather than Viet Cong (VC) guerrillas.

The Battle of Ia Drang Valley was the result of a strategy devised by the North Vietnamese in 1964 and 1965. Their plan was to deploy NVA troops from bases in Cambodia in an east-west attack across the Central Highlands south of Pleiku. After crossing the border, NVA troops were to continue their attack until they reached the coast, thereby cutting South Vietnam in two. It was a strategy they adhered to throughout the next ten years. On the other side, meanwhile, American president Lyndon B. Johnson had made the decision to commit regular U.S. combat forces to supporting the Saigon regime of the Republic of Vietnam (RVN).

The NVA operation began with a siege on a U.S. Special Forces base at Plei Me on October 19, 1965. General William Westmoreland, commander of the Military Assistance Command, Vietnam (MACV), responded to the attack by sending in the First Cavalry Division (Airmobile) of the U.S. Army to relieve the base. Soldiers were flown in by helicopters, in one of the first experiments using helicopters as vehicles of mass transport (as well as the evacuation of wounded). After the base was secured with the help of RVN forces on October 26, Westmoreland ordered American troops to go on the offensive with reconnaissance missions in the surrounding hills.

From the standpoint of NVA commanders, the siege of Plei Me had turned into an opportunity to examine the operations of American combat units in hopes of removing them from an important base at An Khe, a town that stood on the route the NVA hoped to take to the coast. Between November 1 and November 26, numerous engagements took place between U.S. cavalry and infantry and NVA regulars; the NVA usually fought from fixed positions while American troops mounted raids assisted by artillery and air support, including B-52 raids on NVA posts. Although U.S. units were often dispersed and difficult to locate, which hindered the usefulness of air and artillery fire because of the fear of American fire hitting American troops, cohesion was finally reached by mid-November. NVA commanders gave the order to disperse and retreat on November 18, and by November 26, U.S. and RVN forces had secured the area. The NVA thrust to the coast had, this time, been blocked. Casualties at Ia Drang included 305 Americans killed as well as over 3,000 North Vietnamese fatalities. **See also** First Cavalry Division.

# International Commission for Supervision and Control (ICSC)

A body established at the 1954 Geneva Conference, which ended the First Indochina War. It was charged by the hosts of the conference, Great Britain and the Soviet Union, to maintain neutrality while ensuring that the Geneva Accords were implemented. As it happened, the main task of the three member nations of the International Commission for Supervision and Control, India, Canada, and Poland, was encouraging diplomacy in the independent nations of North Vietnam, South Vietnam, Cambodia, and Laos. The ICSC had no enforcement powers and was unpopular among peoples who wanted to determine their own destinies regardless of what the Geneva Accords contained.

In Vietnam, ICSC delegates practiced a sort of shuttle diplomacy between Saigon and Hanoi, the only diplomats with freedom to travel, via Vientiane in Laos, between the two capitals. A major question they had to deal with early in the war was the extent to which Viet Cong insurgents in the south were supported by Hanoi, which would have been a violation of the accords. In 1963 the ICSC released a report, over the objections of the Polish delegate, that accused Hanoi of supporting the insurgents, a complaint that became an article of faith in the United States.

In Laos and Cambodia, ICSC delegates operated at the whim of local authorities. Cambodia's Prince Sihanouk had little use for the organization, and except for a temporary request to investigate American and South Vietnamese bombings of Cambodian territory in 1969, the ICSC remained inactive in that country. In Laos the ICSC played a more active role in promoting negotiations among the main interest groups, including the Royal Lao government and the Communist Pathet Lao. The negotiations collapsed, however, as the fighting in Indochina widened after 1964. The final ICSC delegates left Laos in 1975; their counterparts had already been requested to leave Cambodia six years before.

After the 1973 Paris Peace Accords, which were intended to settle the conflict in Vietnam but only had the lasting result of removing American forces, another version of the ICSC was set up to oversee implementation of the new agreement. Member nations included, once again, Poland and Canada. India declined and was replaced by Indonesia, while Hungary joined as a fourth member. This newer version, based at Tan Son Nhut airport in Saigon, was even less meaningful than the first, since both North and South Vietnam appeared intent on continuing the war despite the departure of the Americans. The ICSC finally disbanded in 1975. **See also** Geneva Conference on Indochina; Paris Peace Accords.

# Iron Triangle

The name given by U.S. and South Vietnamese forces to a major Viet Cong (VC) base area located less than twenty miles northwest of Saigon. The region contained 125 square miles that became crisscrossed with tunnels; it included ammunition and supply depots as well as fortifications. The Iron Triangle served as the base for VC attacks on Saigon and surrounding regions. Several major attacks by U.S. and South Vietnamese forces, such as Operation Cedar Falls, failed to completely dislodge the VC from the area. So also did attempts to negate VC infrastructure by destroying villages and relocating villagers while cutting back the jungle to reveal hiding places. Even bombing raids had little effect. The Iron Triangle remained a major thorn in the side of American and South Vietnamese forces till the end of the war, a constant reminder that the enemy lived, in effect, right next door. **See also** Cedar Falls; Cu Chi tunnels.

## Jackson State College shootings

An incident on May 14, 1970, in which two students were killed by Mississippi state law enforcement officers during an anti–Vietnam War protest. Jackson State College was a predominantly African American institution located in Jackson, Mississippi. As at dozens of other colleges and universities across the country, students gathered there to protest the American incursion into Cambodia, announced on April 30, as well as the shootings of four students at Ohio's Kent State University on May 4 during a similar protest. Local police and state highway patrol officers tried to contain the demonstrations, which grew increasingly tense. The night of May 14, officers shot into a student dormitory. Two people were killed, and twelve more were wounded. Although the officers maintained that they were responding to sniper fire, investigations later found no such activity. The Jackson State incident received little nationwide attention in the wake of the Kent State shootings and the broadening national protests. Some contended that this was because of a perception that the deaths of African American students were less newsworthy than those of young white people. **See also** antiwar movement; Cambodia, invasion of; Kent State University shootings.

## Johnson, Lyndon B. (1908–1973)

President of the United States during the major escalation of American involve-ment in the Vietnam War from 1963 to 1968, and in the end a political victim of the turmoil the war inspired. Lyndon Baines Johnson was born in Stonewall, Texas, on August 27, 1908. After graduating from Southwest Texas State Teachers College (now the University of Texas at San Marcos), he worked for a number of years as a teacher. He was elected to the U.S. House of Representatives in 1938 on the Democratic Party ticket and served in the House until 1947. A skilled negotiator and political insider, Johnson was elected to the Senate from Texas in 1948 and became Senate majority leader in 1953, thus becoming the most influential Democrat in Congress. He agreed, during the 1960 Democratic National Convention, to be John F. Kennedy's running mate, although he had hoped to get the presidential nomination himself. Never close to Kennedy, whose background as a wealthy Northeasterner was vastly different from his hardscrabble Texas origins, Johnson remained on the fringes of Kennedy's inner circle of advisers. When Kennedy was assassinated on November 22, 1963, Johnson took the oath of office as the new president of the United States.

Johnson's interest in domestic policy was far greater than his expertise in foreign affairs. As president, his accomplishments include the passage of a number of measures as part of his Great Society program. These ranged from civil rights measures to social welfare measures and included a major overhaul of America's immigration laws. As the months passed, however, events in Southeast Asia absorbed more and more of his time and energy. His fundamental belief was that communism had to be contained, and he remembered from his years in the Senate the uproar that the supposed "loss of China" had inspired in 1949. Johnson did not want to "lose" Vietnam to the Communists.

After taking office, Johnson retained Kennedy's main foreign affairs team, including Robert McNamara, McGeorge Bundy, and Dean Rusk. To the extent that they paid attention to Vietnam in the early 1960s, these men favored most measures to assist South Vietnam (the Republic of Vietnam, or RVN) in defending itself against the Communist aggression of North Vietnam (the Democratic Republic of Vietnam, or DRV) and the Viet Cong (VC). Johnson's initial impulse was to simply continue along the lines Kennedy had begun, which was to support the RVN with financial aid and military advisers. U.S. help for the RVN, however, began to escalate rapidly, with Johnson's approval. In February 1964 he authorized direct U.S. aid for RVN operations against North Vietnam, as opposed to U.S. support for anti-VC measures in South Vietnam. Soon after, he named as the top American officials in Vietnam two men who were strongly in favor of a heavier American military presence: William Westmoreland as U.S. military commander and General Maxwell Taylor as ambassador.

Over the rest of 1964 and the first months of 1965 Johnson's decisions to commit American combat troops to Vietnam proceeded step by step in response to actual or perceived DRV and VC actions. One of these actions was the Gulf of Tonkin Incident of August 1964. In response to supposed DRV attacks on American ships, Johnson approved a retaliatory bombing raid against North Vietnam. The incident also inspired the Gulf of Tonkin Resolution, a measure passed by a sympathetic and cooperative Congress that allowed Johnson to personally authorize military force throughout Southeast Asia in order to contain Communist aggression.

By February 1965, in response to VC attacks on U.S. military bases in South Vietnam, Johnson had approved a steady stream of bombing raids over the north, a measure known as Operation Rolling Thunder. He also approved the sending of the first American combat troops to Vietnam: two battalions of marines for the defense of the American air base at Da Nang. On April 1, 1965, Johnson authorized the use of American troops for offensive as well as defensive operations. For the next three years the escalation continued, both in response to circumstances and because of Westmoreland's requests for more troops. By 1968, there were 500,000 American troops in Vietnam. Meanwhile, the American bombing of North Vietnam continued, and American planes extended their targets to locations in Cambodia and Laos.

In addition to this gradual military escalation, Johnson approved steps to provide for "nation building" in South Vietnam. This nation building had several goals, including the fostering of American or American-style legal, educational, and economic institutions. Indeed, the number of American civil officials, civilian advisers, academics, technicians, and private businessmen in Saigon soon rivaled that of the U.S. military. A second goal was, of course, to strengthen the ability of the people of South Vietnam to resist both the DRV and the VC. Although well-enough intentioned, these efforts proved to be unsuccessful as Americans failed to take into account Vietnamese history and culture. Moreover, many South Vietnamese saw Johnson's nation building as simply another form of Western imperialism, the force the DRV claimed to be fighting against. In the end, these somewhat heavy-handed attempts to "win the hearts and minds" of the South Vietnamese proved to be failures.

Johnson was criticized for his gradual escalation in Vietnam from many sides. Some felt that U.S. military intervention should be strong and direct rather than gradual and piecemeal. Johnson, however, was worried that stronger U.S. actions might provoke a broader conflict by involving China or the Soviet Union. He also did not want the Vietnam conflict to deter his administration from his Great Society goals by devouring too much of the budget or by alienating important members of Congress. From another angle, and especially as the war began to result in substantial American casualties, Johnson found himself the target of criticism from the emerging antiwar movement. Leaders of the movement often pointed out that Americans were being killed in a war that, they argued, was illegal since it had never been declared by Congress. One chant at antiwar demonstrations ran, "Hey, hey, LBJ, how many kids did you kill today?" Partly because of conflicting reports from his advisers, Johnson was also accused of fostering a "credibility gap" in which his administration's generally positive statements that the war was going well proved to be misleading. The Vietnam War also became increasingly costly, and in 1967 and 1968 Johnson was forced to take federal money away from his Great Society programs and devote it to defense spending. Despite these moves, the national deficit increased rapidly and the U.S. populace faced higher taxes.

As criticism increased, American escalation in the war proceeded, the costs of the war in casualties and wealth mounted, and Johnson and his advisers became graphically aware of the quag-

mire they had involved the nation in, doubts began to arise over the course of U.S. involvement in Southeast Asia. Johnson, who as early as 1965 had realized that Vietnam was a "damned mess," was always willing to open negotiations with North Vietnam. On a number of occasions he called for bombing halts in hopes of drawing DRV representatives to the negotiating table. These almost invariably failed, primarily since Hanoi demanded that the bombings be completely discontinued without conditions. By the end of 1967, meanwhile, Johnson showed he was ready to consider a deescalation of American involvement despite the calls of Westmoreland and other military leaders for more troops, more bombing runs, and an all-out ground war. In November 1967 he requested Clark Clifford, an old Democratic foreign policy adviser who was soon to replace McNamara as secretary of defense, to convene a group known as the Wise Men. Their task was to advise Johnson on Vietnam. Although at the end of that year the group's consensus was that the war was going reasonably well and that America should continue on its present course, opinions were divided to an extent they had not been before.

The dramatic events of the Tet Offensive of January and February 1968 altered Johnson's approach to Vietnam by convincing him that the war was not, in fact, going well. The massive North Vietnamese and Viet Cong offensive suggested to Johnson that the American plan of winning over the South Vietnamese people was failing and that the United States had underestimated North Vietnam's will to continue fighting despite the years of Rolling Thunder bombing raids. In the aftermath of Tet, the president asked Clifford to convene the Wise Men once again, this time to consider the request of Westmoreland and the Joint Chiefs of Staff for over 200,000 more troops to serve U.S. needs both in Vietnam and around the world. Clifford was asked to take into account not only military circumstances but also public opinion, the budget, and the likelihood of opening negotiations with the DRV. Toward the end of March 1968 Clifford's task force made its report to Johnson, and the president accepted many of its provisions. Among them were a rejection of the military's request for more troops aside from a relatively small increase and a recommendation that more of the war be turned over to the RVN, which would also be asked to reduce corruption and mismanagement.

Meanwhile, the campaigning for the 1968 U.S. presidential election had begun. Johnson was eligible for another term in office, and most Democrats assumed that he would run again. Vietnam, however, had become a burden that Johnson was unable to throw aside. On March 12, Senator Eugene McCarthy, who was running on a pledge to stop the war, won 42 percent of the vote in the bellwether New Hampshire primary, a sign that support for Johnson was very thin among Democratic voters. Four days later Robert Kennedy, John F. Kennedy's charismatic younger brother and the former attorney general, announced that he too was running for the Democratic nomination on an antiwar platform.

On March 31 Johnson appeared on national television to address the nation. He announced, first, that he was ordering an immediate bombing halt of North Vietnam except for a small area north of the demilitarized zone (DMZ). He hoped that the DRV would respond positively by entering into peace talks. At the end of his speech Johnson went on to say that he would not seek or accept his party's nomination for president, an announcement that shocked the nation. It may well also have convinced the North Vietnamese to accede to peace talks, which began in Paris

*On March 31, 1968, Lyndon B. Johnson announces he will not seek reelection as president.*

in May 1968. For the remainder of his lame-duck presidency, Johnson watched as the Paris negotiations proceeded inconclusively and while the United States suffered some of the worst urban unrest in its history over both Vietnam and the Democratic nomination.

Johnson retired to his ranch in Texas after leaving the White House in January 1969. He continued to follow developments in Vietnam while noting to biographers that he knew that, as president, he was presented with a no-win choice: supporting the Great Society or pursuing the war in Vietnam. He could not give up the first. But he was forced to devote time, energy, and money to the second or be accused of cowardice and allowing the United States to be seen as an ineffectual superpower and Communist appeaser. Johnson died in Texas on January 22, 1973, just days before the Paris Peace Accords ending U.S. involvement in Vietnam took effect. **See also** Gulf of Tonkin Resolution; Kennedy, John F.; McNamara, Robert; Nixon, Richard M.

## Joint U.S. Public Affairs Office (JUSPAO)

The public relations wing of the U.S. military in Vietnam. The main responsibilities of the JUSPAO were to provide journalists with news about the war and conduct propaganda, or psychological warfare, campaigns directed at ordinary Vietnamese. The office was organized in 1965 and placed under the authority of the Military Assistance Command, Vietnam (MACV). It eventually was housed in a substantial headquarters in central Saigon and had over six hundred employees. JUSPAO was most known to journalists because of the daily military briefings it held. The briefings were criticized as the "five o'clock follies" because of the wide gap between official military reports and the stories told by reporters who had been in the field.

The propaganda campaigns included the production of leaflets and other printed materials, films, speeches, and broadcasts. These materials were then distributed through official military channels engaged in psychological warfare campaigns. Their messages often urged ordinary North Vietnamese soldiers and civilians as well as Viet Cong fighters to ask themselves whether their efforts were truly helping the welfare of their families or whether their leaders were being truthful to them. One propaganda effort focused on the 1972 meeting between U.S. president Richard Nixon and Chinese Communist leaders Mao Tse-tung and Chou En-lai, the latter two of whom were referred to as "elder brothers" in propaganda coming from Hanoi. JUSPAO workers also devised messages that they thought might encourage Communist fighters to desert. **See also** five o'clock follies; media and the Vietnam War; psychological operations.

## Junction City

A major operation involving a total of twenty-six U.S. and South Vietnamese battalions that took place from February 22 to May 14, 1967. One of the largest offensive operations of the war, Operation Junction City was designed to clear Viet Cong (VC) fighters from a region strategists had dubbed War Zone C. War Zone C lay along the Cambodian border east of Saigon. It was a marshy region of some fifty by thirty miles and was thought to be the headquarters for the Central Office for South Vietnam (COSVN), the body that coordinated VC political and military activities with the North Vietnamese regime. Military strategists planned to first secure the northern and southern boundaries of War Zone C to the border, thus creating a sort of horseshoe that would contain any further fighting and prevent Communist forces from escaping.

Operation Junction City involved heavy fighting, not only against VC contingents but against regulars from the North Vietnamese Army (NVA). Taking advantage of their superiority in mobility and firepower, U.S. and South Vietnamese forces steadily cleared Communist forces from War Zone C despite numerous counterattacks. The use of combat helicopters was one great advantage, as it allowed U.S. commanders to withdraw fatigued units and insert fresh ones. Most of the fighting was concluded by the beginning of March; further activity mostly consisted of sweeps across the countryside in search of VC infrastructure.

Operation Junction City had few lasting effects although U.S. commanders declared it a tactical success. VC commanders, for their part, often simply shifted locations or withdrew until peace returned, afterward regrouping. In fact, War Zone C reappeared as a major staging area for the VC during the 1968 Tet Offensive. U.S. or South Vietnamese troops, meanwhile, never located COSVN headquarters. Apparently, NVA commander in chief Vo Nguyen Giap, concerned about a repeat of Operation Junction City, moved the headquarters across the border to Cambodia, where he knew American forces could not follow. Casualties during the operation included 282 American and South Vietnamese killed and 1,576 wounded. Among the Communists, more than two thousand were killed and thousands more wounded. **See also** Cambodia, invasion of; Central Office for South Vietnam.

# Kennedy, John F. (1917–1963)

President of the United States from January 1961 to November 1963, and the first president to substantially escalate American involvement in Vietnam. The son of a wealthy Massachusetts family and a World War II hero, Kennedy was elected to the House of Representatives in 1946 and to the Senate in 1950. Rising quickly through the ranks of the Democratic Party, he was elected president in 1960 over Republican Richard M. Nixon. Kennedy was the first Roman Catholic to ever be elected president of the United States, and many Americans were inspired by the youthful vigor, optimism, and intelligence of the young politician and war hero.

In foreign policy, Kennedy took a particular interest in stopping the spread of communism in developing nations like Vietnam. In order to do so, he favored the development of a flexible military establishment featuring counterinsurgency capabilities rather than the buildup of conventional forces or the unwieldy nuclear deterrent policy favored by his predecessor, Dwight D. Eisenhower. In 1961 he approved the sending of U.S. Special Forces to the Republic of Vietnam (RVN, or South Vietnam) to help RVN president Ngo Dinh Diem in his effort to stem Communist infiltration along the Ho Chi Minh Trail. He also began to send over greater numbers of military advisers while earmarking enough funding to increase the size of the Army of the Republic of Vietnam (ARVN) by thirty thousand men. At this point Kennedy wanted to avoid a direct commitment of U.S. combat troops but considered it America's responsibility, under the cold war containment policy, to aid any regime fighting to prevent Communist insurrections.

The first true test of Kennedy's policy of counterinsurgency in Indochina came in Laos, where the president fully supported the efforts of the Central Intelligence Agency (CIA) to arm and train Hmong soldiers. In Laos, Kennedy hoped to both contain the Pathet Lao, the local Communists, and cut the part of the Ho Chi Minh Trail that passed through the country by reiterating the neutrality of Laos that had been established by the 1954 Geneva Accords. This required negotiations with the Soviet Union, which began providing supplies to the Pathet Lao in 1960. To show that he was serious, Kennedy dispatched the U.S. Navy to the region and sent a contingent of U.S. Marines to the border between Laos and Thailand. The result was a new conference in Geneva, in 1962, at which the Soviets pledged to exert their influence over North Vietnam, getting them to stop sending supplies along the Ho Chi Minh Trail through neutral Laos.

Kennedy's hopes for Laos were dashed when the North Vietnamese ignored the directives of the 1962 Geneva Conference. Disturbed by this diplomatic failure, Kennedy recommitted himself to containing communism in Vietnam by aiding Diem's regime. Relations between Kennedy and Diem, however, grew increasingly worse over the short course of Kennedy's presidency. Diem's stubbornness with regard to democratic reforms grew increasingly frustrating to Kennedy and his advisers. Over the spring and summer of 1963, Diem's repression of Buddhist protesters, which resulted in the self-immolation of a total of seven monks, strained relations between the two leaders even further. In time Kennedy made it clear that the United States would not interfere if South Vietnamese military leaders plotted a coup against Diem. When the coup finally took place on November 1, 1963, and Diem and his brother Ngo Dinh Nhu were assassinated the next day, Americans simply stood by, although Kennedy himself was reportedly shaken by the event.

The removal of Diem could have no effect but to alter U.S. policy in Vietnam. Even before the coup, in fact, Kennedy and his advisers were considering a greater U.S. military presence, although the president continued to have grave doubts about a wider war involving combat troops. With the loss of Diem, it quickly grew clear that South Vietnam might have to rely on the United States more and more. Kennedy, of course, saw none of this. He was assassinated in Dallas, Texas, on November 22, 1963. **See also** counterinsurgency; Johnson, Lyndon B.; Ngo Dinh Diem; Nixon, Richard M.

# Kennedy, Robert F. (1925–1968)

Younger brother of John F. Kennedy and attorney general during his brother's presidential administration. Robert Kennedy was at the center of the president's inner circle of advisers and had a part in creating Vietnam policy, although his greatest interest was in domestic affairs. In 1968 he ran for president himself on a platform of strong opposition to what, by then, he

saw as a misguided U.S. effort in Southeast Asia.

John F. Kennedy asked his brother Robert, who had made a name for himself as a Washington, D.C., prosecutor, to serve as attorney general in 1961. As one of the president's chief advisers, Kennedy generally approved of the slow escalation of U.S. financial and military support for the South Vietnamese regime. After his brother's assassination in November 1963, he stayed on as attorney general under Lyndon B. Johnson, the new president. Kennedy resigned, however, in August 1964 to make what turned out to be a successful bid for election to the U.S. Senate from New York. As a senator, Kennedy continued to support the administration's policies in Southeast Asia, although he wondered out loud whether Vietnam might end up drawing needed funds away from domestic programs such as Johnson's Great Society initiatives. Kennedy began to speak out against Johnson's Vietnam policy only in 1966, following a decision to resume American bombing runs against North Vietnam. Kennedy's change of heart was partly due to the rising tide of antiwar sentiment among the American population, a phenomenon related to the civil rights and social justice concerns that Kennedy prided himself on. Still, he hesitated to criticize Johnson overtly for fear of being accused of political opportunism.

Kennedy entered the race for the Democratic nomination for president in March 1968 after the strong showing of Eugene McCarthy in the New Hampshire primary. The success of McCarthy, who campaigned almost entirely on an antiwar platform, seemed to indicate that Johnson, the incumbent, could be beaten (Johnson, in the end, chose not to run). Still partly the beneficiary of his brother's popularity, as well as because of the sense that McCarthy was too much of a leftist to gain the presidency, Kennedy quickly became the Democratic frontrunner. On June 4, he won the important California primary. Early the next morning, after a speech at Los Angeles's Ambassador Hotel, he was shot by an assassin and died the next day. Kennedy's assassination came only weeks after that of Martin Luther King Jr. and helped turn the summer of 1968 into one of massive protest and violence, notably at the Democratic convention in Chicago. **See also** Johnson, Lyndon B.; Kennedy, John F.

## Kent State University shootings

An incident taking place on May 4, 1970, that resulted in the deaths of four students and the wounding of nine others at Kent State University in Ohio. The occasion for the incident was an antiwar protest that began on May 1 as part of a national impulse to express indignation over President Richard M. Nixon's announcement, on April 30, that U.S. forces had taken part in an "incursion" into Cambodia. The announcement seemed to belie Nixon's promises to draw down the war and bring American troops home, and it inspired some of the widest antiwar protests of the entire Vietnam era. Students on more than one hundred college campuses took part, and anti-Nixon sentiments were heard across the country in newspapers, on the streets, and even in Congress.

The demonstration at Kent State got particularly violent when, on May 1, protesters committed vandalism against buildings and the local mayor called in the National Guard to maintain order. The next day, and despite the presence of the National Guard, much of which was made up of soldiers the same age as university students, protesters burned the building in which the campus's Reserve Officers' Training Corps (ROTC) offices were located. After this, the Ohio governor increased the number of National Guard units. As was often the case in such incidents, individual National Guardsmen were often engaged in conversation by protesters, conversation ranging in nature from kind exhortation to outright harassment.

For reasons that remain mysterious, guardsmen opened fire after failing to disperse a crowd of about two thousand protesters on May 4. Investigations later concluded that guardsmen had fired sixty-one rounds over a period of thirteen seconds at a group of students gathered in a parking lot. Two of the four people killed had not even taken part in the protest. The incident at Kent State further raised tensions, especially on college campuses, hundreds of which were briefly shut down. Along with a similar incident at Jackson State College in Mississippi in which two students were killed, the Kent State shootings also helped inspire a protest that drew over 100,000 people to Washington, D.C. As for the National Guardsmen, although the investigations later showed that the shootings were unnecessary and unjustified, none were found guilty of crimes. **See also** antiwar movement; Cambodia, invasion of; Jackson State College shootings.

## Khe Sanh, Battle of

One of the major battles of the Tet Offensive of 1968. Khe Sanh was a U.S. Marine base located on a mountaintop in a sparsely populated area of central Vietnam. It stood only six miles from the Laotian border, close to an important stretch of the Ho Chi Minh Trail, and fourteen miles south of the demilitarized zone (DMZ). Originally founded in 1962 as a U.S. Special Forces base, Khe Sanh became part of a string of bases and outposts stretching east to west across Vietnam in hopes of preventing incursions by the North Vietnamese Army (NVA) across the DMZ or the Laotian frontier. Beyond this, General William Westmore-

*Marines charge from a helicopter near Khe Sanh, a U.S. military base located on a mountaintop in central Vietnam.*

land, U.S. commander in Vietnam, had plans to use Khe Sanh as a base for a possible invasion of Laos. By April 1967 there were thousands of marines stationed at the site, which also had large-scale artillery pieces and an airstrip. It was supported by isolated gun emplacements and smaller camps in the surrounding mountains.

The first fighting around Khe Sanh took place in the spring of 1967. Because of an increase in communications traffic as well as a larger number of transports along the Ho Chi Minh Trail, Westmoreland came to believe that the NVA planned to besiege Khe Sanh. American patrols instigated fighting with NVA units in the hills around the base, including one major battle that left 160 marines dead. In the process, Americans discovered not only NVA patrols but fixed bases

and gun emplacements, which supported Westmoreland's contention that the NVA was planning a siege. In order to counter the growing NVA presence, Westmoreland called in U.S. bombers from faraway air bases to conduct raids in the hills around Khe Sanh. The success of the raids in quieting NVA activity helped convince him that Khe Sanh could hold, with sufficient aerial support, even if the U.S. troops at the base were vastly outnumbered by the NVA. By January 1968 there were six thousand American troops at Khe Sanh, most of them from the First Marine Division. They were ready not only to defend the base but to patrol the region and, when given the word, mount incursions into Laos.

NVA commander in chief Vo Nguyen Giap considered Khe Sanh as the possible site of a major diversionary tactic in the upcoming Tet Offensive, and West-moreland took the bait. Giap sent a huge force to the area, numbering between twenty and thirty thousand men, suggesting that he envisioned a major battle. Among Giap's tactics was one he had employed to great effect at Dien Bien Phu, the siege in an area not unlike that around Khe Sanh that defeated the French in the First Indochina War. The tactic was to place long-range artillery emplacements around the base in locations that were difficult to find and destroy from the air. Giap could then pound Khe Sanh with constant artillery fire. Meanwhile, fighting around Khe Sanh began more than a week before the Tet Offensive was launched on January 30–31, further serving its diversionary function; American commanders suspected that Khe Sanh might be the site of the first major strike in an NVA march to the coast. American journalists hopped on helicopter transports to the base in search of a major story, while, back in Washington, D.C., President Lyndon B. Johnson was determined to prevent another Dien Bien Phu. He asked for a written guarantee from the Marine Corps that their men would be able to hold the base, and as the fighting proceeded, he had a detailed replica of the Khe Sanh area constructed in the White House basement and asked for reports on the battle to be sent to him hourly.

Despite heavy artillery bombardments and occasional sorties between NVA forces and marine patrols, including one in the Vietnamese village of Khe Sanh some five kilometers from the base, American forces maintained control of the base throughout the entire Tet Offensive. The NVA began its withdrawal on March 6 and the Battle of Khe Sanh formally ended on April 1. Soon after, the base was linked by road with American and South Vietnamese outposts to the east by Highway 9. April 8 was the first

day since January 21 that the base received no NVA artillery fire. American casualties numbered over three hundred killed and some sixteen hundred wounded, along with hundreds more South Vietnamese and Montagnard troops. American officials estimated that between ten and fifteen thousand Communist soldiers were killed, mostly as a result of bombing operations sent in support of the defense of Khe Sanh.

The question of who won the Battle of Khe Sanh remains controversial. If the North Vietnamese truly intended it to be a diversion, it worked, since large amounts of American firepower, particularly planes and bombs, were directed toward Khe Sanh and away from the battle sites of the Tet Offensive. On the other hand, the siege was costly to the NVA in terms of manpower, and the Communists never managed to seize full control of either the base or surrounding hills and villages. Although U.S. forces did not lose the battle, they chose to abandon the base at Khe Sanh in June 1968, inspiring many Americans to wonder what the fighting had been all about in the first place. After the end of the Vietnam War, much of the region was turned over to coffee plantations until the government of the Socialist Republic of Vietnam realized the site's potential as a tourist attraction. **See also** Dien Bien Phu, Battle of; Tet Offensive.

# Khmer Rouge

The largest Communist insurgency in Cambodia during and after the Vietnam War. Meaning the "Red Khmer" (the Red Cambodians), the Khmer Rouge took power in April 1975 and instituted one of the most brutal regimes in human history. The "killing fields" of Khmer Rouge Cambodia remain one of the saddest legacies of the more than thirty years of warfare in Indochina.

The founder of the Khmer Rouge was Saloth Sar, who adopted the name Pol

Pot. Pol Pot had been educated in France, where he was exposed to the revolutionary doctrines of Karl Marx, Lenin, and Mao Tse-tung and came to see a form of peasant communism as a possible salvation for his nation. After returning to Cambodia in the early 1960s, he helped form the Khmer Rouge along with like-minded, and often also foreign educated, Cambodians. In those years the war in Vietnam was expanding, but the Khmer Rouge was unable to get support from North Vietnam, which was supporting insurgencies in South Vietnam and Laos. The North Vietnamese had made a deal with Cambodian ruler Norodom Sihanouk to allow supplies and troops to move across the country; in exchange, they refrained from backing the Khmer Rouge.

Cambodians traditionally held a strong dislike of the Vietnamese, and in fact, aside from rare instances of cooperation, the Khmer Rouge considered the North Vietnamese their enemies. The form of communism the Khmer Rouge professed was different than that of North Vietnam, and indeed it continued to consider North Vietnam an enemy. Pol Pot and his subordinates, notably Ieng Sary and Khieu Samphan, believed that their version of communism was purer and more sanctified than that across the border. It required complete ideological and physical devotion, and members of the Khmer Rouge were required to completely obey their leaders and ignore any suffering they went through in order to achieve their vague revolutionary goals. Dissension or disobedience was not to be tolerated. To the extent that Pol Pot had a consistent ideology, it was built around the establishment of a kind of peasant utopia in which all individuality would disappear; everyone would be a "worker" or a "comrade."

Sihanouk was forced from power in March 1970 by General Lon Nol, a leader identified with South Vietnam and the United States. That same year, the Vietnam War spilled over into Cambodia to a far greater extent than ever before. South Vietnam launched a U.S.-backed invasion of the country in order to prop up the Lon Nol regime and cut Communist supply lines; in addition, the United States began a massive bombing campaign of the Cambodian stretches of the Ho Chi Minh Trail. In these circumstances the Khmer Rouge grew more powerful. It established a brief alliance with the Vietnamese Communists and a more fateful one with the ousted Prince Sihanouk. Moreover, many young Cambodians, especially villagers in the north and east, joined the Khmer Rouge out of anger over the bombing campaigns or because their lands and villages had been destroyed. Between 1970 and 1975 the Khmer Rouge managed to not only enlarge its forces but absorb or defeat all of its opponents, which included other Communist groups. The black-clad Khmer Rouge "forest army," as it was known by many Cambodians, established control over ever larger areas of the countryside as Lon Nol's army, which was partly trained and supplied by the United States, collapsed. The Khmer Rouge launched its final, victorious offensive on the capital city of Phnom Penh in April 1975, just as the North Vietnamese triumphantly entered Saigon to finally unify that country.

Cambodia largely disappeared from the awareness of the world for the next few years, although a few who escaped from this new state told horrifying stories of the methods the Khmer Rouge used to transform the nation. Calling April 17, 1975, the first day of Year Zero, Pol Pot and his soldiers and henchmen attempted a complete makeover of Cambodian society. All of the major cities, including Phnom Penh, which had a population of over half a million, were forcibly evacuated. Patients were even removed from hospital beds; those who could not walk or who resisted were either abandoned or shot by young Khmer Rouge soldiers, many of whom were barely in their teens. In the countryside, the evacuees were forced to work as laborers on state farms, although these more often resembled slave labor camps. Clad always in black to diminish individuality and the risk of dissent, these peasants were told constantly that they were working for "Angka," or the party, which would take care of them and help them create a perfect society as long as they did not resist. There was rarely enough food, and thousands died from malnutrition or disease.

Thousands more died from the Khmer Rouge's attempts to cleanse the nation of its foreign or unhealthy elements; indeed, nearly 2 million people, one-quarter of Cambodia's population, were thought to have died at the hands of Pol Pot's regime. Educated people, for instance, were strongly targeted; anyone who practiced a profession such as teaching, law, or journalism was suspect and often simply murdered. Even those who wore eyeglasses, thought to be a sign of education and wealth, were sometimes killed. Other groups marked for execution included merchants, those with foreign contacts, and Cambodia's large Chinese population. In Phnom Penh a former high school was turned into a torture and interrogation center known as Tuol Sleng. There, some twenty thousand people were condemned to death and their interrogations carefully documented. In the countryside, far more were killed for hoarding food, speaking out of turn, or practicing stronger forms of protest or resistance.

This brutal attempt to create a peasant utopia, and the hundreds of thousands of civilian deaths, finally ended in 1979. In December 1978, after a series of border clashes, the army of the Socialist Republic of Vietnam invaded Cambodia. The Vietnamese took Phnom Penh in mid-January 1979 and occupied the country until 1989. The Khmer Rouge, as it had before 1975, regrouped in the jungles and mountains of the countryside, where it fought a long guerrilla war with the Vietnamese and the puppet government they had set up in Phnom Penh under Heng Samrin, a former Khmer Rouge official. **See also** Cambodia, invasion of; Lon Nol; Pol Pot.

## kill ratio

One of the statistical measures used by U.S. officials, notably General William Westmoreland, head of the Military Assistance Command, Vietnam (MACV), and Secretary of Defense Robert McNamara, to judge success in the Vietnam War. It was used mostly in the years from 1965 to 1968 and was based on the notion that large numbers of enemy dead would result in a decision by Communist leaders to stop fighting or enter into peace negotiations. Frequently, U.S. strategists received reports of engagements with a kill ratio of 15:1 in favor of the United States, which suggested, falsely, that the United States was winning the war. **See also** attrition strategy; body count.

## King, Martin Luther, Jr. (1929–1968)

American civil rights leader and strong anti–Vietnam War spokesman. Born in Atlanta, his wide education taught him how Mahatma Gandhi used techniques of nonviolent resistance to help remove British rule from India. King was to use similar tactics to fight for civil rights for African Americans. He made a name for himself in the late 1950s when, under the banner of the Southern Christian Leadership Conference (SCLC), he began to stage nonviolent protests. These included marches, sit-ins, and, when necessary, jail terms. By the early 1960s King had become famous nationwide, and the work of the SCLC had begun to ensure equal rights for African Americans in regions where those rights were restricted.

After Lyndon B. Johnson took over the presidency in late 1963, King supported him vocally because Johnson promised a wide agenda of domestic reforms and civil rights legislation known as the Great Society program. The two began to diverge, however, over the Vietnam War. King considered the war simply an example of American imperialism rather than a struggle against communism, and he also questioned why frontline soldiers, those most likely to be killed or wounded, were often poor African Americans. In a concern echoed by Johnson, but not always acted on, King feared that the Vietnam War would threaten the domestic and civil rights reforms that he thought were necessary by taking away money and diverting attention. For these reasons King considered opposition to the Vietnam War a way of fighting for civil rights on a new front, and he could frequently be found at antiwar protests calling for an end to bombing campaigns against North Vietnam and the opening of peace negotiations. Other civil rights leaders, however, criticized King for combining the two issues.

King was shot to death in Memphis, Tennessee, on April 4, 1968. His assassination and that of Robert F. Kennedy in early June inspired some of the most violent civil unrest in U.S. history, exemplified by, for instance, the rioting during that summer's Democratic National Convention in Chicago. **See also** antiwar movement; Democratic National Convention of 1968.

## Kissinger, Henry (1923– )

From 1969 to 1973, national security adviser to President Richard M. Nixon, and

*Martin Luther King Jr. shakes the hand of President Lyndon B. Johnson at the signing of the Civil Rights Act in 1964.*

from 1973 to 1976, secretary of state to Nixon and then Gerald R. Ford. Kissinger was a major architect of Nixon's Vietnam policy and the central American figure in the negotiations that produced the Paris Peace Accords of January 1973.

In earlier years a foreign affairs and arms-control consultant in Washington, D.C., Kissinger was appointed national security adviser in 1969. He went on to have far more influence on Nixon's foreign policy than any other official, including the secretary of state. This was partly due to Nixon's approach to governance, an approach that Kissinger shared. Both men felt that traditional bureaucracies, such as the State Department, moved too slowly and that decisions were best made by a small, loyal circle of advisers.

With regard to Vietnam, Kissinger clung to the notion that it was impossible for the United States to win the war. The political costs of raising a sufficient army, accepting a high number of casualties, and paying for the enterprise were simply too high. On the other hand, the United States could not simply leave Vietnam because that would send a message to the world that the United States was weak and lacked credibility. Kissinger was especially concerned that this perception of weakness would harm the United States in its relations with the Soviet Union and China.

Kissinger and Nixon ultimately settled on a plan that would, to their minds, allow the United States to withdraw from Vietnam with its honor intact. The plan involved first what came to be known as Vietnamization. According to this notion, the fighting of the war against Vietnamese Communists would be turned over, gradually, to the South Vietnamese. At the same time, there would be a gradual withdrawal of U.S. ground troops, although Kissinger warned that troops not be removed too rapidly. The Saigon government, however, could still rely on American training, military equipment, and supplies. In addition, Kissinger and Nixon pursued peace negotiations with North Vietnam.

The plan was carried out between 1969 and 1973. It worked to remove American troops from Vietnam, but events complicated the process. One was the takeover of Cambodia in March 1970 by Lon Nol. This precipitated a combined U.S.–South Vietnamese invasion of Cambodia as well as a massive bombing campaign. Kissinger, in particular, was accused by many Americans of trying to expand the Vietnam conflict rather than drawing it down, and, indeed, several members of Kissinger's staff resigned because of the Cambodian incursion. Meanwhile, negotiations went slowly, since many North Vietnamese leaders figured that they were winning anyway.

In July 1971 Kissinger made a secret trip to China. Both he and Nixon wanted to open up negotiations with this Communist superpower as part of their larger strategy for global affairs. Kissinger arranged for a visit to China by Nixon himself, which took place in February 1972. This historic rapprochement had a significant impact on the Vietnam negotiations, as did similar gestures toward the Soviet Union. Thanks to this new American openness, both China and the Soviet Union grew somewhat less friendly toward North Vietnam, and Hanoi found itself forced to take Kissinger's peace negotiations more seriously. In order to further show that the United States was not withdrawing from Vietnam out of weakness or the lack of will, Kissinger supported a massive bombing campaign against North Vietnam in retaliation for its Easter Offensive of 1972.

By the fall of 1972, presidential election season, Nixon had made peace with North Vietnam a high priority, and Kissinger, meanwhile, found himself frequently shuttling between Washington, D.C., and Paris, where he held meetings with his North Vietnamese opposite number Le Duc Tho. The two reached an agreement on October 8 that would include a cease-fire, a removal of all remaining U.S. forces, and the return of American prisoners of war. It would also allow the United States to continue providing aid to South Vietnam. Kissinger returned to the United States and announced on October 26 that he was confident that peace was around the corner.

The Kissinger–Le Duc Tho accord was rejected, however, by South Vietnamese president Nguyen Van Thieu. Thieu refused to accept the notion that he would be forced to rule in conjunction with South Vietnamese Communists, and in the face of Thieu's vociferous disapproval, Le Duc Tho walked out of negotiations. The result was another show of American power ordered by Kissinger and Nixon, the so-called Christmas bombing of 1972 directed at the cities of Hanoi and Haiphong. Although many Americans, and many more worldwide, were outraged by the Christmas bombing, the attacks appear to have convinced Le Duc Tho to return to the negotiating table. Kissinger announced the Paris Peace Accords on January 20, 1973, the day of Nixon's second inauguration. They were signed soon after.

Kissinger's role in ending American involvement in Vietnam made him a political celebrity, and many Americans were fascinated by his global shuttle diplomacy, which, again, worked outside traditional State Department channels. He was named the most admired American in a 1973 poll, and *Time* magazine had named both Kissinger and Nixon "Men of the Year" for 1972. The Vietnam settlement, moreover, earned Kissinger and Le Duc Tho the Nobel Peace Prize for 1973. The Vietnamese official refused to accept the prize; Kissinger donated the prize money to a scholarship fund for the children of soldiers killed in Vietnam. In September 1973, meanwhile, Nixon appointed Kissinger secretary of state, a post at which he remained through the administration of Gerald R. Ford. **See also** Le Duc Tho; Nixon, Richard M.; Paris negotiations.

## Komer, Robert (1922–2000)

As deputy assistant to the commander of the U.S. Military Assistance Command, Vietnam (MACV), in 1967 and 1968, an office that also provided him with ambassadorial rank, Komer was instrumental in implementing the pacification aspects of the U.S. effort to construct and protect the South Vietnamese state.

A former Central Intelligence Agency (CIA) official with expertise in Middle East affairs, Komer joined Johnson's administration in 1966 when the president named him special assistant to the president for national security affairs. It was in this position that Komer took an interest in pacification in South Vietnam, first as the coordinator for such matters in Washington, D.C. As he examined the problem and worked with military officers, Komer became convinced that pacification, rather than military action alone, was the key to stopping the Viet Cong (VC) insurgency. He informed Johnson of his opinion that the only way to secure a victory in Vietnam was to pacify the villages, an effort that would both clear out the VC and provide villagers with the necessary confidence in the Saigon regime. Johnson, in turn, gave Komer free rein to develop a plan that would allow pacification efforts to work in tandem with U.S. military efforts by creating a new organization. This came to be known as Civilian Operations and Revolutionary Development Support (CORDS), and in May 1967 Komer was sent to Saigon to be the initial head of the organization. CORDS would allow pacification officers to use military resources and knowledge but remain under civilian control.

CORDS had mixed results, at least under Komer's tutelage. It helped to coordinate various U.S. attempts at political and economic improvement already under way, and it also had an effect in providing villagers with more of the responsibility for their own defense. Komer's efforts, however, did little to stop the VC. Komer was assigned to be the ambassador to Turkey in November 1968, where he remained until the new president, Richard Nixon, replaced him in early 1969. CORDS, meanwhile, came under the control of William Colby, another former CIA officer. **See also** Civilian Operations and Revolutionary Development Support; pacification.

## Kontum

Aside from Pleiku, Kontum was the most strategically important city in the Central Highlands of Vietnam. This provincial capital was the headquarters of a South Vietnamese army division as well as several American infantry units. Their tasks were to try to contain Viet Cong (VC) units in the surrounding regions and halt any offensive by North Vietnamese Army (NVA) units entering South Vietnam from across the Laotian border. The major fixed battle at Kontum took place in the spring of 1972, when the NVA launched its Easter Offensive. At the Battle of Kontum, a series of engagements taking place from March 30 to mid-June, South Vietnamese forces halted the NVA advance with the help of American air support. In 1975, however, Kontum was abandoned to the NVA. **See also** Central Highlands; Easter Offensive.

## Korea

The cold war conflict in Korea was a precursor to the Vietnam War and set the pattern for the American approach to the Vietnam conflict. The Korean War was fought from 1950 to 1953, and was the first test of what some American strategists had begun to think of as the domino theory. According to this idea, Asian nations were like dominoes; if one was allowed to fall to communism, the others might quickly be toppled over as well. The first Asian dominoes, then, were China, which became Mao Tse-tung's People's Republic of China in 1949, and North Korea, which China supported.

The Korean War started when, in June 1950, North Korea invaded South Korea, a neighbor with which it shared a rather uneasy peace. To stop the invasion, a United Nations force was dispatched to South Korea. Much of the force was made up of American units. By November the North Korean advance had been stopped, but China had also formally entered the conflict on behalf of its smaller client state. At that point the war settled into one of attrition.

The Korean War, like the Vietnam War later, was unpopular among many Americans who feared that it might grow into a much larger conflict. Americans were also hesitant to accept paying the cost of a larger war. Such concerns helped the U.S. president, Harry S. Truman, make the decision to keep the war a limited one by, for instance, firing General Douglas MacArthur, U.S. commander and World War II hero, when MacArthur proposed a wider conflict. Events in Korea also had an impact on the negotiations over Vietnam taking place in 1953 and 1954 in Geneva. Fearful of allowing China a second avenue in which to fight, American leaders urged a peaceful and rapid settlement with Ho Chi Minh's Viet Minh. Meanwhile, the Korean War ended with a cease-fire that took effect on July 27, 1953. The conflict had cost the United States over thirty-three thousand killed and more than 100,000 wounded. A

Communist regime remained in place in North Korea while in South Korea the democratic Republic of Korea took shape.

This north-south split was obviously repeated in Vietnam. The Korean War, moreover, continued to influence American decision making in Vietnam for years to come. In terms of military strategy, for instance, Americans assumed that the North Vietnamese, like the North Koreans, would fight a conventional war rather than a guerrilla war. This proved to be a major miscalculation until, at least, 1969. In addition, U.S. strategists hesitated to accept anything other than a limited war in Vietnam for fear that, again, China might become involved. Finally, U.S. military commanders themselves hesitated to be too outspoken or ambitious, or to challenge the decisions made by politicians, because of concern that they might suffer the same fate as MacArthur.

The Republic of Korea, for its part, became an important ally to both the United States and South Vietnam. It sent some fifty thousand troops to fight in the Vietnam War, and the top Korean officer, along with the head of the South Vietnamese armed forces and the commander of the U.S. Military Assistance Command, Vietnam, served on the joint commission that decided overall strategy. The cease-fire in Korea itself, meanwhile, never resulted in a peace treaty, and tensions between North and South Korea remained strong into the twenty-first century. **See also** cold war; domino theory; Free World Assistance Program.

## Laird, Melvin (1922– )

U.S. secretary of defense from 1969 to 1973, during the first presidential administration of Richard M. Nixon. Laird's main responsibility in office was to preside over the gradual withdrawal of U.S. troops from Vietnam in accordance with the Vietnamization policy, which was intended to turn more of the fighting over to the South Vietnamese. He understood that the U.S. Congress wanted a fairly steady withdrawal of troops and was inclined to reduce the military budget during those years, so he was forced to work within a rising number of constraints. This necessity brought him into conflict with other members of the Nixon administration, notably Henry Kissinger. In fact, Laird was left out of the planning for the joint U.S. and South Vietnamese invasion of Cambodia in 1970, an operation he hesitated to enforce until U.S. forces were committed. Afterward he claimed that the Cambodian incursion was justified because it would aid in the safe departure of American troops. Others, including Military Assistance Command, Vietnam, commander Creighton Abrams and pacification chief in Vietnam, William Colby, as well as Nixon himself, recognized that Laird's efforts were vital to the success of Vietnamization. **See also** Kissinger, Henry; Nixon, Richard M.; Vietnamization.

## Lam Son 719

Code name for the South Vietnamese invasion of Laos, which began on February 8, 1971. The operation was a major test of the Vietnamization policy begun by U.S. president Richard M. Nixon in 1969 to shift more of the fighting of the war to South Vietnamese forces while gradually withdrawing American troops. Since U.S. forces, by law, could not cross the border into Laos, only South Vietnamese troops could take part in the actual invasion. However, the United States could—and did—provide support for cross-border operations. Such support included diversionary operations in the A Shau Valley and off the North Vietnamese port of Vinh; clearing a route along Highway 9 from the South China Sea to the border; providing airlift and bomber support; and even lobbing artillery shells from bases in South Vietnam, including Khe Sanh, across the border.

The objective of Lam Son 719 was to sever the Ho Chi Minh Trail by, first, clearing Communist forces from the town of Zepon and, second, destroying the infrastructure of the trail itself in the vicinity, a district also called Xepon. On February 8, a force of fifteen thousand troops made its way along Highway 9 across the border. Encountering little initial resistance, the force established temporary fire support bases along the way, which, among other things, served as points where U.S. helicopters could drop supplies or troops or, if necessary, lift them out. Intelligence advisers, however, had underestimated the number of Communist troops in the region and by the end of February the advance had bogged down. Moreover, bad weather prevented U.S. aircraft from providing effective bomber support, as did North Vietnamese antiaircraft fire. Rain also turned Highway 9 into a mud pathway, which made forward advances even more difficult and hindered resupply by ground units.

On March 6, under the orders of South Vietnamese president Nguyen Van Thieu, the force launched an airborne assault on Zepon. The town was taken easily, since Communist troops, according to their custom, had simply abandoned it, knowing they could return another day. Having secured the objective, Thieu ordered his commanders to withdraw from Zepon on March 9. The retreat was ill led and undisciplined, and again poor weather hindered American air support. Communist leaders understood that American bombers, moreover, would not drop bombs on sites within one hundred yards of friendly troops; therefore they stayed close to the retreating South Vietnamese even when not engaging them directly. The retreat turned into a rout in which thousands of South Vietnamese soldiers were killed by Communist raiders. The fighting even spilled over across the border, thus involving American forces directly.

Operation Lam Son 719 resulted in heavy losses. Half the South Vietnamese force, up to nine thousand men, were either killed or wounded. American casualties included 253 killed and 1,149 wounded. In an indication not only of the losses but of the magnitude of American support, 108 U.S. helicopters were destroyed in Laos and 618 damaged; seven air force planes were also shot down.

The operation provided important lessons about the progress of Vietnamization, and South Vietnamese commanders took steps to improve their operations. Despite the heavy losses, Nixon proclaimed in a televised speech on April 7 that the operation was a sign that Vietnamization was working. **See also** Commando Hunt; Dewey Canyon II; Vietnamization.

## land reform initiatives

Measures used by the governments of both North Vietnam and South Vietnam to reorganize their societies and ensure the support of ordinary people, the vast majority of whom were farmers or peasants. In its simplest form, land reform in Vietnam involved taking land away from wealthy landlords and redistributing it, in smaller parcels, among the peasants. An added benefit was that the peasants would no longer be tenants of those landlords and therefore subject to all sorts of restrictive and oppressive measures. To cite one indication of the scope of the problem, in 1954 almost half of the available agricultural land was held by only 2.5 percent of the total number of landlords.

The Viet Minh began to implement land reform in areas it controlled during the First Indochina War (1946–1954), although it focused its energies on confiscating land from those who supported the French. The effort continued, among virtually all large landowners, after the establishment of the northern Democratic Republic of Vietnam (DRV) in 1954. The result was a massive land reform campaign that was to transform North Vietnam. Village by village, Communist agents or their lackeys sought out "reactionaries," those who wanted to hang on to their land. Many of those who were found were either executed or sent to reeducation camps. Others escaped to South Vietnam. Once DRV officials had corrected some of the excesses of the effort, these landholdings were then distributed among loyal Communists or made available at extremely low rents. Even Ho Chi Minh recognized that by redistributing land, he would inspire ordinary Vietnamese to support him.

Meanwhile, in South Vietnam, President Ngo Dimh Diem did little to alter the domination of the agricultural sector by large landords. Indeed, he relied on such landlords to support his regime. Despite a number of land reform decrees beginning in 1955, South Vietnamese peasants remained hemmed in by high rents, little control over their crops, and an inability to acquire land of their own. To make matters worse, Diem often made land available to people who had migrated from North Vietnam seeking to escape Communist rule. Many of these migrants, like Diem and his family, were Roman Catholics, and Diem saw in them a wide base of support. It was not unusual for South Vietnamese villagers to be displaced to make way for these newcomers. Diem's unwillingness or inability to carry out effective land reform measures was likely one of the factors that helped turn many villagers into supporters of either North Vietnam or the Viet Cong; the Communists promised them much more extensive land reform. In areas controlled by the Communists during the Vietnam War, notably the Mekong Delta, substantial land reform took place and many peasants were freed from tenancy.

South Vietnamese president Nguyen Van Thieu revived the land reform effort in 1970 with a major piece of legislation. It took land away from large landlords and redistributed it among peasants at no cost. The measure, carried out with surprising efficiency, helped to solidify support for Thieu, at least temporarily. **See also** Vietnam, Democratic Republic of; Vietnam, Republic of.

# Lansdale, Edward G. (1908–1987)

A U.S. Air Force officer who played an important part in developing the American strategy of counterinsurgency in Southeast Asia. He was also influential in stabilizing the regime of Ngo Dinh Diem

as president of the Republic of Vietnam (South Vietnam) in the mid-1950s.

After working in the advertising business in San Francisco for a number of years, Lansdale served as an officer in the Office of Strategic Services (OSS), the predecessor of the Central Intelligence Agency (CIA), in 1941. He later became an officer in the U.S. Army. He elected to remain in the army after World War II but transferred to the air force in 1947. He spent some of the next years in the Philippines, where he worked with both American and Filipino intelligence to subvert Communist movements there.

By 1954 Lansdale was a lieutenant colonel in the air force with a reputation for expertise in counterintelligence and grassroots anticommunism. President Dwight D. Eisenhower assigned him to South Vietnam to serve as the chief of the Saigon Military Mission, an organization affiliated with the U.S. embassy but given outside authority to engage in covert actions. Lansdale's responsibilities were to seek ways to strengthen the Saigon regime while weakening the Communist Democratic Republic of Vietnam (DRV) to the north. He arrived in Saigon in June 1954.

Lansdale spent only two and a half years in South Vietnam, but he likely exerted a major influence on the subsequent course of events. He befriended Ngo Dinh Diem, who at first served as premier and minister of defense in the government of the former emperor, Bao Dai. Over time, in fact, Lansdale grew to be one of the few people outside of Diem's family whom Diem marginally trusted. Lansdale advised Diem to strengthen his position by encouraging huge numbers of people to leave the DRV for South Vietnam, by building governmental service organizations, and by promising economic and social reforms. Lansdale also helped prevent a coup against Diem by a group of rebellious army officers. In order to stabilize Diem even further, Lansdale helped find ways to remove the threats of the Hoa Hao and Cao Dai, two popular religious sects with their own armies, and the Binh Xuyen, a wide-ranging criminal operation. One of Lansdale's last gestures was to help Diem create a new government in late 1955 by devising a new constitution and staging an election that removed Bao Dai from power. Meanwhile, Lansdale remained the guiding force behind the activities of the Saigon Military Mission, which in addition to its duties in the south was also engaged in covert operations, mostly unsuccessful ones, in the DRV.

Lansdale's influence with Diem began to wane once the South Vietnamese president felt secure in his position and began to turn to his brother Ngo Dinh Nhu for advice. Lansdale returned to Washington, D.C., in February 1957, where he took up the post of deputy director of the Office of Special Operations within the Department of Defense. Because of Lansdale's local knowledge, President John F. Kennedy later considered naming him ambassador to South Vietnam, but other administration officials balked at placing a covert operator in such a politically sensitive position, and Kennedy backed off on the appointment. Lansdale, now a major general, retired from the air force in October 1963. He returned to Vietnam on a special assignment given by President Lyndon B. Johnson from 1965 to 1968. His new responsibilities involved implementing the various pacification programs aimed at the ordinary people of South Vietnam.

Lansdale retired from public life in 1968 but remained a controversial figure. Many people distrusted him because he was an intelligence officer who worked outside of standard diplomatic channels. Although many applauded the goals he seemed to have achieved in South Vietnam, others saw him as the best example of America's heavy-handed, idealistic, and ineffective approach to the problems of the country. To some, Lansdale remained a foreigner who never understood Vietnamese culture or the Vietnamese people, and his efforts, therefore, would result only in misunderstandings, if not further violence or chaos. This point of view, and Lansdale himself, was thought by some to be the inspiration for two major novels about misguided Americans overseas: Graham Greene's *The Quiet American* and Eugene Burdick and William Lederer's *The Ugly American.* Lansdale himself sought to clarify his actions in a 1972 memoir, *In the Midst of Wars: An American's Mission to Southeast Asia.* **See also** Central Intelligence Agency; Ngo Dinh Diem; Saigon Military Mission.

## Lao Dong

The familiar Vietnamese name for the Vietnamese Workers' Party, or Dang Lao Dong Viet Nam. It governed North Vietnam (the Democratic Republic of Vietnam, or DRV) from 1951 until 1976, when the party was reorganized. For all intents and purposes, Lao Dong also meant the Vietnamese Communist Party.

The formation of the Lao Dong in 1951 was the culmination of years of efforts by several Communist groups in Vietnam, most notably the Indochina Communist Party (ICP) formed in 1930. The ICP's first general secretary was Tran Phu, who presided over the creation of two basic goals that were to help guide Vietnamese Communists from that point on: ridding Vietnam, as well as Cambodia and Laos, of French colonial rule and taking land away from rich landlords, a basic tenet of the kind of peasant communism the ICP professed. As an organization the ICP survived until 1951. The one major exception to this came in 1945. That year, Ho Chi Minh, who had emerged as the leading Vietnamese Communist and who understood the importance of practical tactics as well as revolutionary ideology, dissolved the ICP, at least officially. He did so in order to seek support from the United States and China in establishing a free Vietnam. French intransigence, however, brought the ICP back out into the open as the guiding force behind Vietnamese independence.

Ho officially changed the name of the ICP to Lao Dong in 1951. The ICP, moreover, split along nationalist lines, with separate organizations being formed in Cambodia and Laos. The name change, to Ho's way of thinking, was necessary to expand nationalist support against the French, especially among those Vietnamese opposed to communism. Meanwhile, the military wing of the Lao Dong, the Viet Minh, fought the French army to a stalemate, and in 1954 the Geneva Accords split independent Vietnam into two nations. The Lao Dong became the sole ruling party of the DRV. Truong Chinh was named general secretary of the Lao Dong, or the leader of the party, while Ho remained head of state.

Over the next few years, with North and South Vietnam nominally at peace, Ho worked through the Lao Dong to institute Communist reforms in the DRV. These included land reform and redistribution as well as various reeducation programs. The efforts were not always peaceful, and in 1956 the Viet Minh, now the North Vietnamese Army, had to put down a major peasant revolt. Le Duan replaced Truong Chinh as general secretary of the Lao Dong in 1959. In the same years, the Lao Dong established itself as an important player in international communism, but its relationships with the Communist superpowers, the Soviet Union and the People's Republic of China, remained largely uneasy. In 1959 and 1960 the Lao Dong approved proposals to increase support for the Communist insurgency in South Vietnam. This support was in accordance with the party's overall goal of reuniting Vietnam under a Communist regime based in Hanoi, but over the next years it resulted also in a vastly expanded struggle against the United States, a struggle the Lao Dong ultimately won. After Ho Chi Minh's death in 1969, Le Duan effectively replaced him as head of state as well as head of party, where he remained until his death in 1986. **See also** Ho Chi Minh; Le Duan; Viet Minh; Vietnam, Democratic Republic of.

## Laos, secret war in

A companion conflict to the Vietnam War that lasted from 1962 until 1973. Laos was a landlocked country that shared a long border with Vietnam. The 1954 Geneva Accords established it as an independent nation, but the Royal Lao government was unstable from the beginning. Indeed, beginning in 1955 Laos relied on American aid to prop up the government and help it counter the insurgency staged by the Communist Pathet Lao. Ineptitude and corruption among leaders in the capital, Vientiane, simply increased support for the Pathet Lao, however, and by 1960 some 20 percent of the country was controlled by the Communists. Outgoing U.S. president Dwight D. Eisenhower, meanwhile, warned his successor, John F. Kennedy, that Laos was the key to Southeast Asia, apparently because it stood as a buffer between Communist China and the states to the south.

Various coups and countercoups in the early 1960s resulted in Lao factions being supported by the U.S. Central Intelligence Agency (CIA) on the one hand and by the North Vietnamese and the Soviet Union on the other. The 1962 Geneva Accords temporarily settled the matter, but fighting arose again quickly. Numerous factions coalesced around the Pathet Lao, which enjoyed regular military assistance from North Vietnam. The CIA, meanwhile, took on the task of building up an alternative coalition made up of the Vientiane government and members of the Hmong tribe, a large group traditionally opposed to the lowland Lao. In this way, the secret war took shape.

With CIA training and supplies, the Hmong built up a large army of tens of thousands under the leadership of an able warlord known as Vang Pao. The Vientiane government, meanwhile, continued to enjoy massive amounts of aid and training as well in its attempt to field an effective Royal Lao army and air force. These forces fought against the combined might of the Pathet Lao and its North Vietnamese patrons; North Vietnam deemed control of eastern Laos as vital to its interests because much of the Ho Chi Minh Trail, the North Vietnamese supply line into South Vietnam, passed through Laotian territory. American involvement in Laos was extensive but largely unknown outside the region. In addition to arming and training the Hmong, the CIA employed an ostensibly civilian airline known as Air America to transport troops and supplies. Some also claim that the CIA partly funded its effort by taking part in the opium and heroin trades that had long been a fundamental way of life for many of the hill tribes in Laos. As was against the custom for such bodies, the U.S. embassy in Vientiane was also deeply involved in the war.

Also kept largely secret were massive U.S. bombing raids conducted against Laos. Between 1964 and 1973 U.S. planes conducted 580,944 sorties over Laos and dropped 2,093,100 tons of bombs, making the ostensibly neutral country the most heavily bombed nation in the history of warfare. Bombing sorties increased beginning in 1969, when bombers were no longer needed in the Vietnam War due to the cessation of raids over North Vietnam and as all parties came to believe that the war there no

longer needed to remain secret. In 1971 the South Vietnamese, with extensive American support, even launched an unsuccessful invasion of Laos code-named Lam Son 719.

The Pathet Lao and the Royal Lao government signed a cease-fire agreement that took effect on February 21, 1973. One major feature of the agreement was the end of U.S. bombing runs. Subsequent attempts to assemble an effective ruling coalition were to no avail and, in August 1975, the Pathet Lao entered Vientiane, forcing the king to abdicate. Soon after, Pathet Lao politicians proclaimed the Lao Democratic People's Republic, a Communist companion to the Socialist Republic of Vietnam. **See also** Air America; Geneva Conference on Laos; Hmong; Pathet Lao.

# Le Duan (1907–1986)

General secretary of the Central Committee of the Lao Dong, the Vietnamese Communist Party, from 1959 to 1969. After the death of Ho Chi Minh in 1969, he assumed the leadership of the Lao Dong, making him the most powerful politician in North Vietnam (the Democratic Republic of Vietnam, or DRV).

After serving long prison terms for anti-French activities from 1931 to 1945, Le Duan joined Ho Chi Minh as a leading member of the Viet Minh, where he proved to be a capable military leader. He was placed in control of Viet Minh efforts in the Mekong Delta during the First Indochina War (1946–1954) and in 1952 was named military commander for all of southern Vietnam. After the 1954 Geneva Accords split Vietnam into two nations, Le Duan remained an active member of the North Vietnamese Communist leadership, continually pressing for reunification with the south. He replaced Truong Chinh as general secretary of the Lao Dong, the North Vietnamese Communist Party, in 1959. The position was an acknowledgment of his long and aggressive service in not only fighting against foreign imperialists but installing a Communist system in the DRV in the years since 1954. After visiting South Vietnam in 1959, Le Duan urged the DRV to take urgent action to support the Viet Cong insurgency against the American-supported Saigon government. For the next several years he helped preside over a rash of revolutionary activities on the part of the Viet Cong, including stepped-up campaigns of assassinations and bombings as well as recruitment and education.

Le Duan also understood the importance of conventional military operations, and he encouraged the DRV government in Hanoi to send regular North Vietnamese Army (NVA) troops to South Vietnam, especially after the arrival of American combat troops in 1965. Meanwhile, he continually took a hard line in negotiations, insisting that all U.S. bombing raids be stopped unconditionally before DRV representatives would sit down to peace talks. Le Duan's parallel approach to the conflict continued after he replaced Ho Chi Minh as head of the Lao Dong. Le Duan refused to seriously consider a continued division of Vietnam, and he grew increasingly confident that a military victory would be achieved once the Americans left. Along with military commander Vo Nguyen Giap, negotiator Le Duc Tho, and DRV prime minister Pham Van Dong, Le Duan accepted the Paris Peace Accords of January 1973.

After Vietnam was formally reunified in 1976 following the military victory over Saigon a year earlier, Le Duan remained head of the Lao Dong and effective head of state over the new Socialist Republic of Vietnam until his death in 1986. **See also** Pham Van Dong; Vietnam, Democratic Republic of; Vo Nguyen Giap.

# Le Duc Tho (1910–1990)

Important North Vietnamese politician; member of the Central Committee of the Lao Dong, the Vietnamese Communist Party, from 1959 to 1986; and the chief North Vietnamese negotiator at the Paris peace talks from 1968 to 1973.

A founder of the Indochina Communist Party, the precursor to the Viet Minh, Le Duc Tho spent much of the 1930s in prison before reemerging as a Communist leader during World War II. He proved to be especially skillful as a theoretician and intellectual, and in the 1950s and 1960s he played a major part in both devising and explaining the policies of North Vietnam (the Democratic Republic of Vietnam, or DRV). Reports suggest that even Ho Chi Minh highly valued his contributions. Tho insisted that the struggle to reunify Vietnam under the Lao Dong's Communist regime was both military and political in nature.

Le Duc Tho was sent to Paris as the chief negotiator for the DRV when peace talks with the United States began in May 1968. He was instructed to take a hard line that real negotiations could not begin until the United States stopped bombing North Vietnam unconditionally. In addition, the United States and South Vietnam would have to accept a new government for Saigon that included the National Liberation Front, the ostensible political leadership of the South Vietnamese Communists. Chief U.S. negotiator Henry Kissinger refused these demands. Tho and Kissinger returned to Paris in 1970 to engage in secret talks in hopes of striking a deal, Tho now allowed a larger degree of latitude in negotiation.

Tho ended up getting most of what he wanted, even to the extent of Kissinger allowing the DRV to maintain troops in South Vietnam after a cease-fire. During the fall of 1972, the intransigence of South Vietnamese president Nguyen Van Thieu threatened to torpedo the peace

*U.S. representative Henry Kissinger meets with Le Duc Tho. The two were awarded the Nobel Peace Prize for their efforts in arranging the 1973 peace accords but Tho refused the award.*

talks, resulting in Tho walking out in December. The infamous American Christmas bombing of 1972, however, brought Tho back to Paris, and all parties concluded a peace agreement on January 27, 1973. Not only would American bombings cease, but American troops would leave Vietnam altogether. Thieu would be forced to accept a coalition government including the National Liberation Front, now known as the Provisional Revolutionary Government, pending future elections. Neither North nor South Vietnam, however, observed the cease-fire that the peace agreement called for, a state of circumstances the DRV leadership decided justified a continuation of the war against Saigon.

Le Duc Tho, along with Kissinger, was awarded the Nobel Peace Prize for his efforts in arranging the 1973 peace accords. Tho refused the award, however. In 1975 he helped direct the final campaign, which led to the DRV victory over Thieu and the Saigon regime in April. After Vietnam was reunified, Tho continued to play an important role as a member of the Central Committee of the Lao Dong, helping to devise policies to instill the Communist system in the south and to guide the 1978 invasion of Cambodia. Tho's influence waned after 1986, when Hanoi began wide-ranging economic reforms. **See also** Kissinger, Henry; Paris negotiations.

## light antitank weapon (LAW)

A lightweight, portable rocket launcher carried by many infantrymen in both the U.S. and South Vietnamese armies. Known also as the M79, the LAW was even disposable, consisting of a long fiberglass tube and a plastic sight. It released a 66-millimeter charge that could penetrate tanks and concrete bunkers if the charge exploded correctly to release a white-hot cloud of gas and molten metal. Thanks to better training, South Vietnamese troops used the weapon more effectively than their American counterparts, who found it difficult to fire the LAW with accuracy. **See also** artillery; grenades; mortars.

## Linebacker I

A months-long aerial operation mounted by the United States against North Vietnam. It was conducted in support of the South Vietnamese defense against the north's Easter Offensive of 1972, although U.S. strategists carried it out with the added goal of forcing the North Vietnamese to negotiate a peace agreement. From another angle, Linebacker I marked a transformation in the form of American involvement in Vietnam. Thanks to Vietnamization, most American ground troops had been withdrawn by the time Linebacker I began on May 10, 1972. This left overwhelming airpower as the most distinct American advantage.

Between May 10 and October 23, 1972, when the operation ended, U.S. Air Force, Navy, and Marine pilots flying from bases in South Vietnam and Thailand and from carriers in the South China Sea carried out more than forty thousand sorties and dropped tens of thousands of tons of bombs. The goal of these flights was interdiction rather than simply destruction, and bombers were instructed to target roads, bridges, tunnels, railroads, warehouses, power plants, and petroleum storage depots. They were helped by the first widespread use of smart bombs, or munitions equipped with electronic or laser guidance systems, which were thought to minimize civilian casualties.

North Vietnam's Easter Offensive bogged down over the summer of 1972, and observers gave Linebacker I a great deal of credit for interfering with the North Vietnamese Army's supply chain and thus making it much easier for South

Vietnamese ground troops to mount a defense. After nearly twenty-eight thousand tons of bombs were dropped in September alone, Hanoi politicians finally also agreed to seriously consider the peace proposals then being discussed in Paris. Only when those negotiations broke down did U.S. president Richard M. Nixon authorize Operation Linebacker II, or the Christmas bombing. **See also** Christmas bombing; Easter Offensive; Paris negotiations; smart bombs.

## literature and the Vietnam War

The Vietnam War inspired, and continues to inspire, a substantial body of literature, both fiction and nonfiction. The great early novels of the Vietnam experience included *The Quiet American*, by Graham Greene, and *The Ugly American*, by Eugene Burdick and William Lederer. Published during the 1950s, both questioned the wisdom of America's involvement in a region about which Americans knew little and for which they may have had unreasonable expectations. In a similar vein was Asa Barber's *The Land of a Million Elephants* (1970), which asked similar questions with regard to Laos. One of the more popular early novels about the Vietnam War was Peter Derrig's *The Pride of the Green Berets*, a depiction of the exploits of Special Forces troops. Published in 1966, it inspired both a hit song and a Hollywood film.

Later novels of the Vietnam War often focused on the individual soldier's experience. Tim O'Brien's prizewinning *Going After Cacciato* (1978) is a nonrealistic, imaginative story of an infantry unit's search for a comrade who has decided to lay down his gun and walk to Paris. O'Brien's *The Things They Carried* (1992) is a collection of powerfully imagined vignettes of soldiers' experiences and emotions. Other important books in this genre written by veterans were *Fields of Fire* (1977), by James Webb and *The*

*Thirteenth Valley* (1982), by John Del Vecchio. Both tell the stories of individual units made up of diverse characters offering a variety of personal viewpoints. Del Vecchio also published the novel *Carry Me Home* (1994), which added to his earlier themes the difficulties veterans encountered upon their return home. Some Vietnam novels were more ambitious epics, including two books by Robert Olen Butler: *On Distant Ground* (1985), in which a combat veteran returns to Saigon in its last independent days to look for a child he fathered with a Vietnamese woman, and *A Good Scent from a Strange Mountain* (1992), a Pulitzer Prize–winning collection of short stories that explored the experiences of both Vietnam veterans and South Vietnamese immigrants to the United States. Anthony Grey's *Saigon* (1981) traced the experiences of French, American, and Vietnamese characters from the 1920s through the fall of Saigon in 1975. *The Tale of Kieu* (1987), by Vietnamese writer Nguyen Du, explores the impossibility of love in the context of war and insurmountable cultural differences.

Many of the more memorable literary documents of the Vietnam experience are memoirs rather than fictional accounts. Tim O'Brien's *If I Die in a Combat Zone* (1973) is among the most eloquent, dealing with the complexities of fighting a war one does not believe in. Others include *Nam* (1981) by Mark Baker, in the form of anonymous oral history; *A Rumor of War* (1976) by Philip Caputo; and *Home Before Morning* (1990) by military nurse Lynda Van Devanter. All highlight the moral ambiguity and clear futility of the fight in Vietnam. Occupying a special category is *Dispatches* (1977), by war journalist Michael Herr, a revised collection of magazine pieces that inspired controversy because of the author's lack of neutrality as well as praise for its unflinching accuracy. Many veter-

ans of the war, meanwhile, published military-style histories for the popular market, including Larry Chambers's *Recondo: LRRPs in the 101st Airborne* (1992), Eric Bergerud's *Red Thunder, Tropic Lightning* (1993), and Otto Lehrack's *No Shining Armor: The Marines at War in Vietnam* (1993).

Some memoirs written by Vietnamese people have also appeared in English. Most well known is Le Ly Hayslip's *When Heaven and Earth Changed Places* (1989), the story of the author's transformation from village girl to Viet Cong sympathizer to black-market operator to American businesswoman and housewife. Hayslip wrote a follow-up titled *Child of War, Woman of Peace* (1992). Another is Duong Van Mai Elliot's *The Sacred Willow* (1999), an epic account of her family from the time of the French takeover through the American war. **See also** film and the Vietnam War; music and the Vietnam War.

# Lodge, Henry Cabot (1902–1985)

Twice U.S. ambassador to South Vietnam (the Republic of Vietnam, or RVN) and a major figure in the implementation of U.S. Vietnam policy in the 1960s. His first term came when President John F. Kennedy appointed Lodge to the ambassadorship in Saigon in June 1963. He was sent to replace Frederick R. Nolting, whom Kennedy found to be overly sympathetic to the oppressive regime of RVN president Ngo Dinh Diem. When Lodge arrived in Saigon in August, he found indeed that his initial challenge was to deal with Diem. Many elements of South Vietnamese society were in open protest against Diem, including Buddhist monks, who Diem attacked openly and violently. Lodge initally approached Diem with the proposal that the president remove from power his brother Ngo Dinh Nhu, who was most directly involved in the oppressive acts of the regime.

Diem refused. Meanwhile, Lodge also received from Washington permission to signal to a group of generals plotting a coup against Diem that the United States might well approve of an overthrow of Diem.

After having a number of frustrating confrontations with the RVN president, Lodge hesitated to agree with members of Kennedy's administration who, in late October 1963, urged him to try to continue working with Diem to institute reforms. The ambassador simply let them know that, by that time, the matter was out of American control. When the generals began their coup on November 1, Lodge told Diem that he knew nothing of it. He offered the newly deposed leader the opportunity of foreign exile, but Diem refused him. The next day, after taking refuge in a church in Cholon, Saigon's Chinese district, Diem and Nhu were captured and assassinated.

In May 1964 Lodge resigned the ambassadorship and was replaced by General Maxwell Taylor. His reason for resigning was to run for the Republican nomination for president, but he was also unhappy with the inept government of the generals who had overthrown Diem. President Lyndon Johnson, however, convinced Lodge to stay on as an informal adviser on Vietnam policy. Over the next months Lodge proved instrumental in arguing for a stronger U.S. military presence on the ground in the RVN as well as bombing campaigns against North Vietnam. Meanwhile, he lost the Republican nomination, which he was arguably unenthusiastic over anyway, to Barry Goldwater.

Lodge returned to South Vietnam as ambassador in July 1965, once Johnson administration officials had made the decision to commence bombing and commit U.S. ground troops. His responsibility this time was to ensure that the Saigon regime held the line against Communist infiltra-tion, both political and military. In the first category, he strongly supported the government of Generals Nguyen Cao Ky and Nguyen Chanh Thi against various political opponents, knowing that the two generals would work closely with U.S. officials. Lodge was also instrumental in subduing the so-called struggle movement, a renewed Buddhist uprising against the Saigon regime that, combined with elements of the South Vietnamese army led by General Nguyen Thanh Chi, took control of the important central Vietnam cities of Hue and Da Nang in the spring of 1966. With regard to containing Communist guerrilla infiltration, Lodge took an active role in reviving the various pacification programs, including educational and economic reforms, aimed at South Vietnamese civilians.

Lodge resigned as ambassador in April 1967. He later turned up again as one of the Wise Men, a group of elder statesmen who gathered informally to advise Johnson on Vietnam policy in the wake of the Tet Offensive of January and February 1968. In 1969, new president Richard M. Nixon, his old running mate, sent him to Paris to take the chief role in peace negotiations with North Vietnam, a post he left after a few months because he found that the talks were going nowhere. **See also** Bunker, Ellsworth; Kennedy, John F.; Ngo Dinh Diem.

## Long Binh

The major U.S. Army base in South Vietnam. Established in 1967, it was located twenty miles north of Saigon near the town of Bien Hoa. Ultimately covering over twenty-five square miles, Long Binh could house fifty thousand soldiers. It was the headquarters of not only American army units but also units of the Army of the Republic of Vietnam (ARVN), the South Vietnamese army. Long Binh also served as a supply depot, equipped with facilities able to handle the thousands of tons of equipment shipped up the nearby Saigon River. For thousands of American soldiers, Long Binh was the first base they saw after arriving in Vietnam and the last place in the country they saw before being shipped home. In time Long Binh contained many of the features of American life, including movie theaters, restaurants, shops (or post exchanges), offices, and hospitals; many of these facilities enjoyed what little air conditioning existed outside of Saigon proper. The base also contained the major U.S. Army prison, known locally as LBJ, which stood for both "Long Binh Jail" and "Lyndon B. Johnson." The jail was the site of a major riot in August 1968, a faraway echo of the civil unrest taking place in the United States as a result of the war.

Long Binh was the frequent target of small-scale attacks by the Viet Cong, whose fire was considered little more than harassment, and it was the site of a major battle during the Tet Offensive of 1968. The base and its vast infrastructure were turned over to the ARVN command after the departure of the last U.S. combat troops in early 1973. It was largely destroyed by attacks of the North Vietnamese Army in their final attack on South Vietnam in 1975. **See also** Bien Hoa; military regions.

## long-range reconnaissance patrols (LRRPs)

One of the major military tactics developed by American forces during the Vietnam War. It was also used by the South Vietnamese army as well as other allied contingents, notably the Australians. Military strategists conceived the long-range reconnaissance patrols in order to effectively challenge the Viet Cong (VC) and North Vietnamese Army (NVA), enemies who were difficult to find, especially in mountainous or jungle-covered areas. The tactic also suited the overall American goal of victory through attrition and interdiction of supply lines rather than conventional warfare involving front lines and the taking of territory.

The first LRRP units were formed in May 1964. They consisted of small teams formed from U.S. Special Forces and either South Vietnamese or Montagnard groups. Their purposes were to collect intelligence on enemy troop movements and supply lines and, at times, to conduct sabotage raids. LRRP units were also called on to set coordinates for air or artillery attacks. The program was expanded in 1966 to include regular U.S. combat troops from army infantry divisions as well as larger numbers of South Vietnamese or Montagnards. LRRP bases were established at Nha Trang, Ban Me Thuot, and on the outskirts of Saigon. In 1967 most American LRRP operations were placed under the jurisdiction of the so-called Studies and Observation Group, a cover organization for intelligence-gathering and behind-the-lines operations. Their missions took LRRP units across South Vietnam and on occasion into Cambodia. The LRRPs proved to be such a success that in 1966 Military Assistance Command, Vietnam, commander General William Westmoreland ordered all divisions to form their own LRRP units. **See also** Civilian Irregular Defense Groups; Special Forces, U.S. Army.

## Lon Nol (1913–1985)

President of Cambodia from 1970 to 1975, the years when Cambodia was a main area of conflict in the Vietnam War. Lon Nol came to power in the aftermath of a complex series of events that swept the previous leader of the nation, Norodom Sihanouk, from office. By 1969 Cambodia was suffering from a great deal of economic distress as well as incursions by both the North Vietnamese Communists and indigenous Communist groups such as the Khmer Rouge. Sihanouk had managed to maintain an uneasy balance that had allowed Cambodia to remain neutral in the war in neighboring Vietnam, but the balance was growing increasingly tenuous. An army officer, Lon Nol was chosen by Sihanouk to be the prime minister of a new government in late 1969. He was, however, a reluctant leader, suffering, among other things, from a number of medical problems.

In early 1970, while he was in Paris receiving medical treatment, Lon Nol met with Sihanouk, who was still technically the head of state. Although evidence is scanty, he reportedly convinced Sihanouk to end his support of the North Vietnamese Communists, which included an open supply line connecting the Cambodian port of Sihanoukville (Kompong Som) to the Cambodian stretches of the Ho Chi Minh Trail. Soon after, Lon Nol used his influence with the army to arrange attacks on North Vietnamese emplacements on Cambodian soil. In March 1970 he asked Sihanouk, publicly, to dramatically increase the size of the Cambodian armed forces. Sihanouk objected furiously but found he had little support among leading Cambodians. On March 18, after a vote of no confidence in the National Congress in Phnom Penh, the capital, Sihanouk left office and went into exile in China. Lon Nol, at times remarkably timid in his actions, only supported the ouster after being threatened by Sirik Matak, a rebellious member of the Cambodian royal family. After another series of power struggles, he found himself named president of the nation.

Soon after, Cambodia was brought into the Vietnam War in a larger and more dramatic way when, in April 1970, a joint force of South Vietnamese and American troops crossed the border into Cambodia to root out North Vietnamese sanctuaries and halt the shipment of supplies along the Ho Chi Minh Trail. Seeing Lon Nol as a potential ally in this effort, the United States and South Vietnam began sending him military aid, including the arming and training of a new Cambodian army known as Forces Armees Nationale Khmer, or the Khmer National Army.

Lon Nol proved to be an inept and sometimes unwilling leader, still beset with medical difficulties and basing many of his decisions on advice from his astrologers. Despite the expansion of his armed forces, he lost most of the countryside to either the North Vietnamese or the Khmer Rouge. His capital city, Phnom Penh, became choked with refugees and increasingly lawless, and the economy collapsed. After leading a successful defense of Phnom Penh against the Khmer Rouge in early 1975, he departed for Hawaii to receive medical care. While he was gone the Khmer Rouge mounted another attack, and on April 17 it took control of the capital. Lon Nol later moved to Fullerton, California. **See also** Forces Armées Nationale Khmer; Khmer Rouge; Sihanouk, Norodom.

# M-14 and M-16 rifles

The standard weapons carried by U.S. infantry troops during the Vietnam War. Both capable of semi-automatic or fully automatic fire, the larger M-14 was replaced by the M-16 in 1966 after the U.S. military determined that the latter was better suited to jungle warfare. The M-14 weighed 9.3 pounds and was accurate to

*South Vietnamese soldiers fire M-16 rifles. Troops from both sides complained about the frequent malfunctions of the rifles.*

a range of five hundred yards. The M-16 was just as accurate but weighed two pounds less and fired a smaller cartridge, and it proved to be a more effective counterpart to the Soviet-made AK-47s carried by North Vietnamese troops. The usefulness of the M-16 was first made apparent at the Battle of Ia Drang Valley in November 1965, where officers on the scene praised its efficacy in helping them to win the battle. Slow production and quality-control problems meant that not until 1967 were most U.S. ground troops provided with M-16s, and the South Vietnamese army was not supplied with them until 1968. Problems with the weapons continued to plague soldiers in the field, who complained about the frequent maintenance and cleaning the rifles required, excessive vibration and lack of control, and jamming as much as 50 percent of the time. Malfunctions were repaired in the field and by manufacturers, and the rifles remained standard issue. **See also** AK-47; grenades; light antitank weapon.

## madman strategy

The name given to a plan to force North Vietnam to end the war by encouraging leaders in Hanoi to think that U.S. president Richard M. Nixon was crazy enough to use nuclear weapons. Nixon adopted this so-called madman strategy from his predecessor Dwight D. Eisenhower, whom Nixon had served as vice president. In 1953 Eisenhower had made it known to the North Koreans that he was considering the use of nuclear weapons in the Korean War, although the notion was a bluff. The Korean War ended with a negotiated settlement soon after. In 1969 Nixon, according to his aides, felt that it might help bring Hanoi to the negotiating table if subtle hints were dropped that hc, Nixon, was so obsessed with defeating communism and so short-tempered that he might decide to use nuclear weapons. Few on either side were fooled, partly because using nuclear weapons would risk the involvement in Vietnam of the Soviet Union or China. **See also** Eisenhower, Dwight D.; Nixon, Richard M.

# Manila Conference

A meeting to discuss ways of negotiating an end to the Vietnam War. It was held in Manila, the capital of the Philippines, on October 24 and 25, 1966. Representatives from South Vietnam and the United States were joined there by representatives of the other nations that were militarily involved in supporting the South Vietnamese: South Korea, Australia, New Zealand, Thailand, and the Philippines. The conference was an attempt to respond to growing international pressure to settle the conflict. However, the allies discussed negotiating terms that the North Vietnamese would clearly never accept, leading some to argue that the purpose of the conference was public relations rather than a serious effort to deescalate the war. **See also** Free World Assistance Program; Honolulu Conferences.

# Mao Tse-tung (1893–1976)

The leader of the Chinese Communist Party and founder, in 1949, of the People's Republic of China. Mao was one of the most influential leaders of the twentieth century and a central figure, along with Karl Marx and Lenin, in Communist thought. Among his contributions to Communist ideology were the notion of a perpetual revolution and the notion that peasant masses, such as those found throughout Asia, were potentially just as revolutionary as industrial workers. Indeed, he was able to muster the support of millions of Chinese peasants in his struggle to take over China, an effort that took some two decades. The success of his movement made Mao an idol to potential peasant revolutionaries worldwide. This was partially true even among Ho Chi Minh and the Vietnamese Communists despite the traditional dislike between the two countries.

The success of Mao's Chinese revolution in 1949 was central to the development of future events in Vietnam. On the one hand, it suggested to anti-Communists, especially in the United States, that the spread of communism was a threat in Asia as well as Europe and that that threat had to be checked at all costs. On the other hand, Mao's successes provided a model for Ho Chi Minh as well as a degree of confidence that a persistent peasant struggle could work. From a more practical standpoint, Mao proved willing to provide Ho with weaponry and other forms of military aid. Some have even suggested that, after hearing about the escalation of the Vietnam conflict with the arrival of American combat troops in 1965, Mao gave the order to send some Chinese troops to fight for North Vietnam wearing Vietnamese uniforms.

Mao ended his support for North Vietnam in 1969, a clear sign that American policy had been guided by at least a partial misapprehension since 1949, namely that all Asian Communists were the same and inevitably allies. The reasons why Mao turned away from North Vietnam included not only the traditional Chinese disdain for their southern neighbors but also a major split with the Soviet Union, the world's other Communist superpower. U.S. president Richard Nixon, meanwhile, made plans to exploit the split between China and the USSR by cultivating better relations with Mao, a move he also hoped would help in the American withdrawal from Vietnam. Mao saw many of the same advantages, and the two held a historic meeting in China in February 1972. Mao died in 1976, by which time the major foreign benefactor of the Vietnamese Communist regime was the Soviet Union. **See also** Ho Chi Minh; Vietnam, Democratic Republic of; Chou En-lai.

## Marble Mountain

One of five sizable mountains outside of Da Nang which, collectively, were simply referred to as Marble Mountain. Lined with tunnels, Marble Mountain was a Viet Cong (VC) outpost that was never rooted out by American and South Vietnamese forces despite regular attacks. It was the site of some of the most intense ground fighting in the Vietnam War. **See also** China Beach; Cu Chi tunnels; Da Nang.

## March on the Pentagon

An early landmark of the anti–Vietnam War movement in America that occurred on October 21, 1967. The march also marked the turning point for many in the antiwar movement away from peaceful protest and toward more active forms of resistance, including civil disobedience. The planning for the event combined two branches of the antiwar movement: a student mobilization committee, which had already planned for a mass turn-in of draft cards that October, and the National Mobilization Against the War, a broader group led by A.J. Muste and Jerry Rubin.

The day began with a rally at the Lincoln Memorial in Washington, D.C., attended by some 100,000 people. Then, about 35,000 began a march through Washington toward the Pentagon, U.S.

military headquarters. A group of as many as 1,000 of them planned to engage in civil disobedience by sitting down in front of the Pentagon, a site where demonstrations were forbidden by law. The group sat down near a line of military police (MPs) and federal marshals, often urging the soldiers to join them. The argument of the protesters was that they were not against common soldiers but against those making decisions to endanger the soldiers' lives in what the protesters believed was an illegal and unjust war. When night fell, numerous protesters burned their draft cards.

The event remained peaceful until, late at night, MPs and federal marshals were given the order to clear the steps of the Pentagon. Since the protesters refused to move, the MPs and marshals resorted to violence. Many protesters were injured; forty-seven people were treated at local hospitals, and numerous others refused or did not need elaborate treatment. The next day several hundred protesters returned to the scene, where most were peacefully arrested. In total, 647 people were arrested over the two days. Government officials and the media were generally critical of the March on the Pentagon, yet it provided a sign of things to come in the antiwar movement, a turn toward harsher protests, increased illegal activities, and violence. **See also** antiwar movement.

## Marine Corps, U.S.

The U.S. Marine Corps played a central role in the Vietnam War by providing a large number of the ground troops involved in jungle fighting. The marines also made up much of the first line of defense against possible North Vietnamese incursions across the demilitarized zone (DMZ). Consequently, the casualty rate among marines was significantly higher than casualty rates in the other U.S. service branches.

*U.S. Marines watch over Viet Cong prisoners of war. The U.S. Marine Corps had an active role in Vietnam, providing a large number of ground troops and the first line of defense in many areas.*

The first U.S. Marines, helicopter crews, arrived in Vietnam in April 1962, where they joined the expanding U.S. effort to support South Vietnamese military forces. The first American ground troops to arrive in Vietnam were also marines; two battalions of the Ninth Marine Expeditionary Brigade landed on a beach near Da Nang on March 8, 1965. The battalions were tasked at first with guarding a local air base, but their commitment grew steadily until the marines were the largest U.S. force in I Corps, the northernmost military region in South Vietnam. Within I Corps, whose top U.S. commander was a marine general, marines took part in both counterinsurgency efforts against the Viet Cong and more conventional bat-

tles. They were heavily represented in such engagements as the Battles of Dong Ha and Khe Sanh. U.S. Marines were also heavily involved in pacification efforts in the region such as the formation of Civic Action platoons in conjunction with their South Vietnamese counterparts. In 1969 many of their tasks in I Corps were turned over to either the U.S. Army or the South Vietnamese in accordance with Vietnamization. By 1972 few marines remained in Vietnam. Those who did included jet pilots, spotters, advisers to the South Vietnamese Marine Corps, and embassy guards.

Marine units in Vietnam, under the overall structure of the III Marine Amphibious Force (MAF), included two full divisions and a large aircraft wing. They were supported by a huge combat force consisting of, among other aspects, twenty-four infantry battalions, ten artillery battalions, and two tank battalions stationed with the U.S. Navy's Seventh Fleet offshore. Marine facilities in Vietnam included major bases at Da Nang and Dong Ha as well as a large airfield at Chu Lai. A total of 14,840 marines died in Vietnam, and 51,392 were wounded. **See also** Khe Sanh, Battle of; Seventh Fleet.

## Market Time

The name for the long-term operation to patrol the South Vietnamese coastline, mainly to prevent supplies from reaching South Vietnamese Communists by ship or boat. Under the operational command of the U.S. Seventh Fleet when it began in 1965, Operation Market Time was transferred in 1966 to the commander of naval forces, Vietnam. Lasting until 1975, the operation involved both aircraft and seaborne patrols using an elaborate network of bases, rallying points, refueling stations, and intelligence centers. Airplanes, for instance, flew from bases at Tan Son Nhut in Saigon, Sangley Point in the Philippines, and U-Tapao in Thailand.

The greatest challenge to Operation Market Time was to differentiate between potential Communist smugglers and the everyday fishing junks and other craft that plied the coastal waters off South Vietnam. To assist in the effort, U.S. Navy officials got permission from the South Vietnamese government to search any boat located within twelve miles of the coast. The effort was also supported by a South Vietnamese Junk Force, which was an arm of the regular South Vietnamese navy, and by the use of small craft such as gunboats and fast transports. As U.S. forces began their withdrawal from Vietnam in 1969, the operation was gradually turned over to the South Vietnamese navy. **See also** Navy, U.S.; Sea Dragon; Seventh Fleet.

## Martin, Graham (1912–1990)

The last U.S. ambassador to South Vietnam, serving from June 1973 to the fall of Saigon in April 1975. After serving at many posts in a long foreign service career, Martin became ambassador to Thailand in 1963, where he stayed for four years. There, he developed a strong belief in the importance of the American effort to stop the spread of communism in Southeast Asia.

After serving as ambassador to Italy, Martin was appointed to the Saigon embassy in June 1973, replacing Ellsworth Bunker. His brief was to convince South Vietnamese president Nguyen Van Thieu that, despite the Paris Peace Accords and the departure of U.S. troops, Washington, D.C., still strongly supported the South Vietnamese regime. In this he was only marginally successful, a record some have attributed to his gruff, straightforward personality and his lack of understanding of both South Vietnamese mores and the corruption of the regime. Nevertheless, Martin remained convinced that the Saigon government was strong and would stand in the face of military action from North Vietnam. He even disputed reports from his military advisers that claimed, as Communist forces approached ever closer to Saigon in March and April 1975, that South Vietnam was in great danger.

On April 21, finally recognizing the danger, Martin helped encourage Thieu to resign. Over the next days he quietly began to encourage nonessential U.S. personnel, as well as key South Vietnamese personnel who worked for U.S. agencies, to leave Saigon. Martin was concerned that too rapid a withdrawal would be a clear sign to the Communists that Washington no longer supported

Saigon. Events overtook him, however, and many South Vietnamese were unable to get away in time. On April 29, as Communist forces entered Saigon, Martin ordered the evacuation of all remaining U.S. personnel. He was among the last to leave, along with his wife and the embassy flag, early in the morning of April 30, having been ordered to stop the evacuation by President Gerald Ford. **See also** Frequent Wind; Ho Chi Minh campaign.

# Masher/White Wing

One of the first major combat operations in which regular U.S. ground troops played an important role and an early exercise in the so-called search-and-destroy strategy. Originally known simply as Operation Masher, the goal of the operation was to clear both Viet Cong (VC) and North Vietnamese Army (NVA) forces from a wide swath of territory in central Vietnam in Binh Dinh province along the coast. While the operation was already under way, U.S. president Lyndon B. Johnson asked that it be renamed White Wing, concerned that the earlier name's brutal connotations might garner negative publicity.

Operation Masher/White Wing included heavy forces from both the United States and South Vietnam, including massive air support. It began on January 24, 1966, and involved brief but intense firefights against both VC and NVA contingents. The overall plan was to drive the Communist forces, using assaults from various points, into waiting units from either the United States or South Vietnam. Then the Communists could be attacked from both sides. The operation ended on March 6, by which time it was apparent that most of the Communist forces had withdrawn from the area or been defeated.

Officially, Operation Masher/White Wing was declared a success, having cleared Communist forces from a wide

and important area in central Vietnam. The ostensible victors failed to press their advantage, however, and the Communists soon returned to infiltrate local villages. Meanwhile, critics claimed that the violence of the operation, most notably defoliation and air strikes, had produced tens of thousands of refugees. **See also** defoliation; search and destroy.

# *Mayaguez* Incident

The final confrontation in Southeast Asia in which American forces were involved and, historians argue, the last battle of the American phase of the Vietnam War. It took place from May 12 to May 14, 1975, some two weeks after the abandonment of the American embassy in Saigon and over two years after the withdrawal of the last U.S. combat troops from Vietnam. The incident began when forces of the Cambodian Communists, the Khmer Rouge, fired on the *Mayaguez*, an American freighter sailing in the Gulf of Thailand. Soon the Khmer Rouge took the vessel and imprisoned its crew, claiming that it was sailing in Cambodian territorial waters.

U.S. president Gerald Ford refused to negotiate over either the ship or its crew with the Khmer Rouge, who only one month before had completed their conquest of Cambodia. Concerned over complaints about his hesitation that had dogged him since becoming president, Ford was prepared to use decisive force to protect the crew, which was being taken, intelligence reports suggested, to Kompong Som (Sihanoukville), the major port on the Cambodian coast. The first engagement took place on May 12 when the *Mayaguez* began to move toward Kompong Som. Although American officials were unsure whether the crew was aboard, they took steps to ensure that the ship not reach the mainland. Fighter planes intercepted the ship after being dispatched from bases in nearby Thailand. After the planes fired across the bow of the ship, it changed course toward an island, Ko Tang, off the Cambodian coast. Ford ordered that no vessel of any kind be allowed to leave Ko Tang, and that evening, when some Cambodians tried to leave, U.S. forces prevented their escape. Ford now grew convinced that the crew was being held on the island, although intelligence sources could not confirm the fact.

On May 13 Ford approved a military plan to end the incident. It would involve three separate actions. One was an assault to retake the *Mayaguez* itself, conducted by helicopter. Second was a series of bombing raids on Kompong Som to prevent Cambodian reinforcements from reaching Ko Tang. The third element of the plan was the riskiest: an amphibious assault on the island by U.S. Marines. The evening of the following day, May 14, the plan went into effect. American forces quickly took possession of the *Mayaguez*, but after it was boarded by men from an American destroyer, they found that the crew was not aboard. On Ko Tang, meanwhile, the marines found themselves in a major firefight with a substantial force of Khmer Rouge fighters, far larger, in fact, than U.S. intelligence had believed. Despite the loss of forty dead and fifty wounded, the marines took the island quickly, although they soon found that the crew was not there either. The bombing of Kompong Som lasted until midnight, when President Ford ordered it stopped. His press secretary had earlier announced that the operation would stop only when the crew of the *Mayaguez* was recovered.

As it happened, the crew was located by a navy pilot flying a reconnaissance mission over the gulf. They had been transferred to a small fishing boat. The pilot, seeing their waving hands, notified his superiors, who then sent an American naval vessel to retrieve them the evening of May 14. **See also** Ford, Gerald R.; Khmer Rouge.

## Mayday Tribe

A group of anti–Vietnam War protesters organized by Rennie Davis, one of the Chicago Seven. Most members of the group were college students who were attracted to Davis's proposal to stage a huge act of civil disobedience that would shut down Washington, D.C., for three days. The group, known as the Mayday Tribe because their protest was to start on May 3, 1971, first issued an ultimatum to the U.S. government requiring it to accept a so-called People's Peace Treaty, which would end the war in Vietnam. The subsequent protest mostly resulted in over twelve thousand arrests, the largest number of arrests during any political demonstration in U.S. history. Because of a lack of other facilities, those arrested were kept in Washington's pro football stadium. Although these events attracted the attention of prominent antiwar congressmen who arrived to give speeches, the protest dissipated on May 5. **See also** antiwar movement; Weathermen; Youth International Party.

## McCain, John, Jr. (1911–1981)

Admiral in the U.S. Navy and, from July 1968 to September 1972, commander in chief of the Pacific Command (CINCPAC). A submarine commander during World War II, McCain rose steadily through the navy bureaucracy. He replaced Admiral U.S. Grant Sharp as CINCPAC in July 1968. The position provided him with command over all U.S. forces in the Pacific Ocean region, including those in Vietnam.

McCain was a strong anti-Communist who held the wide view that China was the greatest threat to the region. Vietnam, while important, was a relatively smaller threat. McCain supported President Richard Nixon's Vietnamization policy while also advocating intensified U.S. air bombardment of North Vietnam and, in 1972, the mining of Haiphong Harbor. McCain was accused by some, particularly army commanders, of failing to sufficiently coordinate his efforts with theirs, notably the ground war in South Vietnam. Complicating his understanding of the Vietnam situation, perhaps, was the fact that McCain's son, navy pilot John McCain III, had been a prisoner of war in Hanoi since 1967. McCain retired from the navy and left his post in September 1972 after the South Vietnamese army had effectively wiped out most of the Communist gains during that year's Easter Offensive. **See also** Honolulu Conferences; McCain, John, III; Pacific Command.

## McCain, John, III (1936– )

Navy pilot, prisoner of war (POW), and son of Admiral John McCain Jr., commander in chief of the Pacific Command from 1968 to 1972. The younger McCain proved to be a highly skilled naval aviator after being sent to the Vietnam theater of war in the mid-1960s. On October 26, 1967, McCain was shot down over North Vietnam and suffered serious injuries in his fall. North Vietnamese forces took him to Hoa Lo Prison in Hanoi, known by the Americans held there as the Hanoi Hilton. There, he recovered from his injuries to become one of the most respected POWs.

McCain was released along with other remaining POWs in February 1973, according to terms mandated by the Paris Peace Accords. After leaving the navy he entered politics; he was elected to the House of Representatives from Arizona in 1982 and to the Senate in 1986. Quickly becoming an influential senator, particularly on matters of foreign and military policy, McCain was a strong advocate of normalized relations with the postwar Socialist Republic of Vietnam.

In 2000 he sought the Republican nomination for the presidency. **See also** McCain, John, Jr.; prisoners of war.

## McCarthy, Eugene (1916– )

U.S. senator from Minnesota and leading antiwar politician. McCarthy's surprise run for the presidency in 1968 greatly altered the political dynamics of the United States during a year that marked the major turning point in the Vietnam War. As a senator McCarthy supported President Lyndon B. Johnson's Gulf of Tonkin Resolution in 1964, although he later maintained that he did not see the measure as one that supported war. As U.S. escalation in Vietnam proceeded in 1965 and 1966 McCarthy developed the view that the government had engaged the country unwittingly in what amounted to an imperial war. Along with other senators he began to make his opposition to the war known in 1966, advocating a cessation of bombing strikes against North Vietnam and a negotiated peace. By 1967 McCarthy was one of the most outspoken critics of Johnson's Vietnam policy. On January 3, 1968, he announced his candidacy for the Democratic nomination as president. Over the next months McCarthy, whose strongest drawing card was his vehement antiwar stance, attracted the support of young people across the country. These young supporters provided him with an extensive grassroots political base, and the candidate made a very strong showing in the bellwether New Hampshire primary in March 1968. Political observers were extremely surprised since his main opponent was a standing president, albeit one whose popularity was in free fall. McCarthy's success in New Hampshire suggested that the Democratic race was wide open, and Senator Robert F. Kennedy quickly announced his candidacy as well. President Johnson, for his part, announced at the end of March that he would not, in fact, seek reelection in the wake of the Tet Offensive in Vietnam, an event which suggested that, contrary to Johnson's optimistic assessments, the war was not being won.

After Johnson's withdrawal, and in the face of Kennedy's charisma and popularity, McCarthy's star faded, although many young people continued to support him. After Kennedy was assassinated in early June, the Democratic Party threw its weight behind Hubert Humphrey, who seemed to offer a better chance to win in the presidential race. Humphrey went on to defeat McCarthy for the nomination at the Democratic convention in Chicago in August while violent riots and protests raged in the streets outside. **See also** antiwar movement; Democratic National Convention of 1968; Humphrey, Hubert H.

## McNamara, Robert (1916– )

Secretary of defense during the presidential administrations of John F. Kennedy and Lyndon B. Johnson and a central figure in the course of American escalation of the Vietnam conflict. A technocrat with expertise in statistics and production control, McNamara was named president of the Ford Company in 1960. Soon after, Kennedy tabbed him to be secretary of defense, and he brought to bear his technical training and business background on defense policy.

McNamara hoped to revitalize American military operations by bringing in some of the strategies he had used successfully in the corporate world, such as greater centralization of authority and decision making and systems analysis. With Kennedy's blessing he also took steps to restore America's strength in conventional forces, as opposed to the massive retaliatory capacity emphasized by his predecessors in the Eisenhower administration. Thus was born the so-called flexible response capability of the American military. Kennedy proved to be so confi-

dent in McNamara's management abilities that the defense secretary found himself with an important role in not only military but also foreign policy.

McNamara proved to be inconsistent in his approach to the Vietnam War. While personally he wondered whether a military solution was possible, especially after 1965, he generally supported the requests of both the Johnson administration and General William Westmoreland, military commander in Vietnam until 1968, for increased levels of men and equipment as well as for air strikes against North Vietnam. He made his first visit to Saigon in the fall of 1963, along with General Maxwell Taylor. Although he had stated in 1962 that the United States had no plans to send combat troops to Vietnam, the visit convinced him that the United States had to support the South

*Robert McNamara served as secretary of defense under Presidents John F. Kennedy and Lyndon B. Johnson.*

Vietnamese in their struggle against a Communist takeover. At first, the U.S. military was to continue in its advisory capacity, although McNamara reported to President Kennedy that the United States might be able to reduce the number of advisers by 1965. That strategy was soon revised in light of events, namely attacks by Viet Cong (VC) forces against U.S. bases in South Vietnam and the offshore episodes that resulted in the Gulf of Tonkin Resolution of 1964, authorizing President Johnson to use necessary force in Vietnam. McNamara supported U.S. air strikes against North Vietnam in retaliation for VC attacks and, in March 1965, supported Westmoreland's request for combat troops by sending over the first official, regular American soldiers: thirty-five hundred marines sent to the American air base at Da Nang. Soon after he approved Westmoreland's request for 200,000 more troops as well as a call-up of reserves, a measure Johnson opposed for political reasons. Meanwhile, however, McNamara also let Johnson know in writing that he was not sure that a military solution in Vietnam was possible and that there was a reasonable risk that the conflict would extend beyond Vietnam.

In 1966 McNamara was implicated in a tactic that was to play an important part in coming years: the use of bombing, or threats of bombing, to force the North Vietnamese to the negotiating table. This tactic, which was supported by Johnson and other administration officials, inspired some resentment among military commanders. American generals already chafed somewhat over McNamara's top-down, micromanaging style and felt that political concerns interfered too much with their ability to fight an effective war. McNamara first got Johnson to authorize a stop to the bombings in December 1965 with the condition that bombings would increase if the North Vietnamese failed to negotiate. When the North Vietnamese

indeed failed, the bombing began again. However, McNamara and other officials protected the right to review all potential targets, implying that military commanders did not choose the most advantageous ones. In particular, by the end of 1966 McNamara was unsure whether the massive bombings of the Ho Chi Minh Trail were serving the purpose of interdicting the transport of equipment.

McNamara's inconsistency continued into 1967. In May he wrote to Johnson that he felt it was time for the United States to change its goals in Vietnam and did not approve Westmoreland's request for 200,000 more troops. He also tried to encourage peace negotiations and played a major role in devising the San Antonio Plan, which, again, promised the North Vietnamese that bombing would stop if they began meaningful peace negotiations. North Vietnam rejected the notion. In November, the defense secretary proposed to Johnson that the United States stop bombings, send no more troops, and turn the fighting of the war over to South Vietnam, proposals the president rejected. Meanwhile, in July 1967, after another trip to Saigon, McNamara returned to report to Johnson that he felt they would win the war if they stuck with the strategies they had put in place already. In February 1968, with the administration in turmoil after the Tet Offensive, Johnson chose to ask for McNamara's resignation. The defense secretary was replaced in March.

In later years McNamara himself appeared to realize that his centralized approach to the management of the American defense establishment may have been mistaken in some regards. As he suggested in a 1995 memoir, *In Retrospect: The Tragedy and Lessons of Vietnam*, the attempt to bring a system of order to defense and foreign policy (as well as their budgets) simply left him too busy to deal effectively or consistently with Vietnam. After all, the Southeast Asian struggle was only one of a number of other problems that were part of his responsibility, and his approach toward Vietnam may have left American forces greatly weakened elsewhere in the world. Far too late for the millions of dead in Vietnam, Cambodia, and Laos and for the more than 200,000 dead and wounded Americans, McNamara noted that "we were wrong, terribly wrong. We owe it to future generations to explain why" (McNamara, *In Retrospect: The Tragedy and Lessons of Vietnam*). **See also** Clifford, Clark; Johnson, Lyndon B.; Rostow, Walt; Rusk, Dean.

## McNamara Line

A plan announced by U.S. secretary of defense Robert McNamara in September 1967 to construct a "wall" made up of watchtowers, land mines, and electronic sensors to be built just south of the demilitarized zone (DMZ) in central Vietnam. Its purpose would be to alert military commanders of infiltrations of North Vietnamese Army (NVA) forces past the DMZ.

The McNamara Line was modified from a proposal made by Roger Fisher, a professor at Harvard University, to construct a barrier of electronic sensors that could be used to help stop the transport of supplies down the Ho Chi Minh Trail in Laos. At the heart of the plan, which was ultimately implemented by a group of scientists affiliated with the Defense Department, were electronic sensors dropped from aircraft that operated similarly to land mines. When the sensors were stepped on or driven over, they would emit a noise that could be tracked by an acoustic sensor. The acoustic sensor could then relay the data to a central computer, which would provide air commanders with the precise positions of transports along the trail. The commanders could then send in their bombers to interdict the transports.

Known officially as Operation Dye Marker, the plan to construct the McNamara Line across Vietnam just south of the DMZ began in September 1967. The construction ran into difficulties quickly, however, because of a major NVA offensive against the DMZ, an operation which, in effect, was the first phase of the later Tet Offensive. Preoccupied with the fighting, the forces building the line failed to complete it by the time Tet began in late January 1968. Soon afterward, American commanders diverted the sensors to the area around Khe Sanh, where huge numbers of NVA troops were massing for a diversionary operation against the American outpost there. Around Khe Sanh, as it happened, the sensors proved effective in alerting American commanders to NVA troop movements. The effort to complete the McNamara Line was halted after the evacuation of Khe Sanh since many officers suspected that, although the sensor technique worked effectively in tracking enemy movements around the center of a circle, as at Khe Sanh, it might be less effective when the sensors were deployed in a straight line. **See also** demilitarized zone; Ho Chi Minh Trail.

## medevac program

The rapid withdrawal of wounded servicemen from the battlefield so that they could receive medical treatment. The term *medevac* is formed from the beginnings of the words *medical* and *evacuation*. The efficiency of the medevac program in Vietnam greatly reduced the number of deaths from wounds among both American and South Vietnamese forces.

The value of medevac by helicopter first became apparent to U.S. commanders during the Korean War. That country's rugged terrain and poor road system made it necessary to bring out the wounded by air, and both medical helicopters and regular combat or transport craft removed more than seventeen thousand wounded by the end of the war. Vietnam, with its mountainous terrain, thick jungles, and lack of a front line, made medevac by helicopter even more necessary, and helicopters became the accepted means of withdrawing the wounded to secure areas.

In April 1962 the first specially modified medevac helicopters arrived in Vietnam. They were UH-1 Hueys that were equipped with up to nine stretchers and a variety of medical equipment. They carried trained medical corpsmen, or medics, who were kept constantly on alert for takeoff. In 1966 the medevac arsenal was expanded with the invention of a "jungle penetrator," a rescue hoist that could be lowered to the ground while the helicopter hovered overhead. Medevac missions, known as dustoffs, were responsible for removing 800,000 to 900,000 wounded during the Vietnam War years, and other helicopters no doubt removed thousands more. The system was so efficient that wounded soldiers could reasonably hope to be on a hospital table only fifteen minutes after takeoff. One statistic notes that, of those who survived the first twenty-four hours after being hit, only 1 percent died. **See also** Chinook; Huey; medical services; search and rescue.

## media and the Vietnam War

Thanks to widespread television, radio, and newspaper access, as well as to energetic and creative professionals, the Vietnam War was the most extensively covered war in history. This coverage was thought to have had a powerful influence on public opinion and therefore on political decision making, thus making the role of the media in Vietnam a controversial one. Some claimed that the U.S. government manipulated the media to serve its own ends, while others argued that the media helped to undermine the U.S. war effort.

At their greatest concentration in 1968, some five hundred reporters, photographers, and their staffs covered the Vietnam War, compared with only around forty in 1964. Not all were Americans; most countries with substantial media services sent journalists to Vietnam. Many journalists worked for specific newspapers, magazines, or news services, but others were "stringers," or freelance journalists. This total does not include the hundreds of military staffers working in military media outlets such as the newspaper *Stars and Stripes* or the Armed Forces Radio and Television Network. It also does not include the staff of the Joint U.S. Public Affairs Office (JUSPAO), the official liaison between the military and journalists.

Much of the controversy over the media in Vietnam stemmed from the different roles of military staffers and journalists. The job of JUSPAO and the military media outlets was not only to inform but to present a positive version of events in order to shore up morale among troops and ensure support for the war among politicians and ordinary citizens. Journalists receiving briefings from JUSPAO often noted discrepancies between these reports and what they themselves had seen on the battlefield. One common example was JUSPAO's description of a military encounter as a victory when in fact the enemy, usually Viet Cong (VC), had simply melted away, as was their tendency. Another involved the official inclination to ignore negative aspects such as large numbers of U.S. casualties or frequent VC attacks. These tactics had at least the tacit approval of President Lyndon Johnson and other top officials, and reporters began to call their daily JUSPAO briefings the "five o'clock follies." JUSPAO also tried to manage reporters by threatening to revoke their credentials if, for instance, they took close-up pictures of dead soldiers or interviewed the wounded without proper permission.

Reporters, on the other hand, were professionally sworn to objectivity in this era, to simply report on what they saw in Vietnam, and even critics of the media noted that field reporters remained consistently objective. Their reports often changed, however, during the editing process. In part, this was due to the necessity of shortening reports to suit news broadcasts or column space, especially in the new media climate when news had to be put out quickly. Some claimed, however, that editors and news managers had an antiwar bias and that they altered reporters' work to suit that bias. Alternatively, and since the media market was so competitive in the United States, editors and news managers may have altered reports to match shifting public opinion and therefore attract wider audiences.

Reporters themselves, meanwhile, were generally free to move about in Vietnam, and there was no attempted censorship on the part of military officials, although on occasion reporters complained of harassment from military police. Many battlefield reporters faced the same dangers as armed troops, and some of their names became well known: Dan Rather, Peter Arnett, Michael Herr, and Peter Braestrup were only a few of the reporters who built their reputations in Vietnam. A total of sixteen American journalists were killed in Vietnam and forty-two remained missing in action. This latter total included Sean Flynn, a photographer for *Time* magazine and son of the swashbuckling actor Errol Flynn, who disappeared in Cambodia in 1972. Dozens more foreign journalists also were killed or went missing. **See also** five o'clock follies; Joint U.S. Public Affairs Office; television and the Vietnam War.

## medical services

U.S. troops in Vietnam enjoyed the best medical services of any American military force in history, and the South Viet-

namese were also able to benefit from the expansive military medical apparatus mounted by the United States. At the front lines, wounded soldiers first received attention from medics, as they were known in the army, or corpsmen, as they were known in the navy and marines. Medics and corpsmen received special training in medical care, battlefield situations, and triage. Ideally, two medics accompanied each platoon. High casualty rates among medics themselves generally reduced that rate in the field. The skill and courage of medics and corpsmen helped provide U.S. forces with the lowest mortality rate of any American war; only between 1 and 2.5 percent of wounded servicemen died. Sixteen medics and corpsmen received Congressional Medals of Honor, and over two thousand died in combat.

Rapid medical evacuation also helped keep down the mortality rate. Medical evacuation (medevac) helicopters performing so-called dustoff flights were able to move severely wounded soldiers to hospital tables within minutes. The seriously wounded were taken to large hospitals in rear areas, as opposed to base camp facilities, or in extreme cases to hospitals in Japan, the Philippines, or the United States. Base camp hospitals were largely staffed by military physicians, who were joined at rear-area locations by large contingents of American and Vietnamese nurses as well as civilian medical professionals.

In the history of warfare more troops have died from disease than from enemy fire, and the tropical climate of Vietnam presented medical services with unique challenges. Thanks to preventative measures such as vaccinations as well as rapid treatment, few U.S. troops suffered from such tropical diseases as malaria, dengue fever, or various intestinal maladies. Hospitalization for such complaints was substantially reduced from

*Soldiers carry a wounded comrade on a stretcher through a swamp. Highly trained medics and corpsmen saved the lives of many wounded soldiers.*

levels in either the Korean War or World War II.

According to military records, 153,303 military personnel were wounded in Vietnam. Most of this total were lightly enough wounded to return fairly quickly to combat, another testament to the skill of medics and corpsmen. The remainder were seriously enough wounded to be hospitalized in rear areas or overseas. **See also** medevac program; search and rescue; women in the Vietnam War, U.S.

## Mekong Delta

An intricate network of rivers, canals, and rich agricultural lands that made up much of the southern portion of Vietnam. South of Saigon, it became a major center of conflict between the South Vietnamese army (ARVN) and its American allies and Viet Cong rebels, who found the labyrinth of waterways and islands an effective place to establish outposts. Indeed, during both the First Indochina War (1946–1954) against the French and from 1962 to 1966 Communist forces controlled much of the delta.

The Mekong Delta lay at the end of the Mekong, one of the world's great rivers. The source of the Mekong River was in the mountains of Tibet, 3,050 miles to the northwest. The river flowed through China and Laos before forming much of the border between Laos and Thailand. After entering Cambodia, it split into two major branches. One, the Hau Giang in Vietnamese, flowed directly into the South China Sea after crossing the Vietnamese border. The second, the Tien Giang, further divided into nine tributaries. Arguably, the South Vietnamese government never fully controlled the delta during its entire period of existence, and it was the site of some of the most intense fighting of the thirty-year Vietnam conflict. By 1974 most of it was under the control of the South Vietnamese Communists. **See also** military regions; Mobile Riverine Force; Saigon.

# Menu

The code name for the bombing of Cambodia, a plan devised by officials of the Nixon administration in early 1969. While Lyndon Johnson, Richard Nixon's predecessor, had refused to violate Cambodia's neutrality, Nixon had no such qualms. He also had access to hundreds of bomber aircraft, recently freed from bombing missions over North Vietnam due to peace negotiations. The ostensible targets of Operation Menu were the sanctuaries maintained in Cambodia by North Vietnamese Army (NVA) and Viet Cong (VC) forces as well as the Central Office for South Vietnam (COSVN), the mysterious and apparently mobile headquarters that coordinated VC activities with Hanoi. In time the targets were expanded to include Cambodian Communist insurgents such as the Khmer Rouge. The first attacks, code-named Breakfast, took place on March 18, 1969. Subsequent attacks were called Supper, Lunch, Dessert, and Snack.

U.S. officials managed to keep Operation Menu secret from the public for over a year. Even B-52 pilots did not always know they were crossing the border to drop their payloads because their radar navigators in the planes, who controlled the headings, were radioed new directions shortly before the planes reached their designated bomb sites. Secrecy proved impossible to maintain, however, and in early May 1970 the *New York Times* published reports of the bombings. By that time, in any case, the war had already spilled over into Cambodia after General Lon Nol overthrew King Norodom Sihanouk on March 18, 1970. Lon Nol asked for military help against the Khmer Rouge and Vietnamese Communists from Saigon officials, and the Americans also fell into line. A U.S.-supported invasion of Cambodia began on April 30, 1970. Along with news of the invasion, news of Operation Menu inspired some of the largest antiwar protests in U.S. history.

Operation Menu alone, meanwhile, dropped some 110,000 tons of bombs in 3,630 B-52 sorties between March 1969 and April 1970. By the time the operation officially ended under a mandate from the U.S. Congress in August 1973, 16,527 B-52 sorties had dropped 383,851 tons of bombs over Cambodia. Their impact on Communist sanctuaries was minimal, and the devastation caused by the bombing probably helped the Khmer Rouge recruit more fighters to oppose Lon Nol, whom many Cambodians saw as a puppet of the Americans and South Vietnamese. **See also** antiwar movement; Cambodia, invasion of; Khmer Rouge; Lon Nol.

# Michigan State University Vietnam Advisory Group

A group of American academic experts in such fields as public administration, economics, and sociology who were sponsored in the 1950s by both the American and South Vietnamese governments. Its task was to assist President Ngo Dinh Diem in assembling a functioning government. The group was guided by Professor Wesley Fishel of Michigan State University (MSU). Making their first trip to South Vietnam in 1955, the group represented a clear indication that the United States was taking a very direct interest in the political stability of the Republic of Vietnam (RVN).

The success of the MSU group was mixed, mostly because Diem and even American military officials decided not to follow its advice. It was unable, for instance, to set up an efficient civil service, corruption being a constant temptation to officials who saw the examples of Diem and his brothers. In perhaps a more telling example given what later happened, Diem as well as the U.S. Military Assistance Advisory Group (MAAG) rejected the MSU group's suggestion that the RVN establish an extensive network of police, divided into the popular forces and the Civil Guard, to defend the provinces and prevent Viet Cong infiltration. Diem and the MAAG decided instead to train and organize their forces for military action, thus treating the presence of the Viet Cong as a military rather than a civil problem. As it happened, of course, RVN forces had little success in either controlling the countryside or increasing support among local people for Diem's regime.

By the early 1960s some members of the MSU group had lost their faith in Diem as well as his brother Ngo Dinh Nhu and said so in published articles. Fishel, however, continued to defend Diem's authoritarianism on the grounds that the South Vietnamese people were not prepared for full democracy. In 1962 Diem removed his support from the MSU group because of the public criticism, and it disbanded. **See also** American Friends of Vietnam; Ngo Dinh Diem.

## Midway Island Conference

The first meeting between Nguyen Van Thieu, president of South Vietnam, and American president Richard M. Nixon. It took place in June 1969 on Midway Island, a remote American outpost in the Pacific Ocean, after Nixon vetoed a Honolulu meeting because of concern over antiwar protests. At the meeting Thieu hoped to secure further American support for his regime since Nixon had been a vocal anti-Communist throughout his political career. Nixon, however, had been elected partly on the promise that he would remove American troops from Vietnam; he was more interested in ensuring that Thieu would support the withdrawal as well as negotiations with the North Vietnamese to settle the conflict. The result was a series of misunderstandings on both sides. Thieu came away

from the meeting believing that the U.S. withdrawal would be slow and that Nixon planned to sponsor conferences between North and South Vietnam at which they would negotiate as equals. He hoped, apparently, that the result would be similar to what had happened in Korea in 1953, where the north and south were split by a line that was defended by the U.S. military. Nixon, on the other hand, simply wanted to inform Thieu of his plans for withdrawal and ensure that he had Thieu's support to begin negotiations with North Vietnam on behalf of Thieu's government. Thieu was also offended by what he saw as a number of slights at Midway, including the fact that he had to meet with Nixon in the presence of Henry Kissinger, the American president's national security adviser, whom he disliked. Nixon, for his part, was pleased by the outcome, sure that Thieu would not object to either a U.S. troop withdrawal or secret talks with the Hanoi government at which Thieu would be excluded. **See also** Honolulu Conferences; Nguyen Van Thieu; Nixon, Richard M.

## Military Assistance Advisory Group (MAAG)

The first U.S. military body to participate in the conflict in Vietnam. The Military Assistance Advisory Group, Indochina (MAAG-Indochina), was formed in September 1950 after U.S. president Harry S. Truman had determined that the United States should provide supplies to the French and their Vietnamese allies in their effort against the Communist Viet Minh in the First Indochina War. Until 1954 the organization remained concerned only with the proper requisition and distribution of supplies, even though American officials wanted to take a larger role in training a strong, independent Vietnamese National Army (VNA) in accordance with their larger goal of supporting colonial independence. The French refused, hesitant to see a too-strong VNA, until the military debacle at Dien Bien Phu in the spring and summer of 1954. At that point France formally asked MAAG-Indochina to take part in training and organizing the Vietnamese force.

Before the final French departure from Indochina in the aftermath of the Geneva Accords, many U.S. officials hesitated to give permission for training operations to begin for fear that U.S. soldiers might be drawn in to the still-continuing war. The new U.S. president, Dwight D. Eisenhower, however, was convinced that the best way to stabilize the South Vietnamese state then being negotiated in Geneva was with a strong army. In August Eisenhower approved National Security Memo 5429/1, which provided for U.S. assistance in helping to create a force that would provide security to South Vietnam. In October MAAG-Indochina was ordered to develop and implement a widespread military training plan for the South Vietnamese army. In June 1955, when French forces finally withdrew, the United States found itself in a state of affairs in which it alone was responsible for the further preparation of the South Vietnamese army. In recognition of the new situation in the region, MAAG-Indochina was renamed MAAG-Vietnam on November 1, 1955.

Over the next nine years MAAG worked closely with the South Vietnamese Defense Ministry and Joint General Staff. The large number of U.S. advisers tied to MAAG included personnel from the U.S. Army, Navy, Air Force, and Marines, and by 1960 advisers worked in tandem with South Vietnamese field commanders and combat units in their new war against North Vietnam. MAAG helped develop an overall strategy, however, that downplayed the importance of guerrilla warfare, which may have been the greatest threat to South Vietnam in the early 1960s. Instead, MAAG prepared for a conventional invasion across the demilitarized zone (DMZ) by regular North Vietnamese Army troops. In May 1964 MAAG-Vietnam was closed down and its responsibilities and personnel shifted to the larger Military Assistance Command, Vietnam (MACV). **See also** Military Assistance Command, Vietnam; Ngo Dinh Diem; Saigon Military Mission.

## Military Assistance Command, Vietnam (MACV)

The organization that controlled all U.S. military efforts in South Vietnam from 1964 to 1973. Technically, the Military Assistance Command, Vietnam, lay under the authority of the U.S. Pacific Command based in Hawaii. In practice, however, the MACV commanders exercised a great deal of autonomy and worked closely with the U.S. ambassador to Saigon, the secretaries of state and defense, and their South Vietnamese counterparts. The Pacific Command, however, retained direct authority over operations outside of South Vietnam proper, for instance the actions of the Seventh Fleet in the South China Sea or the U.S. Air Force in Thailand. The MACV commanders in chief, in order, were General Paul D. Harkins, from February 1962 to June 1964; General William Westmoreland, from June 1964 to June 1968; General Creighton Abrams, from June 1968 to June 1972; and General Frederick C. Weyand, from June 1972 to March 1973. Most American participation in the Vietnam War took place during the terms of Westmoreland and Abrams. First based in central Saigon, MACV headquarters moved late in the war to Tan Son Nhut air base.

Under orders from U.S. president John F. Kennedy, MACV was established on February 6, 1962. For the first two years of its existence, MACV performed mainly an administrative role and left actual military advising to its predecessor, the Military Assistance Advisory Group (MAAG).

When MAAG was overwhelmed by the expansion of advisers, from some five hundred in 1960 to over twenty thousand in 1964, the entire advisory effort was placed under MACV authority. MACV remained, however, a "unified subordinate command," in the parlance of military bureaucracy, under the authority of the U.S. Pacific Command in Hawaii. By 1964 it had responsibility over a wide range of military and military-related operations. Most obvious were the advisers working with various elements of the South Vietnamese armed forces, but there were also Americans involved in intelligence operations, medical services, communications, and other areas. When regular U.S. ground troops began to arrive in South Vietnam in 1965, they were placed under MACV authority as well.

The ability of MACV to conduct its military responsibilities was limited by the fact that it existed, ostensibly, to help South Vietnam defend itself against Communist aggression rather than win an American war. Saigon politicians and South Vietnamese military leaders refused to consider building a joint command for fear that they would then be accused of being American puppets. The solution was to form a Free World Military Assistance Council, which would produce an annual combined campaign plan. The council consisted of the chief of the South Vietnamese Joint General Staff, the top officer of the forces from South Korea, and the MACV commander. The combined campaign plans, the first of which appeared in 1965, did not provide an overall coordinated combat strategy. Instead, they broke up planned campaigns based on geographical areas over which the South Vietnamese, the Americans, the Koreans, and other Free World forces would have responsibility. The South Vietnamese retained overall responsibility for operations within the four military regions (Corps Tactical Zones I through IV), the main geographical designations under which all military forces operated.

As the war developed, MACV commanders and staff found that their task was political as well as military. The organization retained its primary responsibility of advising the South Vietnamese armed forces, which meant that MACV staff continued to concern themselves with the internal problems of South Vietnam. Indeed, the MACV commander also held the office of top adviser to the joint general staff of the South Vietnamese armed forces. Moreover, MACV worked closely with the U.S. embassy to develop and implement pacification programs. These goals and practices, to some minds, muddied the ability of MACV to operate as an effective military command.

Nevertheless, MACV remained closely tied with perceptions of the American war effort in Vietnam. Under General William Westmoreland, who like the other MACV commanders was also the head of the forces of the U.S. Army in Vietnam, MACV developed the strategy known broadly as search and destroy, a source of extremely bad publicity for the larger American effort. Westmoreland's successor, General Creighton Abrams, meanwhile, was designated with the task of overseeing the Vietnamization of the war. MACV was ostensibly disbanded in February 1973 after the signing of the Paris Peace Accords, but its headquarters at Tan Son Nhut remained in place, as did some of its operations. **See also** Abrams, Creighton; Military Assistance Advisory Group; Pacific Command; Westmoreland, William.

## military regions

The official names used by U.S. forces beginning in 1970 to denote what had been known until then as Corps Tactical Zones I through IV. The corps tactical

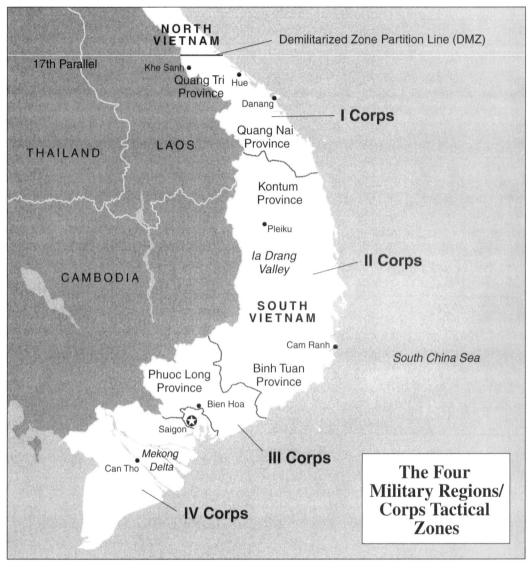

NORTH VIETNAM

Demilitarized Zone Partition Line (DMZ)

17th Parallel

Khe Sanh
Quang Tri Province
Hue
Danang

I Corps

Quang Nai Province

THAILAND

LAOS

Kontum Province

Pleiku

Ia Drang Valley

II Corps

CAMBODIA

SOUTH VIETNAM

Cam Ranh

South China Sea

Phuoc Long Province

Binh Tuan Province

Bien Hoa

Saigon

Mekong Delta

Can Tho

III Corps

IV Corps

**The Four Military Regions/ Corps Tactical Zones**

zones were a South Vietnamese designation, but U.S. forces inevitably used them as well. The four military regions separated South Vietnam into four areas. The division was first made by the Army of the Republic of Vietnam in 1961 following a model that was devised during the First Indochina War (1946–1954).

**I Corps.** The first military region, or I ("eye") Corps, stretched southward from the demilitarized zone (DMZ) in Quang Tri province to Quang Nai province. Containing the cities of Da Nang and Hue, as well as numerous American and South Vietnamese military installations,

notably the marine base at Khe Sanh, I Corps was the site of extremely heavy fighting during the Vietnam War. South Vietnamese headquarters was at Da Nang, which also became an important center of American installations.

**II Corps.** The second military region, or II ("two") Corps, was the largest, a region of central Vietnam stretching from Kontum province in the north to Binh Tuan province in the south. Most of what were known as the Central Highlands were located in II Corps, and like I Corps it was the site of heavy fighting. North Vietnamese strategists had determined that the key to defeating South Vietnam was to cut the nation in half, and they planned several attacks designed to do so across II Corps. At the western border of the region stood areas of both Laos and Cambodia through which long stretches of the Ho Chi Minh Trail ran, and North Vietnamese armies were well positioned to mount attacks into II Corps from the border regions. II Corps contained the strategically important city of Pleiku as well as the major deepwater port at Cam Ranh Bay. It was the site of the first major engagement between American forces and North Vietnamese Army regulars, the Battle of Ia Drang Valley in November 1965.

**III Corps.** Strategically, III ("three") Corps was the most important military region, since it contained the city of Saigon, the South Vietnamese capital, as well as the headquarters and bases of numerous American military and civilian organizations. III Corps extended from Phuoc Long province southward to the Mekong River, and it was bordered on the west by Cambodia. Military headquarters for III Corps was located at Bien Hoa, a massive base outside of Saigon. The region was a major target for both the North Vietnamese and their southern comrades in the Viet Cong (VC). Between them, they hoped to keep Saigon and its outskirts in a constant state of siege so that South Vietnamese and American forces would be kept there, leaving them less of a threat in the other regions of South Vietnam. The terminus of the Ho Chi Minh Trail was located in III Corps, as was the vast web of VC installations and hiding places known as the Iron Triangle.

**IV Corps.** IV ("four") Corps was located in the Mekong Delta south of the Mekong River proper. It was partly bordered by Cambodia on the west but was more a peninsula, surrounded by the South China Sea and the Gulf of Thai-

land. The major base in the region was in the town of Can Tho, the headquarters of one of South Vietnam's four army groups. There was less of an American presence in the region than in the other three tactical zones because of the nature of the fighting that took place there. Most of the combat was against small VC contingents or guerrillas from the North Vietnamese Army. Consequently, American forces in IV Corps consisted mainly of Special Forces groups, often used to prevent infiltration from Cambodia, and the various mobile riverine units.

Since the four tactical zones, and their respective South Vietnamese army groups, were already in place when American forces arrived in large numbers beginning in 1965, American commanders had to adjust to the arrangement. One problem that arose, at least from the perspective of some Americans, was that military operations were not coordinated across the four zones; instead, the respective South Vietnamese commanders at Da Nang, Pleiku, Bien Hoa, and Can Tho exercised a great deal of autonomy. **See also** Field Force I; Field Force II.

# Military Revolutionary Council (MRC)

The group of generals who ran the government of South Vietnam after the assassination of President Ngo Dinh Diem in November 1963. The council proved to be completely unstable and was never able to muster the strong support of the people of South Vietnam. At first, the Military Revolutionary Council consisted of twelve men, with General Duong Van Minh as head of state. Minh hoped that splitting authority among the twelve would prevent a repeat of the authoritarian and nepotistic rule of Diem. In January 1964, however, General Nguyen Khanh mounted a coup against Minh, who in any case had shown little interest in day-to-day governance. U.S. officials applauded the move, believing that Khanh would be a strong ruler. He enjoyed little trust among his comrades, though, and he settled for a compromise government in which Minh actually remained as a figurehead leader.

The instability continued throughout 1964, when South Vietnam underwent seven changes of government in which, it appeared from the outside, the members of the MRC were merely switching seats. Khanh remained an important official, declaring himself premier as well as, at one point, president. Other important officials included Minh; Nguyen Ton Hoan, a Catholic who led the Dai Viet, or Vietnamese Nationalist Party; and General Tran Tien Khiem. The MRC failed dramatically, however, to gain the support or respect of the South Vietnamese and faced rising challenges on the streets from such groups as Buddhists and students. When the pressure forced Khanh, who in the meantime had declared a national emergency, implemented strict state censorship, and drawn up a new constitution, to resign in August, the MRC met once again to construct a new government. This time the MRC settled on a committee of three men: Khanh, Minh, and Khiem. Khanh, however, effectively refused to serve and left Saigon. That autumn, South Vietnam threatened to descend into total chaos as riots continued and as units of the South Vietnamese army threatened to betray their government. The situation was finally calmed when a group of younger officers overthrew the MRC in December 1964. Among them were Generals Nguyen Van Thieu and Nguyen Cao Ky. **See also** National Leadership Council; Ngo Dinh Diem; Nguyen Cao Ky; Nguyen Van Thieu.

## mines

Explosive devices set in position for future detonation when tripped. Mines were used heavily by all sides during the Vietnam War. Among the most common were the claymore mines that were carried by U.S. and South Vietnamese infantrymen as standard equipment. The United States also dropped millions of antipersonnel mines from aircraft. These land mines could be tripped through a wire mechanism by being stepped on or having other pressure applied or, in some cases, remotely through electronics. Communist forces heavily employed larger tank mines that required greater pressure to detonate.

Another form of mining was water mining. Often using homemade devices, Communist forces used water mines throughout the rivers and along the coasts of South Vietnam in order to reduce both civilian and military transports. Countering such mines was a major task of the various riverine and naval forces in Vietnam. The only significant episode of the United States using water mining was the controversial decision in 1972 to mine the harbor at Haiphong, North Vietnam's major port, as well as other harbors.

Casualties from mines were heavy on all sides. In a notable legacy of the war, citizens of Vietnam, Cambodia, and Laos continued to suffer injuries and deaths from leftover mines into the twenty-first century, and mine-clearance efforts are expected to continue for decades. **See also** bombers; booby traps; grenades; unexploded ordnance.

## missing in action (MIA)

Military personnel whose whereabouts remain unknown, a controversial, unresolved legacy of the Vietnam War. When American participation in Vietnam ended after the 1973 Paris Peace Accords, the whereabouts of more than twenty-five hundred troops were unknown. A few were accounted for over the next years, but the vast majority, 2,483, were not. Historian Stanley Kutler explains in *The Encyclopedia of the Vietnam War* that about half of this number were "aviators who were shot down in remote jungle areas and were not seen parachuting to safety." These men, officially unaccounted for, were presumed dead but their bodies were not recovered. Along with the remaining 1,172 missing men they fell into the category of missing in action (MIA). Political advocates and popular movies led many Americans to insist into the 1990s that many of these servicemen were alive and imprisoned in Vietnam. The efforts of such organizations as the National League of Families of American Prisoners Missing in Southeast Asia also sought to keep the matter at the forefront of government decision making.

In the years since 1973 the governments of the United States and the Socialist Republic of Vietnam (SRV) sought to reconcile the MIA issue, and the United States made its resolution one of the necessary conditions for its official recognition of the SRV. At various points in the late 1970s and early 1980s the SRV returned the remains of MIAs to U.S. personnel, and in 1987 an official MIA mission under retired general John Vessey was allowed into Vietnam to search for more remains. These efforts resulted in a reduction of the total number of MIAs in 1996 to 2,143. More than sixteen hundred of these were thought to be in Vietnam, the remainder in Laos and Cambodia. **See also** prisoners of war.

## Mobile Riverine Force

A special force designed for operations on the labyrinth of waterways in the Mekong Delta from 1966 to 1969. Involving servicemen from the U.S. Army and Navy as well as their South Vietnamese counterparts, its operational names were the Mekong Delta Mobile Riverine Force or Task Force 117. The idea for a rapid strike force that could operate from the water was adapted from similar French experiments during the First Indochina War, and included not only a waterborne capability but also the ability to move ground troops rapidly. Ultimately, Task Force 117 could muster a force of five thousand men, with reinforcements or air support called in if necessary. They traveled on floating troop carriers or modified landing craft equipped with a range of weaponry supported by special boats ready for rapid refueling, first aid, and even as landing sites for helicopters. This "Brown Water Fleet" could cover as much as 150 miles in twenty-four hours.

Task Force 117 was based at Dong Tam, a town near the major Mekong Delta city of Mytho. After becoming operational, it was used in a number of attacks against suspected Viet Cong outposts in the delta. The force also played an important role in the Southeast Asia Lake, Ocean, River, and Delta Strategy (SEALORDS), launched in 1968. After the introduction of the Vietnamization policy by the new presidential administration of Richard Nixon in 1969, mobile riverine operations were turned over to the Army of the Republic of Vietnam (ARVN). **See also** Mekong Delta; Seventh Fleet; Southeast Asia Lake, Ocean, River, and Delta Strategy.

## Montagnards

The non-Vietnamese inhabitants of the mountain highlands that define much of the western portion of the country, beginning just north of Saigon and extending to the Chinese border. English speakers adopted the French word *montagnard*, or mountaineer, to describe them. Many Vietnamese, however, considered them racially inferior or uncivilized and referred to them by the word *moi*, which meant "savages." The Montagnards themselves, who belong to many different tribal groupings, including the Rhade, Jarai, Cham, Mien, and Kojo, began to refer to themselves recently as Dega

(Sons of the Mountains) in their search for an honorable place in either Communist North Vietnam, the southern Republic of Vietnam (RVN), or in the postwar Socialist Republic of Vietnam.

The Montagnard tribes belonged to one of two groups, both of which practiced a similar, seminomadic lifestyle involving slash-and-burn agriculture and hunting and gathering. In northern Vietnam the tribes were thought to have descended from the same Chinese peoples who settled coastal Vietnam; the southern tribes were related to Malay and Polynesian peoples, suggesting settlement from Indonesia. The Montagnards paid little attention to national borders, often moving back and forth across the frontiers of Cambodia, Laos, China, and even Thailand, all countries with their own populations of seminomadic tribes. Their isolation meant their customs and traditions remained distinct from those of lowland Vietnam, and there was little mixing outside a tribal group.

Despite this traditional isolation, the Montagnards inevitably were swept up in the long Vietnam conflict. As early as 1946 the French tried to enlist them to fight against the Viet Minh by promising them that their traditional lands would be designated a special administrative region. The promise proved false when, as a result of the 1954 Geneva Accords, the Montagnards in the south were designated as ethnic minorities under the authority of the Saigon government of the RVN. Indeed, the centralization of the RVN government under Ngo Dinh Diem (from 1955 to 1963) resulted in further setbacks for the Montagnards. Not only were their lands placed under central authority, they were often forced to resettle in new areas as a result of Diem's various programs to ensure the support of South Vietnam's peasants and prevent the growth of the Viet Cong. In 1955 some Montagnards

from the Front for the Liberation of the Montagnards, which became a highly organized interest group by the late 1950s, agitated against Diem for greater freedom for the highlanders. By 1964 the group had become FULRO (Le Front Unifié de Lutte des Races Opprimées, or United Struggle Front of Oppressed Races), prepared to add militant action to its lobbying efforts. FULRO staged a number of uprisings at South Vietnamese bases in 1964. The Saigon government, which hoped to gain the support of the Montagnards, responded not by granting them further autonomy but by instituting programs to improve their educational and social levels and their living conditions.

The traditional life of Montagnard tribes, meanwhile, was greatly disrupted by the war. Thousands of highlanders were killed in bombings or encounters on the ground, and casualties among Montagnard fighters were high relative to those of the Americans or South Vietnamese. In addition, hundreds of villages were abandoned or destroyed, and their inhabitants had to be resettled, often forcibly, in an ironic continuation of the land-use policies introduced under Diem. Historians estimate that altogether perhaps 200,000 of the Montagnard population of 1 million in 1959 were war casualties, and as much as 85 percent of the surviving population was resettled. Indeed, even after the fall of Saigon in April 1975 and the reunification of Vietnam under the Hanoi government, groups of Montagnards continued to struggle against the encroachment on their traditional ways and the seizure of their lands. **See also** Civilian Irregular Defense Groups; Hmong; long-range reconnaissance patrols; refugees.

## Moorer, Thomas (1912– )

Top naval commander from 1962 to 1974 and an advocate of strong U.S. military action against North Vietnam. In October 1962, after a distinguished career as a navy pilot, he was named commander in chief of the U.S. Seventh Fleet, much of which was stationed off the coast of Vietnam for the next several years. In June 1964 Moorer was named commander in chief of the entire U.S. Pacific Fleet. He played a key role in convincing President Lyndon B. Johnson to launch air strikes against North Vietnam in the aftermath of the mysterious events in the Gulf of Tonkin in late July and early August 1964. He also vocally supported wider air strikes over both North Vietnam and Laos, extensive seaborne intelligence and interdiction work along the Vietnamese coast, and the deployment of U.S. Marines. He differed strongly with many Washington politicians, who to his mind were both limiting and overmanaging the war for political reasons.

In 1967, after a stint as commander in chief of the Atlantic Command, Moorer was appointed chief of naval operations in Washington, D.C., and rose to be chairman of the Joint Chiefs of Staff from 1970 to 1974. In that position he had to oversee President Richard Nixon's withdrawal of American troops from Vietnam as well as the ongoing U.S. logistical and air support for the South Vietnamese. Throughout, and even after his retirement in 1974, he criticized U.S. strategies in Vietnam as not being strong enough. **See also** Navy, U.S.; Pacific Command; Seventh Fleet.

## mortars

Small artillery pieces that could be hand carried. Mortars were widely used by all sides during the Vietnam War. Each American infantry company was issued three 81-millimeter mortars that could fire a charge a distance of thirty-six hundred meters; 60-millimeter mortars and large 4.2-inch mortars were also available. Mortars proved most effective when

soldiers fought from relatively fixed defensive positions. Soldiers generally left them behind on patrols or search-and-destroy missions due to their weight, which was 132 pounds, and the fact that their activities were often already covered with longer-range artillery fire. North Vietnamese forces also used mortars, generally Soviet- or Chinese-made 82- or 120-millimeter weapons. **See also** artillery; light antitank weapon; M-14 and M-16 rifles.

## music and the Vietnam War

Rock and roll, the music of the young and indeed a new musical form during the Vietnam War years, provided the soundtrack to the war. Rough and irreverent enough to inspire shock among older generations, rock and roll music provided both solace to soldiers in the field in Vietnam and inspiration to antiwar protesters at home.

Until about 1966 music connected to the war effort, as in earlier American wars, was supportive of American policies. One of the most popular songs of 1966, in fact, was "The Ballad of the Green Berets," a paean to U.S. Special Forces troops written and sung by Sgt. Barry Sadler, himself a Green Beret. The political and cultural climate among the younger generation soon changed, however, and so did their music. Psychedelic rock, rhythm and blues, and folk rock emerged as popular counterculture genres and often took on a directly antiwar tone or encouraged various forms of protest and drug use. One especially popular song among troops in Vietnam was "We Gotta Get Out of This Place" by the Animals. "Purple Haze," by former 101st Infantry paratrooper Jimi Hendrix, was a direct reference to the purple smoke that was used in landing areas and an indirect reference to drug use. Some otherwise mainstream songs had a particular poignancy to servicemen, including

"Leaving on a Jet Plane," by Peter, Paul, and Mary, and "Galveston," by Glen Campbell, a soldier's musings on his hometown. Meanwhile, the antiwar movement developed its own soundtrack with such songs as "For What It's Worth," by Buffalo Springfield; "Universal Soldier," by Donovan; and "I Feel Like I'm Fixin' to Die Rag," by Country Joe and the Fish. A performance of the latter was a highlight of the Woodstock Music and Art Fair in August 1969, attended by up to 300,000 people, where opposition to the war in Vietnam was a prominent theme.

By 1970 antiwar sentiment had become mainstream and a number of protest songs found widespread acceptance. These included "War," by Edwin Starr, which chanted that war was good for "absolutely nothing," and John Lennon and Yoko Ono's "Give Peace a Chance."

Meanwhile, some singers, often from the country and western genre, released songs more sympathetic to the war effort. These included Johnny Cash's "Ragged Old Flag" and Waylon Jennings's "Okie from Muskogee." In the 1980s songs appeared reflecting a persistent memory of the Vietnam years and their effects. Most famous was Bruce Springsteen's "Born in the USA," which, despite its rousing chorus, sang of the difficulties faced by Vietnam veterans, and Billy Joel's "Goodnight Saigon." In 1989 Vietnam provided the setting for a very popular work of musical theater, which played for a decade on both Broadway in New York and in London's West End: *Miss Saigon*, by Alain Boublil and Martin Schoenberg, told the story of a Vietnamese woman ready to give up her Amerasian child to the American marine who had loved and

*The Woodstock music festival in 1969 provided peace activists with a soundtrack for the antiwar movement.*

left her. **See also** antiwar movement; film and the Vietnam War; literature and the Vietnam War.

## My Lai massacre

The most infamous of the atrocities committed by U.S. forces in Vietnam and the source of a scandal involving a subsequent military cover-up. The My Lai massacre was the work of C (Charlie) Company, First Battalion, Twentieth Infantry, Eleventh Infantry Brigade, Twenty-third (American) Division. The Americal Division was assembled from various components in 1966 and therefore suffered, some claimed, from weak leadership and lack of cohesion. In March 1968 it was engaged in operations to quell Viet Cong (VC) disturbances and beat back North Vietnamese Army (NVA) attacks in the aftermath of the Tet Offensive in Quang Nai Province in I Corps, the northernmost of South Vietnam's military regions.

On March 16 C Company was assigned to enter the hamlet of My Lai in Son My village, an area thought to be a VC stronghold. Till that point, C Company had not engaged in combat. Brought to My Lai by helicopter, the company found no active VC fighters there. Over the course of four hours, however, led by Captain Ernest L. Medina and Lieutenant William Calley, they proceeded to round up the women, children, and old men who were left in the hamlet and kill almost all of them in cold blood. In one instance, dozens of people were taken to a ditch and gunned down. Others were shot in their homes, which were then burned down. Members of C Company apparently also raped as many as twenty women and girls, some as young as ten years old, before shooting most of them

to death. The total number of deaths was somewhere between two hundred and five hundred, the uncertainty arising from discrepancies in testimony and disagreements over whether the massacre spread to a neighboring hamlet. The memorial museum that was later constructed at My Lai claimed 504 deaths.

These atrocities were not reported to higher authorities by Medina or his superiors, but news of the incident reached authorities via members of C Company who had refused to take part in the massacre and via the helicopter crews who ferried the company in and out of the area. An investigation into the incident only began a year later, thanks to letters to military officials and politicians written by Ron Ridenhour, an infantryman who heard about My Lai secondhand. The formal inquiry was headed by Lieutenant General William Peers, who spent a year collecting testimony from C Company, higher-level officers in the Americal Division, helicopter crews, and villagers from Son My. A number of officers were mildly reprimanded for covering up the incident, and thirteen officers and enlisted men, including Medina and Calley, were court-martialed for war crimes. Only Calley was found guilty, and his initial sentence of life imprisonment was reduced in stages until finally, in 1974, he was paroled by President Richard M. Nixon, evidently bowing to the sentiment of those who believed that Calley was being used as a scapegoat. Hugh Thompson, a helicopter pilot who reportedly stopped the killings by landing his ship between C Company troops and a group of fleeing Vietnamese, was given the soldier's medal for gallantry. **See also** atrocities; Calley, William.

## napalm

An incendiary weapon made up of gasoline thickened to a gel. Its widespread use in the Vietnam War, and vivid images of rice paddies and hillsides bursting into flames when struck by napalm bombs broadcast to the American public, inspired intense protest against not only politicians and the military but also Dow Chemical, the company that produced most of the napalm used in Vietnam.

Napalm was invented during World War II by Harvard University professor Louis Fieser. Fieser's team developed a procedure of thickening gasoline using naphthenic and palmetic acids, the first syllables of which gave the substance its name. Thickening allowed gasoline to both burn longer and spread more effectively. In the later months of World War II, U.S. forces began using napalm in bombs and flamethrowers.

During the Vietnam War, napalm was used by the American military, North and South Vietnamese forces, and the Viet Cong. The Americans and South Vietnamese employed napalm, by that time an advanced chemical formula that could burn even longer and spread farther than the original, mostly in aerial bombardments. The North Vietnamese and Viet Cong used it mainly in flamethrowers. Napalm proved to be devastatingly harmful to human beings, since the substance stuck to almost any surface and was difficult to remove. People caught in napalm attacks often died from burns or suffoca-

tion, since one of its effects was carbon monoxide–filled smoke. **See also** defoliation; dumb bombs.

## National Coordinating Committee to End the War in Vietnam

The product of an early attempt to build a nationwide anti–Vietnam War movement in the United States. The National Coordinating Committee (NCC) was originally formed in Wisconsin to coordinate a major protest, the so-called October International Days of Protest, in 1965. The primary purpose of the NCC was to act as a sort of clearinghouse for information about the activities of local protest groups. Any attempts by leaders to provide a more straightforward leadership role were stymied by factionalism among antiwar groups. Liberal groups, for example, hesitated to work too closely with more radical groups like doctrinaire socialists, and other activists disapproved of the NCC's refusal to hold demonstrations during the summertime because university students were mostly off-campus during those months. Nevertheless, as a center for information gathering and distribution, the NCC greatly helped organize both the October 1965 protests and an even larger Second International Days of Protest in March 1966. In the latter event, demonstrations took place in up to one hundred cities, involving more than 100,000 protesters, and the effort even spread to other countries. In time the NCC was effectively replaced by the Spring Mobilization Committee, which had trouble uniting the movement beyond large, uncoordinated events. **See also** antiwar movement; March on the Pentagon; Youth International Party.

# National Council of Reconciliation and Concord (NCRC)

A body created by the Paris Peace Accords of January 1973 to foster a peaceful reunification of Vietnam through slow, gradual means and, in the short term, to prepare for internationally supervised elections in which the South Vietnamese people would determine their own fate. The National Council of Reconciliation and Concord included representatives of the South Vietnamese government of Nguyen Van Thieu, the Provisional Revolutionary Government (PRG), which represented the South Vietnamese Communists, and a third group of neutralists.

The NCRC unfortunately accomplished little. Any decision made by one of the three representatives had to be ratified by the other two, meaning that each held effective veto power. Moreover, Thieu resisted the organization, having committed himself to a stance of not negotiating with Communists; Thieu and the PRG representatives even refused to stand in the same room to place their signatures on the Paris accords. The South Vietnamese president was concerned that the NCRC was simply a mechanism to increase Communist control over his regime and a way to force him to accept the blame for slowing down the process. In any case, the NCRC was quickly rendered irrelevant by renewed fighting between North and South Vietnam. **See also** cease-fire war; International Commission for Supervision and Control; Paris Peace Accords.

# National Leadership Council (NLC)

The formal name of the regime that governed South Vietnam from June 1965 to April 1975. The National Leadership Council was formed in the aftermath of a year and a half of political infighting among politicians and military officers, which had resulted in eight prior changes of government since former president Ngo Dinh Diem was ousted and assassinated in November 1963. All these governments were manned by a revolving series of generals, and were mildly subject to a body known as the Armed Forces Council. On June 9, 1965, after Premier Phun Huy Quat approached the Armed Forces Council to solve a personal dispute, he was forced out by a group of three young officers concerned with political stability and ensuring American support for their war against the Communists. These three "young Turks," Generals Nguyen Cao Ky, Nguyen Van Thieu, and Nguyen Huu Co, formed the NLC on June 12. It eventually expanded to include ten members, though it remained tied to the Armed Forces Council and largely constituted a military government.

The main figures in the NLC until the fall of Saigon in April 1975 were Ky and Thieu. Ky was initially elected premier, or head of the government, while Thieu, even though his military rank was higher, found himself in the largely ceremonial position of chairman of the NLC, or head of state. In September 1967, by which time the NLC had drafted a constitution, Thieu and Ky found their roles reversed as they were elected to the leadership of the nation on a joint ticket. Meanwhile, the NLC faced American pressure to increasingly liberalize its regime, a task made difficult by the demands of the war. Nevertheless, by the time American forces began to withdraw as part of the Vietnamization program, the NLC under

Thieu had brought to South Vietnam a political stability it had not known since the early years of Diem's regime. **See also** Military Revolutionary Council; Nguyen Cao Ky; Nguyen Van Thieu.

# National Liberation Front (NLF)

The political wing of the Communist insurgency movement in the Republic of Vietnam (RVN), with purported control over Viet Cong (VC) guerrilla operations. The NLF was formed in December 1960 in Tay Ninh province, South Vietnam, under the official name National Front for the Liberation of South Vietnam. By this time the Vietnamese Communist Party, the Lao Dong, had decided that a turn toward violent revolutionary action was necessary to overthrow the regime of Ngo Dinh Diem in Saigon and reunite the nation under the guidance of the Communist regime in Hanoi. At first, the NLF was a cover organization for a wide variety of interests opposed to both Diem and American intervention in Vietnam. Certainly not all were Communists; the first head of the NLF, Nguyen Huu Tho, was known to be not Communist in his sympathies. Over time, however, it grew clear that the organization was controlled by Communist cadres, who proved best able to mobilize manpower and resources. Diem, meanwhile, gave the organization the somewhat demeaning name Viet Cong, which simply meant "Vietnamese Communists." Strictly speaking, however, the NLF was the political arm of the insurgency while the People's Liberation Armed Forces (PLAF) were the guerrilla fighters.

From 1960 to 1965 the NLF managed a steadily rising series of attacks against the Diem regime and, after Diem's ouster in November 1963, his successors. It also worked to build up strong networks of support in the hundreds of villages of the RVN. In addition, the NLF won the sym-pathies of ordinary people through educational programs and other efforts, emphasizing a reasonably benign agenda of land and tax reform and anti-imperialism. To ensure a steady supply of equipment from North Vietnam, meanwhile, Hanoi officials expanded the so-called Ho Chi Minh Trail through the mountains and jungles of the border regions of Vietnam, Cambodia, and Laos. For Americans, the existence of the Ho Chi Minh Trail was proof enough that Hanoi was puppet-master over the NLF and PLAF. When PLAF fighters attacked American instal-lations at Pleiku and Quy Nhon in February 1965, U.S. president Lyndon Johnson decided that strong measures had to be taken against North Vietnam, or else the NLF would prevent a stable society from ever emerging in the RVN. Among the re-sults were Operation Rolling Thunder, years of massive bombing raids against the north, as well as the escalation of di-rect involvement in the fighting by Amer-ican combat troops. From 1965 until 1968, in fact, most American fighting was against the PLAF, or forces made up of both PLAF and North Vietnamese Army (NVA) troops.

The NLF enjoyed its greatest moment during the Tet Offensive of ealry 1968 when its forces launched operations against nearly one hundred towns and cities in the RVN. For a few hours NLF forces even managed to seize control of the U.S. embassy in Saigon, shocking American and RVN leaders who had never suspected that the guerrilla fighters of the Viet Cong were capable of mount-ing major operations against cities. The price of Tet, however, was huge, espe-cially in losses of manpower. On the battlefield, American forces quickly re-gained the upper hand after the initial surprise of the offensive, and historians claim that, after Tet, the NLF could no longer mount effective military opera-tions. Tet remained, however, a major psychological victory over both the RVN and its American allies. Indeed, Tet brought about a rapid reevaluation in Washington, D.C., of Vietnam policy, one element of which was to open peace negotiations with North Vietnam.

When these negotiations began in May 1968 in Paris, the NLF sent representatives to sit alongside those from Hanoi and Washington. In 1969 the NLF began to reform itself into an organized political entity or, as some put it, a government in waiting. NLF leaders began to assemble the Provisional Revolutionary Government (PRG), which, according to the state of negotiations, was to take its place alongside the sitting regime in Saigon or replace it entirely. Indeed, the true status of the PRG was to be a major sticking point in negotiations; North Vietnam insisted on its place in any future South Vietnamese regime, while South Vietnam considered it little better than a full takeover by the north. Meanwhile, on the battlefield, the losses of Tet rendered the PLAF small and ineffective, and most of the fighting from 1969 to 1975 was between the armies of North and South Vietnam. From the standpoint of many northern leaders, the ultimate victory over South Vietnam in April 1975 rendered the PRG, as well as the NLF, irrelevant, although a few NLF leaders were brought into the new government of unified Vietnam. **See also** guerrilla warfare; Provisional Revolutionary Government; Viet Cong; Vietnam, Democratic Republic of.

## Navarre Plan

A scheme devised in 1953 by French general Henri Navarre, the commander of French forces in Indochina, to bring an end to the First Indochina War and secure continued funding from France's patron in the region, the United States. Navarre's plan was to begin negotiations to grant independence to Vietnam, Cambodia, and Laos in exchange for their support for a broader war against Communist insurgents. As part of the plan Navarre hoped to build a substantial army from among the peoples of Indochina to fight alongside a substantial French force. The American government approved of the Navarre Plan and pledged several hundred million dollars in assistance. Events, however, proved it moot in 1954 when Navarre pursued another scheme, the ill-fated hope of drawing the Viet Minh into a decisive defeat at Dien Bien Phu. **See also** Dien Bien Phu, Battle of; First Indochina War; Vietnamese National Army.

## Navy, U.S.

The U.S. Navy's sizable role in Vietnam was predictable given Vietnam's thousands of miles of coastline, inland waterways, and geographic position on the South China Sea. Its most visible component was aircraft carrier operations supporting bombing flights; a total of nineteen U.S. carriers rotated in and out of the South China Sea during the war years. Outside of these operations, the responsibility of the U.S. Seventh Fleet, the navy conducted shore bombardments in support of ground operations, interdicted supply runs along the Vietnamese coastline, and engaged heavily in riverine combat operations in the Mekong Delta. The navy was also responsible on numerous occasions for providing amphibious assault capability; indeed the first ground troops in Vietnam, a contingent of marines from the Third Marine Division, landed on the beach via navy amphibious vessels on March 8, 1965.

Administratively, navy operations were handled by the staff of the Seventh Fleet offshore and by a small Saigon office that, among other things, provided coordination with the South Vietnamese Navy. Further up the chain of command, navy operations were controlled by the naval commander of the Pacific Command and his superior, the commander in chief of the Pacific Command (CINC-PAC), in Honolulu, Hawaii. According to custom, CINCPAC was inevitably a navy admiral.

Over 229,000 naval personnel served in Southeast Asia during the Vietnam War, and 1,628 navy men were killed in action, most of them in the so-called brown-water operations in the Mekong Delta. Another 934 navy men died of non-hostile causes and 4,178 were wounded. Fourteen navy men received the Congressional Medal of Honor. **See also** aircraft carriers; Pacific Command; Seventh Fleet; Southeast Asia Lake, Ocean, River, and Delta Strategy.

## Ngo Dinh Diem (1901–1963)

President of South Vietnam from 1955 to November 1963. America's commitment to Diem linked U.S. interests with the preservation of a non-Communist regime in South Vietnam; Diem's failure to create a strong, stable government, and his ultimate removal from power, encouraged a wider American involvement in Southeast Asia.

Ngo Dinh Diem was born in central Vietnam in 1901, one of many sons in a family of prominent Vietnamese Roman Catholics. He first entered politics as a provincial official in Quang Tri Province during the era of French rule, holding various offices from 1930 to 1933. These included, at one point, a subordinate position to the puppet emperor Bao Dai. After learning that neither he nor Bao Dai exercised any real power, Diem resigned his post. The French, for their part, blacklisted him from further participation in politics, a move that may have encouraged Diem's latent nationalism. For much of the rest of the 1930s, and even during the Japanese occupation during World War II, Diem remained largely in seclusion in the city of Hue, although he maintained contacts among nationalist groups. Diem had a powerful reputation among these groups not only because of his own authority and experiences but because of his brothers, several of whom were important officials in their own right. Ngo Dinh Khoi, for instance, had been a provincial governor before being ousted by the French, and Ngo Dinh Thuc was a powerful man in the Vietnamese Catholic Church. His most influential brother was Ngo Dinh Nhu, whose skills lay in organization, political intimidation, and intelligence work rather than in overt leadership.

After the Japanese surrender in 1945, Diem set out for Hanoi to try and convince Bao Dai to avoid making an alliance with the Viet Minh and its leader, Ho Chi Minh. Ho, as it happened, tried to convince Diem himself to throw in his lot with the Viet Minh, but Diem refused. Leading Communists within the Viet Minh later claimed that they had missed an opportunity to execute Diem. During the period of the First Indochina War (1946–1954), and with the help of his brothers, Diem sought to build a political base. He went to the United States in 1951, where he met with, among others, future president John F. Kennedy, then a young senator. He tried to convince American officials and the public that he represented an effective third alternative for Vietnam, a way out of either French colonialism or a Communist takeover. Many Americans, disliking both colonialism and communism, began to support Diem in his efforts. In 1953 he left for Europe, staying at a Catholic monastery in Belgium but making frequent visits to Paris, where he kept contact with other prominent Vietnamese expatriates. These contacts helped him win a secure base of political support, as well as funding, among prominent southern Vietnamese.

The First Indochina War was settled at the Geneva Conference of 1954. The emperor Bao Dai was ready to take the

*President Ngo Dinh Diem (front row, left) stands outside the Pentagon in Washington, D.C., during a 1957 visit to the United States.*

position as leader of the new, and theoretically temporary, South Vietnamese government in Saigon, but he realized that he needed Diem's important contacts. Believing, because of Diem's record of meetings with top American officials, that Diem enjoyed the support ot the United States, Bao Dai summoned Diem to his chateau at Cannes in southern France in June 1954. There, he asked Diem to be his prime minister. Diem returned to Saigon soon after, ready to form a government. American officials, fearful of Viet Minh power and a Communist takeover of all of Vietnam, acquiesced to the situation by sending Diem's new regime a steady flow of financial aid. In addition, the Military Assistance Advisory Group (MAAG) supplied Diem's fledgling armed forces with military advisers,

and the Central Intelligence Agency (CIA) operative Edward G. Lansdale, an expert in anti-Communist counterinsurgency in Asia, was dispatched to provide advice to Diem.

Confident in his American backing, Diem took steps in 1955 to shore up his personal authority, a necessary move since mostly only Catholics and wealthy landowners and businessmen supported him. Through a series of negotiations, bribes, and intimidating gestures, Diem was able to neutralize the powerful religious sects the Hoa Hao and the Cao Dai. He was then ready to deal with the last major threat to his authority, the criminal Binh Xuyen gang, which he broke up as the result of a series of street battles in the spring of 1955. Meanwhile, Diem also ousted members of Viet Minh cadres who had been allowed to remain in South Vietnam because of the Geneva Accords. Unhappy with the disarray and with the increasingly authoritarian rule of Diem and his brothers, Bao Dai tried to remove Diem from office, but Diem ignored his ostensible superior. Instead, he called for elections to be held in October. The result was an overwhelming Diem victory, in what was thought by most to be a rigged election, of more than 98 percent of the vote. Bao Dai bowed out of the picture, and Diem found himself unchallenged in Saigon. On October 26, Diem declared the independent Republic of Vietnam with himself as president. The new state of affairs was officially recognized by U.S. officials, and the planned elections of 1956 never took place.

For the remainder of the 1950s Diem continued to enjoy American aid and became one of the strongest American allies against the spread of communism in Asia. He played host to important U.S. officials, including Secretary of State John Foster Dulles and Vice President Richard M. Nixon, and he was also invited to Washington, D.C., where he was granted the rare honor of speaking before a joint session of Congress.

Diem failed, however, to ensure the support of the South Vietnamese population. He encouraged a mass migration of hundreds of thousands of people from Communist-controlled North Vietnam. Many of those who made the move were, like Diem, Roman Catholics. To reward them, and ensure their backing, Diem often granted these migrants land and other privileges. This alienated many South Vietnamese, who had come to expect land reform and other measures that would benefit them. In addition, Diem channeled the millions of dollars of U.S. aid that arrived in Saigon into private enterprises and into building a police and security force that would protect him, rather than protect the country against the

rising threat of Viet Cong (VC) guerrillas. Many Vietnamese were also frustrated by Diem's nepotism; his brothers exerted an undue amount of authority and reaped special privileges. Ngo Dinh Thuc, for instance, controlled huge amounts of territory and, in the early 1960s, as archbishop of Hue, took steps to alienate local Buddhists. Ngo Dinh Can, a younger brother, maintained a personal army and police force that kept illegitimate order over a wide swath of central Vietnam and engaged in the smuggling of opium and other items. The most infamous of Diem's brothers, Ngo Dinh Nhu, also maintained his own army and police force.

By the summer of 1963 Diem faced widespread social unrest in addition to a growing VC insurgency, and he continually resisted calls from John F. Kennedy, now U.S. president, to reform his government if he expected accelerated American aid. Among those who objected most dramatically to Diem's oppressive regime were Buddhists, who staged a number of demonstrations and, in several instances, held ceremonies in which prominent Buddhist leaders burned themselves to death in public as a protest. As a horrified world called for an end to the self-immolations, police and soldiers continued their violent crackdown on Buddhist protests. American officials were unsure how to react, unhappy with Diem but also concerned that he presented the best hope of preventing a Communist takeover.

Diem's downfall came fairly quickly. A group of South Vietnamese generals, concerned by the growing disorder in 1963, made plans to overthrow the South Vietnamese president. The plotters made their intentions known to CIA official Lucien Conein in the summer of 1963, who in turn told U.S. ambassador Henry Cabot Lodge. The generals wanted to make sure, by going through Conein and Lodge, that U.S. aid would continue if they overthrew Diem. Lodge, who had replaced Frederick Nolting as ambassador partly because of Nolting's uncritical support of Diem, relayed the news to the White House. Kennedy and his staff responded by saying that they wanted to give Diem a chance to get rid of Nhu, but Lodge, after conferring with other American officials in Saigon, reported back that Diem would never repudiate his brother. Moreover, Nhu might not go quietly, and troops loyal to him might cause even further unrest. U.S. officials spent much of September and October debating whether to support the coup, although Lodge, for his part, made it reasonably clear to the generals that the United States would probably not stand in the way.

The coup took place on November 1 when troops loyal to the rebellious generals seized key points in Saigon and laid siege to the presidential palace. Diem telephoned Lodge to ask him of the American position. Lodge pretended ignorance of any coup but in fact had likely helped it along by failing to deliver a last-hour message from Kennedy instructing him to stop the generals, at least temporarily. Diem and Nhu escaped the palace and went to ground in a Roman Catholic church in Cholon, Saigon's Chinese enclave.

On the morning of November 2, Diem contacted General Duong Van Minh, the leader of the coup. Minh refused to negotiate, although coup leaders had earlier told Lodge that the brothers would be allowed to survive and Diem himself perhaps allowed to return someday if Nhu agreed to go into exile. Diem then offered to surrender to another coup leader, General Gran Van Don, who sent a heavily armed contingent to arrest them at the church in Cholon. On the way back to central Saigon, both Diem and Nhu were killed. **See also** Buddhists and Buddhist protest; Kennedy, John F.; Ngo Dinh Nhu; Vietnam, Republic of.

# Ngo Dinh Nhu (1910–1963)

Younger brother of Ngo Dinh Diem, president of South Vietnam from 1955 to 1963. Nhu's ruthlessness and skills in both organization and political influence building helped allow his brother to exercise almost dictatorial control over South Vietnam.

Born in 1910 and, like his brother, Roman Catholic and French educated, Nhu began to demonstrate his political skills as early as 1953 when, in hopes of establishing Diem as the potential leader of an independent Vietnam, he organized demonstrations against the puppet emperor Bao Dai in Saigon as well as against the Viet Minh. In the process, he established important contacts with the Hoa Hao and Cao Dai religious sects and the Binh Xuyen criminal group, which controlled Saigon's police. These efforts continued in 1954, the year the nation of South Vietnam took shape, when Nhu formed an organization known as the Front for National Salvation. The front included the religious sects as well as other non-Communist nationalist groups. It called upon Diem to form a strong anti-Communist government, and Bao Dai, believing that Diem had the support of the Americans as well, asked Diem to be the prime minister of the new state under his leadership.

In 1954 and 1955, Nhu's intrigues helped his brother not only solidify his authority but also oust Bao Dai from any position of power. Using contacts established earlier, Nhu found ways to neutralize the sects by playing them off against one another, or by offering their leaders important positions within the South Vietnamese government or armed forces. He also used the army, solidly under the control of the brothers, to contain the Binh Xuyen. Along the way Nhu built up his own private police force and, after Diem called for elections to decide whether he or Bao Dai would be head of state, this secret police force was instrumental in ensuring that Diem received more than 98 percent of the vote.

Promises to the United States to support a more democratic regime notwithstanding, Nhu was a strong believer in a version of authoritarianism known as personalism. Personalism urged citizens to exercise obedience and loyalty to a single individual, the leader, who was seen as the embodiment of the state. Nhu formed a political organization known as the Revolutionary Personalist Labor Party, or Can Lao Party in its familiar Vietnamese version, to ensure loyalty to his brother. Using the Can Lao Party as a cover, Nhu constructed a vast network of secret police, labor groups, and intelligence operatives that reported on anti-Diem activities and served to intimidate opponents. In addition, Nhu personally maintained command of the Vietnamese Special Forces as his own private army. As the Communist Viet Cong (VC) insurgency began in earnest in 1959, Nhu took control over some of the first attempts to secure the loyalty of South Vietnamese villages. These were the agroville program and its descendant, the strategic hamlet program. Both tried to establish secure villages by relocating thousands of people. Corruption and mismanagement, however, as well as resentment among villagers who were forced to move, meant that both programs had little effect on the growth of the VC.

By the summer of 1963 Nhu and his brother were faced with a variety of challenges. One was the growing VC insurgency, which Nhu seemed to have few answers for despite his private paramilitary and intelligence networks and his influence over the armed forces. Another was increased pressure from the United States for political and social reform, pressure Diem resisted. Finally, public protests against Diem had grown widespread, especially among Buddhists.

Most Vietnamese were Buddhists, but the brothers were Roman Catholics who tended to reward their coreligionists and act with carelessness toward Buddhists. After a Buddhist protest in Hue in May 1963 was violently put down by Nhu's forces, several Buddhists staged public self-immolations as a defiant gesture. Nhu's wife, Madame Nhu, referred to these burnings as "barbecues" and her husband soon followed suit, saying that he would be happy to supply the gasoline for any further burnings. Such blatant and public insensitivity, as well as the mismanagement and brutality of the Ngo brothers in general, helped seal their doom.

In late summer of 1963, U.S. officials, who had been increasing their numbers of advisers and amounts of aid to Diem in hopes of halting the VC insurgency, learned of a plot among many South Vietnamese generals to overthrow Diem. They floated an idea that Diem might be allowed to remain in power provided that he deposed Nhu from his posts and that Nhu and his wife went into exile. It soon became clear, however, that Diem would never denounce his brother. When the coup finally came on November 1, Diem and Nhu left Saigon's presidential palace to seek refuge in a Catholic church in Cholon, the city's Chinese district. Negotiations came to nothing, and the rebels assassinated both Diem and Nhu on November 2. **See also** Buddhists and Buddhist protest; Ngo Dinh Diem; Ngo Dinh Nhu, Madame.

## Ngo Dinh Nhu, Madame (1924– )

The wife of Ngo Dinh Nhu and political hostess of South Vietnam during the presidency of Nhu's unmarried brother Ngo Dinh Diem from 1955 to 1963. Madame Nhu was born Tran Le Xuan in Hanoi in 1924. Her family was closely connected to French colonial authorities and had grown wealthy under French rule. A Roman Catholic, Tran Le Xuan was educated solely in French schools and was never able to speak Vietnamese fluently. She married Ngo Dinh Nhu in 1943.

After Diem had established himself as president, with the extensive help of Nhu's network of covert contacts and paramilitary groups, Madame Nhu and her husband lived in the presidential palace in Saigon. There she became, effectively, the first lady of South Vietnam. She had an extremely strong personality and quickly acquired a reputation of her own as an outspoken leader with an arrogant disregard for anyone outside her own family or circle of acquaintances; critics called her the Dragon Lady. Madame Nhu heavily castigated the United States after Lawton Collins, the first U.S. ambassador to Saigon, urged Diem to get rid of her. Consistent with the pattern of nepotism throughout the Diem administration, Madame Nhu found ways to place her family members in important jobs. Two uncles, for instance, were given cabinet posts, and her father was named ambassador to the United States. Using her personal authority, Madame Nhu also tried to implement a morality campaign, complete with harsh punishments for offenders. She tried to ban divorce, dancing, birth control, boxing, gambling, fortune-telling, and other potential vices. Most ordinary Vietnamese found this campaign, as well as her construction of a paramilitary women's solidarity movement, excessive, if not ridiculous.

Madame Nhu's outspokenness often brought embarrassment to Diem, but his entire political history and personal philosophy was built around family loyalty, and he hesitated to try to restrict her. Her insensitivity reached unprecedented heights during the so-called Buddhist crisis of 1963 when she referred to the ceremonies in which leading Buddhists burned

themselves out of protest to Diem and Nhu's oppression as "barbecues." Such statements, which were publicized worldwide, helped turn U.S. officials against the Diem regime and emboldened the generals who plotted to overthrow Diem. The coup came on November 1; the next day both Diem and Nhu were killed. Madame Nhu was in Los Angeles at the time, and in later years she retreated into exile in Rome. **See also** Buddhists and Buddhist protest; Ngo Dinh Diem; Ngo Dinh Nhu; women in the Vietnam War, Vietnamese.

# Nguyen Cao Ky (1930– )

Leading South Vietnamese military and political official, and head of the government in Saigon from 1965 to 1967. After training as a military pilot in France, Ky took up posts in the South Vietnamese Air Force (SVAF) after the creation of South Vietnam in 1954. By 1960 he was commander at Tan Son Nhut air force base in Saigon, where he worked with American advisers organizing covert missions into North Vietnam. During the November 1963 coup that overthrew South Vietnamese president Ngo Dinh Diem, Ky ensured the support of the SVAF for the plotters, and he was rewarded with promotions to brigadier general and commander of the entire SVAF.

Ky went on to play a key role in the political intrigues that resulted in nine changes of government in Saigon during 1964 and 1965, a period that also saw him promoted to air vice marshal. In June 1965, along with Generals Nguyen Van Thieu and Nguyen Huu Co, Ky announced the formation of the National Leadership Council (NLC), a body that would rule South Vietnam until its fall in April 1975. The so-called Armed Forces Council, which exercised great influence in Saigon, subsequently named the thirty-four-year-old Ky premier, or head of the government, as chief executive of the

NLC. Thieu, who technically outranked Ky, was placed in the position of head of state, a comparatively powerless job.

As premier, Ky had the responsibility of restoring political and social stability to South Vietnam while continuing to fight a war against Viet Cong (VC) insurgents and the North Vietnamese Army (NVA). By this time, fighting the war also meant managing American aid and advice, and the Americans demanded the liberalization of the South Vietnamese state. Ky's responses to these challenges included an anticorruption campaign and various social welfare measures ranging from land reform to school building. Along with Thieu, he also promised a constitution that would provide for free elections and the rule of law. Meanwhile, however, Ky placed various restrictions on civilian freedoms, including limiting freedom of the press. He also allowed his national police to operate with brutality and outside the law to maintain order and reduce VC activities.

The greatest threat to Ky's authority came during a renewed uprising among Buddhists, a group that had been instrumental in creating the circumstances leading to Diem's ouster in 1963. In March 1966, Ky forced General Nguyen Chanh Thi, who led the South Vietnamese army in I Corps, the northernmost military region, to accept exile to the United States. Ky was afraid that Thi had grown too powerful. In response, both Buddhist leaders and students staged demonstrations in Hue and Da Nang, the two largest cities in the region. Thi decided that such gestures were a measure of support for him, and he withdrew his offer to go into exile. As tensions escalated, Buddhist leaders began to demand that Ky step down. They also participated in protests involving, as they had against Diem three years earlier, self-immolations. Even army officers began to express their sympathy for Buddhist de-

mands and for General Thi. Ky's response, however, was a violent crackdown against both Buddhist demonstrators and any rebels in the army. U.S. forces supported Ky in this effort, since they had decided that I Corps had to remain stable for the purposes of conducting the war against the Communists.

The new South Vietnamese constitution was completed in March 1967. The first elections under the constitution were held in September. In these elections Ky found that his position with regard to Thieu had been flipped. Rather than run in opposition to the popular Thieu, who still outranked him, Ky agreed to run as the vice presidential candidate on a joint ticket. The two men received 35 percent of the vote, which was enough to guarantee them victory on a slate that included ten other candidates. As before, however, the two made up an uneasy match. Ky criticized Thieu, later, for being unwilling to accept the unsavory responsibilities that went along with power and he also accused Thieu of being involved in the drug trade. Meanwhile, Ky found his political power being steadily reduced.

In 1971, during a second round of elections, Ky chose not to run against Thieu after Thieu made an attempt to bar him from office. He returned instead to the SVAF, where he continued to serve as air marshal. In early April 1975 he went to Saigon to stage a rally at the U.S. embassy along with dozens of other officers, pledging to never leave Vietnam. They perhaps hoped that their gesture would inspire an American response. But it was to no avail, and on April 29, as North Vietnamese forces surrounded the city, he escaped on a commandeered helicopter to a U.S. Navy vessel. Afterward he settled in Los Angeles and published, in 1976, a memoir titled *Twenty Years and Twenty Days*. **See also** National Leadership Council; Nguyen Van Thieu; Vietnam, Republic of.

# Nguyen Ngoc Loan
# (1921–1998)

Brigadier general in the South Vietnamese Air Force and director of national police from 1966 to 1968. In June 1967 General Nguyen Cao Ky, at that point premier, chose Loan to be a sort of enforcer and influence builder in the Saigon region, working to provide Ky with a solid power base and reduce the activities of the Viet Cong (VC). Loan and his police apparently worked effectively, greatly curtailing VC activity in a city where up to forty attacks per month took place. Loan was not afraid to operate outside the law, using both police terror and opium trafficking to establish control of the streets. He became notorious during the Tet Offensive of 1968 when photographers captured him summarily executing a VC suspect with a gunshot to the head. The footage of the shooting was shown the world over, and a still photograph of the event remained one of the enduring images of the Vietnam War. It was taken by antiwar protesters as a sign of the brutal nature of the Saigon regime, but others maintained in Loan's defense that the vigilante execution was justified; Loan's victim had himself just shot and killed a South Vietnamese man and his family.

Loan was allegedly wounded in an engagement with VC fighters just outside Saigon in May 1968, and he faded from the scene, ultimately retiring to Virginia. **See also** atrocities; Nguyen Cao Ky; Tet Offensive; Vietnam, Republic of.

## Nguyen Thi Binh (1927– )

The most visible South Vietnamese Communist during the Vietnam War. Madame Binh, as she became known worldwide, served as diplomat for the National Liberation Front (NLF), the political wing of the Viet Cong insurrection, from 1962 to 1969 and as foreign minister to the Provi-

sional Revolutionary Government (PRG), the NLF's successor, from 1969 to 1973.

As a diplomat for the NLF, Binh traveled around the world to publicize the cause of South Vietnamese communism and national reunification. She became a familiar figure in many Western countries and certainly the most well-known spokesperson for the NLF. In 1969 the PRG sent her, as foreign minister, to Paris, where peace negotiations among the North Vietnamese, South Vietnamese, and Americans were under way. As the official PRG representative, Binh sought to include the PRG in any potential new regime in South Vietnam. This proved to be a major sticking point in negotiations, since South Vietnamese president Nguyen Van Thieu did not want to share his power with Communists. She also tried to ensure that any release of American prisoners of war would coincide with the release of political prisoners held by the Saigon regime. When the Paris Peace Accords were finally settled in January 1973, Binh signed on behalf of the PRG, although Thieu refused to sign at the same time. After the reunification of Vietnam and the creation of the Socialist Republic of Vietnam in 1976, Binh went on to be one of the few southern officials to hold important posts in the Hanoi government. One of these was the vice presidency, in the early 1990s. **See also** National Liberation Front; Provisional Revolutionary Government; women in the Vietnam War, Vietnamese.

## Nguyen Thi Dinh (1920–1992)

Top South Vietnamese Communist political and military leader. Nguyen Thi Dinh first appeared in the Vietnamese Communist movement when, as a young woman in 1944, she joined the Viet Minh, taking part in at least one uprising. In 1946, as a member of a revolutionary women's union, she traveled to North Vietnam to seek Ho Chi Minh's aid in fighting the war against the French in the south. She remained deeply involved with the Viet Minh effort during the First Indochina War (1946–1954), supervising weapons shipments, disbursing financial aid, and mobilizing villagers. After the Geneva Accords split Vietnam into two in 1954, she remained in the south and kept her hand in Communist guerrilla activities, mostly in Ben Tre province, while keeping close ties with the Hanoi regime.

In 1960 Dinh played a part in organizing a major uprising against the South Vietnamese regime of Ngo Dinh Diem known as the Dong Khoi uprising. She took advantage of the opportunity to form the so-called Long-Haired Army, a group of mostly South Vietnamese women revolutionaries. Their tasks were to organize opposition to Diem and urge South Vietnamese soldiers to desert. By guiding such activities, Dinh proved capable of both the political and military struggle that Hanoi's version of communism demanded. Her abilities continued to lead her into important posts. She helped form the National Liberation Front and, in 1963, became a member of the Central Committee of the Lao Dong, the Vietnamese Communist Party. During the subsequent years she both continued the political struggle and helped organize the military activities of the Viet Cong.

After the Vietnam War Dinh found herself somewhat marginalized, although she remained a member of the Central Committee. She mostly served on posts concerned with the Socialist Republic of Vietnam's women's movement. **See also** Lao Dong; Viet Cong; women in the Vietnam War, Vietnamese.

## Nguyen Van Thieu (1923–2001)

President of South Vietnam from 1967 to 1975. Nguyen Van Thieu was born on April 5, 1923, in Ninh Thuan Province in central Vietnam. A strong nationalist, he joined Ho Chi Minh's Viet Minh in 1945 but left soon after, disheartened by the Viet Minh's ruthlessness and Communist leanings. During the first years of the First Indochina War (1946–1954), he fought with the Vietnamese forces allied with the French. In 1949 he graduated from the Vietnamese National Military Academy and soon after attended an infantry school in France. He was therefore well positioned to take an important post when the French and their Vietnamese allies formed the Vietnamese National Army (VNA) in 1949. Thieu spent the remainder of the war as an infantry commander.

After the formation of the Republic of Vietnam (RVN, or South Vietnam) in 1954, Thieu became the head of the nation's military academy. In 1956 he traveled to the United States, and in 1957 he graduated from the U.S. Command and General Staff College at Fort Leavenworth, Kansas. Soon after, he returned to Vietnam to resume command over infantry units, rising rapidly in rank and responsibility. By 1962 Thieu was a colonel in command of the South Vietnamese army's Fifth Infantry Division near Saigon. He had also begun, like many top officers, to dabble in politics, becoming a member of Ngo Dinh Nhu's Can Lao Party.

The events of 1963, however, which included an expansion of the war, widespread social unrest, and a wavering American commitment, convinced him to turn away from Nhu and his brother, RVN president Ngo Dinh Diem. Thieu played a significant role in the coup d'etat that overthrew Diem on November 1, 1963, by ensuring that the Fifth Infantry supported the coup and by leading a contingent which neutralized Diem's bodyguard forces. Soon after, he was promoted to general and given command over all Vietnamese forces in IV Corps, the military designation for the Mekong Delta region.

By 1964 the new military government of South Vietnam was in disarray, and Thieu began to involve himself with Air Marshal Nguyen Cao Ky, another young officer. Thieu supported Ky in a December 1964 coup that produced a civilian government supported by a so-called Armed Forces Council. Another coup, in June 1965, resulted in the National Leadership Council to run the RVN, consisting of ten military leaders. Thieu was named chief of state, or head of state, while Ky was named premier, or head of the government.

Both Thieu and Ky faced continual pressure from American officials to turn South Vietnam into a true democracy rather than an unstable military dictatorship, and by 1967 the two, who did not personally like each other, responded by producing a constitution and holding elections. In the elections Thieu was elected president of the RVN while Ky was elected vice president. Thieu was reelected in a 1971 election, although that year Ky chose not to accompany him on the ticket. Ky, however, retained a significant base of support and a powerful reputation, partly because he had helped lead the South Vietnamese effort during the 1968 Tet Offensive while Thieu was away in Europe.

By the end of 1968 Thieu was the unchallenged leader of the RVN. He faced substantial challenges. One of these was continued allegations of corruption, charges he never satisfactorily resolved despite various anticorruption campaigns. Another challenge was to find ways to ensure the support of the South Vietnamese population while, in contrast to the continuing urges of the Americans, slowing the spread of democracy for fear it would make South Vietnamese Communists too powerful by giving them a voice. To that end he undertook a major land reform effort, giving land to tens of thousands of peasants and reducing the oppressive measures used by many landlords. He also gave a great deal of autonomy to such local leaders as village headmen, who were given control, for instance, over popular and regional forces.

Beginning in 1969, Thieu was faced with the challenge of Vietnamization, the American plan to withdraw U.S. troops and turn the war over to South Vietnamese forces. Thieu had to find ways to maintain levels of personnel and ensure sufficient equipment and supplies. These needs led to higher taxes, to a more extensive draft, and to the calling up of almost all adult men in the RVN to serve in either the military or local defense forces. Unsurprisingly, these moves inspired resentment and resistance, and may well have enlarged and strengthened the National Liberation Front (NLF), the overall South Vietnamese Communist movement. Meanwhile, Thieu's heavy-handed approach to the 1971 election inspired many to accuse him of seeking to set up a military dictatorship rather than a functioning democracy.

Thieu's greatest challenge, however, may have been how to deal with the peace negotiations that began between North Vietnam and the United States in May 1968 and were to continue, in fits and starts, until the signing of the Paris Peace Accords in January 1973. Thieu refused to send a representative to the first negotiating sessions, hoping instead for direct talks between his government and Hanoi. In time he was convinced by U.S. president Richard M. Nixon to participate in the talks. Nixon used both the carrot and the stick in dealing with Thieu. He threatened Thieu with a cutoff of U.S. military and financial aid if the South Vietnamese president refused to take part in negotiations while assuring Thieu, at vital points, that the United States would continue to protect his regime, mostly with overwhelming airpower but also with economic aid, if the need arose.

Over the years, in fact, Nixon and Thieu entered an informal agreement that, as Thieu understood it, the United States would continue to support the RVN even after almost all American ground troops had departed.

Peace negotiations, however, remained very difficult. When a peace settlement seemed imminent in 1972, Thieu was reluctant to accept either a continued North Vietnamese Army presence in the south or a Saigon government that would include representatives of the Provisional Revolutionary Government (PRG), the political wing of the NLF. He was strengthened in this view by the fact that his armed forces, along with massive U.S. air support, had fended off the 1972 Easter Offensive mounted by North Vietnam. Thieu finally agreed to what became the Paris Peace Accords of 1973 only after Nixon, in an aside, had promised him continued American aid in the event of a North Vietnamese violation of the accords and after the Nixon administration, in Operation Enhance Plus, helped turn the South Vietnamese army into one of the best-equipped military forces on Earth, with the fourth largest air force.

Thieu's regime, and an independent South Vietnam, might conceivably have survived the departure of American forces as a result of the Paris Peace Accords. Though the North Vietnamese and the PRG continued to refer to him as a puppet of the Americans, Thieu actually strengthened his hold over the RVN throughout 1973. His forces regained some territory earlier taken by Communist forces and took steps to ensure loyalty among village leaders.

*Nguyen Van Thieu addresses a crowd upon his arrival in Honolulu, Hawaii. President Lyndon B. Johnson stands by his side.*

Two larger developments, however, converged to doom Thieu's regime. The first was a growing shortage of military personnel and both military and civilian supplies, including food. The matériel provided in Operation Enhance Plus was being used up rapidly, and Thieu's army suffered heavy losses to both battle and desertion. Second, the U.S. Congress, sick of the Vietnam conflict, refused to allow Nixon to continue American support to Thieu even though North Vietnam had blatantly violated elements of the Paris Accords. When Nixon resigned from the presidency in August 1974, Thieu was extremely distressed, suspecting that there was now little chance that the United States would make much of an effort to help him. His fears were confirmed when North Vietnam mounted its final offensive that November, and the new U.S. president, Gerald R. Ford, sent him no assistance. Meanwhile, his regime threatened to collapse from within. From among the population of Saigon, a large antigovernment movement arose known as the People's Anti-Corruption Movement. In addition, many RVN military commanders felt abandoned by their government when, in the face of the North Vietnamese offensive, Thieu decided to abandon large amounts of territory and failed to communicate his intentions.

Thieu resigned as president on April 21, 1975, as four North Vietnamese regiments closed in on Saigon. He boarded a plane for Taiwan on April 26 along with his family and tons of possessions, and he lived quietly in exile in London and then Boston until his death in September 2001. **See also** Frequent Wind; Nguyen Cao Ky; Paris negotiations; Vietnam, Republic of.

# Nixon, Richard M. (1913–1994)

President of the United States from January 1969 until August 1974 and thus director of the deescalation and withdrawal of U.S. forces from Vietnam. Richard Milhous Nixon was born in Whittier, California, on January 9, 1913. He graduated from Whittier College in 1934 and earned a law degree from Duke University in 1937. After serving in the navy during World War II, Nixon was elected to the House of Representatives in 1946 and to the Senate in 1950. He acquired a reputation, meanwhile, as an aggressive anti-Communist.

As vice president under Dwight D. Eisenhower from 1952 to 1960 Nixon continued to take a hard line against Communist expansion. After the Geneva Accords of 1954 divided Indochina into four separate countries, Nixon maintained that communism had to be contained to North Vietnam (the Democratic Republic of Vietnam, or DRV) to protect Southeast Asia. He took his first trip to the region in 1956, meeting South Vietnamese president Ngo Dinh Diem. Nixon came away from the meeting convinced that, despite his authoritarian tendencies, Diem was a good bet to build a stable, democratic regime in South Vietnam (the Republic of Vietnam, or RVN).

Nixon suffered two crushing political defeats in the early 1960s, losing the presidential election to John F. Kennedy in 1960 and the California governor's race in 1962. Over the next years he entered into what he considered a political exile, although he remained interested in events in Vietnam and even visited Saigon to express his support for the RVN and for U.S. military intervention. In 1968, in an atmosphere of strident debate over Vietnam and what many saw as the decline of law and order in the United States because of antiwar protests and other civil disturbances, Nixon became the Republican nominee for president once again. He promised to restore law and order while pledging that he had a "secret plan" for ending the war in Vietnam. In November he won a close race over Democratic nominee Hubert Humphrey.

As president, Nixon drastically changed U.S. policy toward the Vietnam conflict, although he later noted that these changes were not part of some earlier "secret plan." Along with National Security Adviser (later Secretary of State) Henry Kissinger and other men, Nixon developed a complex policy that he hoped would serve a number of foreign policy and domestic goals. In order to dampen domestic criticism for what, by 1969, was an extremely unpopular war losing support not only from the American populace but within Congress, which was responsible for approving military budgets, Nixon adopted the policy of Vietnamization, designed to allow the United States to withdraw from Vietnam incrementally, preserving American strength, honor, and prestige. At the same time Nixon pledged to continue to help the South Vietnamese with training and supplies and accelerate the heavy-handed pacification programs in villages. Meanwhile, Nixon hoped that he could enter into peace negotiations with the DRV. Finally, and according to the larger Nixon goal of foreign policy "linkage," the president wanted to pursue more peaceful relations with both Communist China and the Communist Soviet Union. Among other purposes, Nixon hoped, such actions would inspire both China and the Soviets to reduce their aid to the DRV.

In Vietnam, as well as in Cambodia and Laos, Nixon's policies were supported by massive bombing operations. In 1969 Nixon and Kissinger decided that cutting North Vietnamese supply lines was the key to the survival of the RVN; since they viewed the whole of Indochina as a single theater of operations, Nixon approved Operation Menu, the steady bombing of DRV bases and supply lines along the Ho Chi Minh Trail in Cambodia. The decision proved to be a disaster.

From a military standpoint, it pushed the DRV forces farther into Cambodia and strengthened the hand of the still small Cambodian Communist group, the Khmer Rouge. Meanwhile, at home, word of the bombings was leaked to the *New York Times*, enraging Nixon, who had hoped to keep the operation secret. Critics claimed that, far from deescalating the conflict, Nixon was opening new fighting with these supposedly "secret" bombings. The president, seeking a way to prevent leaks of his decisions to the press, soon began the irregular practices of wiretappings, threats, and underhanded investigations that, in time, were to undermine his presidency.

Nixon remained true to his pledge to gradually withdraw U.S. combat forces from Vietnam. Vietnamization also continued apace with a stepped-up supply and training program for the Army of the Republic of Vietnam (ARVN) combined with pacification operations in the countryside. In July, in hopes of expressing to the DRV a sincere desire to pursue negotiations, Nixon pronounced what came to be known as the Nixon Doctrine, which indicated that the United States would uphold its treaty obligations but each nation was ultimately responsible for its own defense.

In 1970 Nixon continued to present the contradictory picture of deescalating the war by pulling out American troops while escalating it with new incursions into Cambodia and Laos. In order to stop a growing DRV presence in Cambodia after the overthrow of the Sihanouk government there in March 1970, Nixon approved a joint ARVN-U.S. invasion of the country. At the very least, he hoped, his forces could disrupt DRV supply lines and buy time to proceed with Vietnamization. In January 1971, Nixon approved an ARVN invasion of Laos. Both operations proved to be military failures and showed, among other things, that the

ARVN would have difficulty fighting on its own. Meanwhile, the Cambodian incursion inspired some of the fiercest antiwar protests of the entire Vietnam era. The American antiwar movement had been doubtful of Nixon from the beginning, and his troop withdrawals had not stopped the two war moratoriums held in October and November 1969. Nixon's responses, which included a call to what he saw as America's "silent majority" to help maintain civil order and an odd nighttime visit to protesters gathered at the Lincoln Memorial in Washington, D.C., indicated that the president was out of touch with large sectors of the American population.

On the diplomatic front, Nixon kept up his pressure on the DRV to enter into negotiations. One major step in this effort took place in February 1972, when Nixon traveled to China to meet with Communist officials Mao Tse-tung and Chou En-lai. Although Nixon's purposes were larger, he hoped that one benefit of his rapprochement with China would be to force North Vietnamese representatives to negotiate a peace. Similarly, Nixon planned a summit meeting in the Soviet Union for May 1972. This massive and, to a world caught up in decades of cold war rhetoric, surprising diplomatic effort had little effect on the North Vietnamese, who were growing confident of victory without negotiation.

In March 1972, the DRV launched its massive Easter Offensive against the RVN. Furious, Nixon ordered massive bombing attacks against North Vietnam, including the mining of the harbor at Haiphong. Known as Operation Linebacker I, the bombing campaign represented what numerous leaders had been calling for for years: the use of America's greatest military asset, overwhelming airpower, to win a decisive victory. As it happened, this massive show of force influenced the DRV to accelerate peace negotia-

tions. News of the successful negotiations played a major part in ensuring Nixon's landslide reelection victory over Democrat George McGovern in 1972.

South Vietnamese president Nguyen Van Thieu, however, refused the agreement. Hoping to bring him over to his side, Nixon promised Thieu that he could rely on American troops if North Vietnam broke the truce. Hearing about this, DRV representatives walked away from negotiations. Nixon's response was Operation Linebacker II, the infamous Christmas bombing of 1972. DRV representatives returned to the negotiating table, and the truce was signed in Paris on January 27, 1973.

Although the last official U.S. combat troops left Vietnam by April 1973, Nixon was apparently ready to bring them back if circumstances required, and some evidence suggests he had little faith in the Paris accords. What largely tied his hands, and therefore prevented a still-longer American involvement in Vietnam, was the U.S. Congress. The Case-Church Amendment to a funding appropriations bill in the summer of 1973 prevented the president from sending further military aid to the RVN, and the War Powers Resolution, passed over Nixon's veto in November 1973, required the president to consult with Congress before committing U.S. troops to action in any part of the world after a designated period of time.

By the time the War Powers Resolution was passed, in any case, Nixon had grown increasingly unpopular in Congress because of the wide range of presidential abuses of power known collectively as the Watergate scandal. The immediate cause of Watergate was the arrest of a mysterious group of burglars caught rifling through the offices of the Democratic National Committee in the Watergate building in Washington, D.C., in June 1972. The subsequent investigation turned up news of wiretappings, schemes, and strategically withheld information that led many to question Nixon's honesty. In the summer of 1974 special congressional committees devised three articles of impeachment against Nixon. Rather than be tried and, in all likelihood, found guilty and forcibly removed from office, Nixon chose to resign. He left office on August 9, 1974, and turned the presidency over to Gerald R. Ford. It was thus left to Ford to watch as the North Vietnamese mounted their final offensive against the south and as remaining U.S. officials and civilians were forced to evacuate Saigon in April 1975.

After his resignation, Nixon became a sort of elder statesman claiming particular expertise in foreign affairs, the area where he had made his greatest mark as president, perhaps most notably in the establishment of more peaceable relations with China and the Soviet Union. In 1985 he published a book, *No More Vietnams*, in which he defended his Vietnam policy. **See also** Kissinger, Henry; Nguyen Van Thieu; Vietnamization; Watergate scandal.

## Nixon Doctrine

The name given by the media to a foreign policy statement made by U.S. president Richard M. Nixon on July 25, 1969, during a stopover at the Guam naval air station. Nixon's statement appears to have been directly informed by his desire to "Vietnamize" the conflict in Southeast Asia by turning more and more of the fighting over to the Army of the Republic of Vietnam while gradually withdrawing American troops from the region. Nixon promised Asian nations that the United States would remain true to its treaty obligations but that, except in the case of the threat of the use of nuclear weapons, the United States would presume that the greatest responsibility for defense against outside attack would lie with the Asian nations themselves. Some observers, including figures in the South

Vietnamese government, understood this to mean that Nixon might well abandon South Vietnam to its fate once American troops were gone. Yet Nixon continued to defend the statement, and noted that it allowed for ongoing financial and military aid for nations struggling against Communist expansion. As it happened, Nixon remained mostly true to this doctrine, shifting U.S. help for the Saigon government from huge numbers of combat troops to massive bombing and then to training, supplies, and logistical support. **See also** Nixon, Richard M.; Vietnamization.

## Nolting, Frederick (1911–1989)

U.S. ambassador to the Republic of Vietnam (RVN), or South Vietnam, from 1961 to 1963, a central period in the ongoing debate over the nature of U.S. support for the regime. A longtime foreign service officer, Nolting's expertise was in European rather than Southeast Asian affairs. Nonetheless, he was appointed ambassador to the RVN in February 1961 by President John F. Kennedy. Kennedy felt that Nolting's predecessor, Eldridge Durbrow, was wanting in his support for RVN president Ngo Dinh Diem, and Kennedy wanted a representative in place who would improve relations with Diem on a personal level. Indeed, Nolting developed a strong belief in Diem's ability to solidify the society of South Vietnam and came to support his regime wholeheartedly, even if doing so threatened his relationship with the Western press or with Washington. In particular, Nolting criticized South Vietnamese dissidents who refused to throw their support behind Diem.

By 1963 many in the American government were tiring of Diem's false promises and general incompetence and growing concerned whether his regime could stem the spread of communism. In an attempt to contain Diem on an important issue, the State Department ordered

Nolting to encourage Diem to make peace with the wide number of Buddhist dissidents who had emerged or risk losing American support. Since Nolting was on a vacation in Europe, however, the task fell to another embassy official, William Trueheart. After a reprimand from Kennedy, Nolting returned to Saigon, where in August 1963 he got Diem's halfhearted promise to come to an agreement with the Buddhists. Diem proved once again, however, to be less than sincere, and his government troops soon mounted a brutal attack on the Buddhists instead. By the end of August, Kennedy had replaced Nolting with Henry Cabot Lodge and was considering withdrawing his support from Diem, partly due to the Buddhist affair. **See also** Lodge, Henry Cabot; Ngo Dinh Diem.

## North Vietnam

**See** Vietnam, Democratic Republic of.

## North Vietnamese Army (NVA)

Known officially as the People's Army of Vietnam, the North Vietnamese Army grew from a small insurrectionary force in 1946 to the third-largest standing army on Earth in 1975, the year it accomplished the reunification of Vietnam under Hanoi's Communist regime.

The origins of the NVA lay in an armed propaganda team formed by the Viet Minh in 1944 and led by Vo Nguyen Giap. In May 1945, expanding because of alliances with other Vietnamese nationalist groups and taking possession of its first modern weapons, the force became known as the Vietnam Liberation Army and, soon after the August Revolution in which Ho Chi Minh declared the independence of the Democratic Republic of Vietnam (DRV), the Vietnam National Defense Army. When the First Indochina War against French colonialists took shape late in 1946 the force was redesignated the People's Army of Vietnam, with Giap still in command. The army expanded steadily throughout the First Indochina War, fielding its first infantry division in 1951. By the end of the war, the force numbered some 380,000 soldiers. Of these, 120,000 were regulars, the remainder various regional forces. The People's Army also enjoyed a decisive victory at Dien Bien Phu, the battle that forced the French to withdraw from Indochina. Over the next few years the army was strengthened and consolidated along with the DRV's control of North Vietnam. Among other things, it received its first tanks and other heavy equipment from patrons in China and the Soviet Union.

In 1959 DRV leaders decided the time was ripe to strive for the reunification of Vietnam under their authority. Giap was called forward to lead the NVA, as it was generally known by Americans and South Vietnamese, in this effort. Until 1967 much of the fighting on the Communist side was carried out by guerrillas known as the Viet Cong, or alternatively the People's Liberation Armed Forces. But the NVA provided logistical and tactical guidance and from the beginning sent cadres of troops to South Vietnam to assist the guerrillas. On occasion the NVA took part in major engagements, one of the first being the Battle of Ia Drang Valley in November 1965, the first encounter between NVA regulars and U.S. ground troops.

The NVA took over the bulk of the fighting after the Tet Offensive of 1968 decimated the Viet Cong. Until 1975 the NVA conducted a steadily expanding, and more or less conventional, war against the south punctuated by major offensives such as the Easter Offensive of 1972. By these years the NVA had grown to a force of up to 1 million troops, most of whom were conscripts. These troops were equipped with increasingly modern tanks, hand weapons, artillery, and even antiaircraft missiles, thanks again largely to aid from China and the Soviet Union. The NVA also enjoyed the social unity provided by totalitarian communism, which ensured not only a regular supply of conscripts but regular supplies of food, behind-the-lines support, and political backing. By the early 1970s the armed forces of the DRV also included a small navy, mainly engaged in coastal defense, and an air force equipped with more than two hundred MiGs, Chinese-made jet fighters.

The NVA was also effectively led. Few North Vietnamese could fault General Giap until the early 1970s when his star began to wane, due more to impatience among top officials than to bad decisions on Giap's part. Officers trained by Giap, however, continued to devise and lead effective military campaigns. In particular, General Van Tien Dung led the NVA's final assault of the Vietnam War, the Ho Chi Minh campaign that ultimately toppled South Vietnam.

At war's end the NVA had nearly 1 million troops under arms, most of whom were regulars. It had suffered losses of more than 1 million, including Viet Cong losses. The strength of the North Vietnamese Army, now one of the largest, best-equipped, and most cohesive on Earth, proved decisive in encounters with Cambodia in late 1978 and early 1979 and with China in 1979. **See also** Army of the Republic of Vietnam; Viet Cong; Vietnam, Democratic Republic of; Vo Nguyen Giap.

## 101st Airborne Division

Perhaps the most recognizable U.S. Army unit, it played a major role in the Vietnam War. The 101st Airborne Division was founded as an infantry division during World War I. It was reorganized as the 101st Airborne during World War II when its commander was General Maxwell Taylor, later a leading figure in devising early American policy in Vietnam. During World War II, the 101st Airborne, also known as the Screaming Eagles, was involved in important campaigns ranging from D day to the Battle of the Bulge.

A brigade of the 101st Airborne was deployed to Vietnam in July 1965. It was followed by the rest of the division, which was based at Fort Campbell, Kentucky, in 1967. It was the largest single division deployed in its entirety to Vietnam. Most members were infantry, but the division included other components

*Soldiers of the 101st Airborne Division sit onboard a cargo plane bound for the Nhon Co base camp. The 101st Airborne Division began as an infantry division in World War I.*

ranging from artillery to an extensive variety of combat helicopters and gunships. Stationed in both the Central Highlands and the A Shau Valley, the 101st played a major role in 1969's Battle of Hamburger Hill. It was the last U.S. Army division to leave Vietnam in 1973.

The 101st Airborne suffered nearly twenty thousand casualties in Vietnam, both killed and wounded. Seventeen members were awarded the Congressional Medal of Honor. **See also** Army, U.S.; Hamburger Hill, Battle of.

## Office of Strategic Services (OSS)

The U.S. agency concerned with overseas intelligence activities that was the precursor to the Central Intelligence Agency (CIA). The Office of Strategic Services was formed in August 1941 by President Franklin D. Roosevelt, just prior to U.S. entry into World War II, as the Office of the Coordinator of Information under William J. Donovan. Donovan's group was renamed the OSS in May 1942.

The OSS provided the first links between Vietnamese freedom fighters and American officials. As early as 1941, OSS operatives traveling undercover worked to both establish intelligence-gathering networks and support the groups of Vietnamese who struggled to oust the Japanese from the area. Among these groups was the Viet Minh, led by Ho Chi Minh and his guerrilla warfare expert, Vo Nguyen Giap. The situation was muddied by the fact that the Viet Minh sought to oust both the Japanese and the French. Nevertheless, OSS operatives urged support for the Vietnamese independence movement in general and the Viet Minh in particular. By the summer of 1945, after the Japanese had crushed a brief French attempt to reassert power, the Viet Minh was the strongest anti-Japanese force in Vietnam. And Ho Chi Minh himself had become an OSS field agent, establishing

connections between northern Vietnam and U.S. headquarters in southern China. OSS agents accompanied Ho into Hanoi when the Viet Minh leader, taking advantage of a window of opportunity following the Japanese surrender, declared the independence of Vietnam. Ho proclaimed the founding of the new Democratic Republic of Vietnam in a speech on September 2, 1945; parts of the speech were taken directly from the American Declaration of Independence, which was given to Ho, apparently, by OSS agents.

Ho's window of opportunity closed very quickly, however, and the hopes of some OSS agents that the Viet Minh could be turned into an American ally closed along with it. Indeed, during July's Potsdam Conference, where the leaders of the United States, Great Britain, and the Soviet Union made their plans for a post–World War II world, Vietnam was divided into two temporary spheres of influence. The north of the country was to be occupied by China while the south would be occupied by the British pending the return of free French colonial administrators. The wishes of the Viet Minh were largely ignored. For several weeks after Ho's declaration of independence, however, the good relationship between Ho and the OSS continued.

The OSS, considered by many U.S. officials to be a wartime operation, was disbanded by U.S. president Harry S. Truman on October 1, 1945. In early 1946, however, facing the new cold war threat of the expansion of communism, Truman revived the OSS under the name Central Intelligence Group. It became known as the Central Intelligence Agency in early 1947. **See also** Central Intelligence Agency; Ho Chi Minh.

## Operation Plan 34A (OPLAN 34A)

The plan to conduct covert intelligence-gathering missions, mounted by sea, against the North Vietnamese coast. The missions were to instigate the Gulf of Tonkin Incident, which inspired the United States to escalate its involvement in Vietnam.

Operation Plan 34A was authorized by President Lyndon B. Johnson in November 1963. It grew out of the DeSoto missions, earlier seaborne intelligence operations mounted against the Soviet Union, North Korea, and China. The operation consisted of two components. The first was electronic intelligence. Specially equipped ships would be sent north of the demilitarized zone (DMZ) to locate North Vietnamese radar and radio stations and monitor their transmissions and frequencies. The second component was the insertion of teams of South Vietnamese commandos to conduct harassment missions against supply depots and communications sites and to kidnap and interrogate important officials. OPLAN 34A teams were based at Da Nang and used both specially equipped U.S. Navy ships, such as the destroyer *Maddox*, and small craft known variously as "swifts" or "nasties." On occasion, the navy deployed patrol boats to assist with the missions. These smaller craft, which took the commando teams ashore, were armed and manned by U.S. servicemen. The first OPLAN 34A mission took place in early 1964.

Late on the night of July 30, 1964, an OPLAN 34A team mounted a mission against two islands, which concluded with their firing on North Vietnamese communications installations. The smaller craft, which had failed to insert commandos on the islands, were supported by the *Maddox*, which was stationed more than a hundred miles away and was busy collecting electronic intelligence. Three days later on August 2, when the *Maddox* moved to within five miles of one of the islands, it was fired on by a North Vietnamese patrol boat. On August 4 both the *Maddox* and another U.S. destroyer, the *C. Turner Joy*, reported further attacks, although these reports later proved to be inconsistent. President Johnson used the incidents as justification for a series of air strikes against North Vietnam and as a pretext for the Gulf of Tonkin Resolution. **See also** electronic intelligence; Gulf of Tonkin Incident.

# pacification

Along with bombing and combat, the focus of American and South Vietnamese efforts in the Vietnam War; pacification was understood to be the transformation of South Vietnamese society so that it would support the South Vietnamese government and, by extension, its American supporters. In the process, pacification efforts would minimize the number of ordinary people tempted to join or support the Viet Cong (VC) insurgency and provide security against attacks. Pacification was therefore an integral part of the counterinsurgency strategy adopted in the Vietnam War.

Pacification efforts were extensive, beginning before the arrival of U.S. military advisers. The regime of Ngo Dinh Diem, in the late 1950s and early 1960s, mounted the agroville and strategic hamlet programs. Both were attempts to ensure the support of villagers by providing them with "protected" villages along with training and local government responsibilities. Both efforts failed, largely due to mismanagement and the corruption of the Diem regime, but they lay the groundwork for later pacification efforts.

Extensive American involvement in pacification was delayed by disagreements over whether the matter should be handled by officials in Washington, D.C., or Saigon and whether it should be a primarily civilian effort or one coordinated with the military aspects of the war. In 1965 and 1966 President Lyndon B. Johnson allowed pacification efforts to remain conducted by the U.S. embassy in Saigon but, dissatisfied, he turned pacification over to an official named Robert Komer in 1967. Komer was named head of Civilian Operations and Revolutionary Development Support (CORDS), an organization that was to be directly connected to the Military Assistance Command, Vietnam (MACV). CORDS was given jurisdiction over all pacification programs whether civilian or military or conducted by outside agencies such as the Central Intelligence Agency (CIA). Komer also was expected to coordinate his efforts with the South Vietnamese, and he had access when necessary to military equipment and personnel.

CORDS efforts were based around, first and foremost, village security. To that end, Komer and his lieutenants sought to build up the territorial forces, foster economic growth and local government, build infrastructure in the form of roads and communication lines, and involve U.S. military and civilian officials and even troops in pacification programs. Komer also received approval to build what was later known as the Phoenix Program, an intelligence and police effort designed to root out the Viet Cong infrastructure (VCI) of leaders and political cadres. After the shock of the Tet Offensive of 1968, Phoenix was placed under the control of the so-called Accelerated Pacification Campaign (APC), which lasted until 1969. The APC provided for particularly harsh pacification measures, such as Phoenix, and was apparently intended to convince the American public and its leaders that, despite the evidence of Tet, the United States was winning the war. Komer, meanwhile, was replaced as head of CORDS by William Colby, former chief of the CIA Saigon station, in November 1968.

Although the APC failed in its ostensible goal, it shifted the emphasis of pacification efforts even more toward security (and relatively less toward economic or social development). The new emphasis was on increasing the size of the territorial forces through forced conscription, the effort to destroy the VCI, and the Chieu Hoi Program, which provided incentives to desert to Communist soldiers. These efforts were mainly judged successful in slowing the Communist insurgency in South Vietnam, but they had little effect on strengthening the South Vietnamese government or in altering the determination of North Vietnam to one day reunify the country.

After 1971 pacification was mainly conducted under the Community Defense and Development Program, a mostly South Vietnamese effort. As with the military side of the war, pacification was turned over to the South Vietnamese as part of Vietnamization. **See also** Civilian Operations and Revolutionary Development Support; Colby, William; Komer, Robert; Phoenix Program.

## Pacific Command (PACOM)

One of several global "unified commands" into which the U.S. armed forces are divided. The Pacific Command includes not only the Pacific Ocean region but all of southern and eastern Asia. The commander in chief of the Pacific Command (CINCPAC), invariably a navy admiral, therefore had responsibility for American involvement in the Vietnam

War. His authority was subordinate only to the Joint Chiefs of Staff, the secretary of defense, and the president. PACOM was based in Honolulu, Hawaii, and included major forces from the U.S. Army, Air Force, and Navy. In succession, PACOM commanders during the Vietnam War were admirals Harry D. Felt until June 1964; U.S. Grant Sharp until July 1968; John McCain Jr. until September 1972; and Noel Gayler, who remained CINCPAC until after the war was over.

Many have suggested that the fact that PACOM had control over the Vietnam War hindered the U.S. effort there; the U.S. commander locally, the head of the Military Assistance Command, Vietnam (MACV), was merely the head of the U.S. Army within PACOM. He therefore had no direct tactical responsibility over navy or marine operations, and even army activities lay ultimately under the responsibility of officers in Honolulu. In addition, PACOM often based its military decisions either on preset strategies or on larger considerations, making it difficult for commanders in Vietnam to make necessary improvisations. **See also** Honolulu Conferences; Military Assistance Command, Vietnam.

## Paris negotiations

The lengthy and contentious discussions that finally ended direct American involvement in the Vietnam War. They began in Paris, France, on May 12, 1968, after U.S. president Lyndon Johnson announced that he would unilaterally halt most American bombing of the Democratic Republic of Vietnam (DRV) in hopes that the expression of good faith would bring the North Vietnamese to the bargaining table. Hanoi officials agreed, provided that talks would work at the very least toward an unconditional stop to all American bombing raids. Although both sides negotiated with different goals in mind, these goals reinforced each other. The United States wanted to extricate itself from Vietnam while preserving international prestige and minimizing the political costs of retreat—in other words, to achieve "peace with honor." For the North Vietnamese, their goal remained the reunification of Vietnam under the Communist regime in Hanoi, a task made arguably easier by the fundamental American desire to pull out.

A complex chess game, then, began in May 1968. The head American negotiator was Averell Harriman, Johnson's ambassador at large for Southeast Asian affairs. His North Vietnamese counterpart was Xuan Thuy, an experienced diplomat. Almost immediately the talks were deadlocked over the issue of continued bombings. Johnson and Harriman were hesitant to give up one of their few strong bargaining points, the ongoing threat of American airpower. But the North Vietnamese refused to negotiate anything further until all raids over the DRV ended. Johnson finally acquiesced on October 31, 1968.

The next bone of contention was over the participation of the government of the Republic of Vietnam (RVN), or South Vietnam, the regime that American forces had pledged to defend against Communist incursions. Both the DRV and its sister organization in the south, the National Liberation Front (NLF), refused to recognize the Saigon regime of the RVN as a legitimate governing body and thus a legitimate participant in negotiations. Likewise, the Saigon government refused to recognize the NLF, who had guided the civil war in south Vietnam since 1960. The sides reached the face-saving solution of simply referring to the participants in official talks as either "our side" or "your side." South Vietnamese president Nguyen Van Thieu refused, however, to accept the compromise.

Talks continued by fits and starts from 1969 to late 1972. The new American president, Richard Nixon, replaced Harriman with another diplomat, Henry Cabot Lodge, in January 1969. When Lodge resigned, Nixon assigned David K.E. Bruce, a veteran diplomat with Far Eastern expertise, to Paris. The DRV, meanwhile, raised the stakes, growing ever more confident that the Americans would leave eventually regardless of whatever agreement was reached and that their ultimate victory over the RVN was therefore inevitable. DRV leaders insisted that the United States had to break up the government of the RVN, dismantle its armed forces, and build a new coalition government before a real truce could be achieved. To make that likelihood greater, the NLF announced in June 1969 that it was creating the Provisional Revolutionary Government (PRG), which the Communists argued was a true governing body with the same status as the United States, DRV, and RVN. Soon after, Nixon sent his national security adviser, Henry Kissinger, to begin secret negotiations with the North Vietnamese, rather than the public talks, which were clouded by technicalities and bogged down by diplomatic wrangling over issues such as the shape of the bargaining table. Le Duc Tho, a senior member of the Hanoi government, joined Kissinger in the secret negotiations in Paris.

The confidence of the North Vietnamese that victory was at hand was checked in the spring of 1972 when Nixon demonstrated his willingness to use America's overwhelming advantage in airpower with a massive bombing campaign of North Vietnam called Operation Linebacker I. The campaign was conducted in response to the DRV's Easter Offensive of 1972 as well as a suspension of the Paris talks. One effect of the bombings on negotiations was that the DRV eventually agreed to allow

Thieu's regime to remain intact pending negotiations with the PRG, a relaxation of its earlier stance. This compromise allowed Kissinger and Tho to begin work on a final draft. However, when it was presented to the concerned parties in late October, Thieu refused to consider it, largely because it allowed North Vietnamese troops to remain in place in South Vietnam. Thieu also rejected the proposal to form a National Council of Reconciliation and Concord, which would work toward elections and the creation of a new government for the south involving the PRG. The RVN president only agreed to the deal when assured by Nixon, in November, that the United States would provide military support to the RVN if the DRV violated the terms of the proposed agreement. Hearing of this, DRV negotiators again walked out.

Again, Nixon turned toward a show of overwhelming American airpower to force the hands of the North Vietnamese. The resulting Operation Linebacker II,

also known as the Christmas bombing, dropped tens of thousands of tons of explosives on North Vietnam. Targets included, for the first time, locations in the cities of Hanoi and Haiphong. Hanoi signaled its willingness to return to the negotiations and Kissinger and Tho met again in Paris in early 1973 to hammer out the final version of the Paris Peace Accords. The accords were signed by all four parties, the United States, DRV, RVN, and PRG, on January 27 with barely restrained hostility. PRG and RVN representatives, for example, refused to sign the same page of the accords, while the United States and DRV had to sign on yet a third page. **See also** Kissinger, Henry; Le Duc Tho; Linebacker I; Paris Peace Accords.

## Paris Peace Accords

The peace agreement signed by the United States, the Democratic Republic of Vietnam (DRV), the Republic of Vietnam (RVN), and the Provisional Revolu-

*Secretary of State William Rogers signs the Paris Peace Accords. After four years of negotiations, the accords were finally ratified on January 27, 1973.*

tionary Government (PRG) of South Vietnam on January 27, 1973. Its sole lasting effect was to end direct U.S. military involvement in Southeast Asia. Known formally as the "Agreement on Ending the War and Restoring Peace to Vietnam," the Paris accords did not end the fighting largely because both the DRV (North Vietnam) and the RVN (South Vietnam) took advantage of the agreement's vagueness to seek or regain control of territory.

The Paris accords were the end result of more than four years of negotiations, and were entered into hesitantly. The DRV only agreed to sign after the massive Christmas bombing of December 1972, while RVN president Nguyen Van Thieu gave his consent only after being reassured by U.S. president Richard Nixon that U.S. troops would return to support his regime if the DRV violated the truce. The major negotiators were U.S. national security adviser Henry Kissinger and, for the DRV, Le Duc Tho, a top member of the Lao Dong, the Vietnamese Communist Party.

The opening statement reiterated the claim of the 1954 Geneva Accords, which declared that "all countries respect the independence, sovereignty, unity, and territorial integrity of Vietnam"; in other words, recognize that it was an independent nation. Other major provisions provided for a general cease-fire to begin at 8:00 A.M. on January 28 (Saigon time); the departure of all U.S. and other foreign troops within sixty days, along with a release of all foreign prisoners of war; and a recognition of the neutrality of the neighboring countries of Cambodia and Laos. In Vietnam itself, the agreement was to provide for new negotiations to create a peaceful regime for South Vietnam that would reflect the stances of both the RVN and the PRG; in time, new elections would be held, overseen by a National Council of Reconciliation and Concord. Afterward, steps might be taken to reunite the country slowly and peacefully, although those steps were not described.

The Paris accords effectively ended American participation in the Vietnam War and largely removed the conflict from the forefront of American politics. The last U.S. combat troops left Vietnam within sixty days as promised, leaving only the Marine Embassy Guard, Defense Attaché officers, a group of missing in action (MIA) negotiators, and a few observers as the remnants of what had once been a force of half a million. The DRV also released nearly six hundred American prisoners of war, asserting that they were all who remained under North Vietnamese detention. The small remaining forces from Thailand, the Philippines, Australia, New Zealand, and South Korea also left. **See also** cease-fire war; Christmas bombing; Nguyen Van Thieu; Paris negotiations.

## Parrot's Beak

Familiar name for a region in Cambodia that bordered South Vietnam just north of the Mekong Delta. Its name came from the fact that the region jutted into South Vietnamese territory. Because of its strategic location, and its proximity to the Ho Chi Minh Trail, the Parrot's Beak became the site of semipermanent North Vietnamese supply and operations bases. Its population, meanwhile, was divided among Cambodians and Vietnamese.

Although South Vietnamese forces and occasional covert U.S. teams sometimes crossed into the region, and U.S. president Richard M. Nixon authorized bombing raids over it in March 1969, the Parrot's Beak only became a major center of conflict during the so-called Cambodian incursion from April 30 through June 1970. Then, supported by U.S. artillery, airpower, and intelligence, South Vietnamese forces moved deep into the region. As they had done in Vietnam proper, both Cambodian and Vietnamese Communist forces sometimes engaged the invaders and sometimes simply faded away, to return later. In the meantime, the new Cambodian regime led by Lon Nol took advantage of the circumstances by targeting Vietnamese civilians in the Parrot's Beak, resulting in massive refugee movements.

After the Cambodian incursion ended in June 1970, Communist forces returned to their bases in the Parrot's Beak. The region became a major staging area for both the Easter Offensive of 1972 and North Vietnam's final offensive in 1974 and 1975. **See also** Cambodia, invasion of; sanctuaries.

## Pathet Lao

The Communist insurgency in Laos, a landlocked nation with which Vietnam shared a long border. The Pathet Lao, which means "Land of the Lao," was also known as the Neo Lao Hak Sat, or Lao Liberation Front. It was formed in August 1950 by various forces working together in the region, including the Viet Minh, to oust the French from Indochina. One of its early leaders was a scion of the Lao royal family, Prince Souphanouvong, although it quickly became clear that it was controlled by Communist cadres. At first, and like other organizations, such as the Viet Minh and the National Liberation Front, the Pathet Lao attempted to maintain harmony among Communist and non-Communist people by preaching independence and unity. Over time, however, many Lao people turned away from the organization; it was too dependent on the Vietnamese Communists for aid and support, and Laos had a long-standing dislike of Vietnam.

By 1964 the Pathet Lao was engaged in a war with the Royal Lao government based in Vientiane. The struggle was not unlike that in Vietnam, with the Pathet Lao receiving aid from Hanoi while the government, mostly covertly, was helped by the United States. Meanwhile, the nation suffered greatly from U.S. bombing of the areas in central and eastern Laos that the Ho Chi Minh Trail cut through; bombings, in fact, were heavier in Laos than in Vietnam itself. Between 1972 and 1975, and despite peace talks, the Pathet Lao was able to slowly extend its control over much of the large but sparsely populated country. On August 23, 1975, the Pathet Lao entered Vientiane and established the People's Democracy of Laos under a mysterious leader, Kaysone Phomvihane. **See also** Central Intelligence Agency; Hmong; Laos, secret war in; Viet Minh.

## pathfinders

U.S. infantry soldiers who were placed, prior to the arrival of larger units, in regions where U.S. or South Vietnamese forces hoped to establish forward bases or camps. They were used because of the difficult and sometimes hostile terrain. Known also as "black hats" because of the black baseball caps they often wore, teams of pathfinders were dropped by parachute or landed by helicopter. Then they scouted out possible landing sites, determined the best directional approaches, and set up navigational tools. They might also take the responsibility of clearing away jungle foliage or even Communist booby traps in order to make helicopter landings easier. Teams of pathfinders were used extensively in virtually every aviation unit involved in the ground war in Vietnam. **See also** fire support bases.

## peace initiatives

American involvement in Vietnam ended after the Paris Peace Accords were signed in January 1973, but diplomatic efforts to reach a peace had begun years earlier. The first was Operation Mayflower, begun in May 1965. This was an attempt by U.S. president Lyndon B. Johnson, already facing widespread criticism, to bring the North Vietnamese to the peace table with a voluntary bombing halt. Johnson used a backdoor channel, the U.S. ambassador to the Soviet Union, Foy Kohler, to deliver his proposal to North Vietnamese representatives. The North Vietnamese refused to even consider the proposal and Operation Mayflower failed. Its only real legacy was a public relations victory for Johnson, who could now claim that Communist intransigence, not U.S. bombing runs, was preventing peace negotiations.

Mayflower was followed by Operation Marigold in June 1966. Marigold involved a proposal for negotiations from, supposedly, Hanoi, delivered by Janusz Lewandowski, the Polish representative of the moribund International Control Commission, to Henry Cabot Lodge, U.S. ambassador to Saigon, via Lodge's Italian counterpart. The proposal allegedly included a secret meeting to be held between American and North Vietnamese negotiators in Warsaw. Skepticism over these convoluted plans, from both sides, ensured that Marigold would get nowhere.

Operation Sunflower, begun in January 1970, was a more serious attempt to open peace negotiations than its two predecessors. Discussions about beginning talks took place along two channels. The first, from the United States via the North Vietnamese embassy in Moscow, failed due to the unwillingness of either side to grant concessions. The United States still demanded that both sides deescalate, particularly in South Vietnam, while the North Vietnamese insisted that the United States halt all bombings and any other attacks before they would consent to peace talks. The second channel was through British prime minister Harold Wilson and Soviet premier Alexei Kosygin. Wilson apparently received mixed messages from the United States, and this channel failed as well. **See also** Paris negotiations; Rolling Thunder; San Antonio Formula.

## Pentagon Papers

The familiar name for a group of documents whose unauthorized disclosure was to play an important part in American attitudes toward the Vietnam War, as well as affect the course of Richard Nixon's presidency. Their formal title was *United States–Vietnam Relations, 1945–1967;* they were published in book form as *The History of the U.S. Decision Making Process in Vietnam.*

The Pentagon Papers were the product of a special Department of Defense task force organized by defense secretary Robert McNamara in 1967. By that time McNamara had begun to question whether the United States was pursuing an effective course in Vietnam, and the task force was ordered to assemble a history of U.S. policy in the area since 1945 to provide a basis for reconsidering the matter. The result was a collection of reports written using files from the Department of Defense, the State Department, the Central Intelligence Agency (CIA), and the White House. The task force did not conduct interviews of important participants. Accompanying the reports were copies of many of the documents the task force used. Altogether, the Pentagon Papers consisted of forty-seven volumes containing more than seven thousand pages. Only fifteen copies were produced, and the material was highly classified as top secret. Neither McNamara nor other officials ever intended for the Pentagon Papers to be released to the public; among their concerns was that their release would compromise the ability of the United States to collect vital intelligence.

Two copies of the Pentagon Papers, however, were given to the RAND Corporation, an important governmental consultancy and think tank. There, a researcher named Daniel Ellsberg decided that some of the material should be made known to the public. In earlier years Ellsberg, like many others, was a strong war hawk, but by 1969 he had become an antiwar activist. After reading the Pentagon Papers Ellsberg grew convinced that the American effort in Vietnam was not only misguided but immoral. He began to make photocopies of certain sections of the documents. At first he tried to interest antiwar senators in the material. Failing that, he turned in March 1971 to the *New York Times*, in particular a *Times* staffer with a long interest and expertise in Southeast Asia, Neil Sheehan.

Sheehan, along with others at the newspaper, prepared ten articles to be published on ten successive days, working secretly. The articles were to be accompanied by their supporting documents. The first installment was published on June 13, 1971. Immediately, U.S. attorney general John Mitchell sought to halt the publication of any more material by informing the *Times* that it was in violation of espionage laws and should return the material to the Department of Defense. He filed an injunction in the New York courts when the *Times* refused. Mitchell's boss, Richard Nixon, hated leaks of information, even if they tarnished the administration of Lyndon Johnson rather than his own. Moreover, Nixon was concerned that the publication of the Pentagon Papers would reduce support for his own Vietnam policies and make foreign policy overall more difficult by revealing intelligence sources and methods. The New York courts, meanwhile, suspended publication of further material for four days. Ellsberg outflanked his opposition, however, by offering the material to the *Washington Post*, which began publishing the Pentagon Papers on June 18.

Neither Ellsberg, Sheehan, the *New York Times*, nor the *Washington Post* were seeking to sensationalize or sabotage the war effort. Ellsberg, in fact, withheld from the journalists those portions of the Pentagon Papers he thought might interfere with the ongoing Vietnam peace negotiations. The journalists, similarly, edited the material to take into consideration legitimate national security concerns. Meanwhile, after Nixon's administration pursued its attempt to prevent publication at the U.S. Supreme Court, the Court decided that publication had to be allowed. The government, in other words, had failed to present a convincing case for "prior restraint of publication." By the end of 1971 much of the Pentagon Papers had been published in book form, the only major deletions being reports on peace negotiations and unclassified source documents.

For the American public, the Pentagon Papers seemed to suggest that they had been intentionally misled by their government, which at least until 1968 had consistently said that the Vietnam War was proceeding well. Moreover, the documents suggested a pattern of dubious morality and ineptitude among leaders that many Americans found disconcerting. Others have suggested that a long-term effect of the publication of the Pentagon Papers was to make the Department of Defense overly cautious about writing things down, fearing that they too might be leaked, and therefore restricting operations. **See also** Ellsberg, Daniel; Nixon, Richard M.

# People's Self-Defense Forces (PSDF)

Militarized units of South Vietnamese civilians established in the aftermath of the Tet Offensive of 1968 by a general mobilization law proclaimed by the government of the Republic of Vietnam (RVN). Their main purpose was to provide local security, but from the standpoint of the RVN they offered the additional advantages of freeing regular

South Vietnamese army units for other duty and ensuring that civilians were active in the defense of their country. All men ages sixteen to seventeen and thirty-nine to fifty were required to join the People's Self-Defense Forces, except those who chose instead to join the South Vietnamese army or the territorial forces. Men ages eighteen to thirty-eight were already required to be in service, aside from a few categories of exemptions. The rest of South Vietnamese society—women, younger teenagers, people over fifty, and disabled veterans—were asked to serve the PSDF in support roles. The RVN government disbanded all earlier civilian defense organizations to concentrate on this new, larger program.

By 1972 PSDF units included more than 1 million members, and the organization itself permeated every level of South Vietnamese society. Members were given military training, were armed, and sometimes sent out on patrols, but they rarely had occasion to fight. Reports suggested, however, that the PSDF program greatly enhanced local security. **See also** Army of the Republic of Vietnam; pacification; territorial forces.

## Pham Van Dong (1906–2000)

Top official of the Democratic Republic of Vietnam (DRV, or North Vietnam) and first prime minister of the Socialist Republic of Vietnam (SRV). Pham Van Dong, born in central Vietnam in 1906, became an early member of the Indochina Communist Party and an associate of Ho Chi Minh. Dong took part in the Viet Minh insurgency against the Japanese and French during World War II after receiving, on Ho's instructions, military training in China. In this effort he worked closely with Vo Nguyen Giap, military commander of the Viet Minh.

Over time Dong's skills proved to be more political and diplomatic than military. He was the DRV's chief representa-tive at the 1954 Geneva Conference, although he was marginalized in negotiations after insisting that the French stay out of Vietnamese affairs. Indeed, Dong left the conference without approving the General Accords.

With Ho as the leader of the Vietnamese Communist Party and head of state, Dong served as the premier of the DRV, or head of the government, from 1954 to 1975. Committed to the reunification of Vietnam under the authority of the DRV, he was reluctant to consider negotiations with the United States and South Vietnam until bombings of North Vietnam stopped. He also insisted that any negotiations involve representatives of the South Vietnamese Communists. His intransigence on these points ultimately guided the peace talks that resulted in the 1973 Paris accords. He also became the most public of North Vietnam's leaders after the death of Ho Chi Minh in September 1969.

After the DRV's armies entered Saigon in April 1975, Dong stayed on as the dominant politician in the new SRV. He remained premier until 1986, when he resigned amid intractable economic problems. He remained a well-respected and influential adviser to the Central Committee of the Lao Dong, the Vietnamese Communist Party. Considered incorruptible by many Vietnamese, his reputation outlasted even that of Giap and other revolutionary leaders. **See also** Ho Chi Minh; Lao Dong; Le Duan; Vo Nguyen Giap.

## Phoenix Program

A program targeting the Viet Cong infrastructure (VCI) of Communist political leaders, recruiters, and educators. It was established after the Tet Offensive of 1968 had made apparent the strength of the Viet Cong. However, Robert Komer, the head of Civilian Operations and Revolutionary Development Support (CORDS), the organizing agency for pacification efforts, had planned such a program since mid-1967. Komer built numerous intelligence-collecting centers that were to be financed and managed by the Central Intelligence Agency (CIA). Since there were questions as to whether these centers violated South Vietnamese sovereignty, the head of the CIA's Far East Division, William Colby, secured an agreement with South Vietnamese president Nguyen Van Thieu to place the effort under the ostensibly Saigon-managed Phoenix Program.

Divisions of the Phoenix Program collected lists of suspected VCI leaders and then ranked them from A to D. Ranks A and B were the most wanted targets. The lists were then distributed to special Phoenix Program field units, which consisted of members of the South Vietnamese police as well as military men and various U.S. forces. Often, apparently, suspects were killed in the field. Those who were not were brought back to interrogation centers manned by South Vietnamese military intelligence and CIA personnel. While the information from these interrogations proved useful both in enabling further arrests and in dismantling the VCI, many of them were apparently conducted with great brutality. When questioned about the Phoenix Program during an investigation into the antics of the CIA by the U.S. Congress in 1971, Colby noted that some twenty-eight thousand Viet Cong were captured and of those twenty thousand were killed. He claimed that most of those were slain in combat, a claim that was widely disputed by others, including U.S. intelligence officers present during torture sessions. Colby also suggested that seventeen thousand VC sought amnesty.

Congress's investigation helped to draw down the Phoenix Program, as did the Vietnamization program, which turned most of Phoenix's responsibilities over to the South Vietnamese national police by the end of 1972. Later assessments made not only by the CIA but by South Vietnamese officials noted that the program was successful in rooting out the VCI in South Vietnam. Even after the war was over, former North Vietnamese officials said that their efforts in the south were greatly hampered by the loss of so many important VCI personnel. **See also** Central Intelligence Agency; Colby, William; pacification; Viet Cong.

## Pierce Arrow

An important step in the U.S. decision to escalate its involvement in Vietnam, Pierce Arrow was the code name for the air strikes ordered by President Lyndon B. Johnson in retaliation for the alleged North Vietnamese attacks on two U.S. destroyers in the Gulf of Tonkin, the incident that inspired the Gulf of Tonkin Resolution. The alleged attacks took place in August 1964 and gave Johnson sufficient grounds, he claimed, for a major retaliation. Using aircraft from two U.S. carriers, the *Constellation* and *Ticonderoga*, pilots flew sixty-four sorties against targets on or near the North Vietnamese coast. They included patrol and torpedo boats, a few of which were apparently sunk, and an oil storage facility in the city of Vinh, which was destroyed. The American public overwhelmingly approved of Johnson's decisive show of force. **See also** Gulf of Tonkin Incident; Gulf of Tonkin Resolution.

## Plain of Jars

A major area of conflict during the unofficial war in Laos from 1960 to 1974. The Plain of Jars, located in Xieng Khouang province, is so named because of the presence of hundreds of prehistoric ceramic jars of various sizes scattered about the vast plain. They are thought to have been funerary urns, although scholars remain uncertain about their exact origin or purpose. The Plain of Jars was located in between Vientiane, the capital of Laos, and the northeastern regions of the country controlled by the Communist Pathet Lao and their North Vietnamese patrons. It was the scene of frequent combat. The region was heavily bombed by American planes seeking to halt the Communist advance, and over three decades later the plain remained scarred by bomb craters. Moreover, local residents continued to suffer from both land mines and unexploded ordnance (UXO). **See also** Barrel Roll; Laos, secret war in; unexploded ordnance.

## Plain of Reeds

An area bordering the Mekong Delta west of Saigon. It consisted of a flat, marshy basin and was sparsely populated. From the time of the First Indochina War (1946–1954) it served as a base for Communist guerrilla operations, and neither the South Vietnamese nor the Americans ever established control over the region. Due to its proximity not only to Saigon and the delta but to the Cambodian border, the Plain of Reeds served as a staging area for the Communists and, in 1970 during the Cambodian incursion, for the United States and South Vietnam. **See also** Cu Chi tunnels.

## Pleiku

The capital of Pleiku province in Vietnam's Central Highlands as well as the headquarters of II Corps of the South Vietnamese army. Pleiku was therefore one of South Vietnam's four military headquarters and the base for most operations in the Central Highlands. Thanks to its location in the mountains, Pleiku had long been a market town for the various Montagnard tribes who traversed the area, paying little attention to national borders. South Vietnamese efforts there were focused on halting Communist patrols that also moved through the mountains and valleys. An attack on a U.S.

Special Forces camp in Pleiku on February 7, 1965, which killed eight Americans, helped convince American officials to start sending regular U.S. troops to Vietnam. In later years, large U.S. forces, including the 173rd Airborne Division and the Fourth Infantry Division, were also stationed there at intervals. Pleiku fell to the North Vietnamese in March 1975 after being abandoned by the South Vietnamese army. **See also** Kontum; military regions.

## Pol Pot (1928–1998)

Leader of the Khmer Rouge, Cambodia's main Communist insurgency, and the head of one of the most brutal regimes in human history, the Khmer Rouge's Democratic Kampuchea (1975–1978).

French-educated and in his younger days a radical journalist, Pol Pot, who was born under the name Saloth Sar, returned to Cambodia in 1960 to enter politics. He was elected to the Central Committee of the Cambodian Communist Party, at that time a largely secret organization. In 1963 he became its general secretary, and Cambodian premier Norodom Sihanouk, a wily political survivor, asked Pol Pot to join his government. Pol Pot refused, suspicious over Sihanouk's developing friendship with the North Vietnamese Communists despite his confessed neutrality. The Communist leader instead took to the Cambodian hinterlands to form the Khmer Rouge, adopting the name, or title, Brother Number One.

From 1965 to 1970 the Khmer Rouge was a small, Communist guerrilla army, one of several in Cambodia. Pol Pot's ideological devotion, however, helped attract support among peasants, as did his opposition to the ongoing friendship between Sihanouk and the North Vietnamese. Vietnam was a traditional enemy of Cambodia, and even though the North Vietnamese were Communists, Pol Pot usually rejected their support. In 1970

*Pol Pot was the head of Cambodia's Communist Party and led one of the most brutal regimes in history.*

Sihanouk was forced from power in favor of Lon Nol, a pro-American and pro–South Vietnamese general. These new circumstances forced an alliance between Pol Pot and Sihanouk, and until 1975 Sihanouk's army, which was nominally the same thing as the Khmer Rouge, battled Lon Nol's forces in a devastating civil war. Since Sihanouk mostly spent those years in China, Pol Pot emerged as the most powerful figure opposing Lon Nol. Meanwhile, Lon Nol enjoyed a degree of support from the Americans, who supplied him with military trainers, some weapons, and vast airpower. The bombings of Cambodia, which in fact began on the Cambodian stretches of the Ho Chi Minh Trail in March 1969, were massive. They were

thought to have uprooted tens of thousands of Cambodian villagers, forcing many of them, particularly the young, into the Khmer Rouge.

Having already established control over most of Cambodia, Pol Pot's forces took the capital Phnom Penh on April 17, 1975. He then set out to implement the agrarian utopia he had envisioned. He declared that his new Democratic Kampuchea was now in "year zero" of a new era, an era that was to be dominated by a mysterious entity known simply as Angka, "the party." Pol Pot himself remained Brother Number One and over the next three years presided over one of the most brutal regimes in history.

The Khmer Rouge regime was overthrown after a Vietnamese invasion in 1979, and Pol Pot retreated to the jungles to lead a guerrilla campaign against the Vietnamese occupiers and their Cambodian puppets. After the Vietnamese left in 1989 and Cambodia began to stabilize, Pol Pot was placed on trial by Khmer Rouge opponents. He allegedly died under house arrest in April 1998. **See also** Khmer Rouge; Sihanouk, Norodom.

## Poulo Condore

The site of a prison built by the French to house Vietnamese who actively opposed French colonial rule. It was located on one of the Con Son islands in the South China Sea off the Vietnamese coast. Much of the facility consisted of so-called tiger cages, small cells in which as many as three prisoners were shackled, with roofs made of iron bars for the prison guards to walk across to observe what went on beneath their feet. Some of the inmates of Poulo Condore during French times were men who would later play important roles in the movements to oust not only French rule but, as they saw it, American military interference in Vietnam. These included

Le Duan, Le Duc Tho, and Pham Van Dong.

The government of the Republic of Vietnam (RVN, or South Vietnam) continued to use the prison, which they renamed Con Son, after the departure of the French in 1954. It remained a political prison rather than a criminal institution, and its inmates tended to be both Communist and non-Communist opponents to the RVN. Despite the denials of both the RVN regime and American leaders, both the International Red Cross and, in 1970, a special American task force headed by congressional aide Tom Harkin found that conditions at Con Son violated the Geneva Convention and that various political abuses were commonplace. Some thought that Harkin's report on Con Son, in particular, helped inspire the U.S. Congress to begin to reduce its aid to the RVN.

The continued existence of the political prison at Con Son proved to be a major mistake on the part of the RVN, becoming for North Vietnam a symbol of the oppression of the Saigon regime and its American allies. The site remained intact as a memorial on the island, and a replica of the tiger cages was constructed at the War Remnants Museum in Saigon. **See also** reeducation camps.

## prisoners of war (POWs)

During the Vietnam War some 760 American servicemen were taken prisoner of war (POW) by both North Vietnamese and Viet Cong forces. Their brutal treatment, particularly before 1970, clearly violated the minimum requirements of the Geneva Convention of 1949, but the North Vietnamese took the position that because there had been no formal declaration of war, American captives should justifiably be treated as criminals and "international gangsters" rather than prisoners of war. POWs endured a host of physical and psychological hardships, including beatings and torture, severe deprivation and denial of medical treatment, prolonged isolation, and forced confessions and displays for propaganda purposes.

Nevertheless, American POWs in Vietnam displayed a remarkable degree of resilience, discipline, and military organization in captivity. Some studies suggest that as a group POWs were older and better educated than the average serviceman in Vietnam and thus had the maturity and confidence to withstand severe deprivation. Also, many POWs were aviators taken captive when their planes were shot down, and thus shared similar training and professional experience and perhaps similiar character traits, which fostered strong camaraderie. They devised ingenious communication codes by tapping, blinking the eyes, or sweeping a broom; found ways to break the monotony of imprisonment such as mentally constructing a house, piece by piece; and, many reported, bolstered sheer determination with faith and a sense of humor to survive captivity that lasted in many cases more than five years. Held longest was Army Special Forces captain Floyd "Jimmy" Thompson, a POW for nine years (1964–1973).

Vietnam War captivity can be broken down into four overlapping phases. From 1964 to 1969, most POWs were isolated in small groups among several small camps in South Vietnam, North Vietnam, and Laos. Conditions and treatment were particularly harsh in South Vietnamese camps: Starvation, disease, brutal interrogation, and frequent forced movement contributed to a death rate of 20 percent, compared with 5 percent in North Vietnamese camps.

The period from 1968 to 1972 was marked by the movement of American POWs into North Vietnam to a total of thirteen permanent detention camps, five in Hanoi and eight in Hanoi outskirts. These camps, whose official Vietnamese names are unknown, were known by the nicknames given them by POWs: Alcatraz, Briarpatch, Camp Faith, Dirty Bird, Dogpatch, Farnsworth, Hoa Lo (the so-called Hanoi Hilton), Mountain, Plantation, Rockpile, Skidrow, Camp Hope (also known as Son Tay), and Zoo. Some became well known for particular functions or related events: For example, numerous propaganda films and show interviews of POWs came from Plantation; the level of POW organization was extremely strong at the Hanoi Hilton; and in November 1970 U.S. Army Special Forces raided Son Tay in an attempt to rescue the fifty-five POWs held there (the prisoners, however, had already been relocated).

From 1970 to 1972 American POWs were consolidated into five main camps—Camp Faith, Dogpatch, Hoa Lo, Plantation, and Zoo—and the remaining camps were closed. In the final phase (1972–1973), by the terms of the 1972 diplomatic agreement reached on the release of POWs, the North Vietnamese regrouped prisoners, who were to be released in waves by the various forces who officially held them. Altogether 591 U.S. POWs were released to American authorities from February to April 1973 in Operation Homecoming. A total of 144 POWs are known to have died in captivity; the fate of some two dozen others, classified as POW/MIA, officially remains unknown. **See also** Hanoi Hilton; Homecoming; missing in action.

## Project Daniel Boone

The code name for covert reconnaissance missions across the border from South Vietnam into Cambodia. They were first authorized by the American Joint Chiefs of Staff in June 1966 but did not receive final approval until May 1967; the issue was understandably sensitive given American hesitation to expand the conflict into Cambodia or offend Cambodian president Norodom Sihanouk.

Project Daniel Boone missions were carried out by teams made up, usually, of two or three U.S. Special Forces troops and about ten Montagnards or South Vietnamese soldiers. The teams either marched across the border on foot or were taken by helicopter. Their tasks were mostly to gather intelligence information but also included planting mines and sabotaging enemy operations. In October 1967 Project Daniel Boone was expanded to include an area stretching twelve miles into Cambodia, a distance that was later expanded to about eighteen miles. Project organizers also designated two operational regions, Zone Alpha, the northern area stretching to the Laotian border, and Zone Bravo, stretching southward to the Gulf of Thailand. The Ho Chi Minh Trail ran through both regions. The missions remained highly covert, and ventures into Zone Bravo, in particular, required presidential clearance before beginning.

In December 1968 Project Daniel Boone was renamed Salem House. In 1971, under the cover of the Vietnamization plan to turn the fighting of the Vietnam War over to local forces, it was given a Vietnamese name, Thot Not. Altogether, project teams conducted more than eighteen hundred missions. The teams provided important information to both U.S. and South Vietnamese commanders over the years, including, in late 1967, the information that a large force of both Viet Cong (VC) and North Vietnamese Army (NVA) troops was massing on the Cambodian side of the border in preparation for what was to be the Tet Offensive of early 1968. Using this intelligence, General William Westmoreland, American commander in Vietnam, asked for clearance to send somewhat larger attacks into Cambodia. U.S. officials, including President Lyndon B. Johnson, turned him down, still hesitant to extend the fighting into a new country. In 1970, however, with a new Republican president, Richard M. Nixon, in office and in right of changed circumstances, Project Daniel Boone/Salem House information was used to prepare for that year's Cambodian invasion. **See also** Civilian Irregular Defense Groups; long-range reconnaissance patrols.

## Project 100,000

An American attempt at social engineering during the Vietnam War years. It offered the extra benefit of keeping up numbers of military recruits, making less necessary the politically dangerous tactic of calling up reserve forces. The program was announced in August 1966. According to the program's organizers, Project 100,000 would bring 100,000 men from underprivileged backgrounds into the military every year by reducing traditional entry requirements for service. The hope was that the military experience, which so many American leaders appeared to fondly recall from their younger days during World War II, would instill in these young men important values and skills that they might later carry over into civilian life. In the words of one senator quoted in Marilyn Young's *The Vietnam Wars 1945–1990*, "The armed forces are a dramatic and desperately needed change [for the underprivileged], a world away from women, a world run by strong men and unquestioned authority, where discipline, if harsh, is nonetheless orderly and predictable, and where rewards, if limited, are granted on the basis of performance."

Those selected for Project 100,000 were young men who would not have been accepted into the armed forces otherwise, mainly because of low test scores. Of some 350,000 participants between 1966 and 1972, 80 percent were high school dropouts and 40 percent had limited reading skills. Forty-one percent were African American and a majority

were from the American South. Their experiences in the Vietnam-era military were mixed, although it remained clear that those accepted into the program had a much better than average chance of going directly into combat in Vietnam. Anecdotal evidence suggests that units with large numbers of Project 100,000 inductees had more disciplinary and performance problems than other units, although some commanders were said to have preferred men from the program. In either case, court-martial rates were double those of regular inductees, and many Project 100,000 recruits were dishonorably discharged. For those men, whose military records were to follow them for the rest of their lives, they may have been worse off than if they had never entered the military.

Once the numbers of U.S. troops in Vietnam began to lessen, the quotas for Project 100,000 were reduced. In 1972, when the United States shifted to all-volunteer armed forces, the project was disbanded. **See also** Army, U.S.; draft; draft resistance.

## Provisional Revolutionary Government (PRG)

A governing body that emerged in 1969 as a potential alternative to Nguyen Van Thieu's Republic of Vietnam (RVN, or South Vietnam). The Provisional Revolutionary Government was formed by the leadership of the National Liberation Front (NLF), a Communist front organization in South Vietnam with loose contacts with the Hanoi government in North Vietnam, and the Alliance of National, Democratic, and Peace Forces, a smaller group. The impetus behind the formation of the PRG was the beginning of earnest negotiations among the Americans, North Vietnamese, and RVN leadership. Communist leaders wanted the PRG to represent a sort of government in waiting, ready to rule alongside, and in time replace, the

RVN as a preface to the complete reunification of Vietnam.

The first leader of the PRG was Huynh Tan Phat, an important NLF leader. Its public face, and most important spokesperson, was Madame Nguyen Thi Binh, who served as foreign minister and led the PRG delegation at the Paris peace negotiations. Many around the world, in 1969, accepted the PRG as the true, legitimate government of South Vietnam, as they had earlier accepted the NLF. The PRG was given diplomatic recognition by, among others, the Soviet bloc countries, China, Cuba, Cambodia, North Korea, and, unsurprisingly, North Vietnam (DRV).

PRG representatives continued to take part in peace negotiations, and the existence of the PRG was a major hurdle to overcome, especially for RVN president Nguyen Van Thieu. Thieu was hesitant to accept any truce that might require him to involve the PRG in the government of South Vietnam. Nevertheless, Thieu found himself overcome by events, and after the Paris accords of January 1973 he was forced to accept PRG representatives to his government in an advisory role. A PRG general, Tran Van Tra, in fact was on hand when, on April 30, 1975, DRV tanks forced their way onto the grounds of the presidential palace in Saigon. After Vietnam was reunified under the Hanoi regime, which reconstituted itself as the Socialist Republic of Vietnam, the PRG was absorbed into the new state. Few top PRG officials, however, were placed in important posts, although Madame Binh was named minister of education. **See also** National Liberation Front; Paris negotiations; Viet Cong.

## psychological operations (PSYOPs)

The effort to convince ordinary Vietnamese of the justice of the South Vietnamese and American cause. Psychological operations constituted a practical military effort carried out by the Joint U.S. Public Affairs Office (JUSPAO) using a special Psychological Operations Group (POG), which was established in Saigon in December 1967. The POG consisted of four battalions corresponding to the four military regions, with appropriate subdivisions assigned to loudspeaker groups, audiovisual programs, medical assistance, and other tasks.

PSYOPs were directed toward four primary targets: the Viet Cong (VC), North Vietnamese Army regulars who might be induced to desert or give up, and civilians in both North and South Vietnam. POG personnel performed a wide range of tasks, including distributing leaflets, showing films, providing medical or other civil assistance, and collecting information on local Communist activities. They had the support of army and air force aircraft; some transport planes were equipped with loudspeakers, and helicopters proved to be especially effective in leaflet-dropping campaigns. POG units also learned to use newspapers, radio, and television effectively.

PSYOP messages might be either positive or negative in nature. Positive ones emphasized the importance of family, nostalgic reminders of peaceful times now gone, or suggestions that good soldiers might be led by bad officers. One leaflet campaign directed at VC fighters was characterized by pictures of a beautiful woman and encouraged marriage. Another showed U.S. president Richard Nixon meeting with Communist Chinese leaders Mao Tse-tung and Chou En-lai, a suggestion that North Vietnam's allies and enemies in fact got along reasonably well. One of the more successful PSYOP campaigns, although it was coordinated with other efforts, was the Chieu Hoi Program, which encouraged Communist fighters to desert with promises of, among other things, cash payments. Negative PSYOP messages tended to stress the sufferings of the Vietnamese people. **See also** Chieu Hoi Program; Joint U.S. Public Affairs Office.

## *Pueblo* **Incident**

The January 1968 capture of a U.S. Navy ship by the forces of North Korea, a Communist state known officially as the Democratic People's Republic of Korea. The ship the *Pueblo* was a cargo vessel that had been refitted with electronic surveillance and communications equipment but had little in the way of weaponry or armament. On January 23, 1968, the *Pueblo*, apparently on a spy mission off North Korea, was attacked by North Korean forces. Casualties included one sailor killed and several more wounded, and the ship and its crew were all captured. For most of the next year they were held in North Korea, where they were tortured and made to sign forced confessions. Negotiations resulted in their release at Panmunjom Bridge, which separated North from South Korea, on December 22, 1968.

The event proved a humiliation to the U.S. Navy in several ways. An investigation recommended that the *Pueblo*'s captain and chief intelligence officer be court-martialed, although the navy had failed to provide the vessel with adequate protection. The secretary of the navy, however, rejected the recommendations on the grounds that the crew of the *Pueblo* had suffered enough. Meanwhile, news of the mission itself, and the fate of the *Pueblo* and its crew, tarnished American military prestige in a year of increasing disillusionment over falsely optimistic reports from Vietnam. **See also** Navy, U.S.

## pungi stakes

A simple but lethal form of booby trap used mostly by Viet Cong (VC) forces and their sympathizers. Pungi stakes were sharpened sticks of bamboo that were placed vertically in pits in the ground. Small groups of stakes were planted and camouflaged with jungle foliage. For maximum effect, the tips of the stakes were sometimes smeared with dung to increase the likelihood of infection when a stake pierced the skin. Larger pungi stake "fields" were also devised for areas where VC forces anticipated helicopter or airborne insertions of troops. Sometimes the stakes were tall enough to interfere with a helicopter's rotor blades. Estimates suggest that as much as 2 percent of U.S. combat wounds in Vietnam were the result of pungi stakes, an ironic contrast to the largely high-tech nature of the war. **See also** booby traps; casualties.

## Quang Tri, Battle of

Taking place from March to September 1972, the Battle of Quang Tri was one of the last major engagements in the Vietnam War in which the United States played an important part. Quang Tri Province, centered on the city of Quang Tri, was the northernmost province of South Vietnam. At its northern border stood the demilitarized zone (DMZ). The area was targeted for attack by North Vietnamese Army (NVA) strategists as part of their Easter Offensive of 1972, which would strike not only across the DMZ into Quang Tri but also across the Laotian border.

The attack on Quang Tri began on March 30, involving both a ground march and a massive artillery barrage from guns placed several miles away on the other side of the DMZ. At first, the NVA onslaught went badly for the large number of South Vietnamese forces who were stationed in Quang Tri. Partly because of indecisive leadership and conflicts over command, but also because of inexperience among newly formed units, South Vietnamese forces often deserted their posts. In addition, the NVA enjoyed the advantage of heavy cloud cover that hindered U.S. bombing raids.

The skies cleared toward the middle of April, making massive American B-52 raids possible. But the NVA persevered and by May 1 had taken not only the city of Quang Tri but also the town of Dong Ha, located at the important juncture of Highways 1 and 9. The rapid NVA advance, as well as the general destruction caused by the fighting and bombing, sent thousands of ordinary Vietnamese onto Highway 1 as refugees headed south, human migration that would become common over the next two years. NVA artillery, as it happened, did not differentiate between a strategic road that needed to be cut and a road filled with refugees, and Highway 1 was heavily fired on. So many people were killed along one stretch of the road that the refugees later remembered it as the "road of horrors."

By June the NVA advance had stalled. South Vietnamese reinforcements had begun to arrive and American bombing raids had begun to take a toll on NVA strongholds and supply lines. By late August, South Vietnamese troops were ready to begin a counteroffensive, supported, as ever, by B-52 bombers. After several weeks of intense, hand-to-hand combat, the South Vietnamese were able to retake Quang Tri, although it lay largely in ruins. Along with the failure of the other prongs of the Easter Offensive, the South Vietnamese victory in Quang Tri, costly as it was, helped convince the North Vietnamese to take seriously the peace negotiations then under way in Paris. **See also** demilitarized zone; Easter Offensive; Linebacker I.

# Rangers

Specially trained U.S. Army infantry-men who were granted the designation "Rangers" in Vietnam in 1969. This was the first time the army used the designa-tion. Ranger companies evolved from the long-range reconnaissance patrol (LRRP) units that had operated in Vietnam from the early 1960s. Like the LRRPs, the Rangers were trained in survival, jungle warfare, reconnaissance, and intelligence gathering at their special school at Fort Benning, Georgia. They served through-out Vietnam, often in close association with their counterparts in the South Viet-namese army. **See also** long-range recon-naissance patrols; Special Forces, U.S. Army.

# Red River Delta

The agricultural heartland of northern Vietnam, centered around the Red River, which flowed from southwestern China through Vietnam and into the South China Sea. Centuries of cultivation had crisscrossed the region with an array of irrigation canals, dikes, and dams, mak-ing it possible for the region, in most cir-cumstances, to support large populations. Hanoi, the traditional capital of Vietnam and the center of Vietnamese civilization, stood itself on the Red River some sev-enty miles from the seacoast.

During the Vietnam War there were approximately fifteen thousand miles of irrigation canals in the Red River Delta. The system also provided North Viet-nam with a transportation network, since roads were built on top of the dikes. South Vietnamese and American mili-tary strategists frequently considered

*South Vietnamese army rangers stand guard. Rangers in the U.S. and South Vietnamese armies were highly trained infantrymen.*

targeting the dikes with bombing raids, but held back because of the massive threats of flooding and the destruction of crops, which could potentially cost thousands of civilian lives. This, they considered, would be not only a humanitarian disaster but also a public relations one. **See also** Haiphong Harbor, mining of; Hanoi.

## reeducation camps

Special camps established by the North Vietnamese government to help ensure ideological loyalty to its version of communism. The phenomenon was common in countries that embraced communism; other variations of the reeducation camps included the Siberian gulags in the Soviet Union and the rural "retraining" camps in China during its cultural revolution. In Laos and Cambodia, Communist authorities also built their versions of the camps after taking over in 1975. In Laos they were known as seminar camps, while in Cambodia, where conditions were perhaps most brutal of all, almost all of the people who survived the Khmer Rouge purges spent time in labor camps.

The North Vietnamese built their first reeducation camps in 1947. Most, however, were established after the 1954 Geneva Accords split Vietnam in two. Inmates included political enemies to the Hanoi regime, both real and potential, as well as people whose economic interests or background were contrary to North Vietnam's vision of society, such as large landowners and their families and the so-called mandarins, officials of the Nguyen court who had been loyal to the French. Common criminals were also sometimes sent to the camps. Reeducation consisted of ideological training along with physical labor. Regular brutality was not the norm, but torture and executions were both used when camp officials deemed it necessary.

The new Socialist Republic of Vietnam (SRV), which governed the reunified nation after 1975, built many more reeducation camps in southern Vietnam in the attempt to integrate the recalcitrant southerners into the new regime. Scholars estimate that there may have been as many as 150 such camps. Inmates now included officials of the former South Vietnamese government and military; teachers, journalists, lawyers, and other professionals; and Vietnamese employees of American military or civilian organizations. In 1980 the SRV claimed that most "reeducation courses" were short, around three months long, and that 1 million people had passed through them in the previous five years. Tens of thousands, however, were held for longer periods of time, although the camps were allegedly mostly cleared by 1990. Many inmates, as it happened, sought to escape from Vietnam by immigrating to the United States, Australia, or Europe. On occasion the SRV was only too happy to accommodate them; in the 1980s several deals were struck to allow groups of inmates, notably former South Vietnamese officials, to emigrate to the United States.

There was a wide range of conditions within the camps, but it was generally accepted that health care was minimal and that "ideological training," combined with hard physical labor, could be brutal. Many of the hundreds of thousands of South Vietnamese who left the country on their own, the so-called boat people, had passed through the reeducation camps. **See also** boat people; Khmer Rouge; Vietnam, Democratic Republic of; Vietnam, Socialist Republic of.

## refugees

Refugees were a constant by-product of the forty-plus years of fighting that plagued Indochina after 1945. At several points their numbers were massive: Combat itself produced thousands of refugees, and the populations of cities throughout South Vietnam swelled with an influx of people seeking sanctuary from fighting in the countryside. One estimate indicated that in 1967 up to 12 percent of the population of South Vietnam was made up of displaced persons. Similar refugee populations crowded into Vientiane, the capital of Laos, and Phnom Penh, Cambodia's capital, during the 1970s.

The largest wave of refugees comprised the so-called boat people, more than a million South Vietnamese who fled the country after the fall of Saigon in April 1975. Often braving dangerous conditions ranging from bad weather to rapacious pirates, the boat people, many of whom were of ethnic Chinese origin, swelled refugee camps in Malaysia, the Philippines, Hong Kong, and other areas in Southeast Asia. Most hoped for eventual resettlement in the United States, Australia, or Western Europe.

A second group of Chinese made up another large group of refugees from Vietnam. After 1977 ethnic Chinese, known in Vietnam as Hoa, found their livelihoods ruined by Communist economic policies. While large numbers paid substantial amounts to Communist officials to be allowed to join the exodus of boat people, tens of thousands of others migrated north into China. This influx of refugees was one of the factors cited by China to explain its 1979 invasion of Vietnam.

The war in Cambodia beginning in 1970, and then the brutal regime of the Khmer Rouge in that country followed by another war, this time with Vietnam, produced hundreds of thousands of Cambodian refugees. Lacking anywhere else to go they flocked to the Thai border. By 1980 up to 700,000 Cambodians, out of a population in 1975 estimated at 10 million for the entire country, lived in refugee camps on the Thai-Cambodian border. Most were not allowed to settle in Thailand but filtered back into Cambodia as their country began to stabilize over the next decade. Large numbers of Lao, for that matter, also escaped into Thailand during the years of fighting in Laos. Since much of the population of northeastern Thailand was ethnically Lao they fit in relatively easier, and various support networks allowed most of the influx to be absorbed. In fact, in some northeastern Thai towns, large Lao populations lived alongside large groups of Vietnamese who had made it into Thailand. **See also** boat people.

## rest and recreation (R&R)

The program designed to give U.S. servicemen a break from their duties in Vietnam. The standard Vietnam tour of duty was one year; ideally soldiers were provided with an R&R break of five days for every three months in service during that year. Battlefield necessities or other contingencies often limited R&R breaks, however. U.S. commanders designated R&R sites both within Vietnam and in neighboring areas. Chief R&R sites in Vietnam were China Beach near Da Nang and Vung Tau, a seaside resort not far from Saigon. R&R sites outside the country were Honolulu, Hawaii; Tokyo, Japan; Hong Kong; Sydney, Australia; Manila, the Philippines; Bangkok, Thailand; Singapore; Taipei, Taiwan; and Penang and Kuala Lumpur in Malaysia. Servicemen headed for those destinations were transported by civilian carrier Pan American Airways, which reportedly earned nearly $25 million per year in government R&R transportation payments. The servicemen spent their R&R time as soldiers on leave did in all times and places. Some arranged rendezvous with wives or girlfriends. Most spent much of their military pay on consumer goods and gifts and a wide variety of entertainments and diversions. **See also** China Beach.

# Rolling Thunder

The code name for the American bombing raids against North Vietnam conducted from March 2, 1965, to October 31, 1968. In combination with an escalated commitment of ground troops, Rolling Thunder was the primary tactic by which the United States tried to win the Vietnam War, militarily as opposed to politically, during the presidency of Lyndon B. Johnson. Despite the dropping of over 643,000 tons of bombs, however, the operation failed to accomplish either American or South Vietnamese goals.

Johnson, his staff, and military commanders began to consider bombing North Vietnam in 1964, largely because they thought that the South Vietnamese were losing the ground war to the combined forces of the North Vietnamese Army (NVA) and the Viet Cong (VC). The decision to start the raids was predicated on two assumptions and a related hope. The first was that extensive attacks on North Vietnam would result in moves by the Hanoi government to use its influence to reduce guerrilla attacks by Communists in the south. The second was that massive airpower, used to great effect in both World War II and the Korean War, would destroy North Vietnam's industrial infrastructure—factories, refineries, roads, bridges, and other facilities—and thus make it impossible for the country to continue fighting. Meanwhile, strategists hoped that the bombing raids would encourage Hanoi to enter into peace negotiations.

Rolling Thunder raids were nearly continuous, with only occasional interruptions for bad weather or in support of tentative peace feelers. Taking part were U.S. Air Force and Marine planes from bases in South Vietnam and Thailand, navy craft launched from carriers in the South China Sea, and sometimes planes from the South Vietnamese Air Force. The operation proceeded in phases. The first, from March to June 1965, targeted mainly military sites such as barracks and ammunitions depots. The second, from July 1965 to June 1966, focused on infrastructure elements such as roads, bridges, and railroad tracks. The third phase, lasting from June to October 1966, added oil and petroleum facilities to the targets, while the fourth, from October 1966 to March 1968, added factories and power plants. The final phase of Operation Rolling Thunder was more political than strategic in its orientation; in the aftermath of the 1968 Tet Offensive, Johnson ordered restrictions of the bombing to areas south of 19 degrees latitude. In contrast to his initial goals, he now wanted to bring the North Vietnamese to the negotiating table by limiting bombing raids. Johnson, who throughout had exercised close control over Rolling Thunder raids, even to the extent of choosing specific targets, ordered that the program stop on October 31, 1968.

Operation Rolling Thunder was costly and destructive for both sides. Bombing raids destroyed a large portion of North Vietnam's economic and industrial infrastructure and, according to some estimates, killed more than fifty thousand people. In addition, the NVA lost more than nine hundred aircraft in its attempt to provide air defense. The United States lost over eight hundred aircraft and hundreds of pilots and other crew members. In addition, the operation was extremely expensive. By 1967 Pentagon number-crunchers determined that it cost the United States $9.60 to destroy $1.00 worth of North Vietnamese equipment or facilities.

Moreover, the operation largely failed in its objectives. The failure was due partly to false assumptions on the parts of American politicians and strategists and even more to North Vietnamese determination. North Vietnam, much unlike Germany or Japan during World War II, was a largely agricultural country with only a small industrial base. Destroying its infrastructure, therefore, had little effect on its ability to continue fighting a war. Meanwhile, the Hanoi government was able to muster the participation of hundreds of thousands of ordinary people using the bombing raids as a propaganda tool. It built substantial air defenses, sent larger numbers of NVA troops to the south, and even expanded its ability to provide support to the VC, mostly by using the Ho Chi Minh Trail. **See also** antiaircraft defenses; Arc Light; B-52; Paris negotiations.

## Rome plows

Huge tractors equipped with modified bulldozer blades and special spikes that were used extensively in South Vietnam to clear away jungle. They were developed by the Rome Caterpillar Company based in Georgia. Rome plows were used both to clear land designated for U.S. or South Vietnamese base areas and to perform, along with such airborne weapons as napalm and Agent Orange, the task of reducing the jungle area in which Viet Cong or North Vietnamese troops could hide and operate. **See also** daisy cutter; defoliation.

## Rostow, Walt (1916–2003)

A top adviser to Presidents John F. Kennedy and Lyndon Johnson and a major influence on the overall U.S. approach to the Vietnam conflict. A former Office of Special Services official, State Department official, and academic, Rostow held a variety of offices from 1961 to 1969 that kept him at the center of foreign policy decision making. Under Kennedy, he served as deputy national security adviser before being appointed chair of the State Department Policy Planning Council, where he remained until 1966. He continued to serve Johnson as national security adviser from 1966 until 1969. Throughout, he remained one

of the most vocal and consistent of the so-called war hawks.

Rostow was an early supporter of increased American aid to South Vietnam. In February 1961 he endorsed a report by General Edward G. Lansdale, then an intelligence expert based in Washington, D.C., that South Vietnam was in a state of imminent crisis and required American aid. In October 1961 he traveled to South Vietnam to consult with General Maxwell Taylor, Kennedy's top military adviser in the region. The two returned the recommendation that the United States take a more active, rather than merely advisory, role in South Vietnam, including sending American combat troops. They also advocated economic and other forms of civilian aid to prop up the Saigon regime and discourage villagers from turning to the Viet Cong (VC).

The basic American approach to Vietnam was highly informed by what became known as the Rostow thesis, which the official developed as chair of the State Department Policy Planning Council. Its central idea was that, in order to stop a Communist insurgency movement supported by an outside power, military action should be used against that outside power. In time, the outside power would decide that support for the insurgency was not worth the losses it was suffering. In the case of Vietnam, Rostow's thesis worked on the assumption that the VC insurgency in South Vietnam could be contained by attacking North Vietnam, which was supporting the VC with supplies and arms along the rapidly emerging Ho Chi Minh Trail. Moreover, Rostow pointed out, North Vietnam was in violation of the 1954 Geneva Accords, which prohibited Hanoi from sending troops to South Vietnam or Laos. Attacks on North Vietnam, therefore, were both justified and in accordance with the American desire to protect the South Vietnamese regime from Communist insurrection.

After Johnson replaced Kennedy in November 1963, Rostow's notions, which received the support of other administration advisers, were implemented by fits and starts until, by the end of 1965, American combat troops were in place, a naval blockade of North Vietnam was under way, and most vividly, a series of bombing campaigns targeted strategic areas in the north as well as the Ho Chi Minh Trail itself. In ensuing years, as Johnson's national security adviser, Rostow generally advocated the expansion of bombing raids against North Vietnam and opposed the various proposals to unilaterally halt the American bombing in hopes of bringing Hanoi to the negotiating table. He did express willingness, however, to consider measures that might reduce U.S. casualties and, by 1967 and 1968, limit the Saigon regime's dependency on the United States by turning more of the fighting over to the South Vietnamese. **See also** Johnson, Lyndon B.; Kennedy, John F.; Taylor, Maxwell; Taylor-Rostow Report.

## Rubin, Jerry (1938–1994)

Prominent anti–Vietnam War activist. Rubin's first involvement in radical politics was as a member of the Free Speech Movement in Berkeley, California, in the early 1960s. He proved himself to be an effective organizer and speaker and, by 1965, turned his energies toward opposing the Vietnam War. He helped organize a two-day teach-in at the University of California in the spring of 1965. It was one of the first and largest of such events, attended by more than ten thousand students and attracting such famous speakers as the writer Norman Mailer and the child physician Dr. Benjamin Spock. Soon afterward Rubin formed an organization known as the Vietnam Day Committee for the purposes of taking more direct political action. Among its antics were several attempts to halt troop trains headed for embarkation points in Oakland, where many U.S. troops left for Vietnam.

In 1967 Rubin moved to New York City, where he met Abbie Hoffman, another leading protester. The two helped organize the March on the Pentagon in October 1967. The event featured a new emphasis on the part of Rubin, which was to attempt to expose the ridiculousness of the Vietnam War and the Pentagon through what he called guerrilla theater. Tactics included a symbolic "levitation" of the Pentagon building as well as other mysterious rituals. In late 1967, along with Hoffman and Paul Krassner, Rubin formed the Youth International Party, or Yippies, which courted media attention through provocative, theatrical tactics. Famously, Rubin exhorted young Americans not to trust anyone over thirty, and he suggested that the Vietnam War and the protests against it amounted to a struggle between the generations. The Yippies, and Rubin, went on to play a major part in the protests surrounding the Democratic National Convention in Chicago in August 1968. Although Rubin hoped that the Yippies would stage a "festival of life" to counter the Democratic Party's "festival of death," the protests turned violent and hundreds were injured or arrested. Afterward Rubin was one of eight protest leaders arrested on charges of crossing state lines with intent to riot and conspiracy to riot. The trial of this so-called Chicago Eight (later the Chicago Seven because of the separation of the trial of Bobby Seale, one of the defendants) provided Rubin with another opportunity to speak out against not only Vietnam but the proceedings against him. He was ultimately convicted, although the conviction was overturned in 1972.

By 1973 Rubin was ousted from the Youth International Party, as was Hoffman, partly on the grounds that he was getting too old. He went on to undergo a major transformation and, by the mid-1980s, was the archetype of the Yippie turned yuppie, or a former 1960s radical who had become a respectable young, urban professional, replete with an office job, large bank account, suit and tie, and conservative politics. From time to time Rubin engaged in staged debates with Hoffman, who adhered to his radical politics. **See also** antiwar movement; Chicago Seven; Hoffman, Abbie; Youth International Party.

## rules of engagement (ROE)

The rules under which U.S. military forces begin or engage in combat with an enemy. Rules of engagement during the Vietnam War were designed mostly to limit destruction to property, civilian casualties, and casualties from friendly fire. In Vietnam in particular, ROE, designed by the Joint Chiefs of Staff in Washington, D.C., also tried to limit border incidents and set target areas for B-52 bombing strikes. The ROE were implemented by the Military Assistance Command, Vietnam (MACV), which issued over forty ROE directives to military personnel in Vietnam. These dealt with the proper treatment of Vietnamese civilians as well as careful use of firepower. For example, the Joint Chiefs of Staff required that any B-52 bombing strikes in South Vietnam be at least one kilometer away from villages or towns, and free-fire zones could only be established under consultation with South Vietnamese officials.

The nature of warfare in Vietnam involved many violations of ROE, in part because it was difficult to distinguish civilians from combatants both from the air and on the ground. Tactics and strategies such as harassment and interdiction (H & I) artillery fire and the establishment of free-fire zones inspired varied interpretations of ROE, as did the indication, es-

pecially among some infantry company commanders, that soldiers should seek high body counts. **See also** attrition strategy; free-fire zones.

## Rusk, Dean (1909–1994)

Secretary of state under Presidents John F. Kennedy and Lyndon B. Johnson and a figure closely identified with American policy in the Vietnam War.

Long experienced in East Asian affairs, Rusk was a strong anti-Communist. He came to believe that the spread of communism in East Asia was largely due to Chinese influence and that any Communist government in the region was under the wing of the Chinese. There was some support for this viewpoint in orthodox Communist theory which argued that communism was a unified global movement, but it downplayed the long-standing hatred between China and Vietnam as well as their somewhat different versions of communism.

Under Kennedy, Rusk largely supported the growth of counterinsurgency policies, although he hoped to keep the State Department aloof from the matter, thinking South Vietnam was more a military than a political problem. By 1963, however, he found himself forced to become more actively involved. The main issue was the Saigon regime of Ngo Dinh Diem, which hesitated to accept U.S.-sponsored political reforms. Rusk was thought to have supported moves in which the United States either ignored or supported anti-Diem contingents in the South Vietnamese government and military.

Under Johnson, Rusk emerged as a notable war hawk. He supported measures to escalate U.S. involvement in Vietnam in hopes of weakening both the North Vietnamese and the Viet Cong. Only when the United States and South Vietnam were able to negotiate from a position of strength, Rusk argued, should they open talks with North Vietnam. Consequently,

*Secretary of State Dean Rusk defends President Johnson's Vietnam policy at a Senate hearing in 1966.*

he generally opposed proposals to stop or limit bombings of the north as a prelude to negotiations. Meanwhile, Rusk also found himself in the position of being a public defender of America's Vietnam policy, continually being forced to justify the Vietnam War to the press, the public, and congressional opponents. His explanations included the argument that an American effort in Vietnam was necessary for global security and, again, to halt the growing influence, as he saw it, of Communist China. He also cited the psychological need for the United States to present a strong democratic alternative to communism in developing countries. Naturally, his very public position as secretary of state made him a lightning rod for criticism of the war, and, fairly or not, many people began to blame Rusk as the war effort turned against the United States.

Nevertheless, Rusk continued to support escalation. He backed General William Westmoreland's request for more than 200,000 new U.S. troops after the 1968 Tet Offensive. One of his concerns was the weakening of America's presence elsewhere in the world because of the demands of Vietnam, and he knew that some of the new troops would be sent to other global hot spots. The request for more troops was denied as the Johnson administration chose instead to begin deescalating the conflict and begin peace talks with North Vietnam. Unsure that this was the best course, Rusk remained aloof from the peace talks when they began in Paris in May 1968.

Along with Johnson, Rusk left office in January 1969. He later accepted an academic position at the University of Georgia and published a memoir of his years as secretary of state, *As I Saw It*, in 1990. **See also** Johnson, Lyndon B.; Kennedy, John F.; McNamara, Robert; Rostow, Walt.

## Saigon

The capital of the Republic of Vietnam (RVN), or South Vietnam. The city also served as the headquarters of many U.S. military and civilian organizations during the Vietnam War.

Located on the Saigon River, Saigon was originally a small village connected to the Khmer Empire in Cambodia. Its location near both the Mekong and the South China Sea helped turn it into an important trade center, and by the 1700s there were communities of not only Cambodian and Vietnamese but also Chinese, Malay, and Indian merchants living in Saigon. By the end of the eighteenth century, Vietnam's Nguyen dynasty, ruling from Hue, had seized control of the town from the Khmers and renamed it Saigon from the Khmer *Prei Nakor.* The town went on to serve as the dynasty's administrative headquarters in southern Vietnam.

French colonizers seized control of Saigon in 1861, seeing in it a potentially important deepwater port serving the rich agricultural regions of southern Vietnam. In time the French proclaimed it the capital of their colony of Cochin China, and they began to turn it into a large city replete with modern port facilities, broad boulevards, and nineteenth-century French-style architecture, including a number of monumental buildings such as a Roman Catholic cathedral, an elaborate opera house, and world-class hotels such as the Caravelle and the Rex. Many Viet-

namese flocked to the city to take advantage of economic opportunities, as did people from southern China. A major Chinese enclave, in fact, grew up on the outskirts of the burgeoning city. It was known as Cholon. Despite the fact that the bulk of the population was either Chinese or Vietnamese, the city continued to be controlled by the small French community.

When Vietnam was partitioned by the 1954 Geneva Accords, Saigon emerged as the capital of South Vietnam. First RVN president Ngo Dinh Diem proclaimed it the official capital in 1955, and he ruled from a vast presidential palace. After Diem was ousted in a coup, the palace was razed and replaced by a modern structure, also known as the palace, or Doc Lap palace in Vietnamese. But even more importantly, Saigon became a war capital, and American soldiers and civilian officials became common in its streets, as did the various RVN military and police troops. The modernization of the city continued as well, as dozens of buildings, complete with such facilities as air conditioning, were built to supply housing and office space to the Americans. Meanwhile, as the war continued, Vietnamese refugees began to crowd the city.

Saigon was taken by the North Vietnamese in April 1975. The symbolic event marking the takeover was on April 30, when North Vietnamese tanks stormed through the gates of the presidential palace.

In 1975 the Socialist Republic of Vietnam (SRV) renamed Saigon Ho Chi Minh City, although the old name continued to be common among residents and visitors alike. The city's economic dynamism was only temporarily hampered by the SRV's collectivist policies. **See also** Hanoi; Mekong Delta; Ngo Dinh Diem; Vietnam, Republic of.

## Saigon Military Mission (SMM)

The organization that marked the beginning of direct American involvement in Vietnam through its attempt to prop up the South Vietnamese government. The Saigon Military Mission was established in 1954 by John Foster Dulles, the strongly anti-Communist U.S. secretary of state, and his brother Allen Dulles, the director of the Central Intelligence Agency (CIA). It was headed by air force colonel Edward G. Lansdale. Lansdale was seconded to the American embassy in Saigon as the assistant air attaché but in truth his covert activities on behalf of the SMM kept him far busier. Lansdale's two-part writ was to strengthen the Saigon regime, at first headed by the emperor Bao Dai, and support SMM efforts to weaken the Hanoi regime of Ho Chi Minh. To accomplish these tasks, Lansdale was supplied with a substantial budget as well as a staff and agents who came from both the U.S. military and the CIA.

Even before the SMM was fully operational Lansdale cultivated a friendly relationship with Ngo Dinh Diem, the prime minister appointed by Bao Dai. Lansdale established himself as an adviser to Diem, urging him to become a leader whom the ordinary people of South Vietnam could trust. Lansdale's recommendations included economic and political reforms as well as setting up various public service organizations. Lansdale also urged Diem to allow hundreds of thousands of people from North Vietnam to settle in the south, a provision allowed by the 1954 Geneva Accords provided the move took place within three hundred days after the accords took effect. As it happened, Lansdale was able to assist this huge migration, which consisted mostly of Roman Catholics, by enlisting the aid of the U.S. Seventh Fleet and Civil Air Transport, the CIA's covert airline.

In addition to this vote of confidence for South Vietnam on the part of a portion of the Vietnamese population, the SMM was also able to strengthen Diem by helping him oppose his political enemies. Using a variety of means, including, apparently, large CIA bribes, the SMM was able to convince some of the leaders of Cao Dai and Hoa Hao, two major religious sects, to give up their opposition to the Diem regime in exchange for important positions in the South Vietnamese army. The help of the two sects included the transfer of troops, allowing Diem to contain the final major threat to his authority, the Binh Xuyen criminal gang.

At the same time, the SMM tried to conduct covert operations to try to weaken the North Vietnamese regime. Lansdale sent a group of operatives to the north, where they built up groups of Vietnamese agents and laid in supplies of weapons. In addition, the SMM attempted to sabotage the port facilities at Haiphong as well as other transportation lines. These efforts, however, had little lasting effect. In late 1955 Lansdale left Vietnam and the SMM was closed. **See also** Central Intelligence Agency; Conein, Lucien; Lansdale, Edward G.; Ngo Dinh Diem.

## Salisbury, Harrison (1908–1983)

*New York Times* correspondent in Vietnam in the mid-1960s. Salisbury was one of the first journalists to question not only

U.S. policies in Vietnam but whether American authorities were misleading the public regarding the course and nature of the war.

In 1966 Salisbury, the managing assistant editor at the *Times*, made various attempts to visit North Vietnam, a privilege that had not been granted to any American reporters since the beginning of direct American military action. After an American bombing raid in December, Salisbury was given permission to enter by the North Vietnamese and he set off immediately for Hanoi. Over the next several weeks he filed dispatches to the *Times* reporting that, despite American word to the contrary, bombs were dropping on civilian areas in Hanoi and other towns, resulting in large numbers of casualties. Salisbury also reported that North Vietnamese government officials seemed prepared to fight a long war of attrition and that local morale was high despite the bombing.

The publication of Salisbury's reports in the *Times* inspired a new debate over Vietnam in a country that had been led to believe that the war effort in Vietnam was proceeding well and that bombers were ordered to avoid civilian areas, seeking only military targets. Many U.S. officials, including President Lyndon Johnson, expressed regret over civilian casualties while criticizing Salisbury for exacting sympathy for North Vietnam. Salisbury was also attacked by certain fellow journalists, not only for giving aid and comfort to Hanoi but for not revealing his sources. Editors at the *Washington Post* noted that some of the casualty figures Salisbury cited were similar to those appearing in North Vietnamese propaganda pamphlets. A *Times* editor simply retorted that that was because both Salisbury and the propagandists had gotten their figures from the North Vietnamese government.

Other politicians and journalists praised Salisbury for being willing to paint an unpopular picture of American actions in Vietnam. From 1967 on, many more newspapers proved ready to print articles and editorials that were critical of the war or that questioned official government or military reports. Salisbury, meanwhile, published his reports from Hanoi in book form in *Behind the Lines: Hanoi, December 23, 1966–January 7, 1967*. **See also** media and the Vietnam War.

## San Antonio Formula

The name given by officials to a plan devised by advisers to President Lyndon B. Johnson to open negotiations between the United States and North Vietnam. Johnson announced the plan during a speech he gave in September 1967 in San Antonio, Texas. According to the proposal, the United States would promise to end all bombing of North Vietnam by air and sea provided that Hanoi begin peace negotiations and stop sending supplies and men south down the Ho Chi Minh Trail.

The San Antonio Formula was the result of independent peace feelers made by two Frenchmen, Herbert Marcovich and Raymond Aubrac, and Henry Kissinger, at that time a private American citizen. After the Frenchmen opened a diplomatic channel to Hanoi, Kissinger traveled there to present an early version of the San Antonio propositions to North Vietnamese officials. This took place in August 1967, a month before Johnson's speech. Hanoi, however, rejected the offer, demanding an unconditional cessation of bombing before opening peace talks. Despite this rejection, the San Antonio Formula provided both sides with the blueprint to open negotiations, and a bombing halt in exchange for opening negotiations remained the basis for potential peace talks till they actually began after Johnson renewed the offer on March

31, 1968. **See also** Paris negotiations; peace initiatives.

## sanctuaries

The name given to sites where U.S. and South Vietnamese commanders suspected that Communist troops might gather or resupply safe from attack. Officers almost invariably used the term in reference to territory in Laos or Cambodia, although occasionally sites in South Vietnam were also referred to as sanctuaries. From the perspective of commanders, the existence of such sanctuaries provided the Communists with a distinct advantage: Since both Laos and Cambodia were technically neutral until 1970, U.S. and South Vietnamese forces could not approach the sanctuaries. Meanwhile, and generally thanks to the Ho Chi Minh Trail, Communist troops could easily infiltrate and supply areas close to much of the border of South Vietnam. Beginning early in the war, U.S. commanders lobbied for the ability to root out such sanctuaries, but politicians were reluctant to violate the neutrality of Cambodia and Laos. The neutrality became less of a concern in 1969 and thereafter, when U.S. bombing raids targeted suspected sanctuaries and when invasions of both countries were designed, ostensibly, to root them out. **See also** Cambodia, invasion of; Laos, secret war in.

## Seabees

The construction engineers and crews of the U.S. Navy. Their name comes from the pronunciation of "CBs," or "construction battalions." In Vietnam, contingents of Seabees were among the most visible rear-echelon or support troops (although in fact they often worked under enemy fire). Beginning in 1963, when two small units arrived to support U.S. Special Forces units, Seabees were involved in the construction of military camps, roads, airfields, port facilities, ammunition and supply depots, and other sites. They also took part in various pacification tasks, most notably the construction of hospitals and housing, the digging of wells and clearing of land for cultivation, and the building of roads. They often worked side by side with Vietnamese villagers.

In 1969 there were as many as twenty-six thousand Seabees in Vietnam. Most of them were stationed in the northern military region of I Corps at such sites as Da Nang, Dong Ha, and Chu Lai. Although they were strictly speaking noncombatants, Seabees formed combat units when necessary, usually to deal with snipers. Hundreds were wounded and some sixty were killed in Vietnam. By 1971, when most of the facilities that the United States planned to build had been built, most Seabee units had been withdrawn. The last Seabees left Vietnam in 1972. **See also** Navy, U.S.

## Sea Dragon

One of the major naval operations of the Vietnam War. Operation Sea Dragon was designed to hamper any attempts by the North Vietnamese to transport supplies by sea to their comrades in South Vietnam and to directly attack shore installations. In this latter capacity the operation was a counterpart to Operation Rolling Thunder, the bombing campaign against North Vietnam.

Operation Sea Dragon began in October 1966 when two ships of the U.S. Seventh Fleet, the destroyers *Mansfield* and *Hanson*, began patrol operations north of the demilitarized zone (DMZ). By the middle of 1967, operations had expanded to include other destroyers and cruisers and, temporarily, the battleship *New Jersey*, and they ranged as far north as the twentieth parallel. Actual attacks were made by smaller gunboats, which targeted not only North Vietnamese craft but also such shore installations as bridges, radar stations, repair facilities, and gun-sites. These attacks were sometimes supported by artillery bombardments from the larger vessels.

Operation Sea Dragon appeared to be a success. More than two thousand Communist vessels were destroyed or damaged in one year, and the flow of supplies to the south was drastically reduced. The success came with a cost, however, as the North Vietnamese challenged the operations with vastly increased offshore fire, which also reduced the effectiveness of the attacks on shore facilities. Five sailors were killed and twenty-six wounded over the course of the operation. A total of twenty-nine U.S. ships were damaged, although none were sunk.

After President Lyndon B. Johnson declared a bombing halt in April 1968, the area of operations for Sea Dragon was reduced to the region from the nineteenth parallel south to the DMZ. When Johnson stopped the bombings of North Vietnam altogether on October 31, Operation Sea Dragon was officially ended. **See also** Market Time; Navy, U.S.

## SEALs

The elite special forces branch of the U.S. Navy, known by the acronym for SEa, Air, Land. In addition to various specialized skills ranging from hand-to-hand fighting to navigation, members were trained in parachute operations, land combat, and underwater infiltration; thus, the acronym was fully justified.

Navy SEALs were used primarily in the Mekong Delta during the Vietnam War. From bases on specially configured submarines, SEALs mounted various infiltration and interdiction missions as far as twenty miles inland. Their tasks included attacks on Viet Cong (VC) outposts, the destruction of supply and communications networks, and mine removal. In one operation in 1966 the SEALs, formed into special "hunter-killer" squads of three to seven men using

small boats and small arms, virtually cleared an area earlier known for intensive VC activity near Saigon known as Rung Sat. Other SEAL units were assigned to the Military Assistance Command, Vietnam's so-called Studies and Observation Group engaged in covert activities, with the various mobile riverine units in the delta, or in training South Vietnamese counterparts.

After 1970 SEALs continued to engage in covert operations along the South Vietnamese coast, together with affiliated units known as underwater demolition teams (UDTs). They were only withdrawn completely from Vietnam in late 1972. A total of forty-nine SEAL and UDT personnel died in action in Vietnam, and none were captured. **See also** Mobile Riverine Force; Navy, U.S.; Special Forces, U.S. Army.

## search and destroy

A controversial term used to describe the American approach to ground combat in Vietnam in the period from 1964 to 1968. Allegedly developed by General William Westmoreland, commander of the Military Assistance Command, Vietnam (MACV), and some of his staff officers, search and destroy was used to support the strategy of victory by attrition. According to this strategy, American troops would exact such heavy losses on both the Viet Cong (VC) and the North Vietnamese Army (NVA) that both would, in time, lose their willingness to fight. Westmoreland, who denied that search and destroy was ever a specific tactic, hoped that it would simultaneously minimize U.S. casualties.

The key to search and destroy was American superiority in equipment and technology. American forces would be dropped by helicopter, or march in from base camps, to areas that had perhaps already been cleared of jungle cover by napalm or defoliation attacks. They were to locate VC or NVA units, fix them in place, and destroy them as well as their base areas and stocks of supplies. Then, U.S. troops could be lifted out again by helicopter. The strategy was not designed to take and hold enemy territory.

Not all military commanders agreed with Westmoreland's approach, and in time search and destroy proved ineffective. One reason why was a steady supply of NVA reinforcements, which negated the tactic of attrition. Another was the fact that Communist forces, rather than American ones, frequently initiated the fighting and often chose to fade away before search-and-destroy tactics could begin. Moreover, many U.S. politicians and ordinary citizens, when they learned of search-and-destroy missions or saw pictures of operations taken by soldiers or journalists, were horrified at the violence and brutality, especially when it seemed like entire villages were being destroyed for no reason. Still others wondered why

the tactic did not result in taking territory, rather than simply upping the enemy body count.

This approach to ground combat began to shift to more conventional fixed battles in 1969, by which time Westmoreland had been replaced as MACV commander and more of the fighting turned over to the South Vietnamese army. **See also** attrition strategy; enclave strategy; Westmoreland, William.

## search and rescue (SAR)

The program to retrieve aircrew members whose planes were shot down. Both the U.S. Navy, which used navy and marine pilots, and the U.S. Air Force developed extensive search-and-rescue capabilities, and their efforts saved hundreds of pilots and crewmen from death or capture in Vietnam.

The first large SAR efforts were mounted by the navy from destroyers stationed off the Vietnamese coast. They

*Soldiers scour the jungle near Hue for Viet Cong fighters.*

used specially equipped helicopters for both pickups and support. The largest SAR team was the air force's Third Aerospace Rescue and Recovery Group, which began operations in January 1966 and slowly took over SAR from the navy. It was based at Tan Son Nhut in Saigon but also had operations in Da Nang, Tuy Hoa in central Vietnam, and at Udon Thani in Thailand. Rescue operations usually consisted of two helicopters accompanied by fighter jets for security and support. One helicopter made the actual pickup of downed airmen once they were located. This function was greatly helped in 1967 when the so-called Jolly Green Giant jungle penetrator was added to helicopters' equipment. This device could poke deeply through jungle foliage and featured a basket for pickups. The second helicopter was maintained as a backup if the first was shot down. As the SAR system became more refined, pilots were taught that, if their planes became disabled, they should try to fly to a designated region in the Gulf of Tonkin or to one of several specially chosen jungle areas before ejecting or attempting crash landings. They would then be easier to locate and rescue.

SAR teams saved more than forty-two hundred aircrew members and civilians between 1964 and 1973. A total of seventy-one SAR personnel were killed in action and forty-five helicopters were shot down while engaging in rescues, mostly by North Vietnamese air defense batteries. **See also** Huey; medevac program.

## Seventh Air Force

The component of the U.S. Air Force that had responsibility for air operations in South Vietnam. It replaced the Second Air Division on April 1, 1966, once the U.S. commitment had altered from support and advice for South Vietnam to direct military operations. Its chief was the deputy to the commander of the U.S. Military Assistance Command, Vietnam (MACV), but ultimately the Seventh Air Force was under the command of the U.S. Pacific Command based in Honolulu, Hawaii. Its activities were also coordinated with air force commanders at Clark air base in the Philippines and at Udon Thani in Thailand, where air force operations over Laos and North Vietnam were based.

The Seventh Air Force was based at Tan Son Nhut air base near Saigon, and it reached its height in 1969, when air force activities had helped turn Tan Son Nhut into the busiest airport in the world. Other major air bases included that at Bien Hoa, the headquarters of the Third Tactical Fighter Wing; Da Nang, where the 366th Tactical Fighter Wing was stationed; and Cam Ranh Bay, home of the Twelfth Tactical Fighter Wing. In addition, the Seventh Air Force controlled tactical airlift operations, the use of side-firing gunships, and other support operations. Its major contribution to the war, until 1969, was Operation Rolling Thunder, the attempt to saturate North Vietnam with enough bombs to convince the Communists to both negotiate a peace and stop supporting insurgents in the south. **See also** Air Force, U.S.; Rolling Thunder; Tan Son Nhut.

## Seventh Fleet

The component of the U.S. Navy stationed in the western Pacific during the Vietnam War years and therefore the fleet responsible for the navy's contribution to the war. The Seventh Fleet's home port was at Yokusaka, Japan, and its regional commander was the commander in chief of the Pacific Command in Honolulu, Hawaii.

The main components of the Seventh Fleet involved in Vietnam were Task Force Seventy-seven, which conducted air operations using navy pilots and aircraft carriers; Task Force Seventy-six, which mounted amphibious operations along the Vietnamese coastline and in inland waterways; and Task Force Seventy-three, which handled logistics and support and also commanded several hospital ships. The Seventh Fleet also included Task Group Seventy, a collection of warships responsible for naval bombardment in support of onshore combat operations. The most powerful ship in the group was the battleship *New Jersey*, the largest battleship deployed in the Vietnamese theater. The fleet also included a number of destroyers and cruisers. Naval bombardment was extensive from 1965 to 1972. During the Tet Offensive, for instance, the *New Jersey* alone fired nearly fifteen thousand shells in support of U.S. Marine operations near the demilitarized zone (DMZ). No large vessels of the Seventh Fleet were sunk during the Vietnam War, but a number of them took hits from either North Vietnamese planes or shore artillery. **See also** aircraft carriers; Mobile Riverine Force; Navy, U.S.; Southeast Asia Lake, Ocean, River, and Delta Strategy.

## Shining Brass

The code name for the missions of U.S. Special Forces units, accompanied by Montagnard or South Vietnamese troops, who crossed the border into Laos in one of the largest Special Forces campaigns of the Vietnam War. Shining Brass was under the command of the so-called Studies and Observation Group of the Military Assistance Command, Vietnam. It began in 1965 when twelve-man teams entered Laos on foot to scout out possible bombing targets and perform other reconnaissance. In later years the teams were sometimes larger, and their activities expanded to include the placing of explosives and, when necessary, engaging Communist troops from either Laos or North Vietnam. Because of the difficult

terrain, they were sometimes dropped in from helicopters and were often pulled out the same way. The area of operations for Shining Brass was a long stretch of the regions around the Ho Chi Minh Trail in southeastern Laos, and teams were given the freedom to enter the country to a depth of twenty kilometers. In 1968 the operation was renamed Prairie Fire and in 1971, when it was turned over to the South Vietnamese as a result of the Vietnamization policy, Phu Dung. **See also** Civilian Irregular Defense Groups; long-range reconnaissance patrols; Special Forces, U.S. Army.

## Sihanouk, Norodom (1922– )

The nominal leader of Cambodia under various titles for most of the period from 1941 to 1997. During the Vietnam War, until his partial ouster from power in March 1970, he tried to keep Cambodia neutral while war in Vietnam and Laos raged, but ultimately the task proved impossible.

Norodom Sihanouk was born on October 31, 1922. A member of the Cambodian royal family, he was educated in France. He emerged as the dominant figure in Cambodian politics when, in early 1941, he took over the Royal Council to the Cambodian throne on behalf of his father, the aged king. During the World War II occupation of Cambodia by the Japanese, he was kept under house arrest. When the Japanese overthrew the Vichy French administration of Indochina in March 1945, he was released and proclaimed that French rule over his country was over. He remained head of state as king until 1955, when he abdicated the throne in favor of his father. Sihanouk then took the title of prime minister. By that year Cambodia had become fully independent thanks to the Geneva Accords.

In 1960, when his father died, Sihanouk ended the monarchy and took power as head of state. Over the next years he found himself faced with difficult challenges as the Vietnam War expanded and as the United States sent forces to both South Vietnam to his east and Thailand to his west. This encouraged the growth of both anti-Sihanouk exiles in those countries and Communist groups, which took refuge in Cambodia. Partly as a result of bombings along the nation's eastern border by American and South Vietnamese planes, Sihanouk ended formal relations with the United States and South Vietnam. He also found himself forced to compromise with the North Vietnamese, opening the so-called Sihanouk Trail as an extension of the Ho Chi Minh Trail and supplying their troops with rice, trucks, and other goods. Meanwhile, a native Communist insurgency arose in the isolated areas of northern Cambodia; Sihanouk derisively called them Khmer Rouge, or "red Cambodians."

Sihanouk renewed relations with the United States in early 1969. Moreover, in hopes of stifling the growing Khmer Rouge insurgency, he formed a "Government of National Salvation" headed by General Lon Nol. Lon Nol was associated with Cambodians who resented Sihanouk's flirtations with Vietnamese Communists. In March 1970, Lon Nol's government voted Sihanouk out of office. Sihanouk retreated to Beijing, the capital of China, whose leaders he considered old friends. From China he issued statements against Lon Nol's regime, which in time became allied to the United States and South Vietnam, and proclaimed himself willing to work with the Khmer Rouge to form an alternative regime to Lon Nol's. Although he remained in Beijing during the five years that it took the Khmer Rouge to establish domination over Cambodia and seize the capital, Phnom Penh, Sihanouk's support may have lent the Khmer Rouge a legitimacy among the Cambodian populace that it might not have otherwise enjoyed.

After the Khmer Rouge takeover in April 1975, Sihanouk returned to Phnom Penh. The Communist leaders, however, kept him, again, under virtual house arrest. His only purpose to their eyes was bringing the regime a mild projection of legitimacy and a seat in the United Nations (UN). In 1978, just before a Vietnamese invasion ousted the Khmer Rouge from Phnom Penh and replaced it with a puppet regime, Sihanouk left for exile in China. He remained there until the Vietnamese finally left in 1989. As Cambodia sought stabilization over the next years, Sihanouk retained elder statesman status and a large measure of reverence from ordinary Cambodians. **See also** Cambodia, invasion of; Khmer Rouge; Lon Nol.

## Sihanouk Trail

An adjunct to the Ho Chi Minh Trail that was open from 1965 to 1970. The supply line was named after Cambodian president Norodom Sihanouk, a leader who struggled mightily to maintain his country's neutrality while an overt war raged next door in Vietnam and a covert war was under way in neighboring Laos. One of the compromises he was forced to make was to allow the North Vietnamese Communists to use his territory, both on the Ho Chi Minh Trail proper and along the Sihanouk Trail.

The Sihanouk Trail stretched from the ocean port of Sihanoukville (later Kompong Som) to the eastern regions of the nation, which bordered South Vietnam. The pathway allowed the North Vietnamese to bring supplies by ship and then transport them a relatively short distance to maintain their own forces as well as the Viet Cong. The trail also allowed the Communists easy access to Cambodia's rich annual rice crop. Since Cambodia remained a neutral country, neither the United States nor South Vietnam was willing to take the risk of striking out against either Sihanoukville or the trail. The Sihanouk Trail was closed, however, when Sihanouk was ousted from power in March 1970 by Lon Nol and others tired of Vietnamese incursions on Cambodian soil. **See also** Cambodia, invasion of; Ho Chi Minh Trail; sanctuaries; Sihanouk, Norodom.

## slang of the Vietnam War

U.S. soldiers used a wide and colorful variety of slang phrases to foster camaraderie, vent frustration, emotionally distance themselves from the war's horrors and crushing boredom, and demonize the enemy during the Vietnam War. Some slang was a carry-over from earlier eras but much was unique to Vietnam and has since entered general American vocabulary. Much slang was directly related to military activity or to one's fellow troops. A "cherry," for instance, was a soldier who had just recently arrived "in country," particularly one who had not experienced combat. Similarly, experienced soldiers called newly arrived officers without combat experience "shake 'n' bakes." Infantry troops were referred to as "grunts," ostensibly from the sound they made picking up their equipment, which they then "humped" for endless "klicks" (kilometers) through the "boonies" (jungle) or through "villes" (villages) full of "hooches" (huts or houses), always on the lookout for "doubtfuls," or local people whose loyalties could not be discerned. Military maps that indicated little about true conditions on the ground were simply called "comic books." Due to their mysterious missions and covert abilities, Special Forces troops were acclaimed as "sneaky petes."

Soldiers also used a number of Vietnamese words or phrases as well as the odd French term such as *beaucoups* (pronounced *bookoo*), or "much." They learned to say *dung lai*, or "halt"; *khong biet*, or "I don't understand"; and *xin loi*, which meant "excuse me" but which

troops used instead of "too bad" or "that's life." *Di di mau* meant "move quickly," while *dinky dau*, a popular phrase, meant "You're crazy." Shorthand for something good was "number one"; "number ten" was bad and "number ten thousand" was very, very bad.

Soldiers often referred to the Viet Cong as "Charlie," derived from the alphabetic code "Victor Charlie," or VC. Partly because it was difficult to tell enemies from "friendlies" among the "indidge" (indigenous) population, American troops in Vietnam often applied racist generalizations to all locals, a practice characteristic of combatants in all wars who find ways to dehumanize their enemies. A term first used in the Korean War, "gook," was applied to all Asians, as were "dink" and "slope." Soldiers also used the term "roundeye" to refer to people of European descent.

The vehicles and equipment soldiers depended on in Vietnam also drew mostly respectful slang tags. Helicopters in general were "choppers"; medevac choppers were "dustoffs"; and troop or cargo choppers without attack armament were "slicks." F-105 fighter-bombers were "thuds," and the huge B-52 bomber was a "BUF." The standard M-16 rifle was a "widow maker."

Perhaps because it was the overriding concern of almost all American troops in Vietnam, surviving one's tour of duty and returning to "the world" was the source of some of the most vivid slang. A soldier who was "short" was someone who had only a brief time left in Vietnam. Once one's time was up, he had "a duffle bag drag and a bowl of corn flakes," or final meal, before boarding the "freedom bird" for the ride back to the United States, or "the land of the big PX."

## smart bombs

Bombs equipped with electronic guidance systems; also known as precision-guided missiles (PGMs). Evolving from radio-guided missiles developed during World War II, two major types of smart bombs were used during the Vietnam War. The first was a laser-guided bomb that used a pulsing or "strobe" laser beam that would shine off its target, producing reflected light. The reflected light would then indicate to the device's electronics where the bomb should go. The laser-guidance device could be fitted to conventional munitions. The second smart bomb was known as an electro-optical-guided bomb. It employed a small camera that was fitted into the nose of a bomb known as a "walleye." The bombardier first aimed the camera at the target and then the bomb used an internal computer to deliver it to the spot where it was aimed. After a number of refinements, walleyes could travel up to thirty-two miles provided that the target was large enough for the computer's "seeker" to lock onto.

Smart bombs, the great majority of which were the laser-guided variety, were used in Vietnam by the U.S. Air Force and Navy. Altogether some thirty thousand were dropped, a tiny percentage of the total number of bombs dropped. Nonetheless, the smart bombs were far more accurate than conventional, or "dumb," bombs. This accuracy allowed for not only more reliable target destruction but also far fewer casualties among the North Vietnamese civilian population. Another advantage smart bombs provided was to allow for flight strategies that were far less dangerous to bomber crews than conventional bombing runs. **See also** dumb bombs; Linebacker I.

## Son Tay raid

The attempted rescue in November 1970 of American prisoners of war held at Son Tay Prison twenty miles north of Hanoi. Planning for the raid began in the summer of 1970. Final preparations called for a large force of army Rangers to be dropped over the prison compound by helicopter, while being supported by various army and air force aircraft as well as a large diversionary fleet of planes over Hanoi.

The raid began early on the morning of November 21. Although some Rangers were dropped at a North Vietnamese training site by mistake, where they found themselves in a firefight they quickly won, the raiding party reunited and ultimately took control of the prison. They found no American prisoners, however, since all those held there had been shifted to other locations in earlier months because of, supposedly, bad water at the prison. After another brief firefight, the Rangers withdrew by helicopter and headed back to their base in Thailand.

The Son Tay raid was considered by many to be a tactical success, despite the fact that no prisoners were recovered. It proved, among other things, that American forces could easily infiltrate into positions in North Vietnam and cause a great deal of trouble. Moreover, there were no U.S. casualties except for one soldier with a broken ankle, whereas dozens of North Vietnamese soldiers were killed. The greatest lasting effect of the raid was probably the response of North Vietnamese officials. To discourage a repeat of the raid, they moved all American prisoners into several central locations in Hanoi, which provided for greater contact and, apparently, higher morale among the prisoners. **See also** Hanoi Hilton; prisoners of war.

## Southeast Asia Lake, Ocean, River, and Delta Strategy (SEALORDS)

A combined effort on the parts of American and South Vietnamese land and sea forces to secure southern, inland Vietnam, mostly the Mekong Delta. Once implemented, SEALORDS would cut off supply lines between Cambodia and the Viet Cong (VC), provide the means to harass local VC bases, and help pacify the local population. It was conceived in the fall of 1968 by Vice Admiral Elmo R. Zumwalt Jr., American naval commander in Vietnam.

Also known as Task Force 194, SEALORDS used a wide variety of vessels from both American and South Vietnamese waterborne operations, and it had the capability of calling in ground and air support. Its most basic task was the interdiction of supplies and reinforcements from across the Cambodian border, and to that end it constructed a network of barriers, many of them electronic, across waterways. In the process of building these barriers, SEALORDS forces also engaged in the harassment of VC units and showed that it was possible for military operations to proceed effectively in the vast labyrinth of rivers and other waterways in the Mekong Delta. By 1969 SEALORDS units had constructed barriers stretching from Tay Ninh, northwest of Saigon, to the Gulf of Thailand in the south.

The success of SEALORDS in the delta led to its expansion elsewhere, including the rivers of Hoi An and Cua Dai far to the north of Saigon. In 1970, during the brief invasion of Cambodia, a SEALORDS unit made up of South Vietnamese naval forces was able to travel all the way up to the Cambodian capital of Phnom Penh, thus demonstrating its relative mastery of the inland waterways. According to the policy of Vietnamization adopted by U.S. forces in 1969, SEALORDS was slowly turned over to the South Vietnamese completely, and by April 1971, U.S. forces had stopped their involvement. **See also** Mobile Riverine Force; Navy, U.S.; Sea Dragon.

## Southeast Asia Treaty Organization (SEATO)

An organization set up under American sponsorship in 1954. Conceived by President Dwight D. Eisenhower and Secretary of State John Foster Dulles, the Southeast Asia Treaty Organization was an attempt to establish a collective security arrangement to contain the spread of communism in the region. In that sense it was similar to the North Atlantic Treaty Organization (NATO), which provided collective security to Europe. However, unlike the NATO charter, the SEATO charter failed to provide for standing armed forces as a deterrent and therefore proved less effective. SEATO members, who gathered in Manila, Philippines, on September 8, 1954, to sign the charter, included the United States, Great Britain, France, Australia, New Zealand, Thailand, and the Philippines. In a specific protocol negotiated by Dulles at the behest of Eisenhower, the SEATO charter named South Vietnam, Laos, and Cambodia specifically as three states that, if threatened, could undermine the stability of Southeast Asia in general. Therefore, SEATO members could consider fighting there. This protocol was in contradiction to the Geneva Accords, which in any case the United States did not sign, as the accords provided for the ongoing neutrality of all three states. In time, the Cambodians rejected the SEATO charter, as did the Laotians. The South Vietnamese, however, found it an effective diplomatic cover under which to establish a permanent northern border, although they were never full members.

Arguably, SEATO remained effective for a number of years as a deterrent to Communist aggression, especially in combination with the military effort in Vietnam in the 1960s by not only the United States but also SEATO members Australia, New Zealand, Thailand, and the Philippines. The pact was weakened, however, by the refusal of other regional powers, such as Indonesia and Malaysia, to join, as well as by its lack of specific military provisions. Had it been as clear as the NATO pact, for instance, the British and French would have been obligated to send troops to Vietnam as well. The SEATO charter expired in 1977 and was not renewed. **See also** Eisenhower, Dwight D.; Free World Assistance Program.

## South Vietnam
See Vietnam, Republic of.

## Souvanna Phouma (1901–1984)
The prime minister of Laos during the Vietnam War years. A member of the Lao royal family, Souvanna Phouma rose to prominence as a politician when Laos received its independence from France, and he was head of state during the 1954 Geneva Conference. He continued to serve as prime minister over the next years in a series of coalition governments. The greatest challenges faced by Souvanna included the Communist Pathet Lao insurgency, which enjoyed the support of North Vietnam, and the large conflict taking shape across the border in Vietnam itself. At various points Souvanna found himself forced to accept Pathet Lao representatives into his government, and when, in 1958, the Pathet Lao's political wing won a partial electoral majority, he stepped down to become ambassador to France.

In 1960 Souvanna returned to Laos and emerged as head of the neutralist faction hoping to solidify the nation's political structure, stop a Communist advance, and keep their country out of the simmering Vietnam conflict. The neutralists were opposed by, again, the Pathet Lao, and from the other side by militarists who somewhat resembled the leaders of South Vietnam. These militarists enjoyed the covert support of the United States because of their active opposition to communism. Although Souvanna, with the king's support, tried to once again form compromise coalition governments including both the Pathet Lao and the rightists, his efforts came to nothing. Meanwhile, the United States did not recognize him as the legal head of state. By early 1961 militarist attacks had forced Souvanna into exile, first in Phnom Penh, Cambodia, and then a base in a village in Laos's Plain of Jars. To counter the militarists, he accepted military help from the Pathet Lao, North Vietnam, and even the Soviet Union.

This brief war ended in a negotiated cease-fire in May 1961. Soon afterward a conference was convened in Geneva to settle the Laotian problem. It was attended by representatives of fourteen concerned nations, including the United States. At the conference President John F. Kennedy spoke strongly against the spread of communism to Laos. The conference organized yet another coalition government, naming Souvanna Phouma prime minister. The coalition eventually collapsed, and Laos went on to become a major, if somewhat hidden, arena of warfare during the Vietnam War. Souvanna, as titular head of the Royal Lao government, was recognized by all foreign powers, including, in time, the United States. During the Vietnam War, Souvanna remained the Laotian focus of American efforts to prevent a Pathet Lao/North Vietnamese takeover of Laos, the recipient of large amounts of American financial and military aid.

A final coalition government took office in Vientiane, the capital, in February 1973. Souvanna remained prime minister, but with the withdrawal of U.S. financial and military resources from Southeast Asia, he found himself unable to withstand pressure from the emboldened Pathet Lao and its North Vietnamese allies. He was forced to step aside as head of state in December 1975. The new rulers of Laos would come from the Lao People's Revolutionary Party, a mysterious Communist organization that evolved from the Pathet Lao. Souvanna was named a special adviser to the new regime. **See also** Laos, secret war in; Pathet Lao.

## Special Forces, U.S. Army

Specially trained elite U.S. Army troops who were among the first Americans to participate in combat in Vietnam. Officially formed in 1952 and trained at Fort Bragg, North Carolina, U.S. Special Forces units were trained in infiltration, intelligence, communications, sabotage, and medicine in addition to standard combat procedures. President John F. Kennedy, who appreciated the role that Special Forces might play in counterinsurgency warfare, provided them green berets in 1961 as a mark of distinction.

The first Green Berets in Vietnam were members of the First Special Forces Group station in Okinawa. They arrived in Vietnam in the summer of 1957 with instructions to train Vietnamese counterparts. From 1960 to 1964 Special Forces formed the core of the U.S. training effort in South Vietnam. Also, beginning in 1961, Special Forces began working with Montagnards to form the Civilian Irregular Defense Groups (CIDGs), which would attempt to secure South Vietnam's mountainous border regions. Green Berets also took part in pacification programs such as securing villages and working with ordinary Vietnamese.

By 1965 units of Special Forces were being regularly rotated into Vietnam from the First, Fifth, and Seventh Special Forces Groups. They were by then under the operational control of the Military Assistance Command, Vietnam (MACV), which wanted to emphasize their training and paramilitary functions rather than their role in pacification efforts. Among the most notable of the paramilitary functions were the long-range reconnaissance patrols (LRRPs) that troops often went on in the company of CIDGs. Elsewhere,

Special Forces troops constituted most of the personnel involved in the various covert operations of the Studies and Observation Group. Beyond these activities Special Forces also ran a training center for South Vietnamese units near Nha Trang known as the MACV Recondo School.

In 1968, when they were at their greatest strength, there were some thirty-five hundred Special Forces troops in Vietnam, and those commanders with jurisdiction over their activities continually complained that there were never enough Green Berets to fulfill the various "special" jobs that they were suited for. Most Special Forces troops left Vietnam when the Fifth Special Forces Group was withdrawn in March 1971. A number of them remained, however, to continue their training operations as part of a Special Mission Advisory Group. Teams of Special Forces troops continued to train South Vietnamese (and also Cambodian) troops until February 1973.

The Special Forces in Vietnam were immortalized, to some tastes, by a movie called *The Green Berets*, released in 1968 and starring John Wayne, and by "The Ballad of the Green Berets," a 1967 hit song written and performed by Special Forces veteran Sergeant Barry Sadler. **See also** Civilian Irregular Defense Groups; long-range reconnaissance patrols; Studies and Observation Group.

## Spring Mobilization to End the War in Vietnam

The first well-organized nationwide demonstration against the Vietnam War in the United States. It took place on April 15, 1967, and consisted of two major demonstrations: a march to the United Nations building in New York City and a meeting in Kezar Stadium in San Francisco. Organizers included longtime activists from a variety of groups across the political spectrum. They hoped, in fact, that mobilizing support from disparate interest groups would demonstrate to the Johnson administration the depth and breadth of antiwar sentiment across America.

In New York City, an estimated 200,000 people attended the event. The keynote speaker was Dr. Martin Luther King Jr., famous nationwide for his civil rights activities. Other speakers included Dr. Benjamin Spock, a prominent physician; folksinger and political activist Pete Seeger; and African American leader Stokely Carmichael. In San Francisco fifty thousand protesters heard speakers such as Coretta Scott King, wife of Martin Luther King, and then-radical journalist Robert Scheer. Both events were accompanied by draft-card-burning ceremonies.

The reaction of the Johnson administration to the Spring Mobilization was highly critical. Organizers were accused of being Communist sympathizers and of giving comfort to the enemy. Nonetheless, the size of the two events and the broad spectrum of supporters showed that many mainstream Americans opposed the war, and the antiwar movement continued to grow. **See also** antiwar movement; National Coordinating Committee to End the War in Vietnam.

## Steel Tiger

A limited air operation designed to complement Operation Rolling Thunder, the bombing of the economic and industrial infrastructure of North Vietnam. Operation Steel Tiger was intended to supplement this effort by accomplishing a similar sort of interdiction via air strikes on the Ho Chi Minh Trail in eastern Laos.

Begun in April 1965, Steel Tiger was limited in its conception and had little effect on the southward flow of supplies and personnel. Understandably, U.S. president Lyndon B. Johnson and his staff were sensitive to the political fallout from an American bombing campaign against Laos, a nation whose neutrality the United States guaranteed in the 1962 Geneva Accords. They were concerned that an overt and widespread attack might result in military action on the part of China or the Soviet Union, and they were reluctant to give the world reason to accuse the United States of expanding the Vietnam conflict. Therefore the president and his staff maintained control over specific targets, selecting them in Washington, D.C., and then sending the orders to air force or navy commanders in Southeast Asia. These measures helped keep the attacks reasonably secret.

The aircraft used in Steel Tiger were from air force bases in South Vietnam or Thailand and from navy carriers in the South China Sea, and they included, in time, B-52 bombers. The two commands found it difficult to coordinate their actions, especially since they were given direction from Washington politicians, which limited the effectiveness of the bombing raids. Pilots also found themselves hindered by poor weather and visibility. Meanwhile, the attacks had little effect on traffic along the Ho Chi Minh Trail, much of which was either hidden by jungle cover or could be easily repaired.

In 1968 Steel Tiger was combined with a similar operation directed toward another stretch of the Ho Chi Minh Trail, Operation Tiger Hound, to form Operation Commando Hunt. All three operations helped make the small, sparsely populated, and undeveloped nation of Laos one of the most heavily bombed countries in the history of air warfare, and one which suffered the effects of tons of unexploded ordnance for years afterward. **See also** Barrel Roll; Commando Hunt; Ho Chi Minh Trail; Rolling Thunder.

## Stockdale, James (1923– )

Navy pilot who became one of the most prominent American prisoners of war

(POWs) in North Vietnam. Stockdale, at that time holding the rank of air group commander, was shot down over North Vietnam on September 9, 1965. He remained a prisoner until the release of all American POWs in February 1973 following the Paris Peace Accords. The strong-willed Stockdale, who was the highest-ranking navy man imprisoned, emerged as one of the leaders of the American POWs. He devised orders to ensure that fellow POWs held themselves to military codes of conduct and rose to be the head of the so-called Alcatraz Gang, a group of prisoners who resisted North Vietnamese attempts to break POWs and force their cooperation. Meanwhile, Stockdale's wife, Sybil, formed the National League of Families of American Prisoners and Missing in Vietnam, which, by 1969, was engaged in a massive letter-writing campaign thought by many to have improved conditions for POWs. After his release, Stockdale went on to become the president of the Naval War College. In 1976 he was awarded the Congressional Medal of Honor. **See also** Hanoi Hilton; Homecoming; McCain, John, III.

## strategic hamlets

An early pacification program devised by South Vietnamese president Ngo Dinh Diem and administered by his brother and chief adviser, Ngo Dinh Nhu. Evolving from the prior agroville campaign, the strategic hamlet program consisted of constructing new villages across South Vietnam. These new villages would then be provided with fortifications, military protection, and other security measures.

The strategic hamlet program was first implemented in 1961. Nhu, who commandeered the program, hoped that the strategic hamlets would help the Saigon government reach three goals: the establishment of a communications network linking villages for the purposes of de-

fense; an opportunity to impose economic and social reforms; and cementing the support of villagers for the government. The hamlets would be administered by officials sent out from Saigon.

Nhu planned for seven thousand villages to be constructed by 1963 and for an eventual total of fourteen thousand. Many fewer than that were actually built, and few functioned as the brothers had hoped. Many conflicts arose between local officials or village chiefs and Saigon officials over jurisdiction and responsibility. Moreover, local officials often sought to impress Saigon by providing false data or even by simply erecting fences, a measure that allowed their villages to be designated strategic hamlets. Villagers, for their part, resented being forced to relocate away from lands they and their ancestors had inhabited for centuries and where their ancestors' bones were buried, an important concern to rural Vietnamese. Villagers also balked at being forced into such tasks as guard duty.

Viet Cong (VC) groups, meanwhile, found in the strategic hamlet program a useful opportunity for propaganda and infiltration. VC leaflets and recruiters compared the hamlets to prisons, and VC cadres found it easy to enter the villages to seek recruits or speak out against the Saigon regime. By 1963, the VC was attacking strategic hamlets directly, and they found it reasonably easy to disperse South Vietnamese troops and police as well as sever communications links, thus undermining the defense function of the program. **See also** Ngo Dinh Nhu; pacification; Thompson, Robert G.K.

## Students for a Democratic Society (SDS)

A student protest group that played an important role in the anti–Vietnam War movement. Students for a Democratic Society was formed in January 1960 by, among others, Tom Hayden, a student at the University of Michigan. Its initial goals were to support the civil rights movement and take steps to involve poor people in politics. In July 1962 SDS issued the Port Huron Statement, one of the founding documents of the so-called New Left in American politics. The statement called for Americans to take more individual responsibility for the political decisions that affected them, which the SDS considered to be "true" democracy, as well as be willing to take direct, and hopefully nonviolent, political action.

After the Gulf of Tonkin Resolution of 1964, SDS, now a national organization with name recognition, emerged as a powerful antiwar voice. Members continued to focus their efforts on college campuses, and by 1968 there were up to four hundred SDS chapters, with tens of thousands of members on U.S. college and university campuses. SDS activities included demonstrations, teach-ins, and seeking ways to avoid the draft. At least initially, SDS was not connected to the emerging counterculture of hippies and others who seemed to reject American society, but over the years there was inevitably some overlap. In any case, the organization's wide reach and relative respectability lent the antiwar movement a great deal of credibility in mainstream America.

SDS began to splinter in 1967 and 1968. Some members began to advocate more direct action; SDS member Carl Davidson, for example, proposed in October 1967 that the group burn down draft offices. In addition, thousands of SDS members were present during the violent 1968 Democratic National Convention in Chicago. As the United States began to withdraw its troops in 1969, and as the other branches of the New Left sought more violent or solitary paths, the influence of the SDS began to wane. **See also** antiwar movement; Hayden, Tom.

# Studies and Observation Group (SOG)

A subordinate organization within the Military Assistance Command, Vietnam (MACV), designated to carry out intelligence gathering and covert operations. The Studies and Observation Group was first assembled in 1964 to assess the use of military advisers in South Vietnam, but it evolved rapidly into a cover for covert military activities. By 1996 SOG included some two thousand U.S. personnel from across the four military branches. Many of them were Special Forces–trained troops such as navy SEALs and air force special operations. The force also included eight thousand local people, most of them recruited from South Vietnamese or Montagnard units. SOG in its entirety was given a field of operations that included not only the two Vietnams but also Cambodia, Laos, southern China, and Burma.

To increase its effectiveness, officers divided SOG into several divisions, including psychological, maritime, air, and ground studies groups. Psychological group activities consisted primarily of misleading radio reports aimed at confusing Communist forces. The maritime division mounted commando raids behind enemy lines in North Vietnam and the Mekong Delta. The air studies group sent special units into North Vietnam, Laos, and Cambodia on intelligence missions. Finally, the ground studies group conducted the widest variety of missions, including the recovery of prisoners of war and downed pilots, sabotage, and the use of South Vietnamese and Montagnard troops on long-range reconnaissance patrols. SOG was also ultimately organized into three so-called central control commands. This was intended to supplement the larger U.S. strategies of attrition, weakening Communist forces, and pacifying civilian populations at a minimum cost to U.S. forces. After going through several reorganizations, SOG was officially disbanded in April 1972. **See also** counterinsurgency; Military Assistance Command, Vietnam; Special Forces, U.S. Army.

## Sullivan, William (1922– )

The U.S. ambassador to Laos from 1964 to 1969. Still a rather young man for so high a post, Sullivan was granted the ambassadorship after working closely with Averell Harriman, undersecretary of state to U.S. president John F. Kennedy, in ensuring the neutrality of Laos at a conference in Geneva in 1962. After being posted to the U.S. embassy in Vientiane, the capital of Laos, in December 1964, Sullivan took up the responsibility of guiding the "secret war" that America was conducting in the country. It remained secret for the next four years, in fact, largely because of Sullivan's insistence that the war effort not prove to be a diplomatic embarrassment to either the Royal Lao government or the Soviet Union, both of which were signatories to the 1962 Geneva agreement. This required the use of local troops rather than American ground forces, and in a tactic which in any case had already begun, Sullivan supported the expansion of the CIA-trained army of Hmong tribesmen as the main force against the Communist Pathet Lao. Sullivan was willing, however, to allow the use of American air support, a measure that could conceivably be justified by the fact that the Ho Chi Minh Trail, a target of U.S. bombing raids, traversed parts of southeastern Laos.

After leaving Vientiane in March 1969, Sullivan became a deputy assistant secretary of state for East Asian affairs. He played an important part in the creation of peace proposals for negotiation with North Vietnam and served as a deputy to National Security Adviser Henry Kissinger in formulating the Paris Peace Accords of January 1973. **See also** Air America; Laos, secret war in.

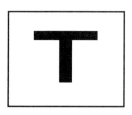

# T

## tanks and armored personnel carriers (APCs)

Armored vehicles, both tanks and armored personnel carriers, were widely used by U.S., South Vietnamese, and North Vietnamese forces. There were three U.S. Army tank battalions deployed in Vietnam, and infantry divisions generally included an armored component as well. The U.S. Marines also sent a tank battalion. The principal tanks used by the United States and its South Vietnamese allies were the M48 Patton and the Sheridan M551. The Patton proved to be better suited to jungle terrain than the Sheridan, although the latter was faster, more mobile, and had greater firepower. In fact, the Sheridan was equipped with a 152-millimeter cannon, the largest tank gun in the world. The M48 was the workhorse of the war, and in 1969 there were over 370 of them on the ground in Vietnam. Tanks were usually used in mop-up and securing operations rather than at the forefront of attacks. The largest operation in which tanks played a central role was Operation Lam Son 719 in 1971, the South Vietnamese invasion of Laos. The North Vietnamese, meanwhile, began using Soviet-made T-54 tanks in 1968. When after 1969 the war in Vietnam became one of more conventional battles rather than guerrilla warfare and search-and-destroy missions, North Vietnamese tank units played a major role. They were used effectively in both the Easter Offensive of 1972 and, especially, the Ho Chi Minh campaign of 1974 and 1975, when North Vietnamese armored units played a role in overwhelming the South Vietnamese military. In their few direct encounters, however, the T-54 proved no match for the M48.

The main APC used by American and South Vietnamese forces was the M113. It could be equipped with a wide variety of guns, including mortars and flamethrowers, and when properly armored was even used as an assault vehicle. In its way the M113 was a workhorse itself, flexible enough to be used in combat operations, construction work, communications, and even psychological warfare. M113s were unpopular with crewmen and other soldiers, however, because they were susceptible to enemy mines and, unless specially modified, did not provide much protection against large guns. **See also** artillery; gunships; mines.

## Tan Son Nhut

The major commercial and military airport in Saigon, the capital of the Republic of Vietnam (RVN, or South Vietnam). It was located only seven kilometers from the center of the city, and for several years in the late 1960s and early 1970s it was the busiest airport in the world. The first American installation at Tan Son Nhut was an air force control unit that was placed there in October 1961 and began sending out reconnaissance missions soon after. The airport already served as the headquarters of the air force of the RVN, and throughout the Vietnam

*American troops sit on an Ontos, an armored fighting vehicle. Smaller and lighter than a tank, the Ontos provided infantrymen with intense firepower.*

War the two air forces worked together closely. In 1964 the army air wing of the Military Assistance Command, Vietnam (MACV), was relocated to Tan Son Nhut as well. In 1967 a large complex was constructed at the airport to serve as headquarters for all of MACV; it came to be known locally as "Pentagon East." Meanwhile, reconnaissance missions, bombing raids, search-and-rescue missions, transport flights, and regular commercial flights expanded in number until, by 1969, Tan Son Nhut was indeed the busiest airport in the world. It was also the main disembarkation point for many American troops sent to Vietnam.

Tan Son Nhut was a frequent target of Viet Cong (VC) attacks, and was therefore tightly defended. The largest attack came during the 1968 Tet Offensive, when Communist forces moved deeply into the base before being turned away by American and South Vietnamese troops. The attack caused a great deal of damage to the airport. After most American troops departed from the RVN in early 1973, Pentagon East was turned over to the Defense Attaché Office attached to the U.S. embassy. Headquarters were also established there for the International Commission for Supervision and Control, which was supposed to preside over the implementation of the Paris Peace Accords.

Tan Son Nhut was again a major target during the final phase of the Ho Chi Minh campaign, North Vietnam's final offensive against the RVN in March and April 1975. Its runways suffered heavy bomb damage on April 28–30 that along with jettisoned bombs and fuel tanks, closed it to all air traffic except helicopters. During the attack, two U.S. Marines were killed by shrapnel, the last

Americans to be killed in Vietnam. Since Tan Son Nhut was designated one of the evacuation points for American and other foreign nationals, as well as for South Vietnamese who would be endangered in the event of a North Vietnamese takeover, the closing of the runways had a major impact on the ongoing evacuation. Nonetheless, some five thousand people were evacuated by navy helicopters on April 29 before the order came to shut down the operation. Afterward, the former MACV headquarters, which had already been wired with explosives, was blown up.

Tan Son Nhut went on to become the major air hub of southern Vietnam and served the Vietnamese air force as an important base. Years after the war ended, the site was still surrounded by empty buildings and the shells of American quonset huts. **See also** Frequent Wind; Seventh Air Force.

## Taylor, Maxwell (1901–1987)

U.S. Army general who served as a top military adviser to Presidents John F. Kennedy and Lyndon B. Johnson from 1961 to 1965. Taylor also served as chairman of the Joint Chiefs of Staff from 1962 to 1964 and as U.S. ambassador to the Republic of Vietnam (RVN, or South Vietnam) from July 1964 to July 1965.

A longtime success as a strategist, administrator, and field commander, Taylor was appointed army commander in chief for the Far East in 1953 and army chief of staff in 1955. In the latter position he expressed concerns that the U.S. military might be growing too reliant on nuclear weapons at the expense of flexible ground forces, a view he explained in a 1959 book, *The Uncertain Trumpet.*

Taylor retired from the army in 1959, but his book brought him to the attention of presidential candidate John F. Kennedy, who was also interested in developing flexible response capabilities

using U.S. ground forces, especially to combat Communist insurgency movements in developing countries. After he was elected in 1960, Kennedy appointed Taylor to a new post: military representative of the president. Among Kennedy's reasons for creating the post was that, supposedly, he had little confidence in traditional military channels of advice, namely the Joint Chiefs of Staff. Taylor, meanwhile, found himself elevated to the post of top military adviser to the president, and he took a particular interest in the situation in Vietnam.

Taylor first traveled to Vietnam in October 1961, sent by Kennedy on a fact-finding mission in the company of Walt Rostow, another adviser. The two returned with a report that was to shape the next years of U.S. policy in Vietnam. Taylor reported that two major problems threatened the ability of the RVN to stave off a Communist overthrow. The first was the imperiousness and corruption of the regime of RVN president Ngo Dinh Diem. The second was the sense that the United States would not act decisively to stop the spread of communism not only in the RVN but throughout Southeast Asia. To remedy those problems, Taylor recommended measures to strengthen the military forces of the RVN through the use of American advisers, training, and weaponry and encouraging Diem to undertake political and economic reforms. He also suggested that Kennedy send over eight thousand U.S. combat troops under the cover of a "flood control team," the first time since 1954 that anyone had meaningfully suggested a direct U.S. military commitment to the region. Although Kennedy rejected the idea of sending troops, he approved of Taylor's other recommendations. The result was a broader U.S. commitment of advisers and funds to the Diem regime, a sign, American officials were sure, of U.S. seriousness about stopping communism in the area.

In the fall of 1962 Kennedy recalled Taylor to active duty and named him chairman of the Joint Chiefs of Staff. Taylor returned to Vietnam several more times while in the position, expressing confidence each time that the expanding U.S. commitment of funds and advisers was working to strengthen the regime of Ngo Dinh Diem. Taylor worked very closely with Secretary of Defense Robert McNamara, who shared his ideas on flexible military response working together with political activities such as pacification. As the American stake in Vietnam grew, the region's importance to overall American security strategy grew as well. Taylor agreed with McNamara that Vietnam was now vital to U.S. security, a fundamental assumption behind the escalation of the Vietnam War in later years. Taylor also expressed a great deal of confidence, which some thought was misguided, in the military capabilities of the RVN. Indeed, Taylor suggested that both Diem's regime and its army would be strong enough by 1965 to allow the United States to withdraw its advisers and trainers. He opposed, on military grounds, the tacit U.S. support for the coup that overthrew Diem in November 1963.

As 1964 began, Taylor began to argue, along with the other members of the Joint Chiefs, that the United States should expand its direct military presence in the RVN, including selected bombing strikes against North Vietnam. In July of that year, President Lyndon B. Johnson named Taylor ambassador to South Vietnam, his most politically sensitive and challenging post yet. He proved unable to work effectively with the South Vietnamese generals who followed Diem as leaders of the RVN, and he had little grasp of Vietnamese culture. Taylor's tendency to be blunt and plainspoken, in addition to his impatience with the subtleties of Vietnamese politics, had Prime Minister Nguyen Khanh at one point considering whether Saigon should ask the United States to recall Taylor. Meanwhile, the ambassador worked with General William Westmoreland, American commander in the RVN, in devising new ways to help Saigon halt the growing threat of both the North Vietnamese Army and local Viet Cong (VC) guerrillas. Although he was reluctant, Taylor ultimately had to consider the possibility of sending regular U.S. combat troops, a measure Westmoreland strongly advocated. Taylor wanted to avoid sending the message to RVN leaders that the United States would be fighting their war for them.

In February 1965 Westmoreland asked for a contingent of U.S. Marines to protect the U.S. air base at Da Nang, a request which was granted. Faced with the arrival of the first regular American combat troops, Taylor took steps to try to restrict their use. He recommended a so-called enclave strategy in which American forces might simply be deployed to help secure important sites such as major cities, military bases, and ports. Over the next months he lost this argument to Westmoreland, who called instead for a larger American ground war and the use of a so-called search-and-destroy strategy, a far more aggressive tactic than Taylor's enclave strategy. Not long after, Taylor left office as ambassador, returning to Washington, D.C., as a special consultant to President Johnson. **See also** counterinsurgency; Kennedy, John F.; McNamara, Robert; Taylor-Rostow Report.

## Taylor-McNamara mission

A high-level fact-finding mission sent to Saigon by President John F. Kennedy in late September 1963. Its members included chairman of the Joint Chiefs of Staff Maxwell Taylor, Secretary of Defense Robert McNamara, Defense Department consultant William Bundy, State Department official William Sullivan, and William Colby of the Central Intelligence Agency (CIA). The purpose of the mission was to assess the security of the regime of South Vietnamese president Ngo Dinh Diem, which was being threatened by both public protest and coups planned by various South Vietnamese generals. The mission was also asked to report on the state of the conflict between Saigon and Viet Cong (VC) guerrillas and to determine whether further U.S. involvement was called for.

The mission remained in Saigon for eight days. Members met with both Diem and General Paul Harkins, the commander of the U.S. Military Assistance Command, Vietnam (MACV). Both Harkins and Diem expressed confidence, Harkins claiming that the situation might even be secure enough to allow large numbers of American military advisers to be rotated home. Diem, for his part, downplayed both the civil unrest and the military threats to his regime. McNamara, however, who had the primary responsibility of meeting with Diem, was uncertain.

After returning to the United States in early October, members of the mission released the so-called Taylor-McNamara Report to President John F. Kennedy. The emphasis of the report was on the American approach to the recalcitrant Diem. Although the mission did not believe that a coup was likely and recommended against U.S. support for such a move, members asserted that Diem had to be encouraged to alter his repressive and distant style of government. For example, the United States could assert pressure on Diem by reducing economic and military aid and make sure that the South Vietnamese president understood that further American help depended on containing his corrupt and aggressive brother Ngo Dinh Nhu. On the other major issue, the state of the war, the report was more optimistic, agreeing with

Harkins's assessment. Those who recommended putting pressure on Diem for reform wanted to make sure that any measures the United States undertook would not interfere with the war effort. **See also** Kennedy, John F.; McNamara, Robert; Taylor, Maxwell; Taylor-Rostow Report.

## Taylor-Rostow Report

A 1961 report that had a major impact on the evolution of U.S. policy in Vietnam. The report was made to President John F. Kennedy after a fact-finding mission to South Vietnam by General Maxwell Taylor, special military adviser to the president, and Walt Rostow, deputy national security adviser. The two visited Saigon from October 18 to 25, 1961, and delivered their findings to the president on November 3.

Taylor and Rostow arrived in Saigon when the South Vietnamese capital was in a state of high tension. Viet Cong (VC) guerrillas had just mounted a major attack on a nearby city, a sign of increased VC activity throughout southern Vietnam. In addition, a large flood had stricken the Mekong Delta region, bringing hardship. As a result, many ordinary Vietnamese were expressing their dislike for the regime of South Vietnamese president Ngo Dinh Diem, who seemed unwilling or unable to respond to either natural disasters or VC attacks. Diem was able to convince the Americans, though, that his regime was strong and remained the best hope for preventing a Communist takeover of South Vietnam.

The Taylor-Rostow Report asserted that the VC activity in South Vietnam, which was supported by the Communist regime in the north, was part of a larger Communist threat to all of Southeast Asia, and therefore implied that South Vietnam was a vital "domino" that the United States could not allow to fall. The Communist threat, however, could be contained by potential American airpower. Meanwhile, Taylor and Rostow suggested that the United States take steps to strengthen Diem's regime. Some of these steps were mostly symbolic at the time, such as signaling to Diem that the United States was serious in its support by expanding the U.S. Military Assistance and Advisory Group (MAAG) into the Military Assistance Command, Vietnam (MACV). Others were more practical, including various advisory and training programs aimed at the South Vietnamese military as well as intelligence-gathering and aid programs. Kennedy concurred with these recommendations and began to implement them in December after Diem, in exchange, promised to institute political reforms. **See also** Kennedy, John F.; Ngo Dinh Diem; Rostow, Walt; Taylor, Maxwell.

## teach-ins

A central tactic of antiwar activists in the United States. Modified from similar practices in the labor and civil rights movements, teach-ins involved lectures, question-and-answer sessions, films and other demonstrations, and rallies. The first anti–Vietnam War teach-in was held at the University of Wisconsin the night of March 24, 1965, and involved more than three thousand students. The success of the event inspired other teach-ins at college campuses across the country, and they became a familiar part of the antiwar movement, providing education and validating the support of protesters. **See also** antiwar movement.

## television and the Vietnam War

The Vietnam War was the first war to be televised, in part because only in the 1960s did most American homes have television sets and because television networks devoted unprecedented resources to coverage of the conflict. From 1964 to 1973, reports from Viet-

nam were featured almost nightly on TV news broadcasts by the three major networks at the time: ABC, CBS, and NBC. The perceived trustworthiness of TV news anchormen, notably Walter Cronkite of CBS, gave further credibility to these broadcasts. Americans became accustomed to seeing battle reports during their evening meals, and television inevitably played a role in shaping public opinions and perceptions of the war.

The influence of television on Vietnam has inspired much controversy. At one extreme, critics charged that television helped lose the war for the United States and that the medium's antiwar bias unfairly prejudiced public opinion. At the other extreme supporters of television coverage demanded that American citizens be given a full, uncensored picture of what their government had involved them in, regardless of morale or security concerns.

Much of the criticism arises from the nature of television broadcasts themselves. News clips and reports were often short and lacking in context, and editors were unable to resist the temptation, right or wrong, to emphasize the sensational: killed or wounded soldiers, hillsides exploding in clouds of napalm, helicopter evacuations, and the like. Since journalists with the proper credentials were granted full access without censorship, they were able to film or describe both the negative and positive aspects of the U.S. experience, and news editors at home were as prone to report on mistakes as they were successes. One vivid example was provided by the Tet Offensive of 1968, during which the reports and films of TV journalists caught up in the massive (if ultimately unsuccessful) Viet Cong attacks provided a direct contrast to the years of positive reports of progress from the Johnson administration and military officials. Cronkite, for his part, made it clear after Tet that he felt the Vietnam War might be unwinnable.

It was not until the late 1980s that the television networks felt comfortable presenting fictionalized accounts of the Vietnam War. The most popular TV series based on the war in Vietnam was *China Beach*, running from 1988 to 1992 and centered on the popular rest and recreation (R&R) spot south of Da Nang. Others included *Tour of Duty* (1987–1989) and HBO's *Vietnam War Story* (1989–1990). **See also** film and the Vietnam War; media and the Vietnam War.

## territorial forces

A major part of the total military forces of the Republic of Vietnam (RVN, or South Vietnam). The territorial forces were divided between regional and popular forces (known as "ruffs" and "puffs" to Americans) and resembled an army national guard combined with a national police force. Their primary responsibilities, from the time of their founding in 1955 until the fall of the RVN in 1975, were to provide rural security; guard roads, bridges, communications facilities, and other infrastructure elements; and assist the regular Army of the Republic of Vietnam (ARVN) when needed. Territorial forces soldiers made up as much as half the total manpower available to the RVN.

The regional forces were the more heavily militarized of the two divisions. Originally known as the civil guard, the regional forces, full-time, paid soldiers, were initially assigned to man rural outposts, where they were among the first to fight Viet Cong (VC) guerrillas. In 1964 the regional forces were integrated into the command structure of the ARVN. The popular forces, meanwhile, were made up of volunteers who had outside jobs. They were organized into small teams and generally assigned to guard duty and other tasks around members' home villages. They were also given a salary by the government of the RVN and, from 1964, were under ARVN command.

Within the South Vietnamese military culture, duty with the territorial forces was seen as second best, and regular ARVN officers avoided serving with them. Moreover, the ARVN often used the territorial forces to perform duties shunned by the regular army, such as search-and-destroy missions. Almost always inadequately trained, supplied, and armed, the territorial forces often found themselves without the operational or tactical support necessary to conduct such missions. Nonetheless, many ordinary South Vietnamese preferred service in the territorial forces to the ARVN, which removed them from their homes and forced them, perhaps, into directly supporting a regime they disliked rather than simply protecting their villages.

After the Tet Offensive of 1968, two new developments enlarged both the size and the role of the territorial forces. The first was a general mobilization law enacted in June 1968 that required all men in the RVN between the ages of eighteen and thirty-eight to serve in either the ARVN or the territorial forces. Many chose the latter. Then, in 1969, U.S. combat forces began their gradual withdrawal from Vietnam. Anticipating this move, the Americans had already taken steps to better train and equip the territorial forces. From 1968 to 1972, in fact, the territorial forces bore more of the brunt of the fighting against the North Vietnamese Army than the ARVN, although their budget continued to be far smaller. As a consequence, the territorial forces had far higher casualties. During the final North Vietnamese offensive of 1975, many of these units of "citizen soldiers" dissipated; those that remained were overwhelmed by the better-armed Communists. **See also** Army of the Republic of Vietnam; Nguyen Van Thieu; pacification; People's Self-Defense Forces.

# Tet Offensive

A major offensive mounted by the North Vietnamese Army (NVA) and Viet Cong (VC) in early 1968. Although it was a military failure for the Communists, the Tet Offensive proved to be a political victory that marked the turning point of the Vietnam War.

The Tet Offensive was the brainchild of Vo Nguyen Giap, the top commander of the NVA and an influential political figure as well. In the face of a military stalemate, Giap argued that the Hanoi regime needed to try to end the war with a single master stroke. Following the revolutionary doctrines of Mao Tse-tung, the Communist leader of China, Giap planned a general offensive that would be accompanied by a general uprising of ordinary people in South Vietnam. In the face of both, Giap hoped, the South Vietnamese army would collapse, the government in Saigon would be overthrown, and the Americans would lose their will to continue fighting.

Giap planned the general offensive for Tet 1968. Tet was the most important holiday in Vietnam, marking the beginning of the Lunar New Year. In earlier years both sides observed informal cease-fires during the Tet celebrations, but Giap and other Communist leaders wanted to strike when their enemies least expected it.

Preparations for the Tet Offensive began in the fall of 1967 when NVA and VC forces instigated a series of battles in the border regions and around the demilitarized zone (DMZ), the most notable of which were at Dak To and the U.S. Marine base at Khe Sanh. These actions were designed to draw U.S. and South Vietnamese forces away from the major urban centers, where Giap planned for the major Communist attacks to take place. These diversionary attacks, most notably that at Khe Sanh, proved to be reasonably successful. Fearful that Khe Sanh might represent the American Dien

Bien Phu, a 1954 battle site where the French were surrounded and ultimately defeated, U.S. politicians and commanders committed themselves to defending the base at all costs. The main place where diversionary actions failed to work was in the area around Saigon, where General Frederick C. Weyand, concerned about an increased level of Communist radio traffic, grew suspicious and convinced General William Westmoreland, commander of the Military Assistance Command, Vietnam, to allow him to pull back thirteen battalions of U.S. troops that might have been deployed elsewhere.

Giap planned for the nationwide offensive to commence on January 31, 1968, but VC units in Da Nang, Pleiku, Nha Trang, and a number of other areas in South Vietnam jumped the gun, beginning their attacks on January 30. As a result, South Vietnamese commanders canceled the holiday leaves they had given to their troops and prepared for a defense. U.S. forces also went on alert. The main thrust of the Tet Offensive began early in the morning of January 31 when VC troops attacked the presidential palace in Saigon and the nearby U.S. embassy. By the end of the day, the Communists had mounted attacks on virtually all of South Vietnam's important towns and cities and had taken control of Hue. They also were largely in command of Cholon, Saigon's Chinese district.

Most of the fighting was over within a few days, a resounding defeat for the Communists. Nevertheless, it provided numerous dramatic and tense moments, which were captured by journalists and photographers. The fight at the U.S. embassy, for instance, lasted for ten hours, and even civilian embassy officials found themselves taking part in the defense. The news that VC troops had been able to hold a portion of the embassy grounds even for such a short time was a shock to the United States and the world. The only areas where the fighting dragged on were Hue, which took shape as the major fixed battle of the Tet Offensive; Cholon, where street combat dragged on into early March; and Khe Sanh, which continued to occupy U.S. attention until late March.

The general uprising Giap had hoped for did not take place and, again, Tet proved extremely costly to the Communist cause. Since outside of Khe Sanh the VC bore the brunt of the fighting, it also took substantial losses. Many claimed that these losses destroyed the VC as an effective insurgency force, an argument strengthened by the fact that in the aftermath of Tet the NVA took on the majority of the fighting, which shifted from a guerrilla war to a more conventional war using ground armies. Saigon did not fall, despite the numerous attacks throughout the city, and the South Vietnamese army, for its part, held out reasonably well.

*Civilians flee from Hue during the Tet Offensive. They managed to safely cross the Perfume River despite the destroyed bridge.*

The Tet Offensive only secured the last of Giap's goals, which was to sap the will of the Americans to continue fighting. Much of the fault for this was the Americans' own: Up until Tet, reports from both commanders in Vietnam and politicians in Washington, D.C., had declared that they were winning the war. News of the nationwide offensive, and of such vivid events as shootouts in the U.S. embassy grounds, strengthened the viewpoint among many Americans that they were not winning despite the optimistic reports of officials. As it happened, Tet shifted public opinion markedly away from supporting continued fighting in Vietnam. President Lyndon B. Johnson, who had grown so obsessed with the defense of Khe Sanh that he ordered hourly reports and had a scale model of the base built in the White House situation room, was himself greatly shaken by Tet. Following a gathering of policy advisers known as the Wise Men, whose consensus now was that the war was unwinnable, Johnson announced that he was prepared to declare a bombing halt in order to open peace negotiations with Hanoi and that he would not seek reelection to the presidency. After Tet, the primary American strategy was no longer to win the war but to find a way to withdraw from the quagmire honorably. **See also** Hue, Battle of; Johnson, Lyndon B.; Khe Sanh, Battle of; Vo Nguyen Giap.

# Thich Quang Duc (1897–1963)

Buddhist monk whose self-immolation on June 11, 1963, inspired worldwide protests against the repressive regime of South Vietnamese president Ngo Dinh Diem. The incident was carefully planned as a ceremonial act. Thich Quang Duc, the leader of a monastery near Hue ("Thich" is a Vietnamese honorific for high-level monks), drove from Hue to a busy Saigon intersection where some of his students doused him with gasoline and then ignited him. The monk's calm, captured in numerous journalists' photographs, made him a martyr worldwide, and other monks followed suit. The insensitive response by Diem and his family members, one of whom allegedly approved of such "barbecues," helped turn the U.S. administration of John F. Kennedy away from its steady support of Diem. The car that took Quang Duc to Saigon, meanwhile, was given an honored position at his Hue monastery and was bedecked with both garlands and a photograph of the immolation. **See also** Buddhists and Buddhist protest; Ngo Dinh Diem.

# Third Marine Division

A component of the U.S. Marine Corps that supplied the first official combat unit deployed to Vietnam and went on to provide the first line of defense south of the demilitarized zone (DMZ) in I Corps, the northernmost military region of South Vietnam.

The Third Marine Division was formed during World War II to play a key role in fighting the Japanese in the Pacific theater. It remained in the Pacific, stationed at Okinawa after World War II. Once U.S. politicians made the halting decision to send regular ground troops to Vietnam, it was logical that they be marines stationed nearby. Elements of the Third Marine Division were deployed to Da Nang in March 1965. Their ostensible duty was to guard the airstrip there as well as other key locations such as ports and supply depots, and they were told not to engage in combat. When a few months later troops from the First Marine Division arrived in Da Nang, the Third was redeployed to the area of Quang Tri province south of the DMZ. Until 1969, when it was recalled to Okinawa, the Third Marine Division manned a string of bases that stretched from the coast to the Laotian border. The most famous of these was Khe Sanh. The division provided the bulk of the defense during the Battle of Khe Sanh in early 1968. In addition, it participated in dozens of other combat and reconnaissance actions. I Corps, in fact, was the only military region where the majority of American troops were marines rather than army. Elements of the Third Marine Division were also helicoptered in to help provide logistics and security during the American evacuations of Phnom Penh, Cambodia, and Saigon in April 1975. **See also** Khe Sanh, Battle of; Marines, U.S.

# Thompson, Robert G.K. (1916–1992)

A British counterinsurgency specialist who played an important part in developing counterinsurgency strategy in South Vietnam from 1961 to 1965. Thompson acquired his reputation as an expert on combating Communist insurgencies when he devised a plan to contain such a movement in Malaysia in the 1950s. In 1961 he went to Vietnam as the head of the local British advisory mission, Vietnam being a country the British were mildly obligated to according to the terms of the charter of the Southeast Asia Treaty Organization (SEATO). In that position he tried to bring his Malaysian experience to bear by directly advising South Vietnamese president Ngo Dinh Diem. Following a practice that had proved successful in Malaysia, Thompson urged Diem to adopt a so-called strategic hamlet program. This would involve fortifying and defending villages for the purposes of both enabling a common defense and discouraging Communist infiltration by the Viet Cong (VC). According to Thompson's plan, Diem should help villagers provide for their own defense via police and other local defense forces rather than impose a military and political presence from above, which Thompson argued would alienate people rather than enlist them as potential allies.

Diem adopted Thompson's advice, and when they learned of it, American officials and advisers also endorsed the plan. However, both Diem and the Americans ignored vital differences between Malaysia and South Vietnam. For one, most of the strategic villages in Malaysia had been inhabited by ethnic Malays who had an enmity with the local Chinese, who were, in any case, easy to spot and identify. The VC, on the other hand, was deeply involved in many Vietnamese villages, and it was very difficult to separate VC cadres from ordinary people. Another problem was the presence of soldiers of the highly organized and well-equipped North Vietnamese Army, which helped indicate to villagers the strength of the Communist insurgency. Finally, and in ways diametrically opposed to Thompson's ideas, Diem and his brother Ngo Dinh Nhu, who administered the strategic hamlet program, mishandled the strategy. They forced thousands of villagers to relocate, installed loyal or corrupt officials from Saigon, and both restricted the movement of villagers and conscripted them into various tasks. This heavy-handed, top-down approach, which, as Thompson might have predicted, alienated many villagers, doomed what may have been a promising strategy. It was abandoned in 1964.

Thompson continued to speak and write widely on the Vietnam conflict after leaving the British mission in 1965, often serving the United States as an informal consultant on anti-VC strategies. Among his books were *Defeating Communist Insurgency: The Lessons of Malaya and Vietnam*, published in 1966, and *Peace Is Not at Hand*, a prescient volume published in 1974. **See also** counterinsurgency; Southeast Asia Treaty Organization; strategic hamlets.

## Toan Thang

Meaning "complete victory," Toan Thang was the major focus of American military efforts from the aftermath of the Tet Offensive in March 1968 to the final withdrawal of U.S. troops in March 1973. It involved, primarily, ensuring the security of the city of Saigon and the regions around it, which included the vast military base at Bien Hoa. Operation Toan Thang was a complement to the decision by American political leaders to, first, find a way to reduce America's military commitment and, second, begin the process of Vietnamization, by which more of the military defense of South Vietnam would be turned over gradually to the armed forces of South Vietnam themselves. The operation formally began on April 8, 1968, when eleven different operations around Saigon were combined. Forces involved in the operation included three U.S. infantry divisions, all South Vietnamese units already stationed in the region, and an Australian task force. Their primary tasks over the next years involved preventing Viet Cong (VC) infiltration, which, even after the VC was decimated during the Tet Offensive, proved to be an ongoing threat. Important sites to be defended included bridges, especially those on the road linking Saigon to Bien Hoa, and the air base at Tan Son Nhut. One long-term effect of the American focus on the Saigon region was an identifiable shift elsewhere in Vietnam from the involvement of American ground troops, with some exceptions, such as the Battle of Hamburger Hill, to the use of massive air and artillery support. **See also** Vietnamization.

## Tran Do (1923–2002)

Top North Vietnamese political and military leader. He rose to prominence during the First Indochina War (1946–1954) serving the Viet Minh as both a staff officer, most notably in the execution of operations during the Battle of Dien Bien Phu, and a Communist Party official. After the North Vietnamese government reached the decision, in 1959, to assertively support a Communist takeover of South Vietnam, Do was dispatched to the south to work with local Communists. He emerged as one of the top officials of the Central Office for South Vietnam (COSVN), the liaison organization through which Hanoi sought to direct and aid operations in the south. Do took command of the COSVN's political department, responsible for ideology, propaganda, and the coordination of efforts among various groups. He also served as a field officer during many operations of both the Viet Cong (VC) and the North Vietnamese Army (NVA). Do proved, in fact, to be a capable military leader as well as administrator. Under the name Chin Vinh, Do took the initiative to direct both political and military operations in the south, and he was instrumental in the planning of the 1968 Tet Offensive. Despite the heavy Communist casualties of Tet, Do was politically astute enough to realize that it had been a victory for North Vietnam and the Communists because of its effect on American attitudes toward the war. **See also** Central Office for South Vietnam; National Liberation Front; Viet Cong.

## Tran Van Tra (1918–1996)

Top North Vietnamese politician and military leader. Following a long history of military commands in the Viet Minh and North Vietnamese Army, Tra was infiltrated into South Vietnam in 1963 to take command of a large Viet Cong (VC) cadre group, or group of leaders. In 1964 he was appointed head of the Central Military Committee for the Central Office for South Vietnam (COSVN). This made him the top Communist military leader in South Vietnam.

Over the next years Tra worked to improve the effectiveness of the VC and, in 1968, he led the VC's attack on Saigon during the Tet Offensive, an attack that featured major strikes against both U.S. military installations at Tan Son Nhut airport and the U.S. embassy in the center of the city. In 1969 he was named defense minister in the Provisional Revolutionary Government of Vietnam, a proposed Communist alternative to the U.S.-supported South Vietnamese government. After diplomatic efforts by 1973 had removed U.S. forces but failed to halt the fighting between North and South Vietnam, Tra returned to Hanoi, the northern capital. His task was to help plan the final North Vietnamese offensive against South Vietnam along with Vo Nguyen Giap, Le Duan, and Le Duc Tho, the other Communist leaders and men with whom he had some disagreements.

Rising above their differences, the North Vietnamese leaders launched their final offensive in October 1974 with Tra in overall command. Along with Le Duc Tho, Tra was the top official to enter Saigon on April 30, 1975, to accept the final surrender of the South Vietnamese government. He remained there until January 1976 as head of the military occupation government. Afterward, he remained a member of the ruling politburo of the new Socialist Republic of Vietnam and set to work on a controversial, five-volume account of the long Vietnam conflict. Published in 1982, the book, *History of the Bulwark B2 Theater*, contained material that was critical of the way the North Vietnamese conducted the war, particularly in what he regarded as their reckless use of VC guerrillas. For his pains, Tra found himself ousted from the politburo and his book banned, although in time the ban was rescinded. Tra eventually took his place as one of the elders of the Vietnamese revolution and independence struggle. **See also** Central Office for South Vietnam; Tet Offensive; Viet Cong.

## Truman, Harry S. (1884–1972)

As president of the United States from 1945 to 1953, the first leader to involve the country in the Vietnam conflict. What was then known as French Indochina first came to Truman's attention in July 1945, when the Allied nations of World War II made plans for Southeast Asia in the aftermath of the defeat of Japan. Along with British prime minister Clement Attlee, Truman agreed that French Indochina should be split along the sixteenth parallel. North of that line, the Chinese would accept the Japanese surrender and serve as a temporary occupying force; south of it, the British. No definitive decision was reached on whether to restore full French colonial authority or allow for national independence, which was the goal of Ho Chi Minh, who was working with the American Office of Strategic Services at the time.

Between 1945 and 1949, Truman and his advisers, developed what was to be U.S. policy throughout the cold war. The policy focused on the containment of communism to the nations that already practiced it, notably the Soviet Union and its satellites in Eastern Europe, combined with some sort of U.S. support in nations threatened by the spread of communism. The fall of China to the Communist Mao Tse-tung in 1949 greatly upped the stakes of the containment policy and added

Southeast Asia to Europe as an important cold war battleground. In 1950 Truman ordered U.S. troops into Korea, as part of a larger United Nations force, to halt communism there. That same year, he also took steps to prevent Mao's China from acting too aggressively toward Taiwan and sent aid to anti-Communist forces in the Philippines.

Also in 1950, convinced by Secretary of State Dean Acheson to halt the threat of "monolithic communism," Truman agreed to send aid to the French, who were then engaged in fighting a war against Ho Chi Minh's Viet Minh in Indochina. The aid consisted of a sum of $15 million in financial support and equipment, a sum that was to grow to $3 billion by 1954, at which point the United States was largely financing France's war effort. In addition, Truman gave permission to form a semipermanent U.S. advisory body in Vietnam, the U.S. Military Assistance Advisory Group (MAAG). Given the global nature of the containment policy, Truman supported the French not only because of the threat of communism in Indochina but because the United States relied on France to be a strong ally in Europe. He also had to respond to the fact that the Soviet Union, then seen as the leader of global communism, had in 1949 successfully tested its first atomic bomb; he was responding as well to opposition politicians in the United States, who found in the circumstances an opportunity to accuse the Truman administration of being "soft on communism."

After leaving the presidency in 1953, Truman enjoyed the status of an elder statesman. During the 1960s he refused to endorse the Vietnam policies of either John F. Kennedy or Lyndon B. Johnson, the latter of whom he strongly disliked. **See also** cold war; containment policy; First Indochina War.

## unexploded ordnance (UXO)

Land mines, bombs, grenades, artillery, mortar shells, or other munitions that either failed to detonate when used or were simply left behind by the various forces involved in the long war in Vietnam, Laos, and Cambodia. All three countries remained plagued by this refuse of warfare for decades after the fighting ended, and each year several hundred people are injured or killed by unexploded ordnance. The problem is worst in Laos but is also severe in parts of Vietnam, notably the former demilitarized zone (DMZ) UXO-removal teams from various organizations were busy throughout the 1990s trying to remove the material, but to finish the job will take decades. As much as 30 percent of the bombs that were dropped failed to detonate, and land mines are notoriously difficult to locate and then either remove or defuse. UXO has been found of not only American but also Soviet, Chinese, French, and British origin. **See also** mines.

## Vann, John Paul (1924–1972)

U.S. Army officer and, later, civilian official in Vietnam whose experiences and attitudes were often cited as an example of the paradoxical nature of American involvement in Vietnam; Vann continually evinced a strong desire to support the South Vietnamese and prevent a Communist takeover but remained frustrated by the inability of the United States to develop or implement strategies that might work to accomplish those goals.

Vann's first tour of duty in Vietnam, from March 1962 to April 1963, was as a U.S. Army officer serving as an adviser to contingents of the Army of the Republic of Vietnam (ARVN) in their efforts against Viet Cong (VC) infiltrators in the Mekong Delta. He was present at the Battle of Ap Bac, a daylong skirmish in which the ARVN proved unable to contain a VC contingent despite massive advantages in firepower and air support. Along with a few other encounters, this experience convinced him that the South Vietnamese could not win the war without changes in tactics. In 1963, this message stood in direct contrast to what President John F. Kennedy was hearing from his military and diplomatic advisers. Among other reports, Kennedy was told by General Paul D. Harkins, then U.S. commander in Vietnam, that Ap Bac was a major victory. When Vann's criticisms and recommendations, including the consideration by the United States of the use of massive American force, were ignored by his superiors, he began to speak to reporters, notably Neil Sheehan of the *New York Times.* Unhappy with Vann's outspokenness, the army transferred him back to Washington, D.C. He retired from the army in July 1963 but continued to pay attention to developments in Vietnam as well as question American and South Vietnamese strategy.

Vann returned to Vietnam in March 1965. This time he went as a civilian, an officer in the Agency for International

Development (AID). Vann, who for the time and for an American had a unique understanding of and ability to get along with the Vietnamese, was a great success as an AID officer. In 1966 he was given command over all pacification programs for the Saigon area and, in 1971, he was named senior AID official for the Central Highlands. This gave him tactical command over not only AID personnel but also relevant U.S. military forces and elements of the ARVN in the area. Some have claimed that, for a number of months, Vann was in fact the third most powerful American in Vietnam after the ambassador, Ellsworth Bunker, and the commander of the Military Assistance Command, Vietnam, General Creighton Abrams. Vann remained unhappy, however, with American policies in Vietnam.

He had heavily criticized the tendency of William Westmoreland, Abrams's predecessor, to rely on statistical measures such as kill ratios to judge the success of the war. He also asserted that both Americans and South Vietnamese officials underestimated the strength of the Communists militarily and in terms of their appeal to ordinary Vietnamese.

Vann was killed in a helicopter accident during the Battle of Kontum in central Vietnam on June 9, 1972. He was officially eulogized, somewhat uncomfortably, by President Richard M. Nixon. **See also** Agency for International Development; Ap Bac, Battle of.

## veterans

More than 2.5 million American servicemen and servicewomen served in some

*John Paul Vann (left) discusses strategy with South Vietnamese and American soldiers. Vann served in Vietnam as an army officer and later as a civilian adviser.*

capacity in Vietnam. The vast majority of them successfully adjusted to civilian life after their duty ended, establishing families and careers despite some degree of post-traumatic stress disorder (PTSD), reactions to stress that involve depression, anxiety, and blunting of emotions. However, the Vietnam veterans' postwar experience was significantly different from that of veterans of previous wars. Many complained of the unsympathetic welcome they received and a lack of recognition and thanks for their service. Public opinion over the war was bitterly divided, and many opponents and protesters of the war focused their criticism and even contempt on returning veterans.

Official efforts to ease veterans' transition into civilian life have also been criticized as inadequate. For example, a soldier's tour of duty often ended with disorienting abruptness; many soldiers found themselves in combat one day and on a plane home the next. Moreover, the GI Bill offered Vietnam veterans only about half the benefits that veterans of World War II had been eligible to receive.

Such lack of support, as well as evidence that many draftees had had little education and job training prior to Vietnam service and controversial evidence of the harmful effects of Agent Orange, has been blamed for the fact that as many as 15 percent of veterans returned with severe combat-related PTSD and continue to have difficulties in civilian life, including job trouble, substance abuse, and psychological and medical problems.

Since the mid-1980s a general effort has been made to increase counseling and medical services for Vietnam veterans still suffering from PTSD or addiction; counter the negative stereotype of Vietnam veterans as violent, dysfunctional, and prone to homelessness; and belatedly welcome veterans home with memorials and tributes. Several veterans organizations continue to play an active role in this effort, including Vietnam Veterans of America, the United Vietnam Veterans Organization, and AMVETS.

## Vientiane Agreement

The cease-fire agreement to end the long civil war in Laos. It was signed in Vientiane, the capital of Laos, on February 21, 1973, less than one month after the Paris Peace Accords were signed. The signatories to the Vientiane Agreement were Pheng Phonsavan, representing the Royal Lao government, and Phoumi Vongvichit, representing the Pathet Lao, the nation's Communist insurgency. Among the main articles of the agreement was the establishment of a Provisional Government of National Union, a coalition regime that would prepare the nation for general elections to be held at a date to be determined. In addition, the agreement provided for a National Political Consultative Council to ensure that all relevant points of view were heard. In an echo of the Paris accords, the Vientiane Agreement also called for the departure of all foreign military personnel as well as the disbandment of paramilitary groups. A number of Americans, mostly Central Intelligence Agency (CIA) agents and Air America pilots and support personnel, had served in Laos since the early 1960s. But now they were to leave and the indigenous forces they built up, notably the "secret army" of Hmong tribesmen, were to be disbanded.

Aside from the cease-fire, which began on February 22, the Vientiane Agreement formally took effect on September 14, 1973, after further negotiations. It established two members of the Lao royal family, Prince Souvanna Phouma and Prince Souphanouvong, as prime minister and chairman of the National Political Consultative Council, respectively. Many of its other provisions were never implemented, however, because as in Vietnam neither the Communist insurgents nor government forces stopped fighting. In August 1975, when the Pathet Lao took control of Vientiane, the 1973 agreement was rendered obsolete. **See also** Laos, secret war in; Pathet Lao; Souvanna Phouma.

## Viet Cong (VC)

The common term for the Communist guerrillas of South Vietnam. The term, meaning simply "Vietnamese Communists," was slightly derogatory and was first used by Ngo Dinh Diem, president of South Vietnam from 1955 to 1963, in his effort to identify a challenge he never took seriously. The Viet Cong evolved from the southern remnant of the Viet Minh forces left after the First Indochina War (1946–1954). Their number was small, probably fewer than ten thousand, and they were joined by disaffected members of the Hoa Hao, Cao Dai, and Binh Xuyen armies as well as others who had little love for the Diem regime.

Until 1959 the nascent VC engaged in little more than rare attacks on government outposts. But that year the North Vietnamese government decided to begin its struggle to reunite South Vietnam with North Vietnam, and the VC was to be the center of the effort in the south. Political cadres arrived to give political education to potential members, while military training and supplies also began to flow south from Hanoi. VC recruiters found a number of ordinary villagers ready to join in their cause thanks to the brutality, corruption, and indifference of the Diem regime. It was a strong contrast to the nationalist, pro-Vietnam message of the political cadres.

Officially, the VC was the National Front for the Liberation of South Vietnam, or, more familiarly, the National Liberation Front (NLF). VC fighters, for their part, were organized into the People's Liberation Armed Forces (PLAF). Both organizations were officially formed in December 1960. The NLF took on the tasks of education, recruitment, and policy coordination with Hanoi while the PLAF began a guerrilla war against Diem's regime almost immediately. The successes of this guerrilla war led directly to expanded U.S. involvement in Vietnam. Indeed, PLAF attacks on American bases at Pleiku and Qui Nhon in 1965 convinced American officials that a military presence on the ground was necessary.

The nature of the VC made the Vietnam War different from any major war Americans had fought before. Members of the VC did not wear military uniforms, nor were they necessarily young men or even full-time soldiers. Older people, young women, and even children were involved in bombings and other attacks, and some villagers led a double existence as VC fighters and ordinary farmers. Also complicating the war was the viewpoint adopted by U.S. politicians and commanders that the VC was entirely controlled from Hanoi and was in fact little more than a Communist front organization. The alternative view was that many VC were Vietnamese nationalists first and Communists second, if at all. They simply wanted to see their country unified and foreign interference removed. Thus, among other reasons, membership in the VC could never be accurately estimated.

U.S. and South Vietnamese officials tried to win the war partly by either winning over or destroying the VC. They spent a great deal of time and effort on pacification programs such as securing villages, education, encouraging local government, and improving roads and fields in order to discourage villagers from either joining or supporting the VC. In addition, beginning in 1967, the United States and South Vietnam began a major program to root out what they

*A captured Viet Cong fighter is closely guarded as he awaits interrogation.*

called the Viet Cong infrastructure (VCI) on the principle that, once the leadership was removed, the rank and file would disperse or be ineffective. The VCI was roughly the equivalent of the NLF, in other words the leadership, logistical, and political components of the VC, although military leaders were also targeted by what became known as the Phoenix Program.

The VC played a central role in the Tet Offensive of 1968, the turning point of the war. Massive VC units were directed to move to key towns and cities throughout South Vietnam to not only mount attacks but, hopefully, inspire a popular uprising. The attacks were, in

time, beaten back and the popular uprising never occurred. But the massive concentrations of VC fighters capable of such actions as besieging the U.S. embassy in Saigon for a number of hours provided ample indication that neither pacification nor counterinsurgency warfare was succeeding. On the other hand, the VC was badly defeated militarily during Tet, and the Phoenix Program, despite its brutality, proved effective in disabling the VCI. After Tet, most of the fighting on the Communist side was done by the regular North Vietnamese Army. After Saigon fell in April 1975 and the nation reunified, few VC fighters or political leaders found much of a welcome in the new Socialist Republic of Vietnam, where the highest posts were reserved for northerners. **See also** National Liberation Front; Provisional Revolutionary Government; Vietnam, Democratic Republic of.

## Viet Minh

The cover organization for the broad, North Vietnam–based Communist movement that struggled against Japanese occupation from 1941 to 1945 and then fought France in the First Indochina War of 1946 to 1954. The name is a contraction of Viet Nam Doc Lap Dong Minh Hoi, or the League of Independence for Vietnam.

The Viet Minh was founded in June 1941 at the Eighth Congress of the Indochina Communist Party. Its purpose was to go beyond the traditional tasks of a political party, even a revolutionary one, in the attempt to unite the Vietnamese people against foreign interference. Taking the practical goal of national liberation before Communist revolution, the Viet Minh sought to unite diverse interest groups in Vietnam in pursuit of independence. Some of these interest groups were ideological enemies of communism but recognized the greater organizational and military abilities of the Viet Minh and offered tentative co-operation.

Viet Minh leaders, notably Ho Chi Minh, initially adopted a strategy of wait-ing and preparing, knowing that the Japanese and French, despite wartime agreements, could be counted on to turn against each other. In March 1945, when the Japanese seized formal control of Vietnam from the collaborationist French, the Viet Minh stepped up its preparations, which included a covert military buildup as well as seeking Amer-ican help. After the Japanese surrendered months later the Viet Minh staged the so-called August Revolution and proclaimed the independence of Vietnam from French rule as well as Japanese. Ho's de-claration of Vietnamese independence, made on September 2, 1945, was backed up by a substantial military force led by Vo Nguyen Giap. It took a long war against a resurgent France, backed up by an American government concerned about the Viet Minh's Communist ideol-ogy and connections, to make Viet-namese independence a fact, however.

Meanwhile, in late 1945, Communist leaders dissolved the Indochina Commu-nist Party, which left the Viet Minh as their sole organization. During the war with the French the Viet Minh developed not only a substantial military force but also extensive political capabilities fea-turing educational, administrative, and propaganda branches. The Indochina Communist Party was revived in 1951 under the name Dang Lao Dong Viet Nam, or the Vietnam Workers' Party. Known familiarly as the Lao Dong, it re-placed the Viet Minh as the central lead-ership body of the North Vietnamese Communists, although similar front or-ganizations continued to exist. The Viet Minh was formally dissolved that same year, although the term continued to be used to refer to the Communists until 1954. **See also** Ho Chi Minh; Lao Dong; Pham Van Dong; Vietnam, Democratic Republic of.

# Vietnam, Democratic Republic of (DRV) (North Vietnam)

The official name of the Communist regime that struggled to reunify all of Vietnam under its authority from 1945 to 1975. Since from 1954 to 1975 the De-mocratic Republic of Vietnam governed an independent nation from the seven-teenth parallel north to the Chinese bor-der, the DRV was familiarly and best known as North Vietnam.

The DRV was formed by the Viet Minh, a collection of nationalist groups in Vietnam that emerged during World War II and was dominated by Commu-nists such as Ho Chi Minh, Pham Van Dong, and Vo Nguyen Giap. From a base the Viet Minh already controlled in rural northwestern Vietnam, members entered Hanoi after the Japanese surrendered on August 15, 1945. On September 2, Ho declared the founding of the DRV as an independent state, hoping to make it an established fact before French colonial-ists could restore their control over In-dochina.

In December 1946, after a series of diplomatic maneuvers failed to gain true independence, the DRV and France went to war. When this conflict, the First In-dochina War, began on December 19, the DRV enjoyed a substantial presence in only Hanoi, Haiphong, and other areas in the Red River Valley. After being forced to abandon even Hanoi and Haiphong, Ho, Giap, and the remainder of the Viet Minh retreated to the countryside. Giap, the movement's military leader, slowly built up a substantial military force, the People's Army of Vietnam (PAVN, known by Americans as the North Vietnamese Army), from supporters across Vietnam, but the French remained in control of the important cities.

In 1950 the new People's Republic of China officially recognized the DRV as the government of northern Vietnam, and the Chinese Communists began to filter military aid to the PAVN. Thanks to both French miscues and the persistence of Giap, the Viet Minh was able to seize control of most of rural Vietnam by 1953. It had also begun operations in Laos, clinging to the old idea of an Indochinese as opposed to Vietnamese Communist insurgency. In the spring of 1954 Giap's forces besieged the French outpost at Dien Bien Phu, and their victory there removed the French from Indochina and established the DRV as the strongest political and military entity in the region. The Geneva Conference, which took place roughly at the same time as the siege at Dien Bien Phu, acknowledged the fact: The DRV was granted Vietnam north of the seventeenth parallel pending nationwide elections to be held in 1956. South of the seventeenth parallel, the government was to be in the hands of a nascent Republic of Vietnam (RVN), an unstable collection of nationalists, Roman Catholics, and others led by the former emperor Bao Dai and his dictatorial premier, Ngo Dinh Diem. The Geneva Accords were accepted as a merely temporary expedient by most parties involved. Neither the United States nor the RVN signed the accords, and even the DRV was unsatisfied with the compromise, complaining that it had been sold out by China and the Soviet Union, which wanted to contain any further military conflict.

What Ho, Giap, and the other DRV leaders wanted was full reunification for Vietnam, but they realized after 1954 that they would have to put off any aggressive action to achieve that end. Between 1954 and 1959 the Hanoi regime therefore devoted its energies to consolidating its hold on the north and creating a Communist state. The effort involved extensive land reform measures and the "destruction" of the "landlord class," as well as education, indoctrination, and the expansion of the PAVN. These changes came at a heavy price, prompting a mass migration to the south (which was permitted for three hundred days after the Geneva Accords took effect) and significant social unrest suppressed by the PAVN at a cost of more than thirty thousand lives. Meanwhile, the DRV began to accept economic aid from the Soviet Union in order to foster industrial growth and agricultural self-sufficiency. A major effort was the collectivization of agriculture, a measure resisted by many peasants. Nonetheless by 1962 much farming in the DRV was performed by agricultural cooperative organizations tied to the state. Industrial development was less successful since the DRV lacked an industrial workforce and a sufficiently developed engineering and technical class. The leaders of the DRV also took steps to create a classless society, the goal of Communist ideologists. They provided mass education and guaranteed equality for women, who were then expected to make their contributions to the state. They also reduced income differences among ordinary people, including the leadership class. Rather well disciplined, the leaders of the DRV sought to provide the examples themselves of being "workers" for larger causes, including the development of an egalitarian society, the expulsion of foreign imperialists, and the reunification of the country.

By 1959 DRV leaders were ready to march forward with reunification. The Lao Dong, the Vietnamese Communist Party, went on to commit North Vietnam to a "war of national liberation" in September 1960. Efforts to undermine the Diem regime were already under way, as was the construction of the Ho Chi Minh Trail. Le Duan, the secretary-general of the Lao Dong, helped create the National

Liberation Front (NLF) and its military branch, the People's Liberation Armed Forces (PLAF), in the south to foment a Communist insurrection there. Both the NLF and PLAF were familiarly known among South Vietnamese and Americans as the Viet Cong (VC). The DRV intended the VC apparatus to provide political education along with military insurrection. The Ho Chi Minh Trail would facilitate the transport of both supplies and personnel from north to south, and the whole effort would be coordinated from Hanoi using such mechanisms as the Central Office for South Vietnam (COSVN), a kind of mobile headquarters. The DRV mounted a similar plan for Laos, through which large portions of the Ho Chi Minh Trail ran, by providing support to the Pathet Lao, the local Communists.

From 1960 to 1975 the DRV remained on a total war footing, and the effort to reunify Vietnam by defeating South Vietnam and its American patrons required intensive effort and sacrifice from all segments of the North Vietnamese population. In 1975 more than 1 million citizens were in uniform as members of the PAVN, and well over 500,000 others had died during the war. Civilians as a matter of course worked in defense plants, built defenses, manned communications installations, and performed other rear-echelon functions. Since the DRV had a command economy (i.e., one in which virtually all economic activity was controlled by the state), citizens had little choice in the jobs they did, and due to the demands of the fighting, little access to consumer goods or other comforts. Nevertheless, and in marked contrast to South Vietnam, Ho and other DRV leaders managed to achieve a large degree of social cohesion, convincing northerners that their fight to reunify the nation and expel the foreign invaders was justified. The fact that the regime had little tolerance for dissent, and like other Communist regimes made full use of prison and reeducation camps for political opponents, was no doubt another factor that gave the DRV a solidarity that its southern counterpart lacked.

Military aid from China and the Soviet Union, combined with an awareness among DRV leaders that the United States was growing weary of its commitment to support South Vietnam, kept the DRV confident of ultimate victory in the Vietnam War and hesitant to engage in meaningful peace negotiations that would delay reunification. Circumstances changed somewhat in 1972 when U.S. president Richard Nixon marginalized the Chinese and Soviets diplomatically and began an intensive bombing campaign of the north. Operations Linebacker I and Linebacker II, the latter better known as the Christmas bombing, finally convinced DRV leaders to negotiate seriously. The social cohesion of North Vietnam still showed, however, as reinforcements continued to flow in to the PAVN and when, during the Christmas bombing of Hanoi and Haiphong, leaders were able to organize orderly evacuations that greatly reduced civilian casualties.

The DRV accepted the RVN's surrender on April 30, 1975, a little over two years after American forces withdrew from Vietnam. A year later the DRV was absorbed into the new Socialist Republic of Vietnam (SRV) governing a reunified nation. The long struggle had transformed the DRV into a semi-industrialized nation and both reunified the country and expelled foreign interference, but it came at a heavy price. In 1995 the government of the SRV reported that 1.1 million Communist fighters had died from 1954 to 1975, along with 2 million civilians. Most of their industrial capacity lay in ruins from bombing, and more than thirty towns needed to be rebuilt. **See also** Ho Chi Minh; Lao Dong; Vietnam, Republic of; Vietnam, Socialist Republic of.

# Vietnam, historical overview of

The sweep of Vietnamese history was characterized by many themes that appeared again during the Vietnam War. These included the attempt to assure independence from foreign nations and empires and the effort to build and maintain a unified nation stretching from the Red River Delta in the north to the Mekong Delta in the south. Vietnamese history also supplies a pantheon of nationalist heroes remembered for their efforts to keep Vietnam independent.

According to local legend, Vietnamese history began with a kingdom known as Van Lang founded by a mythical king, Hung Vuong, during the third millennium B.C. Centered in present-day Vinh Phu Province, Van Lang was thought to have been a large empire consisting of not only most of Vietnam but also portions of southern China. Although Hung Vuong and his successors were long celebrated during rituals and holidays by the Vietnamese people, some scholars confine him to legend. Most accept, however, that Van Lang was a reasonably advanced civilization of Bronze Age farmers capable of fine craftwork. Although they built few large towns, the people of Van Lang, known as Lac Viet, built a culture that was distinct from the cultures in neighboring China and Cambodia. Their society was matrilineal in nature, tracing bloodlines through the mothers rather than the fathers, and they supported themselves through rice cultivation. Worshiping many gods and spirits, notably a god of the earth, the Lac Viet also believed that there was a strong distinction between the peoples of the coastal flatlands and the peoples of the mountains.

In 111 B.C. the Lac Viet, by then under the authority of kings who called the country Nam Viet, fell under the domination of China when the Han emperors seized the Red River Delta. Vietnam remained a feudal state under Chinese domination for the next ten centuries. For the first two centuries after 111 B.C. the Vietnamese people felt little influnce from China, which largely ignored them. But during the first century A.D. Chinese officials began an aggressive effort to implant Chinese culture on their southern neighbor. This effort included giving incentives to Chinese immigrants such as land grants. This new aggressiveness inspired the first of a number of revolts against the Chinese. It began in A.D. 39 and was led by two sisters, Trung Trac and Trung Nhi. Their rebellion spread through much of Vietnam and forced the Chinese authorities to flee. Two years later, however, a large Chinese army returned, and it defeated the two sisters in a battle at Lang Bac in 43. Rather than submit to Chinese authority, they committed suicide by jumping into a nearby river.

Now apparently convinced that their southern neighbor was going to be troublesome, the Chinese applied a stricter form of government and stepped up their efforts to sinicize the population, or make them more like the Chinese. The Vietnamese had to accept the new status of being the southern nation, or Nam Quoc, living in the shadow of the northern nation, China, or Bac Quoc. The Chinese introduced, for instance, the Confucian social order that dominated China itself. Confucianism was based on a rigid social hierarchy, respect for the past and for tradition, and domination by learned officials, whom Westerners later called mandarins. Mandarins were often also major landowners. In addition, the Chinese introduced the abstract philosophy of Taoism and the more mainstream religion of Mahayana Buddhism. The latter made room for a generous number of nature and ancestral spirits and became the major religion of Vietnam. Chinese writing eventually became the only form of writing, and social elites spoke Chinese rather than Vietnamese. These influences helped turn Vietnam away from its neighbors in Southeast Asia; Laos, Cambodia, and Thailand, for instance, all adopted the Theravada form of Buddhism and, until the nineteenth century at least, avoided much influence from China. Southern Vietnam, however, evolved in a way more similar to the experience of Cambodia than to Chinese Nam Viet. Under the sway of the Champa emperors based in central Vietnam, that region practiced first Hinduism and then Buddhism, both imported from India. Chinese influence did not extend much beyond the central city of Hue.

Throughout the thousand years of Chinese rule, numerous revolts arose echoing that of the Trung sisters, and their leaders joined the sisters in the pantheon of Vietnamese nationalist heroes. Notable among them were Ba Trieu, who led a revolt in the third century, and Mai Thuc Loan in the eighth century. In 938 a new rebel leader, Ngo Quyen, finally ended Chinese rule with a victory in a battle near the Bac Dang River in the north. Ngo was seen from then on as the founder of independent Vietnam, a status the Vietnamese were to enjoy until the nineteenth century, except for a brief period during the 1400s when they fell under the dominion of the Ming dynasty in China. To ensure their independence, however, Vietnamese kings continued to pay tribute to the Chinese emperors.

Independent Vietnam, or Dai Viet (Great Viet), was ruled by a succession of ten dynasties. The most important were the Ly kings, who ruled from 1009 to 1225; the Tran dynasty, in power from 1225 to 1400; and the Le rulers, who took over in 1428 after ousting the Ming and remained in power until 1728. The Ly kings established the city of Thang Long, which later became Hanoi. The Tran rulers maintained the country's independence by fighting off three invasions

from the Mongols, a Central Asian tribe who conquered much of Asia in the 1200s, including China. All three of them, as well as the others, maintained a Chinese system of government based on Confucianism and the training of mandarins as the country's elite.

One of the major developments of this era of independent Vietnam was the long-lasting "march to the south" (Nam Tien). This was the effort by northern Vietnamese to take control of the rich agricultural lands in central and southern Vietnam, which were already important points in the trade networks of East and Southeast Asia. It involved, first, a war against the kings of Champa, which the Ly kings won in 1069. This gave the Vietnamese control of much of central Vietnam. Further battles, as well as diplomatic arrangements such as noble marriages, allowed Vietnam to extend its sway further by the end of the fifteenth century.

The final stage of the march to the south was to seize the Mekong Delta from the vast Khmer Empire based in Cambodia, whose temples at Angkor provided a reminder of its scope and wealth. Even after the Khmer Empire declined in the fourteenth and fifteenth centuries, the Khmers, or Cambodians, continued to control the delta. Only in the mid-1700s, after centuries of fitful warfare, did Vietnamese kings finally take control of the delta and force the Khmers to retreat up the Mekong River. Nonetheless, the banks of the river up to the Khmer city of Phnom Penh remained inhabited by a mixed population of both Vietnamese and Cambodians.

In 1592, meanwhile, Vietnam was effectively split into two portions. The Trinh lords ruled in the north from their base at Thang Long. The Nguyen lords set up a kingdom at Hue, and it fell to them to conquer the south. In the late 1700s the Trinh and Nguyen lords faced a major uprising known as the Tay Son rebellion. Led by three brothers from the town of Tay Son in Binh Dinh Province, the rebellion was inspired by the excessive corruption of the Nguyens. The brothers built a huge army and managed to oust both the Trinh and the Nguyen, promising land reform and greater justice. All three, however, died in the 1790s before their reforms could take hold. The surviving Nguyen prince, Nguyen Anh, subsequently assembled an army and in 1802 took the throne as the first of the Nguyen emperors of a now, once again, fully united Vietnam. He took the imperial name Gia Long, and he and his successors constructed a palace in Hue known as the Citadel. It was modeled on the Forbidden City in Beijing, the Chinese capital. Indeed, according to their old habits, the Nguyen emperors continued to rely on Confucian mandarins and used both spoken and written Chinese as their court language.

Gia Long took the throne with the help of a French missionary named Pigneau de Behane, one of a line of European missionaries who, along with a sprinkle of merchants, had come to Vietnam since the 1500s. The greatest challenge to the Nguyen emperors, as the nineteenth century progressed, would be controlling European influence in the form of French colonizers. It was a battle they ultimately lost. **See also** French Indochina; Vietnam, Democratic Republic of; Vietnam, Republic of; Vietnam, Socialist Republic of.

# Vietnam, Republic of (RVN) (South Vietnam)

The regime that governed South Vietnam from 1954 to 1975 and which the United States struggled mightily but unsuccessfully to build up and preserve.

The Republic of Vietnam was declared in 1950 as part of the effort to stabilize the area during the First Indochina War (1946–1954). The RVN was to be an affiliated state within the French Union

with, theoretically, an army of its own known as the Vietnamese National Army. Supported by numerous powerful South Vietnamese nationalists, particularly Roman Catholics or those with French ties, the idea of the RVN stuck. At the Geneva Conference of 1954 delegates approved the formation of an independent RVN pending elections, to be held in 1956, on reunification with the northern, Communist Democratic Republic of Vietnam (DRV). The head of the RVN was to be the former emperor Bao Dai and his premier Ngo Dinh Diem, the most prominent of the Catholic nationalists. By the end of 1955 Diem had forced out Bao Dai and marginalized all other challengers. He had also ensured support for his regime from the United States, claiming that the RVN was a bulwark against the spread of communism in Asia. After November 1963, when Diem was ousted in a coup by military officers, the RVN fell under the control of a clique of contentious military officers, only stabilizing in 1965 under the rule of Air Marshal Nguyen Cao Ky followed by General Nguyen Van Thieu.

None of these leaders managed to achieve a large degree of social cohesiveness, and all continued to rely on American financial aid, turning the RVN into a client state of the United States for the duration of its existence. During his years in power, Diem channeled more than 75 percent of this aid into his military and bureaucracy, which left little money available for such social measures as education, health, or housing. The aid also discouraged him from implementing taxes or encouraging economic growth. While the RVN remained largely self-sufficient in terms of food, it experienced very little industrial expansion. After the American phase of the Vietnam War began in earnest in 1965, Ky and Thieu likewise found little incentive to imple-

*Soldiers in the Republic of Vietnam's army prepare to board helicopters for an assault on a nearby mountain range. The South Vietnamese troops fought to preserve their country's regime with the aid of the United States.*

ment social or economic reforms, although they did levy taxes, much to the chagrin of ordinary people. Only in 1970, after intensive lobbying for reforms on the part of American officials, did Thieu institute meaningful land reform measures.

The needs of the war also required RVN leaders to mobilize the population. At its height the armed forces of the RVN included over 1 million men, many of them conscripts as young as sixteen years old. Even older people, young children, and women were encouraged to devote service to the state as part of the People's Self-Defense Forces, formed in 1968. While this mass conscription may have brought some popular support to the regime, it drew millions of people away from productive work on farms and in towns. Younger citizens came to understand that their best hope for a future was to attempt to join the corrupt bureaucracy or army or take part in the vast "black" economy of smuggling, drugs, and prostitution. These unintended consequences of mass mobilization worked against the construction of a viable civil society in the RVN.

The RVN was also riven by ethnic, cultural, and geographic differences. Lowland Vietnamese held long-standing hatreds toward the Montagnards, who lived in the mountainous border regions and agitated for greater autonomy. In addition, most Vietnamese were Buddhists, hesitant to accept the authority of either Roman Catholics, such as those who dominated the Diem regime, or secular Americans. Important northern cities in South Vietnam, such as Hue, were traditional centers of Vietnamese culture, while Saigon, the capital, was seen by many Vietnamese as a corrupt urban center dominated by foreign ideas and practices, whether French or American, and by venal officials. Throughout the nation, the variations in landscape from mountains to lowland flood plains to the labyrinthine Mekong Delta, as well as the fluid borders with Laos and Cambodia, made it difficult for the regime to secure its territory against constant Viet Cong and North Vietnamese incursions. Arguably, in fact, the RVN never entirely controlled its territory as determined by lines drawn on maps.

With American forces long gone and American military supplies dwindling, the RVN collapsed when North Vietnam launched its final offensive in late 1974. Top military and political officials abandoned their posts and tried to escape with their families, and although units of the RVN's army fought on bravely, they proved no match for the larger, better armed, and better disciplined northern army. His last-hour requests for American military aid denied, Thieu resigned as president in favor of his vice president, Tran Van Huong, on April 21, 1975, and fled into exile. In turn, Huong turned the presidency of the RVN over to General Duong Van Minh, a long-standing player in RVN affairs whom remaining leaders considered their best hope for a negotiated settlement with the DRV. Instead, realizing the situation was hopeless, Minh ordered all remaining RVN forces to stop fighting on April 30 and turned the RVN's presidential palace over to Communist commanders. **See also** Duong Van Minh; Nguyen Cao Ky; Nguyen Van Thicu; Victnam, Democratic Republic of;

# Vietnam, Socialist Republic of (SRV)

The nation formed by the reunification of North Vietnam (the Democratic Republic of Vietnam, or DRV) and South Vietnam (the Republic of Vietnam, or RVN) after the conquest of the RVN by DRV forces in 1975. The Socialist Republic of Vietnam was officially established on July 2, 1976, once the former DRV was secure in its control of the south. Hanoi became the SRV capital, and the new nation's political structure was dominated by the politburo of the Vietnamese Communist Party. Few South Vietnamese, even if they were Communists, found themselves placed in important posts in the new regime.

For years after reunification, the SRV continued to maintain a large, well-equipped military establishment. SRV forces, in fact, invaded Cambodia in 1978 and kept an occupation force there until 1989. They also fended off a Chinese invasion in 1979. The SRV was also desperately poor, partly because of the aftereffects of over thirty years of warfare, partly because of Communist economic policies, and partly because of American refusal to allow international aid agencies to provide funds to Hanoi, a prohibition finally lifted in 1993. Indeed, Vietnam, one of the richest rice-producing areas on Earth, was forced to import rice from Japan and Thailand for a number of years, and grew increasingly reliant on Soviet economic aid.

The Soviet flow of aid ended with the breakup of the Soviet Union in 1991, but already Vietnamese Communist officials had begun to loosen economic controls. The model the SRV came to follow was that of China, which consisted of a more or less free-market economy combined with a somewhat repressive Communist government. In 1986 Hanoi officials implemented a major program of economic reforms they called Doi Moi. These reforms included more independence of action on the part of industries, offering higher pay and bonuses to workers to encourage productivity, and an attempt to attract foreign investment. By the early 1990s these reforms were beginning to pay off. Vietnam was once again self-sufficient in rice and also undergoing rapid economic growth, especially in the southern city of Ho Chi Minh City (formerly Saigon). Nevertheless, the nation remains one of the poorest in East Asia. **See also** Vietnam, Democratic Republic of; Vietnam, historical overview of; Vietnam, Republic of.

# Vietnamese National Army (VNA)

A Vietnamese army created by French commanders and Vietnamese nationalists to fight the Communist Viet Minh during the First Indochina War (1946–1954). The Vietnamese National Army was therefore the predecessor to the Army of the Republic of Vietnam (ARVN).

The VNA was formed in July 1949 when France recognized the independence of Vietnam as a member of the French Union. The force, which France intended to fight alongside its own armies, was limited in size and freedom of operation from the beginning. Although it was technically under the command of Bao Dai, the former emperor and now head of state, the French retained effective operational control over the VNA. Moreover, subsequent French commanders differed over how to use the VNA. Some wanted it completely under French command while others hoped to increase its independence using French equipment and training. Almost all French leaders, however, refused to channel American aid directly to the VNA. Another problem the VNA faced was lack of recruits; few nationalist Vietnamese willing to fight wanted to do so under a force that was so beholden to their former colonial overlords. By 1951 the VNA had

only forty thousand members. Various conscription measures and the construction of an officer training school helped increase the number of recruits by 1954, but the VNA was never a major factor on the battlefield. In 1955 it was officially disbanded by South Vietnamese president Ngo Dinh Diem. **See also** Army of the Republic of Vietnam; First Indochina War.

# Vietnam Information Group (VIG)

An organization within the administration of U.S. president Lyndon B. Johnson designed to produce effective public relations regarding the administration's Vietnam War policy. It was established by Johnson in August 1964, after the Gulf of Tonkin Resolution and the decision to commit U.S. ground troops to Vietnam. It was originally known as the Public Affairs Policy Committee for Vietnam, changing its name to the Vietnam Information Group in 1967, and it was directed by Harold Kaplan.

Johnson used the VIG to try to ensure public support for his Vietnam policies while at the same time disparaging his political opponents on both the right and the left. In a preview of Richard Nixon's later championing of the "silent majority," Johnson believed that there was a "silent center" in the United States that could be reached through effective public relations. He asked both military and diplomatic officials in Saigon to send the VIG any optimistic information on the progress of the Vietnam War, which it later released as presidential statements and press releases. These often took the form of statistics on measures such as kill ratios. The material also found its way into many of Johnson's speeches as well as into various position and policy papers that administration officials used to define their Vietnam policies. Journalists, both American and foreign, learned to take many of the VIG's statements with a grain of salt, especially as the "credibility gap" between the actuality of the Vietnam War and the Johnson administration's claims about it grew wider. **See also** Joint U.S. Public Affairs Office; media and the Vietnam War.

## Vietnamization

The term used for the policy adopted toward the Vietnam War by the administration of U.S. president Richard M. Nixon. Vietnamization involved parallel strategies. Along one line, American combat troops would be gradually withdrawn from Vietnam, a decision deemed necessary because of the unpopularity of the war in the United States. Simultaneously, and as an obvious effect of the pullback of U.S. troops, the fighting of the war against North Vietnam would be turned over almost completely to the Republic of Vietnam, or South Vietnam. In many ways the policy of Vietnamization, to use the term employed first by Nixon's secretary of defense Melvin Laird, was a return to the U.S. viewpoint of the early 1960s, when South Vietnam was expected to provide for its own defense against the north, using American support and advice.

The withdrawal of American troops began in July 1969 with the departure of twenty-five thousand men. It continued steadily until the summer of 1972, by which time most combat forces had left Vietnam, leaving only scattered residual support troops. In fact, Nixon and his national security adviser, Henry Kissinger, justified the American involvement in the invasion of Cambodia, which took place in the spring of 1970, by claiming that the action was necessary because it would divert North Vietnamese forces and damage their supply lines, thus making it easier for the withdrawal to continue. In addition, the withdrawal of American troops may well have made it easier for Nixon and

his advisers to decide to deal with North Vietnam by launching massive bombing raids, as they did through much of 1972. In any case, the steady return of American troops, to a rather mixed welcome, helped dampen the vocal and active antiwar movement by 1971. So also did Nixon's decision to end the draft, effective January 1973. **See also** antiwar movement; Lam Son 719; Linebacker I; Nixon, Richard M.

## Vietnam syndrome

The term for the supposed hesitation of both American politicians and the American public to support the use of their armed forces after losing the Vietnam War. The notion was mostly cited by those who could not accept the fact that not only did the United States lose the war, it could not have won it even with complete public support. The Vietnam syndrome had several manifestations. One, and in fact the one that faded most quickly, was a lack of faith in the quality of members of the armed services. During the last years of the Vietnam War, the services were plagued by bad morale, drug use, and indiscipline, and certain organizational aspects, such as excessive careerism among the officer corps, made the services seem inefficient. Top commanders, however, began to address these deficiencies as early as 1973. Former Military Assistance Command, Vietnam (MACV), head General Creighton Abrams was instrumental in this effort. Others have claimed that the shift from a draft to a volunteer armed services also helped markedly to increase the quality of recruits, as did raising minimum requirements for entrance. By the early 1980s, and thanks partly to a change in the political climate, it was again fashionable in the United States to praise the armed forces.

A second manifestation of the Vietnam syndrome was uncertainty over whether the armed services could perform effectively under combat. This notion was tested in 1983 when American forces were sent to the Caribbean island of Grenada to supposedly rescue groups of hostages and in 1989 during an operation in Panama. In both instances the forces performed fairly effectively, albeit in limited circumstances.

A third aspect of the Vietnam syndrome was whether politicians would be able to mount a large-scale military effort involving substantial risk to American lives. The concern was that, as during the Vietnam era, widespread public protests would undermine any such effort by staying the hand of politicians and thereby make it much more difficult for military commanders to carry out their duties. This aspect of the Vietnam syndrome was put to rest, many thought, by the success of the short Gulf War of 1991 and the invasion of in Iraq in 2003, although it remained to be seen whether the American public, or its politicians, would be willing to accept a drawn-out conflict resulting in a large number of casualties.

## Vietnam Veterans Against the War (VVAW)

An antiwar group made up mostly of servicemen who had been to Vietnam. Vietnam Veterans Against the War was formed in April 1967 by a small group of veterans already active in antiwar demonstrations. Their hope was that the fact they had experienced the war firsthand would give their protests added weight and credibility.

Members of VVAW took part in most major antiwar events, and they also staged their own. One VVAW event was Operation Rapid American Withdrawal, a September 1970 march from Morristown, New Jersey, to Valley Forge, Pennsylvania. Along the way the participants, dressed in battle fatigues, staged reenactments of alleged astrocities committed against Vietnamese civilians. In February 1971 VVAW staged a public meeting in Detroit at which members spoke of atrocities they had themselves committed; however, critics contended that not all speakers were citing their own experiences, or were even Vietnam veterans at all. Another VVAW event was Operation Dewey Canyon III, an ironic reference to Dewey Canyons I and II, two military operations in Vietnam. During this demonstration some one thousand VVAW members dumped their medals on the steps of the Capitol building in Washington, D.C.

VVAW was instrumental in bringing attention to the psychological toll that Vietnam service took on the men who had been there. In 1970, working with New York psychiatrists Robert Jay Lifton and Chaim Shatan, VVAW members began holding what they called "rap sessions," which were simply group get-togethers where members could speak openly about what they had experienced in Vietnam and what feelings of guilt, remorse, or shame they carried with them. Throughout the 1970s, even after the end of the Vietnam War, members of VVAW continued to concern themselves with the psychological aftereffects of the war, and their efforts helped establish what came to be known as post-traumatic stress disorder as a legitimate mental condition requiring professional treatment. Veterans Administration hospitals, in fact, adopted the strategy of rap sessions as one way to deal with the disorder.

VVAW was controversial. Many thought it was infiltrated by government informants, and during its wartime protests the organization was often accused of exaggeration or of using nonveterans to pose as victims of the Vietnam experience. In addition, on at least one occasion the group refused to allow women who had served in Vietnam to join them. Nevertheless, VVAW activities helped define the Vietnam veterans' experience for posterity, not only through protests but also through such activities as poetry and literature. A post-war organization, Vietnam Veterans of America, carried on the work. **See also** antiwar movement; Dewey Canyon III.

## Vietnam Veterans Memorial

The chief structure intended to commemorate the 58,198 American men and women who died in the Vietnam War. It stands on the Mall in Washington, D.C., not far from the Lincoln Memorial. The guiding force behind the memorial was Jan Scruggs, a soldier who had been

*People visit the Vietnam Veterans Memorial. The memorial in Washington, D.C., is a solemn reminder of those who died in the Vietnam War.*

wounded in Vietnam in 1969. Scruggs formed a Vietnam Veterans Memorial Fund to raise money for the project in 1979. Money was slow in coming, but in 1980 the federal government agreed to provide land for the structure. Only after the release of American hostages held in Iran in 1981 did momentum for the memorial grow, and by the end of that year the fund had raised over $8 million. Meanwhile, the organization also held a design competition. It was won by Maya Ying Lin, an architectural student at Yale University. Her design, which inspired much controversy from those seeking a more conventional memorial, was a simple V-shaped wall made of black granite and placed against a hillside. The names of all those killed in Vietnam would be engraved in the granite in chronological order. Lin was forced to accept certain compromises in the design, notably the stationing of a flag and the construction nearby of a conventional statue of four soldiers depicting both the ethnic diversity and fatigue of the Vietnam experience. The wall was dedicated in November 1982, the flag and statue in 1984. In November 1993 another statue was added to commemorate the women who served.

The Vietnam Veterans Memorial became one of the most popular sites in Washington, D.C., and from its unveiling provided one means by which veterans and bereaved family members could come to terms with the Vietnam experience. Visitors often left behind flowers, letters, and other mementos or took rubbings of the names of their lost friends or loved ones. **See also** veterans.

# Vo Nguyen Giap (1911–1998)

Top military commander for the Democratic Republic of Vietnam (DRV, or North Vietnam). Giap developed strategies that helped oust French colonial rule over Indochina in 1954 and then, during the 1960s and 1970s, continued to fight in ways that, although costly in terms of North Vietnamese casualties, helped end in victory for his nation.

Giap became a formal member of the Indochina Communist Party in 1937. In 1940 he left for China, where he joined other Vietnamese exiles. Notable among them was Ho Chi Minh, the leader of the Vietnamese Communists. As one of the few formally educated cadres Giap was a natural leader, and Ho ordered him to go to the mountainous regions of northern Vietnam. He stayed there from 1941 to 1945, working to convert local hill tribes to the cause of ousting French rule. Giap's efforts easily fit within the larger goals of the Viet Minh, formed by Ho in 1941. As the effective leader of the groups of cadres working in northern Vietnam, as well as a target of French wartime authorities, Giap gained a great deal of tactical and logistical experience during the World War II years.

In December 1944 Giap took command of his first military-style organization, a small unit of thirty-four men that called itself the Vietnam Armed Propaganda and Liberation Brigade. Over the next months Giap's unit mounted attacks on small French outposts. During one of these attacks, on August 20, 1945, Giap learned that the Japanese had surrendered and were no longer the authority in Vietnam. He quickly marched his men to Hanoi, where they supported Ho Chi Minh in his declaration of Vietnamese independence. Giap was also on hand when, on September 2, Ho announced the formation of the Democratic Republic of Vietnam. He was named the DRV's first interior minister and soon given control over all military forces of the Viet Minh.

At the beginning of the First Indochina War in December 1946, Giap issued a statement asking all patriotic Vietnamese to fight with the Viet Minh against the French. Ultimately, he led an army numbering more than 300,000 men, including civilian volunteers. After a number of setbacks, his troops were able to take and maintain control of most of northern Vietnam outside major cities such as Hanoi and Haiphong, and in 1953 Giap launched an incursion into what was to become Laos. The First Indochina War came to an end when the French commander, Henri Navarre, made an ill-fated attempt to force Giap to commit his forces to a single area. Then, Navarre believed, superior French discipline and firepower would end the Viet Minh threat. The Frenchman chose an isolated valley near a village called Dien Bien Phu to make his stand and stationed it with more than ten thousand soldiers. Giap, in effect, took the bait, but in such a way that the French forces were besieged and overwhelmed. Giap surrounded Dien Bien Phu with well over fifty thousand Viet Minh troops and also moved in a number of large artillery pieces, which were dragged foot by foot up the surrounding mountainsides. This enabled him to continually pound the French with artillery fire, while his troops picked away at isolated French outposts. After fifty-five days the French surrendered, and soon after, the Geneva Peace Accords granted the DRV its independence. Giap, now at perhaps the height of his power and reputation, was named minister of defense of the new nation as well as commander in chief of the North Vietnamese Army (NVA). He was also named to the ruling politburo of the Vietnamese Communist Party.

Giap differed, however, with other politburo members on tactics and strategy. Whereas other top Communists favored a focus on developing a strong Communist state, a so-called political struggle, Giap advocated an "armed struggle" to reunite the DRV with South Vietnam, where the Geneva Accords had established a state known as the Republic of Vietnam (RVN). Giap, in fact, followed the pattern laid down by Chinese Communist leader Mao Tse-tung, which called for, in order, a guerrilla war, defense of your gains, and then a counteroffensive. He thought that the pattern had succeeded against the French and that, given time, it would succeed in reuniting Vietnam as well. Then, once reunification was accomplished, the political struggle could proceed.

The NVA commander was able to test his ideas when fighting in Vietnam surged once again in the early 1960s. He took charge of the military effort to weaken the RVN and, later, to force out American forces. In so doing he often used tactics suggestive of his victory at Dien Bien Phu by trying to trap the enemy in such spots as the Ia Drang Valley in 1965 and Khe Sanh in 1967 and 1968. Giap was concerned that one day the South Vietnamese and Americans might mount an invasion of the DRV, a move they never actually attempted, so he took whatever auspicious occasions arose to try to reduce the strength of the enemy. In 1968, when other top DRV officials made plans for the Tet Offensive, Giap expressed his hesitation with the strategy, thinking that the DRV and its Communist comrades in the south, the Viet Cong, might not yet be ready for an all-out assault. He ultimately acquiesced to the Tet Offensive, however, acknowledging the greater political influence of Le Duan, another member of the politburo, as well as General Nguyen Thi Chan. Although Tet resulted in a sort of victory for the DRV, since it shocked the United States enough to convince it to begin a pullback from Vietnam, it was a very costly victory, suggesting that Giap's instincts may have been correct. The Viet Cong was virtually destroyed, there were large numbers of NVA casualties, and no territory was taken. Giap was ultimately blamed by his opponents in the politburo for his failure to act more aggressively and decisively during the offensive. These attacks did not prevent him, however, from becoming one of a ruling triumvirate in the DRV following the 1969 death of Ho Chi Minh. Giap remained minister of defense and commander in chief while Lao Dong general secretary Le Duan assumed leadership of the Vietnamese Communist Party and, as such, the man in charge of domestic politics. The third member was Pham Van Dong, the foreign minister.

Giap continued to believe that the DRV was not yet ripe for the third stage of the Maoist pattern, counteroffensive, and from 1969 until 1972 the NVA mounted few attacks on South Vietnam. Instead, the action shifted to regions of Laos and Cambodia, where Giap hoped to strengthen the Ho Chi Minh Trail. In the spring of 1972, and still suspecting that the time was not right, Giap led the Easter Offensive against the south, which was ordered by most members of the politburo. The Easter Offensive, like the Tet Offensive, had mixed results. Incursions south of the demilitarized zone (DMZ) by the NVA resulted in the takeover of new territory. But beyond that, the combination of a strengthened South Vietnamese army and massive American air support stymied the offensive. In addition, the NVA suffered huge numbers of casualties, and, for the first time, American bombing raids targeted Hanoi and Haiphong.

In the aftermath of the Easter Offensive and the signing of the Paris Peace Accords in January 1973, Giap was slowly eased from his post as commander in chief of the NVA, although he was allowed to remain in office as defense minister. Military command fell to his longtime subordinate General Van Tien Dung, who had served with him at Dien Bien Phu. Giap was only marginally involved in the planning and execution of the final North Vietnamese offensive against South Vietnam. Dung took overall responsibility. After the fall of the RVN in April 1975 and the establishment of the unified Socialist Republic of Vietnam in 1976, Giap held mainly symbolic roles within the Hanoi hierarchy and had little involvement in the Vietnamese conflicts with Cambodia in 1978 and China in 1979. **See also** Ho Chi Minh; North Vietnamese Army; Viet Minh; Vietnam, Democratic Republic of.

## War Powers Resolution

An attempt by the U.S. Congress to place limits on the war-making powers of the president. According to the U.S. Constitution, only Congress has the right to declare war. Yet on numerous occasions in American history, the president, using the authority as commander in chief of U.S. military forces granted him by the Constitution, deployed American troops in combat situations without a formal declaration of war by Congress. One such occasion was in 1965 in Vietnam.

The War Powers Resolution was introduced in Congress by Senator Jacob Javits of New York in the spring of 1970. The immediate occasion was American involvement in the invasion of Cambodia, which could be seen as yet another violation of the Congress's right to declare war. The source of much debate over the next few years, the resolution was ultimately passed by both houses of Congress in November 1973, over the veto of President Richard M. Nixon. It required the president to consult with Congress before forces were sent into areas where combat was occurring, or was likely, and to present a report in writing within forty-eight hours of any troop deployment. In such a case, however, the president could continue the deployment only for up to ninety days. After sixty days, the president had to inform Congress, again in writing, that thirty more days were necessary for the safety of American troops. Any deployment beyond ninety days required a congressional declaration of war or a similar act by Congress.

The consensus of many was that the 1973 War Powers Resolution was the result of both the Vietnam War and longer-term trends in U.S. foreign policy. Certainly many members of Congress were concerned about the rapid buildup of American forces in Vietnam between 1965 and 1968 and the 1970 invasion of Cambodia, which to most came as a complete surprise. Adding to their concerns was the vocal, widespread, and sometimes violent opposition on the part of ordinary American citizens, some of whom used the Vietnam War as an occasion to question the legitimacy of other actions of the federal government. Javits himself, in 1973, claimed that the resolution provided the United States with an opportunity to learn from its experiences in Southeast Asia.

Beyond the circumstances of the Vietnam War, scholars also claim that the War Powers Resolution was designed to check what some have termed the "imperial presidency," a state of affairs in which the U.S. president, in opposition to American custom and, perhaps, the Constitution, exercised undue influence over foreign policy and other areas at the expense of the legislative and judicial branches of the U.S. government. They trace the growth of this imperial presidency back to 1941 and the events of the cold war, which often required direct and quick presidential decisions and, on occasion, covert or intelligence operations that threatened to get out of control. Nixon, who hated sharing authority and often even information, was particularly reluctant to work with Congress, especially as his presidency became mired in the Watergate scandal. Indeed, by 1973, when almost all American forces had been removed from Vietnam, the Congress, despite Nixon's desire to continue American support of the South Vietnamese, began to use a powerful weapon to ensure that Nixon presided over no more military adventures in Southeast Asia: the denial of funding.

Nixon objected to the War Powers Resolution on the grounds that it could put the nation in great danger if, in a time of crisis, the president was not free to act quickly. He also claimed that it granted Congress rights that belonged to the president according to the Constitution, such as troop deployments. Later critics of the act, as well as some later presidents, repeated these objections and added that the act placed unreasonable limitations on the right of the executive branch to conduct foreign policy. The resolution's many supporters, however, claimed that it was justified because it put a necessary restraint on the president and required consultation between the president and Congress when military action threatened. **See also** Case-Church Amendment; Cooper-Church Amendment; Gulf of Tonkin Resolution; Nixon, Richard M.

## Washington Special Actions Group (WSAG)

A foreign policy advisory group established by U.S. national security adviser Henry Kissinger in early 1969. Composed of staff from the National Security Agency, the Departments of Defense and State, and the chairmen of the Central Intelligence Agency (CIA) and the Joint Chiefs of Staff, the Washington Special Actions Group exerted a major influence on Vietnam policy during the Nixon ad-

ministration. Moreover, according to the methods of decision making preferred by both President Richard Nixon and Kissinger, the WSAG operated outside of traditional diplomatic, military, or bureaucratic channels, which the two men felt moved too slowly.

The WSAG proved instrumental in extending the Vietnam War into Cambodia by, first, supporting attacks on North Vietnamese troops along the Cambodian stretches of the Ho Chi Minh Trail and, second, facilitating arms shipments to new Cambodian president Lon Nol in April 1970 and thus, partly, committing U.S. support to Lon Nol's regime. In 1972 the WSAG also helped plan the mining of Haiphong Harbor and the efforts to supply the South Vietnamese army with the latest equipment in the wake of the American troop withdrawal. **See also** American Friends of Vietnam; Kissinger, Henry.

## Watergate scandal

The scandal that undermined the presidency of Richard M. Nixon and led to his resignation on August 9, 1974, making Nixon the only president ever to resign from office. Along with the Vietnam War, Watergate provided evidence for many Americans that there was something very wrong with American politics in the 1960s and 1970s.

Specifically, the Watergate scandal refers to the break-in of Democratic Party National Headquarters, which was housed in Washington, D.C.'s Watergate office complex, on June 17, 1972. The would-be burglars, who were apprehended by Washington police, were part of a covert team organized and run by Nixon staffers. Their intent was to uncover information that might be damaging to the Democrats in the 1972 presidential election. Over the next months, the investigation of the Watergate burglary spread from the Washington police to the U.S. Congress, and in the process, investigators found what amounted to an unsettling pattern of behavior in the Nixon administration. It included misinformation campaigns, smear attacks on political enemies, and the use of illegal means such as unauthorized wiretappings and property break-ins.

The basis for this pattern of presidential misbehavior was Nixon's obsession with secrecy and loyalty, especially with regard to policy in Southeast Asia. The president believed that information leaks, even over major events that were of great concern to both his colleagues in Congress and the American people, inhibited his effort to carry out effective foreign policy. He was particularly infuriated when, in 1970, the *New York Times* published stories about the secret bombings in Cambodia. In an effort to trace the source of the information, Nixon authorized his national security adviser, Henry Kissinger, to place a wiretap on the telephone of *Times* reporter William Beecher.

In 1971, Nixon was likewise incensed when the *Times* published parts of the so-called Pentagon Papers, a secret Defense Department report on the evolution of Vietnam policy during the administration of Lyndon B. Johnson. Even though the *Times* reports did not implicate his administration directly, Nixon continued to feel that it was imperative that the inner workings of the federal government not be exposed in this manner. After the publication of the Pentagon Papers, Nixon authorized the formation of a special team of operatives known as "plumbers" because of their mandate to stop leaks. Among their activities, and one that became well known during the Watergate investigation, was a break-in of the Los Angeles office of Daniel Ellsberg's psychiatrist. Ellsberg was the former Defense Department staffer who had given the Pentagon Papers to the *Times*, and the plumbers were, apparently, seeking information that would reduce Ellsberg's cred-

ibility and destroy his reputation. It was a later group of plumbers who staged the unsuccessful Watergate burglary.

As investigators exposed more and more examples of this type of behavior, they also grew aware that Nixon and many of his administration staffers were also guilty of attempting to cover up their activities. It was these cover-ups that brought Nixon to a potential state of legal culpability. In July 1974, the Congress brought three articles of impeachment against the president, but he chose to resign rather than face being found guilty and forcibly removed from office. Nixon was later pardoned of all wrongdoing by his successor, Gerald R. Ford. **See also** Nixon, Richard M.; Paris negotiations; Pentagon Papers.

## Weathermen

The most radical of the anti–Vietnam War groups in the United States. The Weathermen were formed out of a much larger group, the Students for a Democratic Society (SDS). At an SDS meeting in March 1967, certain members cited their dissatisfaction with nonviolent protest and began to promote violence as a way to bring about the changes they wanted; soon after they splintered off into the Weathermen. The Weathermen were interested in not only ending the Vietnam War but also transforming American society so that it would be antiracist and egalitarian. In addition, most members professed goals and methods that other Americans identified with communism. These included raising revolutionary consciousness among the working classes, engaging in constant argument and even "self-criticism," and, when necessary, militant action. The most famous of the Weathermen's incidents was the so-called Days of Rage, a staged riot in Chicago in October 1968. The group also considered such methods as bombings and arson attempts against the U.S. government.

The Federal Bureau of Investigation (FBI) kept close tabs on the Weathermen, as it did with most other vocal antiwar groups, and the radicals carried out few incidents beyond the Days of Rage. Most Americans, even those who opposed the war, were against the Weathermen's message and methods, and the group faded from importance by 1972. **See also** antiwar movement; Democratic National Convention of 1968; Youth International Party.

## Westmoreland, William (1914– )

General in the U.S. Army and, as commander of the Military Assistance Command, Vietnam (MACV), from June 1964 to June 1968, the top American military man in Vietnam.

In January 1964, Secretary of Defense Robert McNamara appointed Westmoreland, a general with a long history as both a field commander and administrator, as deputy to General Paul D. Harkins, commander of MACV. He replaced Harkins as the top officer on June 20. At that time, U.S. policy in Vietnam was still focused on providing support to the government of South Vietnam through financial aid and military advice. When the Gulf of Tonkin Resolution was passed by the U.S. Congress later that summer, Westmoreland found himself in charge of a major American military effort, and to give him added authority to go along with his added responsibilities, he was promoted to full general.

Westmoreland felt that the South Vietnamese army lacked organization, purpose, and ten-

acity, and he was prepared to prosecute the war more vigorously. He elected to use a strategy of attrition in which he would draw both factions of the enemy, the Viet Cong (VC) and North Vietnamese Army (NVA), into protracted actions, and the superior American firepower in such actions would result in victory. Alternatively, American forces could eliminate enemy units using "search-and-destroy" missions. The attrition strategy was based on the notion that, with high enough casualties, the Communists would lose their willingness to fight. It came to rely heavily on such statistical measures as kill ratios and body counts, which, MACV

*General William Westmoreland addresses his troops to prepare them for combat.*

analysts argued, were accurate descriptions of the U.S. progress toward victory.

Westmoreland was held largely responsible for the failure of the strategy of attrition, and he became a major target for both antiwar protesters and members of Congress who questioned the way the Vietnam War was being carried out. Westmoreland, however, had little control over political decisions that influenced the American approach to Vietnam, and even the commander in chief of the Pacific Command, based in Hawaii, had control over some U.S. operations in Vietnam. In addition, as a well-trained and highly experienced officer, Westmoreland was using tactics that were reasonable if the objective was military victory, especially given the overwhelming American advantages in firepower and technology. Indeed, by 1967, statistical measures as well as anecdotal reports convinced Westmoreland that his practice of taking the war to the Communists was working. However, Westmoreland's tactics worked in contradiction, many have argued, to the true U.S. goal in Vietnam, which was not necessarily military victory but the strengthening of the South Vietnamese state. His military measures rarely worked smoothly with the effort at pacification that was being carried out by others, and in fact may have worked to alienate many ordinary South Vietnamese.

The 1968 Tet Offensive, though a military victory for the United States and South Vietnam, was a morale breaker resulting in a major shift in U.S. policy. Hoping to press the military advantage, Westmoreland asked for over 200,000 more troops, most of whom would be used in Vietnam. President Lyndon B. Johnson ultimately refused the request, which would have meant calling up reserves and would also have been politically unacceptable. Johnson, acknowledging the change in overall Vietnam policy, recalled Westmoreland in June 1968 and, in effect, kicked him upstairs by appointing him army chief of staff. While Westmoreland busied himself with other army matters, including the planning of an all-volunteer force, it fell to his successor as commander of MACV, General Creighton Abrams, to preside over the withdrawal of American troops from Vietnam. **See also** Abrams, Creighton; attrition strategy; Military Assistance Command, Vietnam; Tet Offensive.

# Weyand, Frederick C. (1916– )

U.S. Army general and last commander of the Military Assistance Command, Vietnam (MACV). An infantry commander, Weyand arrived in Vietnam along with the Twenty-fifth Infantry Division in March 1966. One year later he was named head of Field Force II, with command over army operations in the region around Saigon. He proved instrumental in preparing the Saigon area for the Tet Offensive of 1968 when he, along with his political adviser John Paul Vann, grew suspicious over increased Communist radio traffic. The concern was high enough that he was able to convince MACV commander William Westmoreland to pull back army units that had been deployed elsewhere. This precipitate action was thought to have altered the course of Tet around Saigon.

Weyand left Vietnam later in 1969 but got away from the Vietnam War only briefly. From March 1969 to June 1970 he served as the military adviser to the U.S. side in the Paris peace negotiations. In September 1970 he was appointed to Saigon to serve as deputy to MACV commander Creighton Abrams. He succeeded Abrams in June 1972 and therefore presided over the final pullout of American troops and, after the signing of the Paris Peace Accords in January 1973, shutting down MACV headquarters at Tan Son Nhut air base.

Weyand remained involved with Vietnamese affairs, however, over the next two years. After leaving Saigon he was appointed commander in chief of the U.S. Army in the Pacific region and, soon after, found himself raised to vice chief of staff of the army and, in October 1974, chief of staff after the death of Abrams, who had again preceded him. Weyand returned to Saigon for a final time on March 27, 1975, sent there by President Gerald Ford, who wanted an assessment of the military situation. He had little to report that was positive, and he was forced to inform South Vietnamese president Nguyen Van Thieu that the United States would send no more military aid even as Saigon itself was falling to Communist forces.

Weyand retired from active duty in September 1976 but had already taken an interest in using the lessons of the Vietnam War to build an army that would better serve the needs of the American people. He published several articles on the subject in military journals. **See also** Military Assistance Command, Vietnam; Tet Offensive; Vietnamization.

# Wheeler, Earle G. (1908–1975)

U.S. Army general and chairman of the Joint Chiefs of Staff from 1964 to 1970. A protegé of General Maxwell Taylor, he replaced Taylor as chairman when Taylor left the post to become American ambassador to South Vietnam in 1964. This made Wheeler the senior military officer in the United States for most of the Vietnam War years. He remained, however, as much a politician as a military man, and although he got along well with President Lyndon B. Johnson, Johnson allowed his secretary of defense, Robert McNamara, to be the guiding hand in Washington on Vietnam policy. This happened despite Wheeler's attempts to present a unified front by the Joint Chiefs and therefore prevent McNamara and other civilian officials from exercising

control over military operations. As the months passed, Wheeler and the other Joint Chiefs developed strong doubts about McNamara's attempt to win the war through various gradual means rather than using America's greatest advantage, overwhelming and immediate force. The conflict provided a vivid example of political and military goals for Vietnam that were mutually contradictory.

As chairman, Wheeler was involved not only in Vietnam policy but in American military operations worldwide. As the U.S. commitment to South Vietnam expanded, he grew increasingly concerned about balancing the operations in Vietnam with those elsewhere in the world. In particular, Wheeler worried about manpower; he knew that the U.S. military did not possess the numbers of troops that would be required to both escalate the commitment in Vietnam and maintain strong positions elsewhere, notably in Western Europe. He hoped to strengthen the manpower pool by calling up reserve troops, but this the Johnson administration, for political and economic reasons, hesitated to do. Meanwhile, the Joint Chiefs devised an overall plan for Vietnam that, ironically, supported McNamara's strategy of gradualism and partly recognized political realities. It was a three-pronged approach designed to, first, get the North Vietnamese government to stop interfering in South Vietnam; second, end the guerrilla threat presented by the Viet Cong; and third, ensure that China did not step in to help North Vietnam. To accomplish the third of these goals, Wheeler realized, larger numbers of U.S. troops would be a necessary deterrent.

By 1968, the year of the Tet Offensive, the siege of Khe Sanh, and a fundamental change in the U.S. approach to the Vietnam conflict, relations between the Joint Chiefs and the president were as poor as they had ever been. Indeed, some criticized Wheeler in later years for not being able to bridge this gulf and make sure that Johnson understood that, in the opinions of the Joint Chiefs, McNamara's strategy of gradualism would likely fail. Wheeler, in any case, used the opportunity of the Tet Offensive to press Johnson for a massive call-up of more than 200,000 new troops after conferring with General William Westmoreland, American commander in Vietnam.

Johnson disdained Wheeler's recommendations, however, and chose instead to follow the advice of those who urged a pullback of the American commitment in Vietnam. Although Wheeler remained chairman of the Joint Chiefs, with the approval of both Johnson and his successor, Richard M. Nixon, neither president took much heed of his advice. Wheeler retired from the Joint Chiefs of Staff, and from the U.S. Army, in July 1970. **See also** McNamara, Robert; Taylor, Maxwell.

## Wise Men

An informal group of senior advisers who gathered to discuss Vietnam policy with President Lyndon B. Johnson, a man who understood that his greater expertise was in domestic affairs. Membership shifted, but at various times the group of Wise Men included foreign policy and military experts from the post–World War II era of the beginnings of the cold war and the containment policy as well as current staffers within both the Kennedy and Johnson administrations. Most were Democrats. Among the Wise Men were Dean Acheson and Generals Omar Bradley, Matthew Ridgeway, and John McCloy, who remained prominent from the early cold war years. Others included George Ball, McGeorge Bundy, Clark Clifford, Cyrus Vance, Abe Fortas, Henry Cabot Lodge, and General Maxwell Taylor. The group first met in July 1965.

The Wise Men were apparently most influential on two occasions. The first came early in the period of American involvement in Vietnam, November 1965. At that point Johnson's secretary of defense, Robert McNamara, encouraged the president to limit the American presence in Vietnam and to stop bombing North Vietnam and return to the earlier emphasis, which was to try to strengthen the South Vietnamese regime so that it could fight its own war. The Wise Men, however, with the notable exception of George Ball, favored Johnson's policy of escalated American involvement; Johnson elected not to share McNamara's opinion with them.

The second major appearance of the Wise Men came after the Tet Offensive of 1968. Following an in-depth report on the offensive assembled, partly, by Dean Acheson, Johnson brought them together in late March. They were presented with information that came as some surprise, namely that the Tet Offensive had severely damaged the U.S. effort to pacify South Vietnam and that, mistakenly, the South Vietnamese Communist forces remained strong despite nearly three years of U.S. military efforts. The consensus of the Wise Men was that, in these circumstances, the United States should find a way to begin removing itself from the Vietnam quagmire. Not all of the men felt this way, notably members of the military establishment. But others realized that the risks of continued U.S. involvement were high and that a further expansion of the war would be extremely expensive and politically harmful, and might damage other foreign policy interests in Europe and China. To his disappointment, Johnson found himself forced to agree. **See also** Ball, George; Johnson, Lyndon B.; McNamara, Robert; Tet Offensive.

## women in the Vietnam War, U.S.

More than seventy-five hundred American women served in Vietnam as members of the armed forces. This total included some five thousand in the army, two thousand in the air force, five hundred in the navy, and thirty-five in the Marine Corps. Most of them were nurses, but women also served in various behind-the-lines support positions as administrators, intelligence or personnel specialists, or office workers. Nearly five hundred were officers. Women were also part of medical evacuation teams stationed in Alaska, Guam, and the Philippines. In addition, hundreds of other American women served in civilian posts ranging from embassy and military work to United Service Organizations (USO) and Red Cross volunteers.

Women were in Vietnam virtually from the beginning of the U.S. involvement there. A few served as nurses and advisers to local medical staffs in the early 1960s. As the U.S. escalation proceeded beginning in 1965, so did the deployment of women. The first large group were air force nurses assigned to bases in both Vietnam and Thailand as well as at large military hospitals. Soon after, women arrived to perform support work in various administrative specialties.

Eight service women were killed in the line of duty during the Vietnam War. Several dozen civilian American women were also killed in plane crashes or Viet Cong bombings. In November 1993 the Vietnam Women's Memorial was opened near the Vietnam Veterans Memorial in Washington, D.C. It is a statue of three nurses tending a wounded soldier and commemorates the work that most of the military women in Vietnam performed. **See also** casualties; women in the Vietnam War, Vietnamese.

# women in the Vietnam War, Vietnamese

Women and women's groups played key roles in the three significant Vietnamese forces during the Vietnam War: North Vietnam, South Vietnam, and the Viet Cong (VC). This was especially true for the Communists, who recognized few differences between the genders on ideological grounds and who argued that women as well as men must take part in the struggle for national liberation. As early as 1930 the Indochina Communist Party, the precursor to the Vietnamese Communist Party, or Lao Dong, had an affiliated Women's Union. In 1945 a woman leader of the Viet Minh, Ha Thi Que, formed an all-woman's guerrilla unit prepared to fight against the French; by 1954, hundreds of thousands of women participated in official guerrilla units throughout Vietnam. Most fought the political fight rather than the military one, seeking to educate villagers, mobilize fighters, and provide behind-the-lines support. Untold numbers of women also worked as laborers in providing transport of materials and on building projects.

In 1960, when the Viet Cong movement was rising in South Vietnam, Nguyen Thi Dinh began to form an army of peasant women eventually known as the Long-Haired Army. Their goals were to encourage South Vietnamese soldiers to desert, stage rallies and strikes, and otherwise protest against the corruption of Ngo Dinh Diem's Saigon regime. Within the VC itself up to 40 percent of regimental commanders were women, and large numbers served as political cadres. Nguyen Thi Dinh was herself a VC general and one of its top commanders. Women took part in nearly every aspect of VC attacks, and they found that they made effective operatives in covert attacks, since neither the Americans nor the South Vietnamese were apt to suspect women of being active VC members.

Huge numbers of women also participated in the broader effort to oppose Saigon and its American allies. By 1965, for instance, an organization known as the Women's Liberation Association (WLA) claimed as many as 1.2 million members in South Vietnam. The WLA

*Young women of the People's Self-Defense Force patrol their South Vietnam village. Over 1 million Vietnamese women volunteered to join the war effort.*

recognized the value of propaganda praising women's contributions to the struggle for national liberation, as did the VC in the south. Women were praised in posters, pamphlets, and speeches, which sometimes hearkened back to earlier female heroes in Vietnam such as the Trung sisters who fought against Chinese domination.

In the south, women found their official roles far more limited, which may partly explain the appeal to women of the Communist insurgency. During Diem's regime, his sister-in-law, Madame Nhu, formed a women's solidarity movement to support the government and combat immorality. Few took it seriously. When the Vietnam War got under way in the early 1960s the South Vietnamese army formed a Women's Armed Forces Corps (WAFC) as an affiliate body. The WAFC played a significant, though underreported, part in the South Vietnamese war effort. Members provided behind-the-lines or medical support and often also took part in fighting. In addition, a women's team of paratroopers and a special branch of the national police contributed greatly toward undermining the VC infrastructure in the late 1960s by collecting intelligence and infiltrating VC groups. **See also** Ngo Dinh Nhu, Madame; Nguyen Thi Dinh; women in the Vietnam War, U.S.

continued the effort to encourage soldiers to desert and provided education and communications to the VC. WLA members also constructed booby traps and prepared and delivered food.

By contrast, few women joined the North Vietnamese Army, although almost all women received military training. In North Vietnam, women's contributions consisted of working in factories, forming self-defense teams, and otherwise working for social cohesion. Those women who did join the army generally served as medics or in behind-the-lines roles. The North Vietnamese government

# Xuan Loc, Battle of

The last major battle of the Vietnam War, taking place from April 9 to April 22, 1975. Xuan Loc was a village located some forty miles north of Saigon on the juncture of Highway 1, Vietnam's major north-south artery, and Highway 20, which ran west to east. It served as the gateway to not only Saigon but also the major military bases at Long Binh and Bien Hoa. The North Vietnamese Army (NVA) began its attack on the city on March 17 as part of the final step in the larger Ho Chi Minh campaign designed to finally take Saigon and reunite the country. This first attack, however, was repulsed by the Army of the Republic of Vietnam (ARVN). After waiting for reinforcements, the NVA again attacked Xuan Loc on April 9. It also cut off Highway 1, which effectively ensured that the ARVN could not be reinforced from the ground.

The battle continued for days and proved very costly to both sides. Unable to secure not only reinforcements but supplies, the ARVN fought bravely but found itself steadily being hemmed in by a vastly larger NVA force consisting, ultimately, of four divisions. The ARVN lost some 30 percent of its force in Xuan Loc, and the regional forces that fought alongside it suffered even heavier casualties. The NVA likewise suffered heavy losses, particularly from ARVN air support. Among the weapons used by the South Vietnamese Air Force was the CBU-55, the most powerful weapon available outside of nuclear bombs. The bomb pulled all of the oxygen from the air within a two-acre radius, killing 250 people.

On April 21, the same day that South Vietnamese president Nguyen Van Thieu resigned his office and prepared to go into exile, the ARVN began an aerial evacuation from Xuan Loc. It continued through the following day; the South Vietnamese signaled their departure by dropping the CBU-55. With the NVA now in control of this important juncture, the way to Long Binh and Bien Hoa lay open and clear, and Saigon's days as the capital of an independent nation were numbered. **See also** CBU-55; cease-fire war; Frequent Wind; Ho Chi Minh campaign.

## Yankee Station

One of two fixed points in the open ocean that were used as staging areas for the ships of the U.S. Seventh Fleet. The other, located to the south, was known as Dixie Station. Yankee Station stood in the South China Sea off the North Vietnamese coast at a spot 17 degrees, 30 minutes north latitude and 108 degrees, 30 minutes east longitude. There were usually two aircraft carriers deployed there. Its main purpose was to support the responsibilities of Task Force Seventy-seven, the air wing of the Seventh Fleet. These included bombing strikes and reconnaissance over North Vietnam proper; strikes over other regions were mounted from Dixie Station. **See also** aircraft carriers; Dixie Station.

## Youth International Party (Yippies)

One of the more visible and vocal of the antiwar movements in the United States. The Youth International Party was founded in 1967, ostensibly as a joke, by antiwar activists Abbie Hoffman, Jerry Rubin, Dick Gregory, and Paul Krassner, the last of whom was credited with coining the term *Yippies*. The Yippies organized themselves around sentiments expressed in Rubin's famous motto "Never trust anyone over thirty," and they saw the Vietnam War as a generational conflict. In addition, they portrayed themselves in a way similar to the so-called hippies: They had long hair, espoused increased awareness

through drug taking, and opposed convention and authority. They combined political activism with a cultural movement known as absurdism, a reflection of the awareness of how absurd conventional behavior and attitudes supposedly were.

Outspoken Yippies such as Rubin and Hoffman made good fodder for the media, and the group took advantage of that. In March 1968 the group held a "Yip-in" at Grand Central Station in New York City, a gathering of speakers that turned into a mildly violent protest, which attracted a great deal of media attention. Seeing the upcoming Democratic National Convention in Chicago as a further opportunity, Yippie leaders made plans for a massive protest gathering including, they hoped, up to fifty thousand people. Part of their plan was to stage a rock concert in Chicago's Lincoln Park on August 25. When police refused to allow them to set it up, tensions rose, and the gathering turned into a riot. The violence increased after thousands of protesters gathered in front of the hotel where Democratic Party leaders were staying. Thousands were injured, and Yippie leaders Rubin and Hoffman were arrested, at least partly because of their visibility. Along with other members of the so-called Chicago Seven, the two were tried on charges that included crossing state lines with intent to incite a riot. During their trial, they continued their absurdist behavior, inspiring a number of contempt-of-court charges. Rubin and

Hoffman were convicted, but the charges were later overturned on appeal. Though the Yippies remained active after the trial of the Chicago Seven, they lost their influence as American troops were withdrawn from Vietnam. Rubin and Hoffman were voted out of the organization after the 1972 Democratic Convention. Other Yippies claimed that the two were too old and becoming conventional. They were both pushing forty. **See also** antiwar movement; Hoffman, Abbie; Rubin, Jerry.

# Zumwalt, Elmo, Jr. (1920–2000)

U.S. Navy admiral and commander of naval forces in Vietnam from 1968 to 1970. Appointed to Vietnam in September 1968, Zumwalt was placed in command of U.S. naval operations within Vietnam itself, not of the U.S. Seventh Fleet, which supported U.S. operations from the South China Sea. Zumwalt, therefore, oversaw such matters as riverine activities, coastal surveillance, naval construction, and liaison with the South Vietnamese navy. His largest operation was the Southeast Asia Lake, Ocean, River, and Delta Strategy (SEALORDS), which was intended to interdict Communist supply and communication lines in the vast Mekong Delta and Cambodian border regions. He was also instrumental in beginning the naval aspects of Vietnamization, turning operations over to South Vietnam. In this he enjoyed a close friendship with Commodore Tran Van Chon, the head of the South Vietnamese navy.

Zumwalt was recalled to Washington, D.C., in April 1970 to take the position of chief of naval operations, the highest position in the navy involving membership in the Joint Chiefs of Staff. Although he was inevitably concerned with global affairs, he continued to pay attention to the Vietnam War and was a strong advocate, for instance, of the bombing of Haiphong Harbor. After retiring from the navy in July 1974, Zumwalt took an interest in humanitarian activities. He sought the freedom from Communist captivity of his old comrade Tran Van Chon and spoke on behalf of U.S. servicemen injured by Agent Orange. The defoliant, which Zumwalt had used along the South Vietnamese coast and inland waterways to uncover Communist hideaways, was thought to have injured his son, Elmo R. Zumwalt III, a coastal surveillance officer in Vietnam. **See also** defoliation; Mobile Riverine Force; Southeast Asia Lake, Ocean, River, and Delta Strategy.

**1887**

France forms the Indochinese Union consisting of the Vietnamese colony of Cochin China and the protectorates of Tonkin, Annam, Laos, and Cambodia.

**1930**

Ho Chi Minh and others form the Indochina Communist Party in Hong Kong.

**1932**

Nguyen emperor Bao Dai returns from French exile to become a puppet leader in Vietnam.

**1941**

Japan occupies Indochina but leaves the Vichy French administration in place there; Ho Chi Minh and other Vietnamese nationalists form the Viet Minh to challenge Japanese and Vichy authority.

**1944**

Vo Nguyen Giap assembles the first Viet Minh army.

**1945**

*July*

At the Potsdam Conference, the leaders of the United States, Great Britain, and the Soviet Union determine that when the Japanese surrender, the northern part of Vietnam will be occupied by China and the southern part by Great Britain.

*August 15*

Japan surrenders, ending World War II.

*August 29*

Ho Chi Minh declares a provisional government based in Hanoi.

*September 2*

Ho declares the independence of Vietnam and the formation of the Democratic Republic of Vietnam (DRV).

**1946**

*June*

French high commissioner Georges Thierry d'Argenlieu outflanks Ho and his own government by declaring an independent regime for Cochin China.

*November 23*

French ships bombard Haiphong.

*December 19*

The First Indochina War begins when the Viet Minh attacks French troops in Hanoi.

**1948**

Having committed itself to stopping the spread of communism, the United States begins to send aid to the French to support their war effort in Indochina.

**1950**

*January*

Ho Chi Minh declares that the DRV is the only legitimate government of Vietnam. His regime is recognized by China, the Soviet Union, and other Communist bloc states.

*February*

The United States and Great Britain recognize Bao Dai's nascent Republic of Vietnam (RVN).

*September*
The United States sends its Military Assistance Advisory Group (MAAG) to Vietnam, having provided the French with $15 million in military aid.

## 1951
*February*
Ho Chi Minh creates the Lao Dong, the Vietnamese Communist Party.

## 1954
*May 7*
The French surrender at Dien Bien Phu, marking the effective end of the First Indochina War.

*May 8*
The Geneva Conference turns its attention to Indochina.

*June 16*
Bao Dai selects Ngo Dinh Diem to be his prime minister.

*July 20*
The Geneva Accords recognize the independence of Cambodia, Laos, the DRV (North Vietnam), and the RVN (South Vietnam). (The latter two are to hold a plebiscite on national reunification in 1956.)

*September*
The Southeast Asia Treaty Organization (SEATO) is formed.

## 1955
*January*
The United States begins to send aid to South Vietnam and agrees to take on the responsibility of training the Army of the Republic of Vietnam (ARVN). Edward G. Lansdale's Saigon Military Mission arrives to help Diem consolidate power.

*October*
Diem defeats Bao Dai in a national vote and establishes himself as RVN president. In the preceding year he has already defeated or coopted rivals in the Cao Dai, Hoa Hao, and Binh Xuyen.

## 1959
*January*
The DRV decides to step up its struggle to achieve unification with South Vietnam by adding an "armed struggle" to its "political struggle."

*May*
The DRV authorizes enlargement of the Ho Chi Minh Trail.

*July 8*
The first American casualties in Vietnam are military advisers Major Dale Buis and Sergeant Chester Ovnand. They are part of a U.S. advisory effort of some eight hundred men.

## 1960
*December*
Hanoi forms the National Liberation Front (NLF) to fight the insurgency warfare in the south. Its fighting arm, the People's Liberation Armed Forces, is dubbed the Viet Cong (Vietnamese Communists, or VC) by Diem.

Fighting erupts in Laos among various factions, one of which receives military aid from the Soviet Union. Another, led by General Phoumi Nosavan, is aided by the American Central Intelligence Agency (CIA).

## 1961
*May 16*
The Geneva Conference on Laos begins as the result of steps by the United States, the Soviet Union, and Great Britain to ensure stability in the region. The accords are signed on July 23, 1962.

*October*
Maxwell Taylor, military adviser to President John F. Kennedy, visits South Vietnam with Walt Rostow. Their report on the visit suggests a wider commitment of economic aid and military advisers to Diem.

## 1962

*February 6*
The Military Assistance Command, Vietnam (MACV), is established, officially replacing the MAAG in 1964. Its responsibility is to manage the advisory program that, by mid-1962, employed some two thousand Americans.

*March*
The strategic hamlet program, administered by Diem's brother Ngo Dinh Nhu, becomes the first major pacification effort.

## 1963

*January 2*
During the Battle of Ap Bac, Viet Cong insurgents defeat a larger ARVN force but do not occupy the town, prompting contradictory reports from U.S. military officials and journalists.

*May 8*
ARVN troops fire on Buddhist demonstrations in Hue. In protest, Thich Quang Duc stages a self-immolation in Saigon the next month. Widespread Buddhist demonstrations and further self-immolations follow. The disdainful reactions of Diem and his family members create further hostility toward their regime.

*July*
South Vietnamese generals inform Lucien Conein, a CIA agent, that they are planning a coup against Diem.

*August 21*
Ngo Dinh Nhu's police attack Buddhist temples.

*November 1*
Led by Duong Van Minh, the generals stage their coup. Diem and Nhu seek refuge in a Roman Catholic church in Cholon, Saigon's Chinese district. Diem and Nhu are assassinated the next day.

*November 22*
President Kennedy is assassinated in Dallas.

## 1964

*January*
General Nguyen Khanh seizes control of the RVN government, beginning a year and a half of coups and countercoups.

*June*
General William Westmoreland replaces General Paul D. Harkins as commander of the MACV.

*July*
With U.S. assistance, South Vietnamese vessels begin covert intelligence-gathering missions along the North Vietnamese coast.

*August 2*
The Gulf of Tonkin Incident begins with an attack on the U.S. destroyer *Maddox* by North Vietnamese patrol boats.

*August 4*
Naval commanders on the *Maddox* and a second destroyer, the *C. Turner Joy*, report further attacks, probably falsely. President Lyndon B. Johnson authorizes U.S. air strikes against North Vietnam in response.

*August 7*
Congress passes the Gulf of Tonkin Resolution.

*October*
North Vietnam begins sending North Vietnamese Army (NVA) regulars to South Vietnam via the Ho Chi Minh Trail.

*October 30*
The Viet Cong attacks Bien Hoa air base, killing five U.S. servicemen.

*December*
U.S. bombing of the Ho Chi Minh Trail and other targets in Laos begins as part of Operation Barrel Roll.

*December 24*
The Viet Cong attacks U.S. facilities in Saigon, killing two servicemen.

## 1965

*February 7*
Viet Cong attacks take place on American installations at Pleiku and Qhi Nhon.

In response, Johnson authorizes American air raids against North Vietnam.

*March 2*

Rolling Thunder, the sustained U.S. bombing campaign against North Vietnam, begins.

*March 8*

The first official U.S. combat troops, marines from the Third Marine Division, land in Vietnam. Their task is to guard installations in and around Da Nang.

*April 15*

Students for a Democratic Society (SDS) stages an antiwar rally in Washington, D.C.

*June*

Air Marshal Nguyen Cao Ky becomes the head of the National Leadership Council, a reasonably stable regime in Saigon.

*October*

Large antiwar demonstrations take place across the United States.

*November*

The Battle of Ia Drang Valley, the first engagement between American forces and NVA regulars, occurs.

## 1966

*February 8*

At the Honolulu Conference, the United States and South Vietnam officially recognize the need to "pacify" South Vietnam as a complement to winning the war on the battlefield.

*March*

Buddhist demonstrations in Hue and Da Nang inspire a violent response from Ky's government.

*September*

The United States announces that it is using Agent Orange and other defoliants in Vietnam.

*December*

U.S. military forces number 362,000. Allied with them are more than 600,000 South Vietnamese regulars and irregulars as well as 50,000 troops from the Free World Assistance Program.

## 1967

*March*

At a meeting on Guam, Johnson and his advisers urge Ky and General Nguyen Van Thieu to institute democratic reforms in the RVN.

*April 15*

Massive peace demonstrations take place across the United States.

*September*

Westmoreland sends more troops and equipment to the marine base at Khe Sanh in response to word of expanded NVA movements in the region.

*September 3*

Thieu is elected president and Ky vice president in the RVN's first national elections.

*October 21*

The March on the Pentagon, one of the largest and most contentious antiwar rallies yet, takes place. Polls suggest that most Americans now oppose the Vietnam War.

## 1968

*January 3*

In response to the surge of antiwar sentiment, Senator Eugene McCarthy announces his candidacy for the Democratic nomination for president as a "peace" candidate.

*January 21*

The Battle of Khe Sanh begins.

*January 30–31*

The Tet Offensive, a massive attack accompanied by, Communist leaders hope, a "general uprising," begins. Communist troops are defeated quickly aside from lengthy battles at Hue, Khe Sanh, and Cholon.

*February*

Westmoreland asks for 206,000 additional troops to be sent to Vietnam and mobilization of reserve units in the United States. Johnson ultimately approves only 13,500 troops.

*March 12*
McCarthy nearly beats Johnson in the New Hampshire primary election.

*March 16*
Senator Robert F. Kennedy announces his candidacy for the Democratic presidential nomination; the My Lai massacre occurs; Westmoreland is appointed army chief of staff; he is replaced as MACV commander by General Creighton Abrams.

*March 25*
The Wise Men, a group of advisers, recommend that Johnson not escalate the Vietnam War any further.

*March 31*
In a televised speech, Johnson announces both a partial bombing halt and his decision not to run for president.

*May 12*
The United States and North Vietnam open preliminary peace talks in Paris.

*June 5*
Robert Kennedy is assassinated after winning the California Democratic primary. He dies the next day.

*August*
The Democratic National Convention takes place in Chicago amid massive rioting on the city's streets. Hubert Humphrey is nominated as the party's presidential candidate.

*October 31*
Johnson announces a total bombing halt over North Vietnam.

*November 5*
Richard M. Nixon defeats Humphrey and becomes president of the United States.

*November–December*
U.S. forces step up operations in Laos, including both interdiction along the Ho Chi Minh Trail and bombing raids.

*December*
U.S. troop strength stands at nearly 540,000.

## 1969

*January*
Representatives of the RVN and the NLF join in the Paris peace talks.

*March*
Nixon's plan to "Vietnamize" the war by withdrawing American troops while still providing aid to the RVN is announced.

*March 18*
Nixon authorizes the "secret" bombing of Cambodia called Operation Menu.

*May*
The Battle of Hamburger Hill in the A Shau Valley takes place.

*September 2*
Ho Chi Minh dies. He is effectively replaced as leader of the DRV by a triumvirate of Vo Nguyen Giap, Pham Van Dong, and Le Duan.

*October 15*
A national antiwar moratorium takes place across the United States.

## 1970

*February 21*
Henry Kissinger, Nixon's national security adviser, begins secret peace talks in Paris with Le Duc Tho.

*April 30*
U.S. and South Vietnamese forces invade Cambodia.

*May*
Widespread demonstrations across the United States protest the Cambodian invasion. On May 4, four people are killed during a demonstration at Kent State University. On May 14, two more are killed at Jackson State College.

*December 22*
The U.S. Congress bans the use of U.S. forces in Cambodia or Laos. U.S. military strength in Vietnam is down to 335,000.

## 1971

*February*

Lam Son 719, a South Vietnamese invasion of Laos heavily supported by U.S. aircrews and artillery, begins.

*April 20*

Veterans stage a major antiwar protest in Washington, D.C.

*June 13*

The *New York Times* begins publication of the Pentagon Papers. Despite Nixon's fury, the Supreme Court allows publication to continue.

*July*

Nixon organizes the "plumbers," an investigative team intended to stop information leaks. They target Daniel Ellsberg, the former Defense Department staffer who leaked the Pentagon Papers.

## 1972

*January 25*

Nixon reveals that Kissinger has been engaged in secret peace talks.

*March 30*

North Vietnam launches its Easter Offensive against the south. Engagements include the Battles of An Loc and Quang Tri.

*April 15*

Nixon authorizes American forces to resume bombing of North Vietnam after more than three years of no such activity.

*May 10*

The mining of Haiphong Harbor.

*June 17*

Five men affiliated with Nixon's plumbers are arrested during a break-in at the Democratic Party's headquarters in Washington, D.C.'s Watergate building. The subsequent scandal undermines Nixon's presidency.

*July 13*

Paris peace talks resume after being postponed because of the Easter Offensive and the U.S. bombing raids.

*October 8*

Kissinger and Le Duc Tho reach a tentative peace agreement. It is rejected by Thieu.

*November 7*

Nixon is reelected to the presidency in a landslide.

*November 11*

U.S. Army forces turn over the huge base at Long Binh to the Vietnamese.

*December 13*

Further peace talks between Kissinger and Le Duc Tho reach a stalemate. The North Vietnamese depart the negotiations.

*December 18*

Linebacker II, the so-called Christmas bombing, begins. Over the next eleven days American planes drop thousands of tons of bombs on sites in North Vietnam, killing some sixteen hundred civilians. U.S. troop strength is down to twenty-four thousand.

## 1973

*January 8*

Peace negotiations begin again.

*January 27*

The Paris Peace Accords are signed by representatives of the United States, North Vietnam, South Vietnam, and the Provisional Revolutionary Government representing South Vietnam's Communists; the draft in the United States ends.

*February 21*

A cease-fire agreement in Laos is reached, and American bombing over Laos ends.

*March 29*

Remaining U.S. troops are withdrawn from South Vietnam, with the exception of a few advisory personnel and those attached to the U.S. embassy.

*April 1*

The last American prisoners of war are released in Hanoi.

*June 1*
U.S. Congress votes to ban all bombing in Cambodia as of August 15.

*November 7*
Over Nixon's veto, Congress passes the War Powers Resolution limiting the president's war-making abilities.

## 1974

*January*
Thieu proclaims that North and South Vietnam are again at war.

*August 9*
Nixon resigns rather than face removal from office. He is replaced by Gerald R. Ford.

*August 20*
American aid to South Vietnam is reduced substantially.

## 1975

*January*
NVA forces take Phuoc Long Province north of Saigon. Their rapid advance convinces them to speed up their timetable for the conquest of South Vietnam.

*March 12*
The NVA takes Ban Me Thout, beginning the final, successful offensive against South Vietnam.

*March 25*
The NVA takes Hue.

*March 30*
Da Nang falls to the NVA, and South Vietnamese forces are in complete disarray.

*April 12*
The U.S. embassy in Phnom Penh, the capital of Cambodia, is evacuated.

*April 17*
Phnom Penh falls to the Khmer Rouge.

*April 21*
Thieu resigns, having failed to secure help from a no-longer-interested United States. He is replaced by Tran Van Huong.

*April 22*
NVA forces win the Battle of Xuan Loc, the last major engagement of the Vietnam War.

*April 28*
Huong abdicates in favor of Duong Van Minh.

*April 29*
The U.S. evacuation of Saigon, Operation Frequent Wind, begins. It is completed early in the morning of April 30.

*April 30*
Minh surrenders to the NVA. The last two U.S. casualties in Vietnam, marine corporals Charles McMahon and Darwin Judge, occur during an attack on Tan Son Nhut airport.

*August*
The Pathet Lao take Vientiane, the capital of Laos.

## 1976

*July 2*
The Socialist Republic of Vietnam (SRV) is officially declared. Saigon is renamed Ho Chi Minh City.

## 1977

*January 21*
President Jimmy Carter pardons nearly ten thousand U.S. draft evaders.

*November*
A massive repression campaign against ethnic Chinese in Vietnam begins. Thousands of Chinese flee across the border into China or join the exodus of Vietnamese "boat people" across Southeast Asia.

## 1982

The Vietnam Veterans War Memorial is unveiled in Washington, D.C.

## 1993

The United States resumes formal diplomatic relations with Vietnam and lifts its ban on economic aid.

## Books

David L. Anderson, *Trapped by Success: The Eisenhower Administration and Vietnam.* New York: Columbia University Press, 1991.

Dale Andrade, *Ashes to Ashes: The Phoenix Program and the Vietnam War.* Lexington, MA: D.C. Heath, 1990.

Anthony Austin, *The President's War: The Story of the Tonkin Gulf Resolution and How the Nation Was Trapped in Vietnam.* Philadelphia: J.B. Lippincott, 1971.

Chester A. Bain, *Vietnam: The Roots of Conflict.* Englewood Cliffs, NJ: Prentice-Hall, 1967.

David M. Barret, *Uncertain Warriors: Lyndon Johnson and His Vietnam Advisors.* Lawrence: University of Kansas Press, 1993.

Thomas A. Bass, *Vietnamerica: The War Comes Home.* New York: Soho Press, 1996.

Elizabeth Becker, *When the War Was Over: Cambodia's Revolution and the Voices of Its People.* New York: Simon and Schuster, 1986.

Brian Beckett, *The Illustrated History of the Vietnam War.* New York: Gallery Books, 1985.

Philip D. Beidler, *American Literature and the Experience of Vietnam.* Athens: University of Georgia Press, 1982.

Michael Bilton and Kevin Sim, *Four Hours in My Lai.* New York: Penguin Books, 1992.

Thomas D. Boettcher, *Vietnam: The Valor and the Sorrow.* Boston: Little, Brown, 1985.

Joel O. Brende and Erwin E. Parson, *Vietnam Veterans: The Road to Recovery.* New York: Plenum Press, 1985.

David Butler, *The Fall of Saigon.* New York: Simon and Schuster, 1985.

Sucheng Chan, *Hmong Means Free: Life in Laos and America.* Philadelphia: Temple University Press, 1994.

David P. Chandler, *The Tragedy of Cambodian History: Politics, War, and Revolution Since 1945.* New Haven, CT: Yale University Press, 1991.

Kenton J. Clymer, ed., *The Vietnam War: Its History, Literature, and Music.* El Paso: Texas Western Press/University of Texas, 1998.

Charles DeBenedetti and Charles Chatfield, *An American Ordeal: The Antiwar Movement of the Vietnam Era.* Syracuse, NY: Syracuse University Press, 1990.

Peter Dorland and James Nanney, *Dustoff: Army Aeromedical Evacuation in Vietnam.* Washington, DC: U.S. Army Center of Military History, 1982.

James F. Dunnigan and Albert A. Nofi, *Dirty Little Secrets of the Vietnam War.* New York: St. Martin's Press, 1999.

James R. Ebert, *A Life in a Year: The American Infantryman in Vietnam, 1965–1972.* Novato, CA: Presidio Press, 1993.

George Esper and the Associated Press, *The Eyewitness History of the Vietnam*

*War, 1961–1975*. New York: Ballantine Books, 1983.

Bernard Fall, *Hell in a Very Small Place: The Siege of Dien Bien Phu*. New York: J.B. Lippincott, 1966.

———, *Street Without Joy*. Harrisburg, PA: Stackpole, 1961.

Wesley Fishel, *Vietnam: Anatomy of a Conflict*. Itasca, IL: Peacock Press, 1968.

Frances Fitzgerald, *Fire in the Lake: The Vietnamese and the Americans in Vietnam*. New York: Vintage Books, 1972.

Adam Garfinkle, *Telltale Hearts: The Origins and Impact of the Vietnam Antiwar Movement*. New York: St. Martin's Press, 1995.

Michael A. Genovese, *The Nixon Presidency: Power and Politics in Turbulent Times*. New York: Greenwood Press, 1990.

Zalin Grant, *Facing the Phoenix: The CIA and the Political Defeat of the United States in Vietnam*. New York: W.W. Norton, 1991.

Graham Greene, *The Quiet American*. New York: Penguin Books, 1955.

Gene Gurney, *Vietnam: The War in the Air*. New York: Crown, 1985.

David Halberstam, *The Best and the Brightest*. New York: Random House, 1973.

———, *The Making of a Quagmire*. New York: Knopf, 1987.

Daniel Hallin, *The Uncensored War: The Media and Vietnam*. Berkeley and Los Angeles: University of California Press, 1986.

Eric Hammel, *Khe Sanh, Siege in the Clouds: An Oral History*. New York: Crown, 1989.

Le Ly Hayslip, with Jay Wurts, *When Heaven and Earth Changed Places*. New York: Plume/Penguin, 1989.

Philip H. Helling, *Vietnam in American Literature*. Boston: Twayne Books, 1990.

Michael Herr, *Dispatches*. New York: Knopf, 1972.

George C. Herring, *LBJ and Vietnam: A Different Kind of War*. Austin: University of Texas Press, 1994.

Craig Howes, *Voices of the Vietnam POWs: Witnesses to Their Fight*. New York: Oxford University Press, 1993.

Arnold R. Isaacs, *Without Honor: Defeat in Vietnam and Cambodia*. Baltimore: Johns Hopkins University Press, 1983.

Anthony James Joes, *The War for South Viet Nam, 1954–1975*. Westport, CT: Praeger, 2001.

Lawrence H. Johnson, *Winged Sabers: The Air Cavalry in Vietnam, 1965–1973*. Harrisburg, PA: Stackpole, 1990.

Stanley Karnow, *Vietnam: A History*. New York: Viking Penguin, 1983.

Philip Katcher, *Armies of the Vietnam War, 1962–1975*. London: Osprey, 1980.

Francis J. Kelly, *The Green Berets in Vietnam, 1961–1971*. Washington, DC: Brassey's, 1991.

Andrew J. Krepinevich, *The Army and Vietnam*. Baltimore: Johns Hopkins University Press, 1986.

Stanley I. Kutler, ed., *Encyclopedia of the Vietnam War*. New York: Simon and Schuster, 1996.

Michael L. Lanning, *Vietnam at the Movies*. New York: Fawcett Columbine, 1994.

Robert J. Lifton, *Home from the War: Vietnam Veterans, Neither Victims nor Executioners*. New York: Simon and Schuster, 1973.

Norman Mailer, *The Armies of the Night*. New York: New American Library, 1968.

Edward J. Marolda, *By Sea, Air, and Land: An Illustrated History of the U.S. Navy and the War in Southeast Asia*. Washington, DC: Naval Historical Center, 1994.

Bobbie Ann Mason, *In Country.* New York: Harper and Row, 1985.

Robert S. McNamara, with Brian VanDeMark, *In Retrospect: The Tragedy and Lessons of Vietnam.* New York: Times Books, 1995.

Allan R. Millet, *Semper Fidelis: The History of the United States Marine Corps.* New York: Macmillan, 1980.

Harold G. Moore and Joseph Galloway, *We Were Soldiers Once . . . and Young: Ia Drang, the Battle That Changed the War in Vietnam.* New York: Random House, 1992.

John M. Newman, *JFK and Vietnam: Deception, Intrigue, and the Struggle for Power.* New York: Warner, 1992.

Nguyen Cao Ky, *Twenty Years and Twenty Days.* New York: Stein and Day, 1976.

John B. Nichols and Barrett Tillman, *On Yankee Station: The Naval Air War over Vietnam.* Annapolis, MD: Naval Institute Press, 1987.

Richard M. Nixon, *No More Vietnams.* New York: Avon Books, 1985.

Don Oberdorfer, *Tet!* Garden City, NY: Doubleday, 1971.

Tim O'Brien, *If I Die in a Combat Zone.* New York: Delacorte, 1978.

James S. Olson, ed., *Dictionary of the Vietnam War.* New York: Greenwood Press, 1988.

James S. Olson and Randy Roberts, *My Lai: A Brief History with Documents.* Boston: Bedford/St. Martin's Press, 1998.

William O'Neill, *Coming Apart: An Informal History of America in the 1960s.* New York: Times Books, 1971.

Bruce Palmer, *The 25-Year War: America's Military Role in Vietnam.* Lexington: University of Kentucky Press, 1984.

*Pentagon Papers: The Defense Department History of United States Decisionmaking on Vietnam.* Boston: Beacon Press, 1971.

Douglas Pike, *PAVN: People's Army of Vietnam.* Novato, CA: Presidio Press, 1986.

Robert Pisor, *The End of the Line: The Siege of Khe Sanh.* New York: W.W. Norton, 1982.

John Prados, *The Hidden History of the Vietnam War.* Chicago: Elephant Paperbacks/ Ivan R. Dee, 1995.

Christopher Robbins, *Air America.* New York: Putnam, 1979.

Anthony Robinson, Anthony Preston, and Ian V. Hogg, *Weapons of the Vietnam War.* New York: Gallery Books, 1983.

Harrison Salisbury, *Behind the Lines: Hanoi, December 23, 1966–January 7, 1967.* New York: Harper and Row, 1967.

Sidney H. Schanberg, *The Death and Life of Dith Pran.* New York: Viking, 1982.

William Shawcross, *Sideshow: Kissinger, Nixon, and the Destruction of Cambodia.* New York: Simon and Schuster, 1979.

Neil Sheehan, *A Bright Shining Lie: John Paul Vann and America in Vietnam.* New York: Random House, 1988.

David Burns Sigler, *Vietnam Battle Chronology: U.S. Army and Marine Corps Combat Operations, 1965–1973.* Jefferson, NC: McFarland Press, 1992.

Charles M. Simpson, *Inside the Green Berets.* Novato, CA: Presidio Press, 1983.

Richard L. Stevens, *The Trail: A History of the Ho Chi Minh Trail and the Role of Nature in the War in Vietnam.* New York: Garland Books, 1993.

Robert Stone, *Dog Soldiers.* Boston: Houghton Mifflin, 1974.

Harry G. Summers, *On Strategy: A Critical Analysis of the Vietnam War.* Novato, CA: Presidio Press, 1982.

Jon Swain, *River of Time: A Memoir of Vietnam and Cambodia.* New York: Berkley Books, 1995.

Robert Templer, *Shadows and Wind: A View of Modern Vietnam*. New York: Penguin Books, 1998.

William S. Turley, *The Second Indochina War: A Short Political and Military History, 1954–1975*. Boulder, CO: Westview Press, 1986.

Lynda Van Devanter, *Home Before Morning*. New York: Warner Books, 1984.

James C. Wilson, *Vietnam in Prose and Film*. Jefferson, NC: McFarland Press, 1982.

Shelton Woods, *Vietnam: An Illustrated History*. New York: Hippocrene Books, 2002.

Clarence R. Wyatt, *Paper Soldiers: The American Press and the Vietnam War*. Chicago: University of Chicago Press, 1993.

Marilyn Young, *The Vietnam Wars, 1945–1990*. New York: Harper Perennial, 1991.

Samuel Zaffiri, *Hamburger Hill*. New York: Pocket Books, 1988.

## Websites

Air America, www.air-america.org. Tells the story of Air America in Laos, Vietnam, and elsewhere from its founding until the mid-1970s.

Aircraft in the Vietnam War, www.farfrom glory.com/aircraft.htm. Descriptions and photos of the various fixed-wing and rotor aircraft used in Vietnam.

The American Experience: Vietnam, www.pbs.org/wgbh/amex/vietnam. A Public Broadcasting Service site that attempts to describe how the Vietnam experience affected every segment of American society and the course of American history.

Cambodian Genocide Program, www. yale.edu/cgp. The home page of an official information clearinghouse on Cambodia and the Khmer Rouge.

A Guide to the Vietnam War, www.surfnet kids.com/vietnam.htm. An overview of the Vietnam War intended for younger children.

History Place: The Vietnam War, www. historyplace.com/unitedstates/vietnam. Many resources, including timelines, essays, and an analysis of America's role in Vietnam.

Military History of the Vietnam War, www.skalman.nu/history/vietnam.htm. An in-depth listing of military units participating in the Vietnam War and other links.

Music of the Vietnam War, www.battle notes.com. Contains lists of protest songs, combat songs, and other music from the era.

The Peace Movement, www.landscaper. net/peace.htm. Describes the antiwar movement, with links to related topics.

Vietnam Helicopter Pilots Association, www.vhpa.org. A commemorative site for helicopter crews who flew in Vietnam.

Vietnam Veterans Against the War, www. vvaw.org. The home page for the wartime organization, which remains active.

Vietnam Veterans Memorial Wall Page, www.thewall-usa.com. The story of the Vietnam Veterans Memorial in Washington, D.C., including many photos.

The Vietnam War, www.vietnamwar.net. A comprehensive site including histories, descriptions, photos, and links.

The Vietnam War Internet Project, www. vwip.org. A comprehensive site containing memoirs, photos, documents, and other resources.

The Vietnam War Pictorial, www.vietnam pix.com. A photographic tour of the Vietnam experience.

# PICTURE CREDITS

# ABOUT THE AUTHOR

Jeff T. Hay, Ph.D., teaches history at San Diego State University and is the author of Greenhaven Press's four-volume *History of the Third Reich.* His research on the Vietnam War has involved three trips to Indochina.

# ABOUT THE CONSULTING EDITOR

Charles Zappia, Ph.D., is a professor of history and chair of the Department of Social Sciences at Mesa College in San Diego. An expert on the Vietnam War, labor history, and U.S. history, Dr. Zappia has also served as an officer of the American Historical Association.